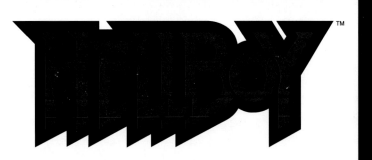

THE CHAINED
COFFIN
and OTHERS

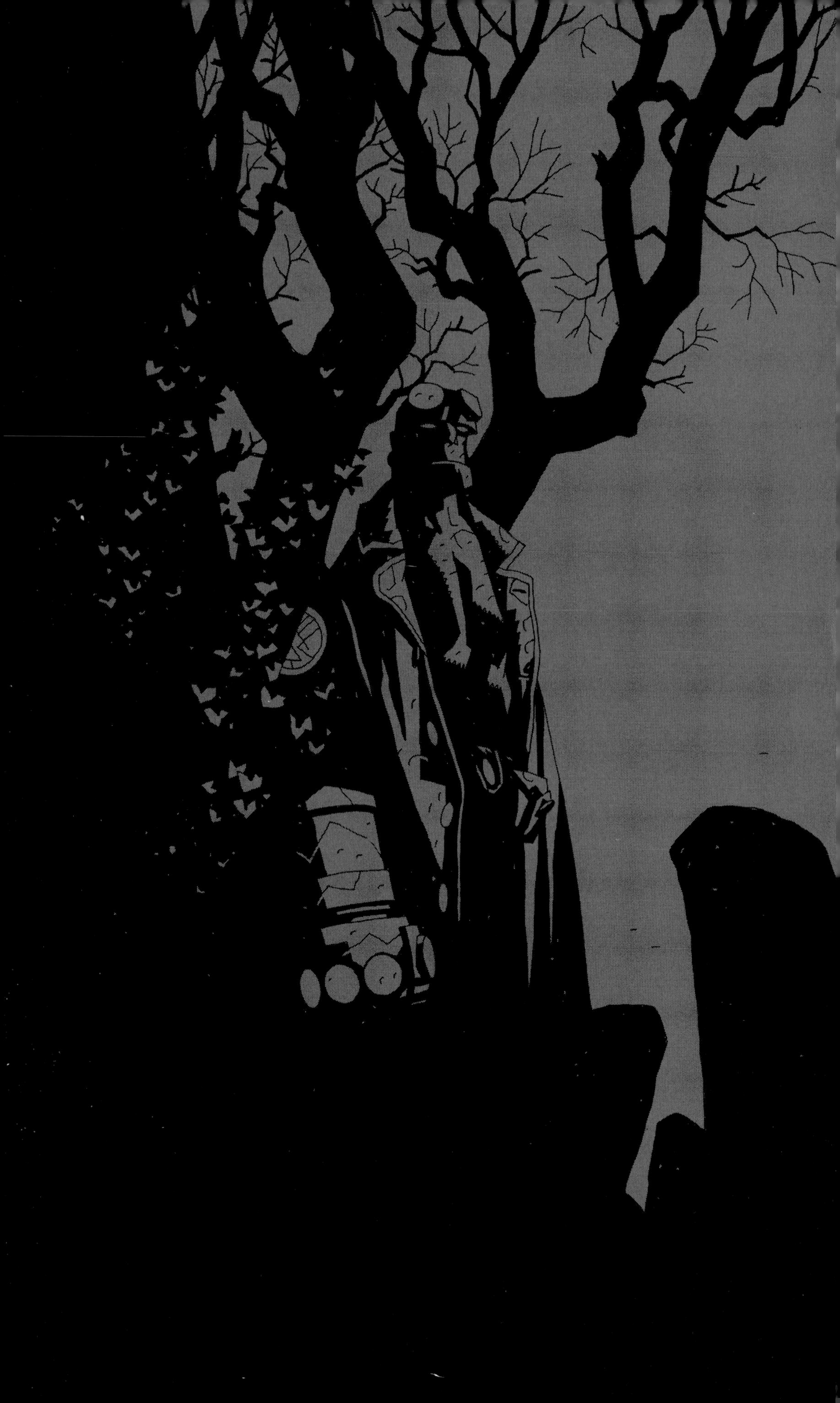

HELLBOY

THE CHAINED COFFIN and OTHERS

by
MIKE MIGNOLA

Colored by
JAMES SINCLAIR,
MATTHEW HOLLINGSWORTH,
& DAVE STEWART

Lettered by
PAT BROSSEAU

✠

Introduction by
P. CRAIG RUSSELL

Edited by
SCOTT ALLIE

Hellboy logo designed by
KEVIN NOWLAN

Collection designed by
MIKE MIGNOLA & CARY GRAZZINI

Published by
MIKE RICHARDSON

DARK HORSE BOOKS

BARBARA KESEL *co-edits on*
"The Corpse" and "The Wolves of Saint August."

BOB SCHRECK *co-edits on "The Chained Coffin."*

JAMES SINCLAIR *colors for "The Iron Shoes," "Almost Colossus,"*
"The Wolves of Saint August," and "A Christmas Underground."
MATTHEW HOLLINGSWORTH *colors for "The Corpse."*
DAVE STEWART *colors and separations for cover, "The Chained Coffin,"*
"The Baba Yaga," and the pinup gallery;
separations and additional colors for "Almost Colossus"
and "A Christmas Underground."

Special thanks to ROB HUMPHREYS *at Seraphim Films.*

NEIL HANKERSON ✠ *executive vice president*

TOM WEDDLE ✠ *vice president of finance*

RANDY STRADLEY ✠ *vice president of publishing*

CHRIS WARNER ✠ *senior books editor*

SARA PERRIN ✠ *vice president of marketing*

MICHAEL MARTENS ✠ *vice president of business development*

ANITA NELSON ✠ *vice president of sales & licensing*

DAVID SCROGGY ✠ *vice president of product development*

DALE LaFOUNTAIN ✠ *vice president of information technology*

DARLENE VOGEL ✠ *director of purchasing*

KEN LIZZI ✠ *general counsel*

Published by Dark Horse Books
A division of Dark Horse Comics, Inc.
10956 SE Main St.
Milwaukie, OR 97222
www.darkhorse.com

First Edition: August 1998
Second Edition: November 2003
ISBN: 1-59307-091-8

This volume collects stories from the Dark Horse comic books *Hellboy: The Wolves of Saint August,*
Hellboy: The Corpse and the Iron Shoes, Hellboy: Almost Colossus, Dark Horse Presents 100 #2, and *Hellboy: Christmas Special* .

10 9 8 7 6 5 4 3

PRINTED IN CHINA

INTRODUCTION

by P. Craig Russell

I own five pages of the original artwork to Mike Mignola's Hellboy story "The Corpse." Five. If you all want to hate me now, it's okay, I can handle it. I own five pages of "The Corpse."

When it comes to the artwork of Mike Mignola, I find I'm still wearing the hat of a fan. It appears every time I pick up his latest work. And it's especially prominent whenever it's one of his short stories, which, let me be up front about this, I consider to be the finest and most consistently successful work, on so many different levels, being done in comics today.

I first became aware of Mike's work about ten years ago when Al Milgrom, editor of *Marvel Fanfare*, knowing I filled time between my personal projects with inking assignments, tried to entice me onto the book by sending me xeroxes of a Submariner story by a young artist I was not too familiar with. It bore little resemblance to the Mike of these days, but it looked good, and one panel in particular, that of Subby casually standing on a wave, seemed fresh and clever. I was enticed.

Over the next six years I inked almost three hundred pages of Mike's artwork and I'm still enticed. For those three hundred pages I had a front-row-center seat to watch his continual development, and watching that evolution was half the fun of inking him (only in comics do we talk about inking "him," as if to ink an artist's pencil drawings is to ink the artist himself).

A digression. Our careers have intersected in some interesting ways. Years ago DC Comics editor Mike Carlin called to offer me the art assignment on a *Phantom Stranger* limited series. I said I was too busy to pencil it, but I could possibly ink it if they could find an interesting penciller, someone, say, like Mike Mignola, who was currently pencilling Michael Moorcock's *Corum* for First Comics. When he was offered the project, Mike seemed to like the idea of the collaboration, and so dropped *Corum* and went over to DC. Almost immediately I got a call from an editor at First saying "For some reason, Mike has left the *Corum* book and we need an artist. Would you be interested?" You can't make up stuff like that. A criminal genius who *wanted* to hijack the *Corum* book couldn't have planned it better. But I didn't want to hijack the *Corum* book, I just wanted to ink Mignola. Besides, Mike was already well on his way to becoming a master of understatement. Inkers love that in a penciller.

Let me get back to the "fan hat" thing.

As a kid I seemed to wear it all the time. In the mid sixties for Steranko's series of Nick Fury and Captain America stories. Then in the early seventies for Windsor-Smith's first flash of brilliance on the Conan stories. Sure, some of these graphic stories, as *stories*, could be naively pulpy, but it was the way these artists worked the form itself that fascinated me, and I was

devoted to these creators not just for the quality of their work, but for the greater excitement of seeing them grow as artists, literally, month by month. Each new work brought some new visual innovation, as they stretched their graphic wings, as influences were assimilated, or dropped, or transformed. To me, the cliffhanger wasn't what would happen to the hero next issue, but what surprising visual development the artist might come up with next. And so it has been with Mike Mignola.

In the past . . . twenty-five (my god) years since the last Windsor-Smith Conan stories, there have been many graphic stories that stretched the form, that have expanded and deepened it and taken it far from any Hyperborean fantasy land. If you read comics at all you probably know which ones I mean. Monumental stand-alones like Spiegelman's *Maus* and Cruse's *Stuck Rubber Baby*, series with names like *Bone* and *Hate* and *Cerebus* and *Eightball*. Documentaries like Joe Sacco's *Palestine*, Pekar's *American Splendor* and Chester Brown's *Yummy Fur*. All of these books, and many more besides, have moved me, provoked me, and challenged me to produce better work. And though already a devotee of Mignola's *Hellboy*, it was the publication of "The Corpse" that rekindled my youthful enthusiasm for the form. It was, and remains, absolutely unique, with a deft wit, a sometimes gruesome sense of humor, and at all times a formal elegance.

It is this formal elegance that hearkens back to those earlier works that so excited my imagination as a young artist. It is not just in Mike's drawing that I take such pleasure, but in all the disparate elements that make simple drawing fit into the larger context of graphic storytelling. It lies in the powerful use of black, the clever use of exposi-tional panels, the careful attention to the rhythm of balloon placement and sound effects, color as mood, architectural detail (Mike seems to be the only artist in comics to realize that not all graveyards come from New England), and, most importantly, the plasticity of his layouts. His panel arrangements seem to breathe, their size and proportion one to the other in quick and elastic response to the needs of the story. It is a sensual pleasure to read these stories.

To bring us up to date. It was just a few weeks ago that I saw an announcement for this volume in the back of the book *Abe Sapien*. And it was only a few days ago that editor Scott Allie asked me, to my great pleasure, to write this intro. As I hadn't seen the as yet unpublished "Baba Yaga" story, I asked Scott for a copy to preview, reasoning that I couldn't introduce a book unless I'd seen all of it. But, really, my motive was not so pure. What I really wanted to do was to wave the unpublished piece before all my friends who are also Mignola fans and say, "Look what I haaaaave."

I have five pages of original art form "The Corpse," did I mention that?

The Corpse

ABOUT FIFTEEN YEARS AGO I discovered an Irish folktale called "Teig O'Kane and the Corpse," and I decided right then and there that one day I would adapt it for comics. Well, that sort of happened. In 1995 someone at Dark Horse approached me with the idea of me doing a Hellboy story that would appear in Capital City's *Advance Comics* catalog in two-page installments. Two pages? How the hell do you do that? The challenge was to come up with a story where some new, strange thing would happen every two pages. I dug out "Teig O'Kane" (thinking of the three different churchyard incidents), added bits and pieces from other English and Irish folktales (the changeling, the bouncing rock, Jenny Greenteeth, etc.), and there you go.

Several people I respect and admire consider this to be the best Hellboy story I've done (see Craig Russell's introduction). I guess I would agree, but when I first did "The Corpse," I was convinced that it was the all-time worst story I had ever done. I don't remember why. Oh well . . .

✠

The Iron Shoes

WHEN IT CAME TIME to collect the two-page "Corpse" installments I was faced with a problem. The story wasn't quite long enough to fill a comic. I added a new first page (the title page), but didn't want to try adding new story pages. By now I liked the story and didn't want to mess it up. So I came up with "The Iron Shoes," because I like the title *The Corpse and the Iron Shoes*.

I will be the first to admit that this isn't really a story, just a weird little incident, but that's okay. I like the use of the experts at the beginning as a way to throw some folklore at the reader. It's a trick I plan to use again one of these days.

The Corpse

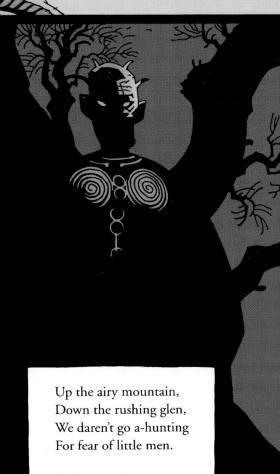

Up the airy mountain,
Down the rushing glen,
We daren't go a-hunting
For fear of little men.

"The Fairies"
 William Allingham

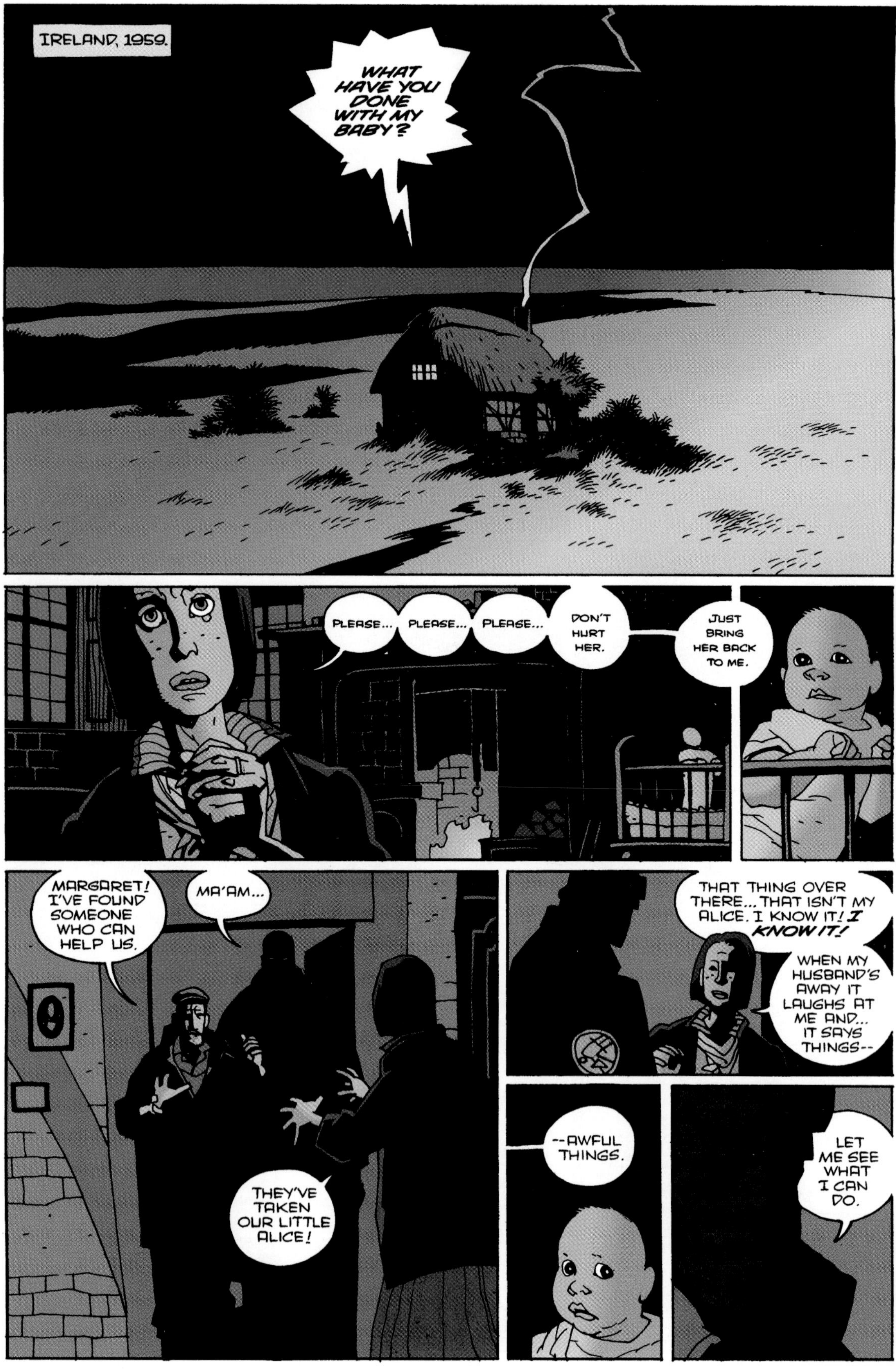
IRELAND, 1959.
WHAT HAVE YOU DONE WITH MY BABY?
PLEASE...
PLEASE...
PLEASE...
DON'T HURT HER.
JUST BRING HER BACK TO ME.
MARGARET! I'VE FOUND SOMEONE WHO CAN HELP US.
MA'AM...
THEY'VE TAKEN OUR LITTLE ALICE!
THAT THING OVER THERE... THAT ISN'T MY ALICE. I KNOW IT! I KNOW IT!
WHEN MY HUSBAND'S AWAY IT LAUGHS AT ME AND... IT SAYS THINGS--
--AWFUL THINGS.
LET ME SEE WHAT I CAN DO.

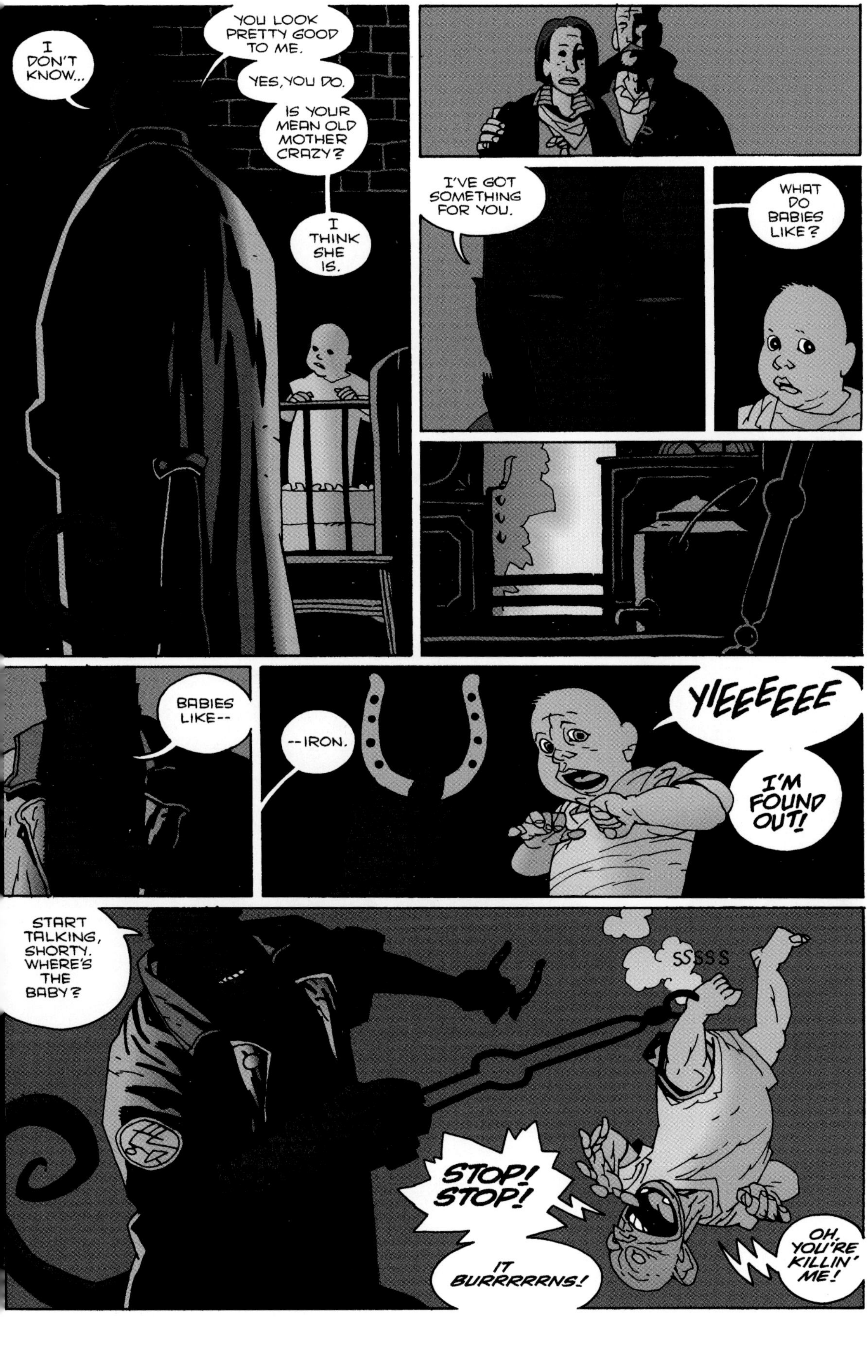
I DON'T KNOW...
YOU LOOK PRETTY GOOD TO ME.
YES, YOU DO.
IS YOUR MEAN OLD MOTHER CRAZY?
I THINK SHE IS.
I'VE GOT SOMETHING FOR YOU.
WHAT DO BABIES LIKE?
BABIES LIKE--
--IRON.
YIEEEEEE
I'M FOUND OUT!
START TALKING, SHORTY. WHERE'S THE BABY?
SSSSS
STOP! STOP!
IT BURRRRRNS!
OH, YOU'RE KILLIN' ME!

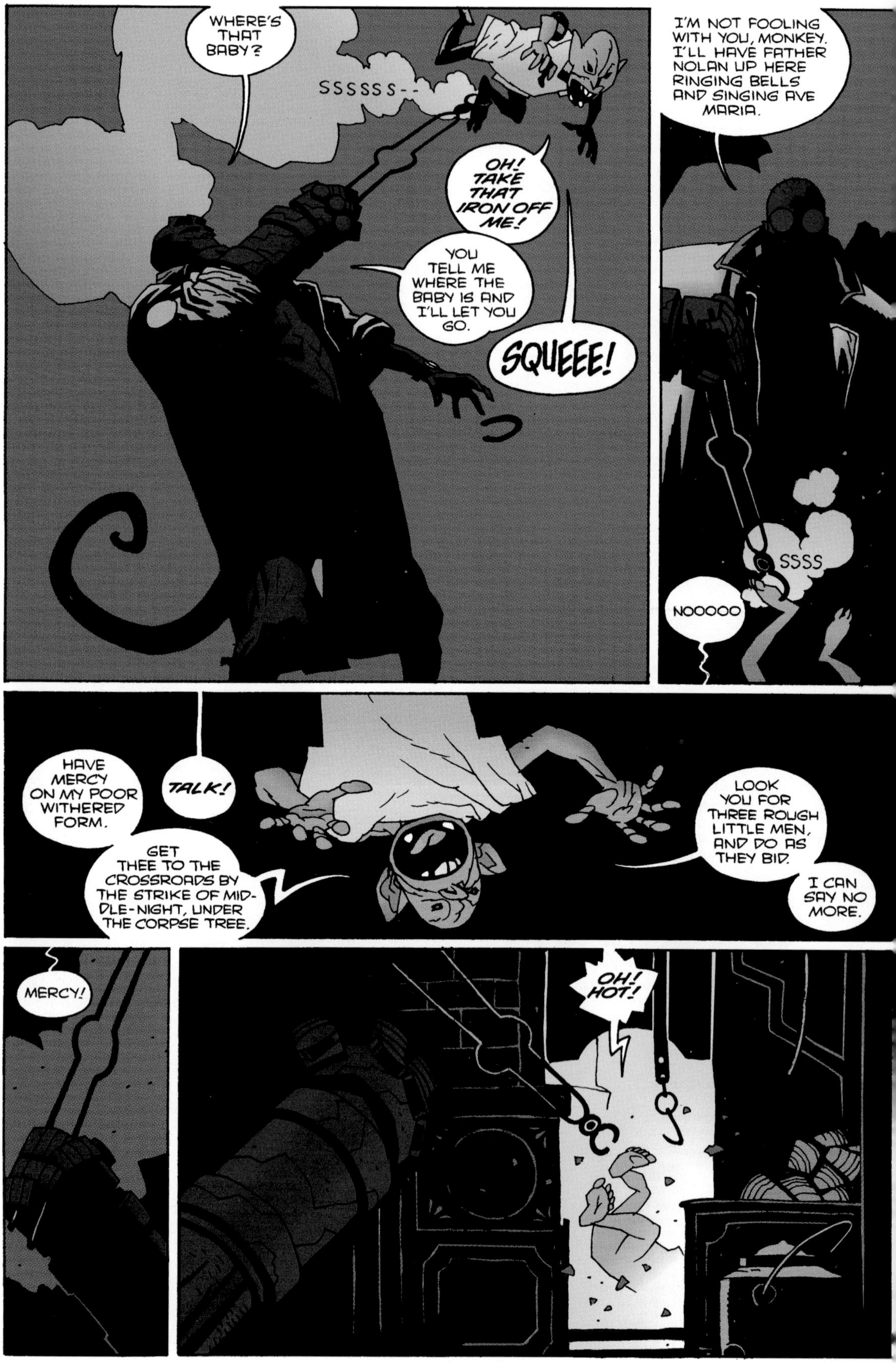
WHERE'S THAT BABY?
SSSSSS--
OH! TAKE THAT IRON OFF ME!
YOU TELL ME WHERE THE BABY IS AND I'LL LET YOU GO.
SQUEEE!
I'M NOT FOOLING WITH YOU, MONKEY. I'LL HAVE FATHER NOLAN UP HERE RINGING BELLS AND SINGING AVE MARIA.
SSSS
NOOOOO
HAVE MERCY ON MY POOR WITHERED FORM.
TALK!
GET THEE TO THE CROSSROADS BY THE STRIKE OF MID-DLE-NIGHT, UNDER THE CORPSE TREE.
LOOK YOU FOR THREE ROUGH LITTLE MEN, AND DO AS THEY BID.
I CAN SAY NO MORE.
MERCY!
OH! HOT!

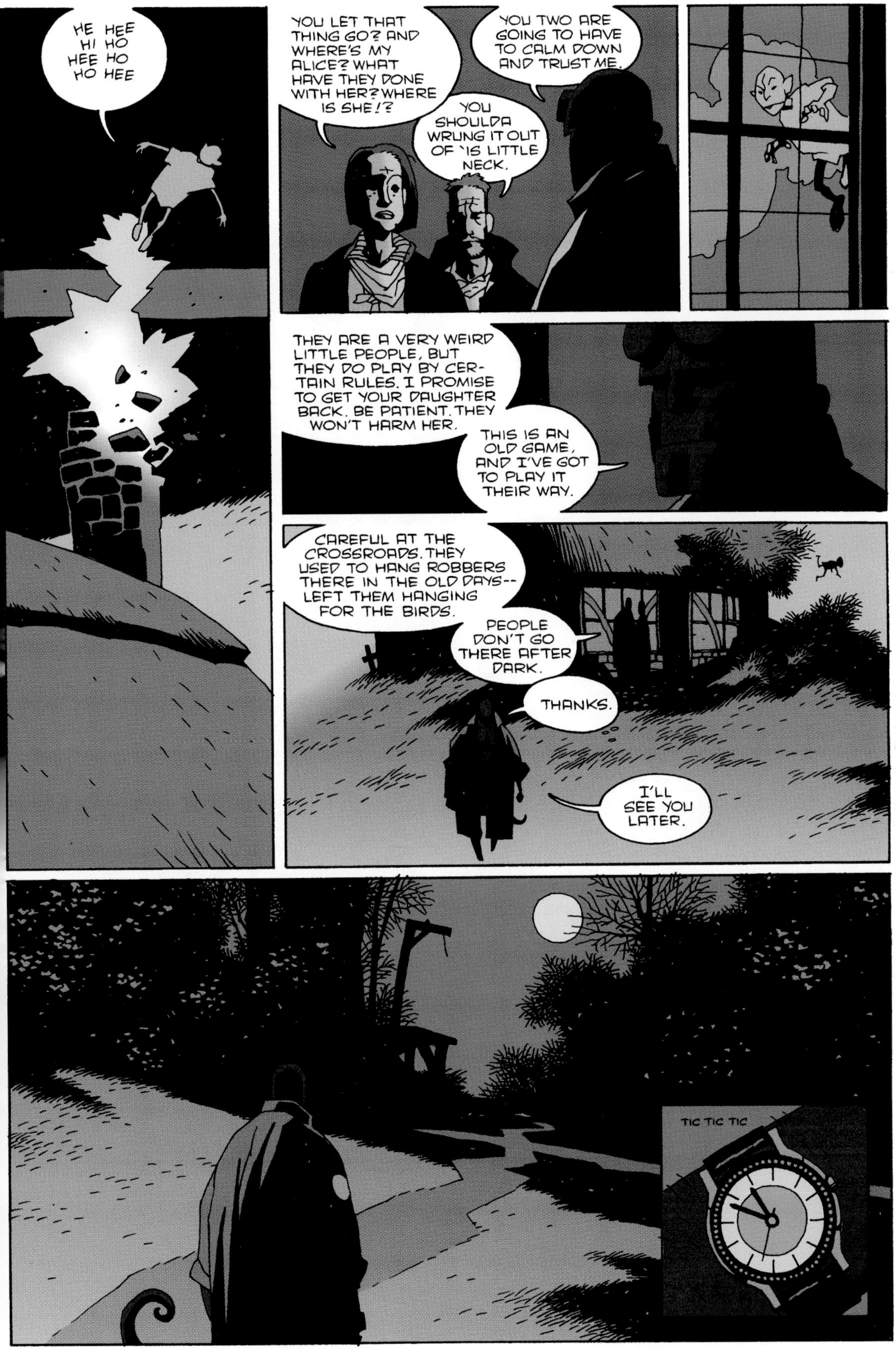
HE HEE HI HO HEE HO HO HEE
YOU LET THAT THING GO? AND WHERE'S MY ALICE? WHAT HAVE THEY DONE WITH HER? WHERE IS SHE!?
YOU TWO ARE GOING TO HAVE TO CALM DOWN AND TRUST ME.
YOU SHOULDA WRUNG IT OUT OF `IS LITTLE NECK.
THEY ARE A VERY WEIRD LITTLE PEOPLE, BUT THEY DO PLAY BY CERTAIN RULES. I PROMISE TO GET YOUR DAUGHTER BACK. BE PATIENT. THEY WON'T HARM HER.
THIS IS AN OLD GAME, AND I'VE GOT TO PLAY IT THEIR WAY.
CAREFUL AT THE CROSSROADS. THEY USED TO HANG ROBBERS THERE IN THE OLD DAYS-- LEFT THEM HANGING FOR THE BIRDS.
PEOPLE DON'T GO THERE AFTER DARK.
THANKS.
I'LL SEE YOU LATER.
TIC TIC TIC

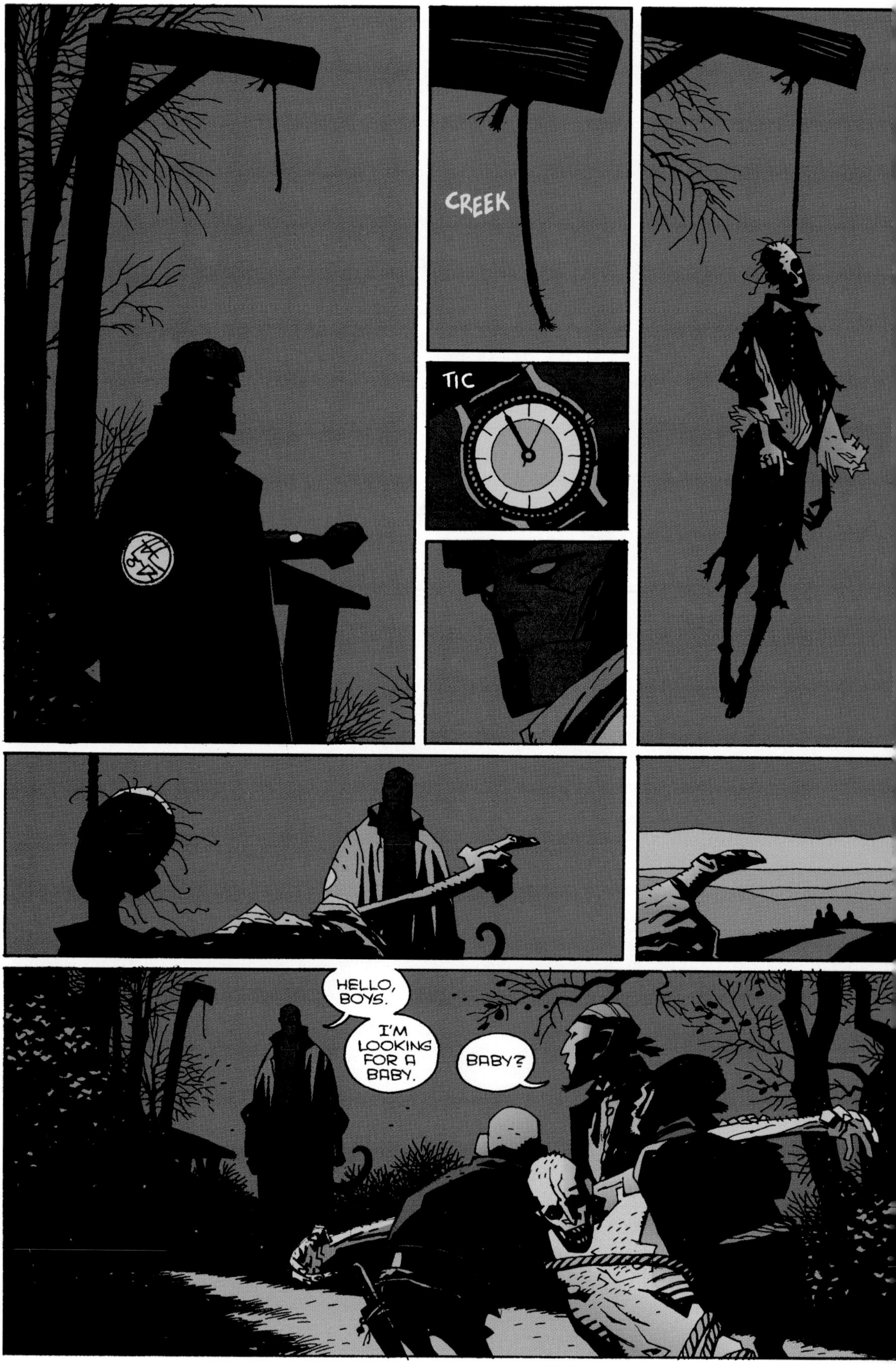

CREEK
TIC
HELLO, BOYS.
I'M LOOKING FOR A BABY.
BABY?

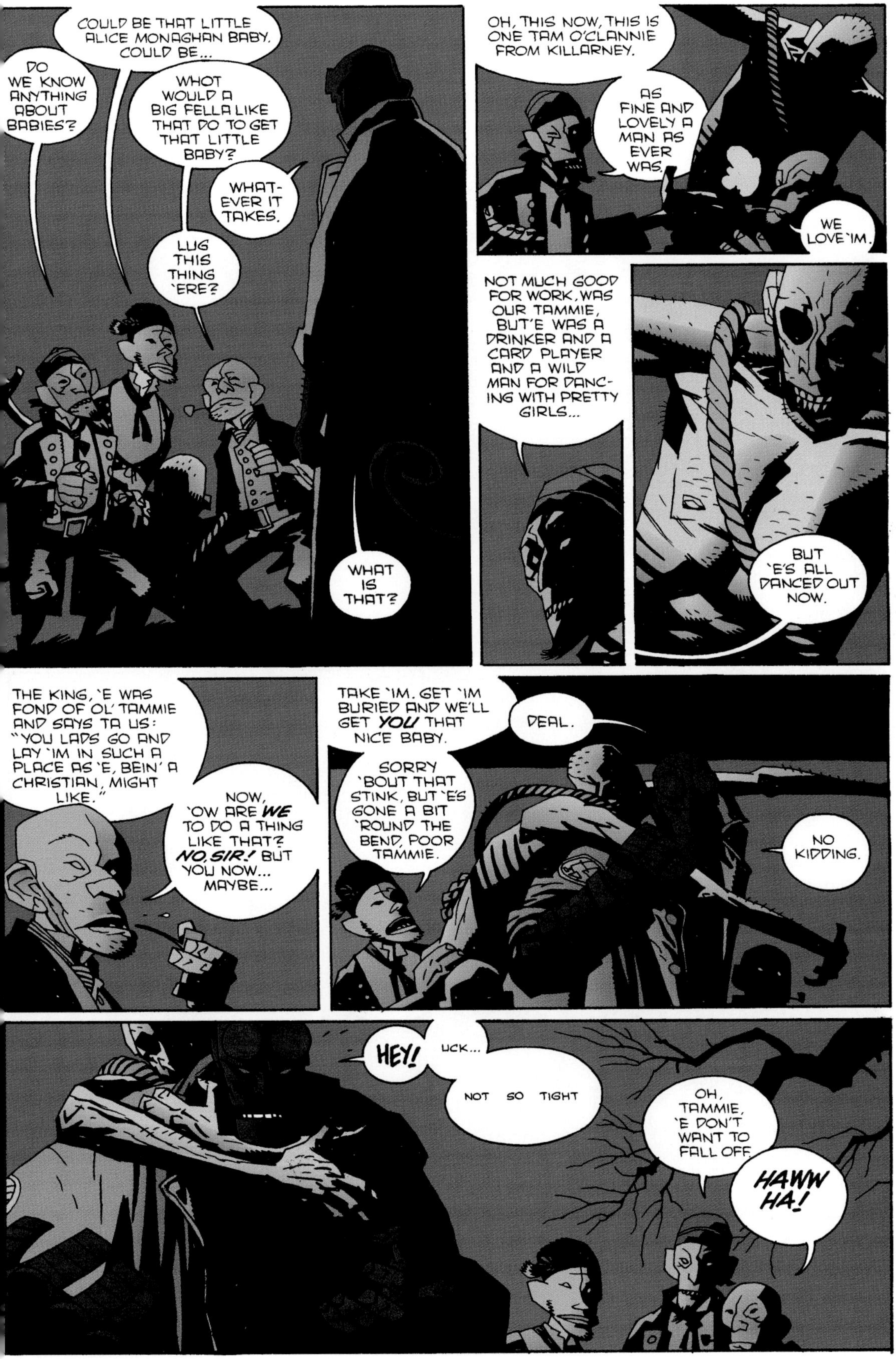

DO WE KNOW ANYTHING ABOUT BABIES?
COULD BE THAT LITTLE ALICE MONAGHAN BABY. COULD BE...
WHOT WOULD A BIG FELLA LIKE THAT DO TO GET THAT LITTLE BABY?
WHAT-EVER IT TAKES.
LUG THIS THING 'ERE?
WHAT IS THAT?
OH, THIS NOW, THIS IS ONE TAM O'CLANNIE FROM KILLARNEY.
AS FINE AND LOVELY A MAN AS EVER WAS.
WE LOVE 'IM.
NOT MUCH GOOD FOR WORK, WAS OUR TAMMIE, BUT 'E WAS A DRINKER AND A CARD PLAYER AND A WILD MAN FOR DANC-ING WITH PRETTY GIRLS...
BUT 'E'S ALL DANCED OUT NOW.
THE KING, 'E WAS FOND OF OL' TAMMIE AND SAYS TA US: "YOU LADS GO AND LAY 'IM IN SUCH A PLACE AS 'E, BEIN' A CHRISTIAN, MIGHT LIKE."
NOW, 'OW ARE WE TO DO A THING LIKE THAT? NO, SIR! BUT YOU NOW... MAYBE...
TAKE 'IM. GET 'IM BURIED AND WE'LL GET YOU THAT NICE BABY.
DEAL.
SORRY 'BOUT THAT STINK, BUT 'E'S GONE A BIT 'ROUND THE BEND, POOR TAMMIE.
NO KIDDING.
HEY!
UCK...
NOT SO TIGHT
OH, TAMMIE, 'E DON'T WANT TO FALL OFF.
HAWW HA!

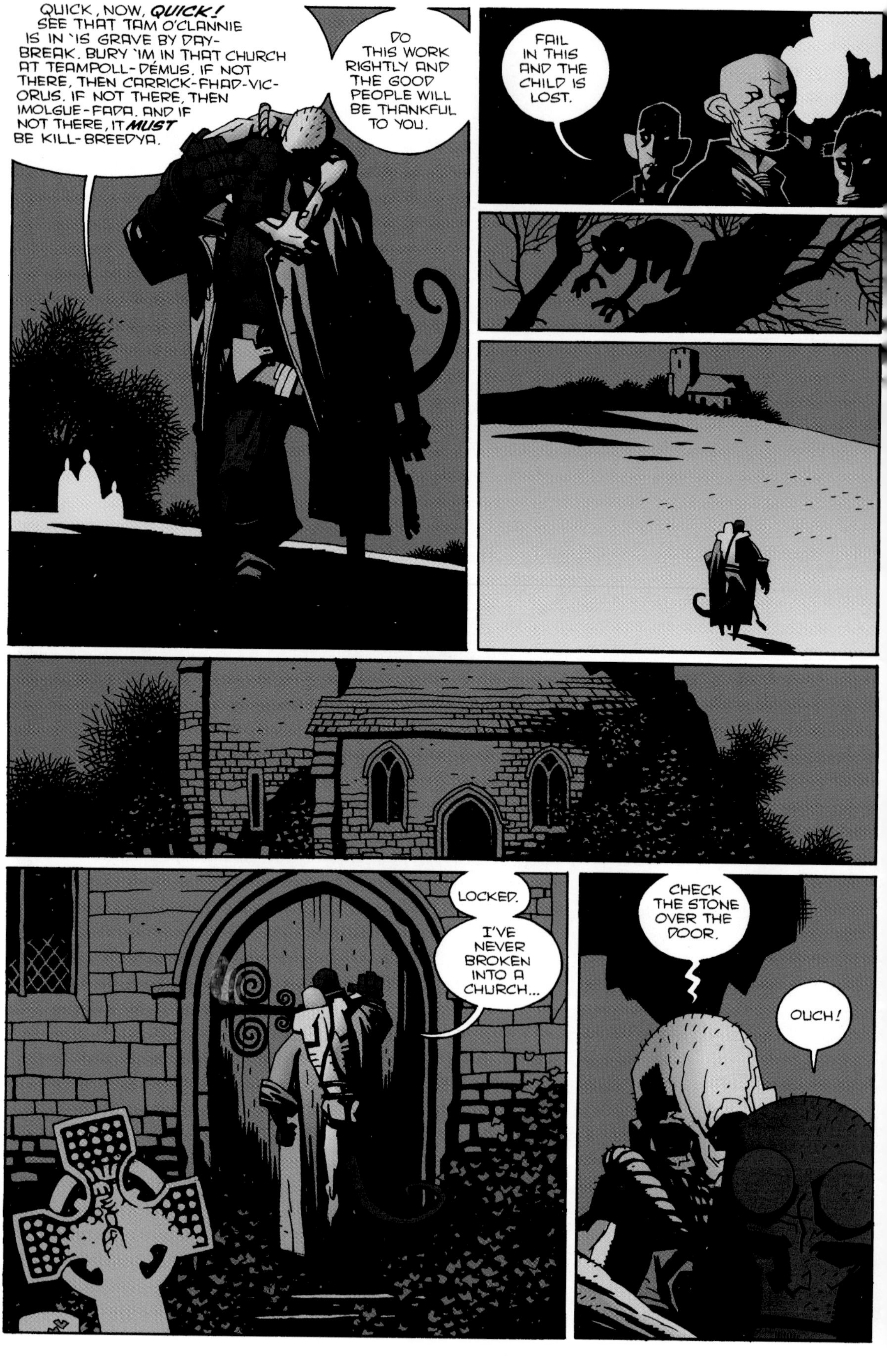

QUICK, NOW, QUICK! SEE THAT TAM O'CLANNIE IS IN 'IS GRAVE BY DAY-BREAK. BURY 'IM IN THAT CHURCH AT TEAMPOLL-DÉMUS. IF NOT THERE, THEN CARRICK-FHAD-VIC-ORUS. IF NOT THERE, THEN IMOLGUE-FADA. AND IF NOT THERE, IT MUST BE KILL-BREEDYA.
DO THIS WORK RIGHTLY AND THE GOOD PEOPLE WILL BE THANKFUL TO YOU.
FAIL IN THIS AND THE CHILD IS LOST.
LOCKED.
I'VE NEVER BROKEN INTO A CHURCH...
CHECK THE STONE OVER THE DOOR.
OUCH!

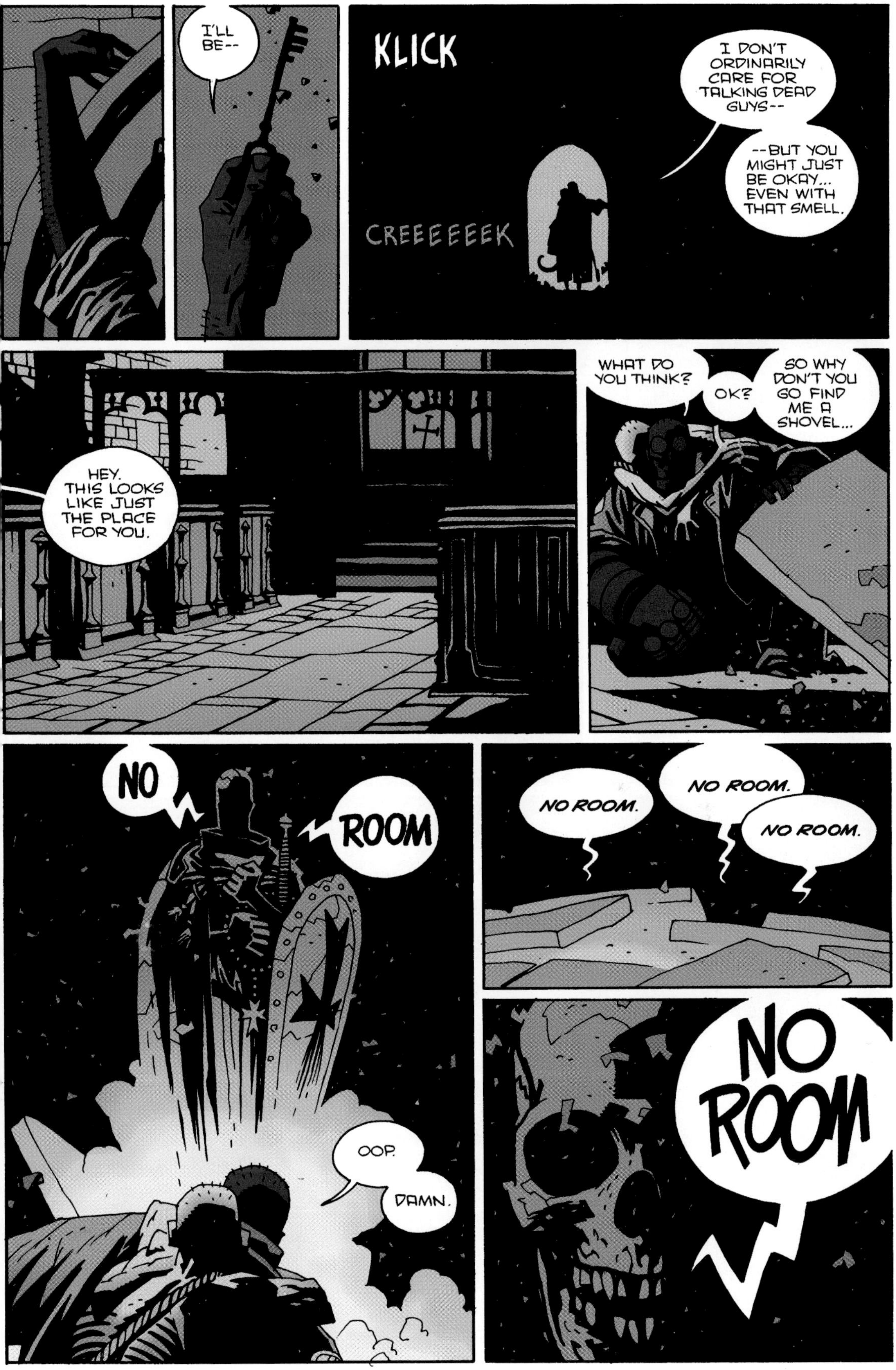
I'LL BE--
KLICK
CREEEEEEK
I DON'T ORDINARILY CARE FOR TALKING DEAD GUYS--
--BUT YOU MIGHT JUST BE OKAY... EVEN WITH THAT SMELL.
HEY. THIS LOOKS LIKE JUST THE PLACE FOR YOU.
WHAT DO YOU THINK?
OK?
SO WHY DON'T YOU GO FIND ME A SHOVEL...
NO
ROOM
OOP.
DAMN.
NO ROOM.
NO ROOM.
NO ROOM.
NO ROOM

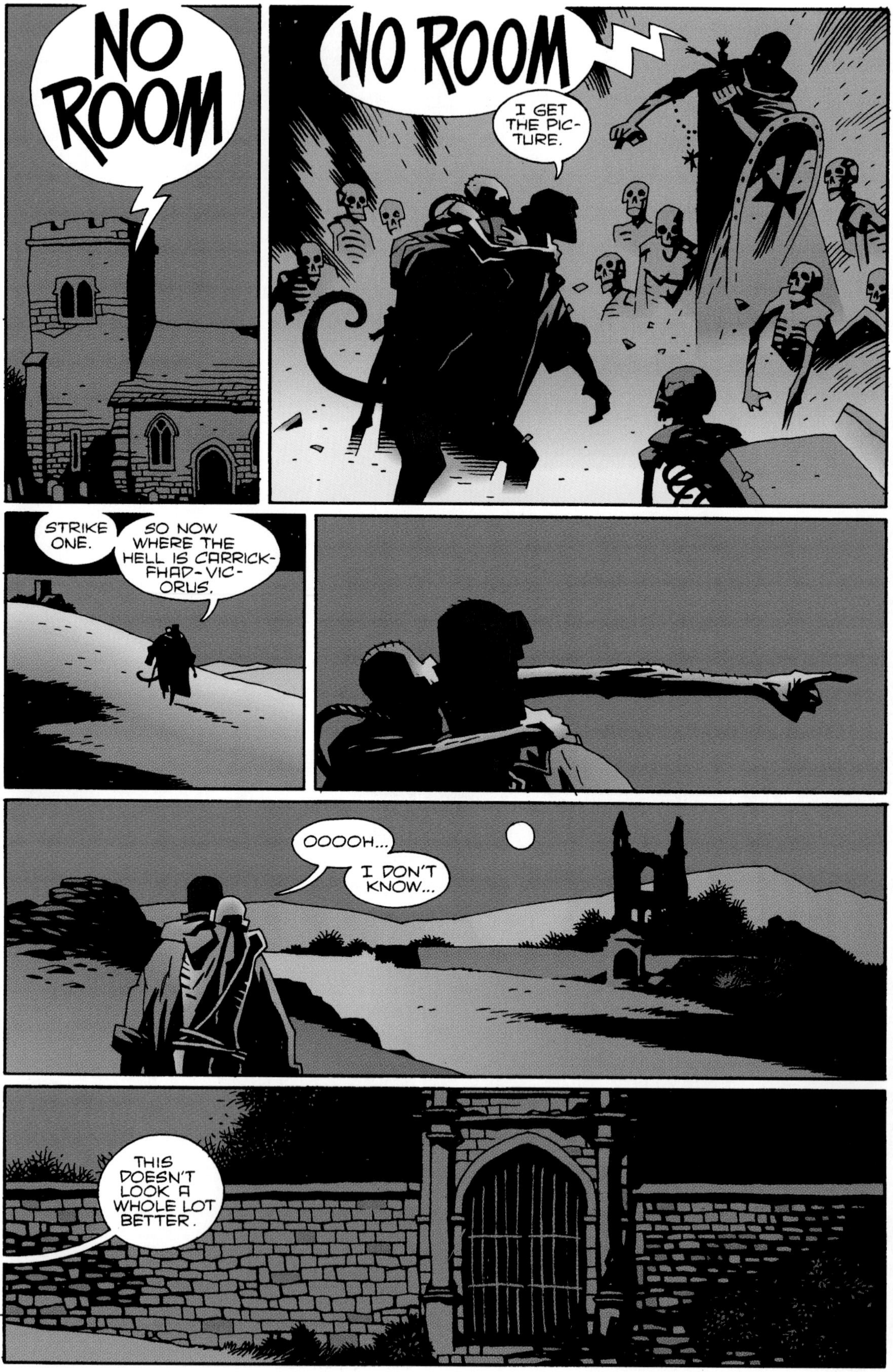
NO ROOM
NO ROOM
I GET THE PIC-TURE.
STRIKE ONE.
SO NOW WHERE THE HELL IS CARRICK-FHAD-VIC-ORUS.
OOOOH...
I DON'T KNOW...
THIS DOESN'T LOOK A WHOLE LOT BETTER.

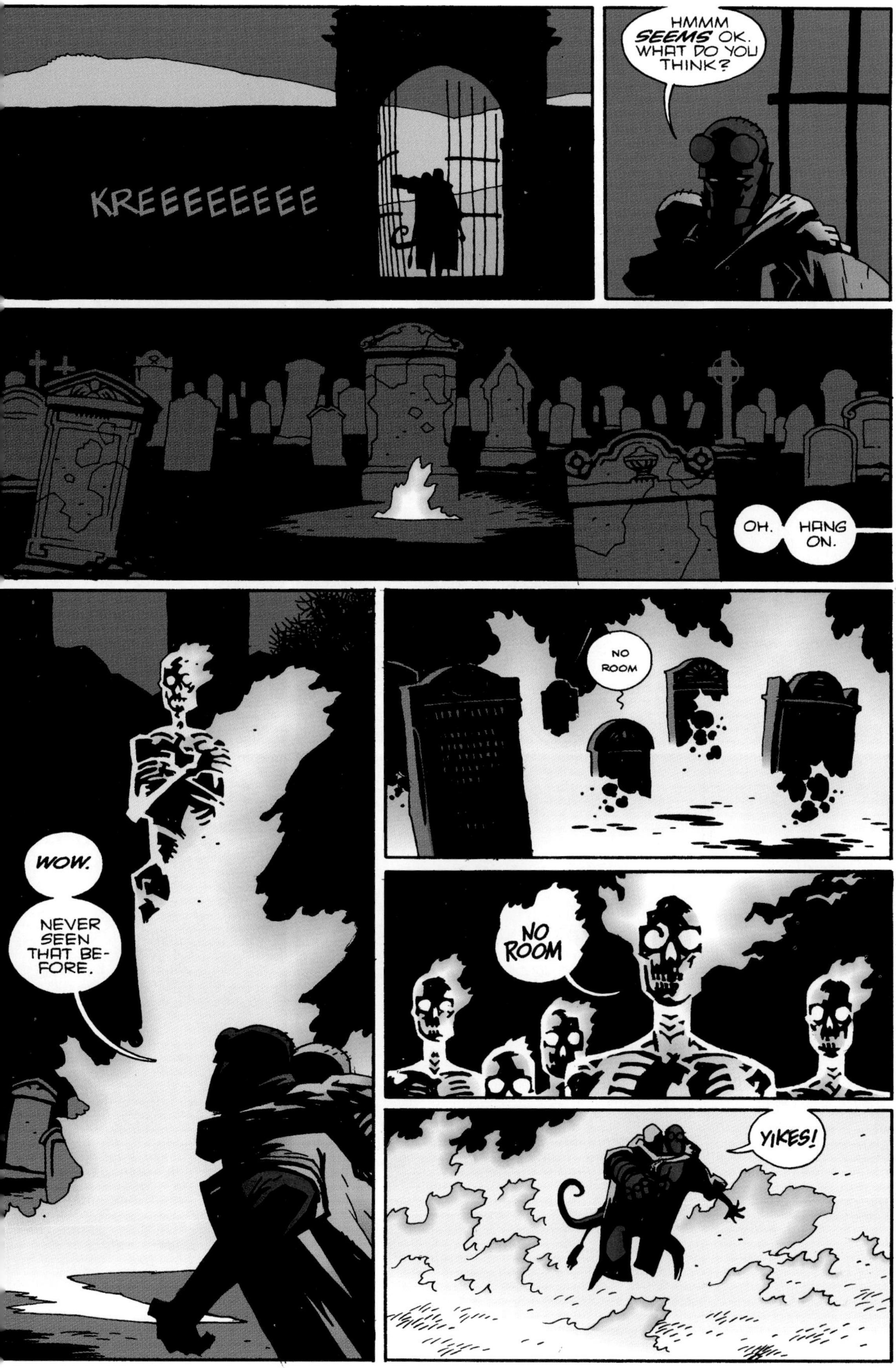
KREEEEEEEEE
HMMM SEEMS OK. WHAT DO YOU THINK?
OH.
HANG ON.
WOW.
NEVER SEEN THAT BE-FORE.
NO ROOM
NO ROOM
YIKES!

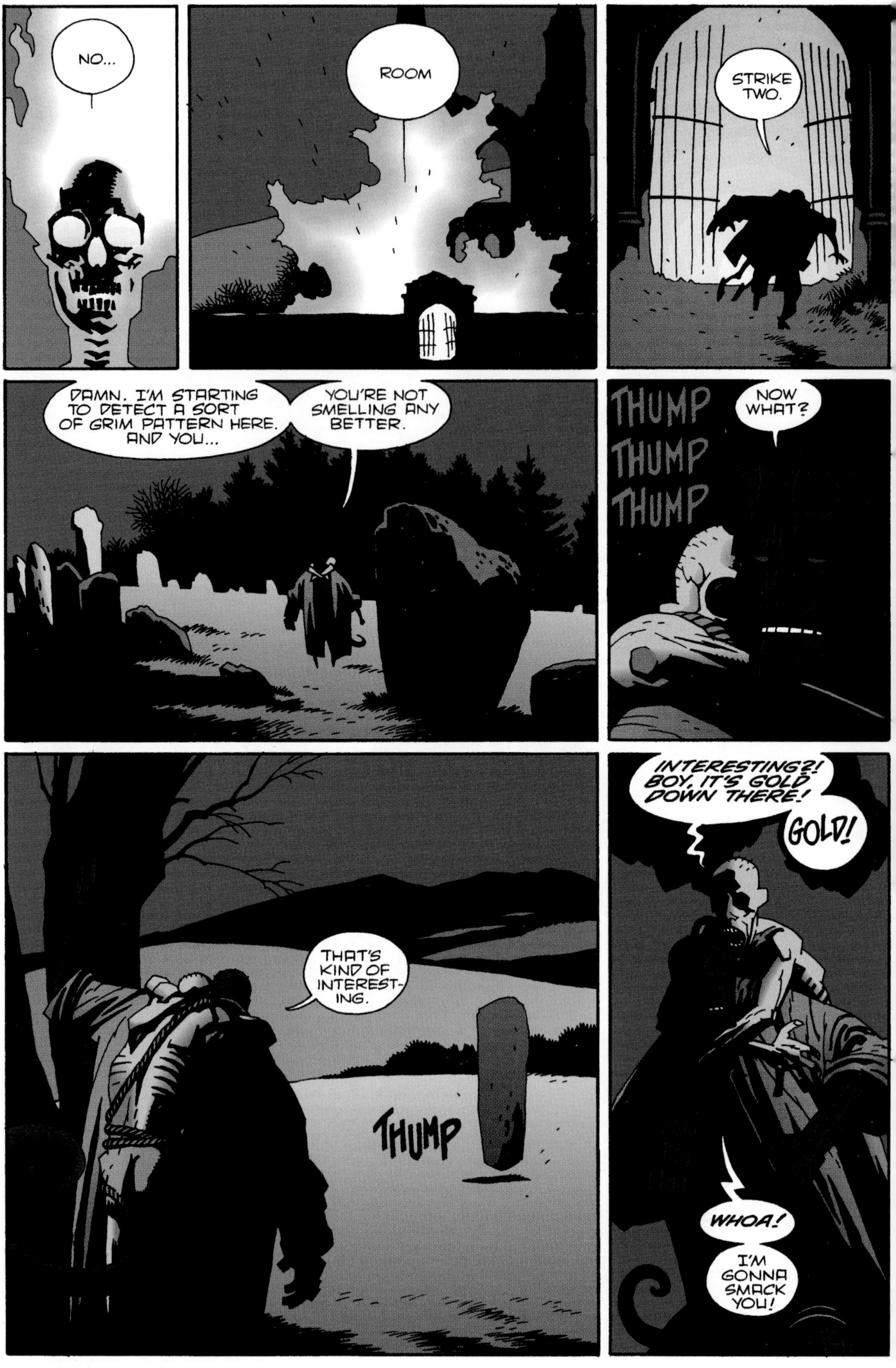

NO...
ROOM
STRIKE TWO.
DAMN. I'M STARTING TO DETECT A SORT OF GRIM PATTERN HERE. AND YOU...
YOU'RE NOT SMELLING ANY BETTER.
THUMP THUMP THUMP
NOW WHAT?
THAT'S KIND OF INTEREST-ING.
THUMP
INTERESTING?! BOY, IT'S GOLD DOWN THERE!
GOLD!
WHOA!
I'M GONNA SMACK YOU!

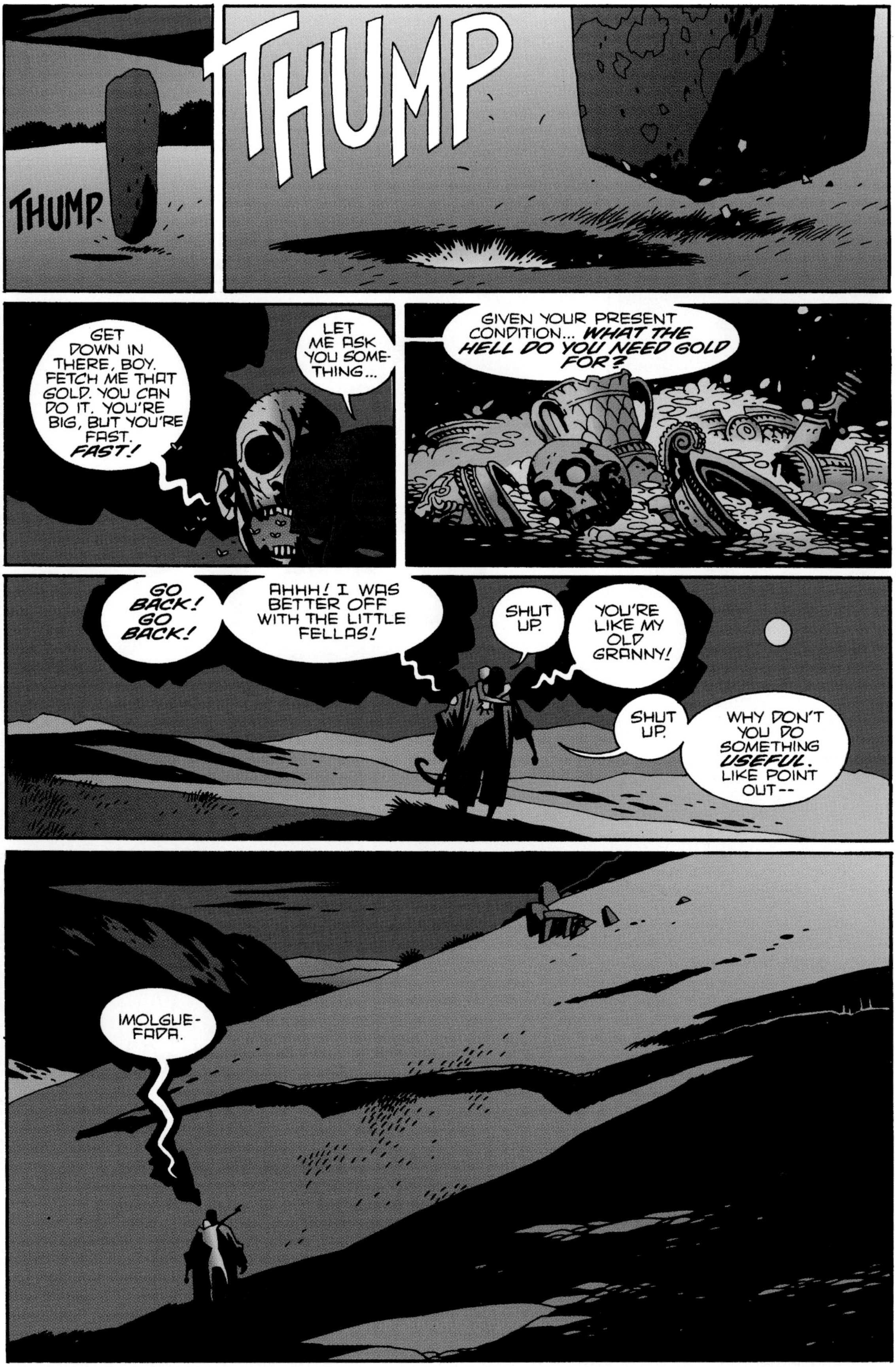
THUMP
THUMP
GET DOWN IN THERE, BOY. FETCH ME THAT GOLD. YOU CAN DO IT. YOU'RE BIG, BUT YOU'RE FAST. FAST!
LET ME ASK YOU SOMETHING...
GIVEN YOUR PRESENT CONDITION... WHAT THE HELL DO YOU NEED GOLD FOR?
GO BACK! GO BACK!
AHHH! I WAS BETTER OFF WITH THE LITTLE FELLAS!
SHUT UP.
YOU'RE LIKE MY OLD GRANNY!
SHUT UP.
WHY DON'T YOU DO SOMETHING USEFUL. LIKE POINT OUT--
IMOLGUE-FADA.

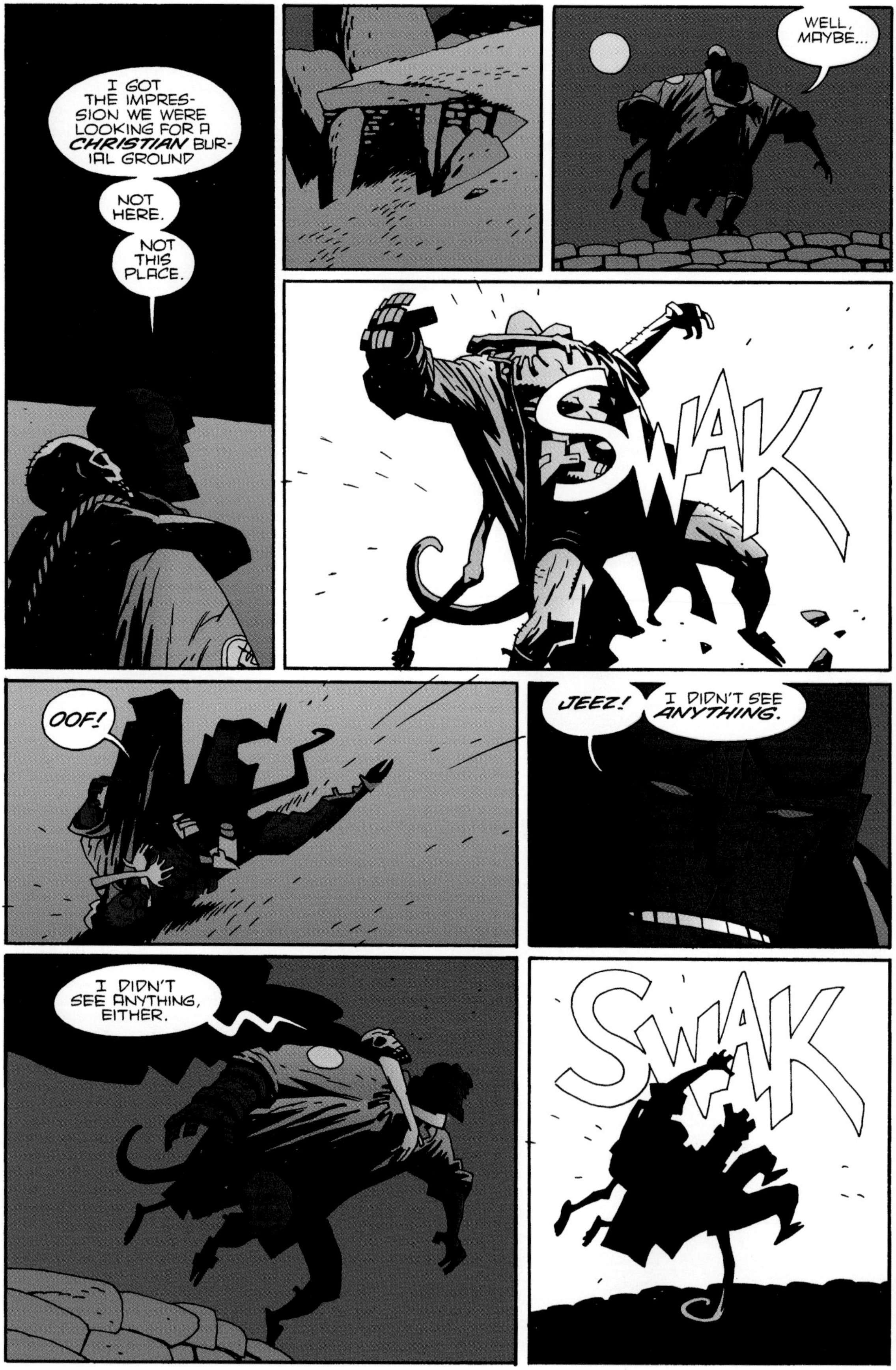
I GOT THE IMPRESSION WE WERE LOOKING FOR A CHRISTIAN BURIAL GROUND
NOT HERE.
NOT THIS PLACE.
WELL, MAYBE...
SWAK
OOF!
JEEZ!
I DIDN'T SEE ANYTHING.
I DIDN'T SEE ANYTHING, EITHER.
SWAK

THIS IS RIDICU-LOUS.

SCREW IT. LET'S GO TO KILL-BREEDYA.

THE BEAST 'AS SURVIVED IMOLGUE-FADA, AND 'AS TIME ENOUGH TO DO 'IS WORK BEFORE THE MORNING.

THEN BRING OUT THE CHILD AND MAKE HER READY TO RETURN. WE HAVE NO CHOICE BUT HONOR. AND WE *SHOULD* HONOR THIS "BEAST" ABOVE ALL THE CREATURES OF THE EARTH. DACCI AB JURA. HEAVEN, HELL, AND HUMAN COME TOGETHER AS ONE. ENCINCTU DAMI.

HONOR THE BEAST. HONOR THE DEAL...

THOUGH BY THE DOING, WE DIE A LIT-TLE MORE.

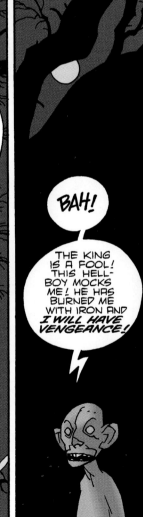

BAH!

THE KING IS A FOOL! THIS HELL-BOY MOCKS ME! HE HAS BURNED ME WITH IRON AND *I WILL HAVE VENGEANCE!*

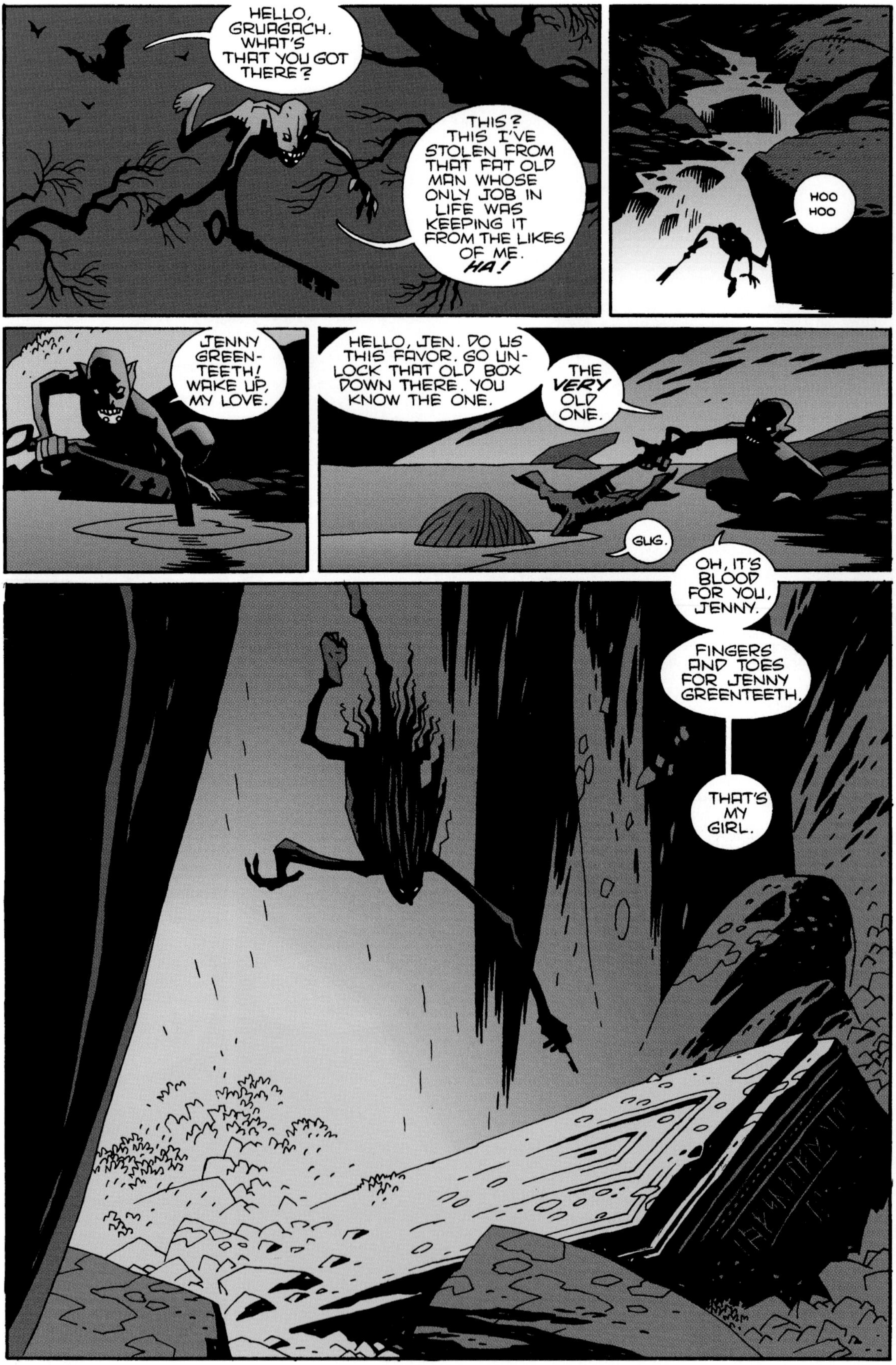
HELLO, GRUAGACH. WHAT'S THAT YOU GOT THERE?
THIS? THIS I'VE STOLEN FROM THAT FAT OLD MAN WHOSE ONLY JOB IN LIFE WAS KEEPING IT FROM THE LIKES OF ME. HA!
HOO HOO
JENNY GREEN-TEETH! WAKE UP, MY LOVE.
HELLO, JEN. DO US THIS FAVOR. GO UN-LOCK THAT OLD BOX DOWN THERE. YOU KNOW THE ONE.
THE VERY OLD ONE.
GUG.
OH, IT'S BLOOD FOR YOU, JENNY.
FINGERS AND TOES FOR JENNY GREENTEETH.
THAT'S MY GIRL.

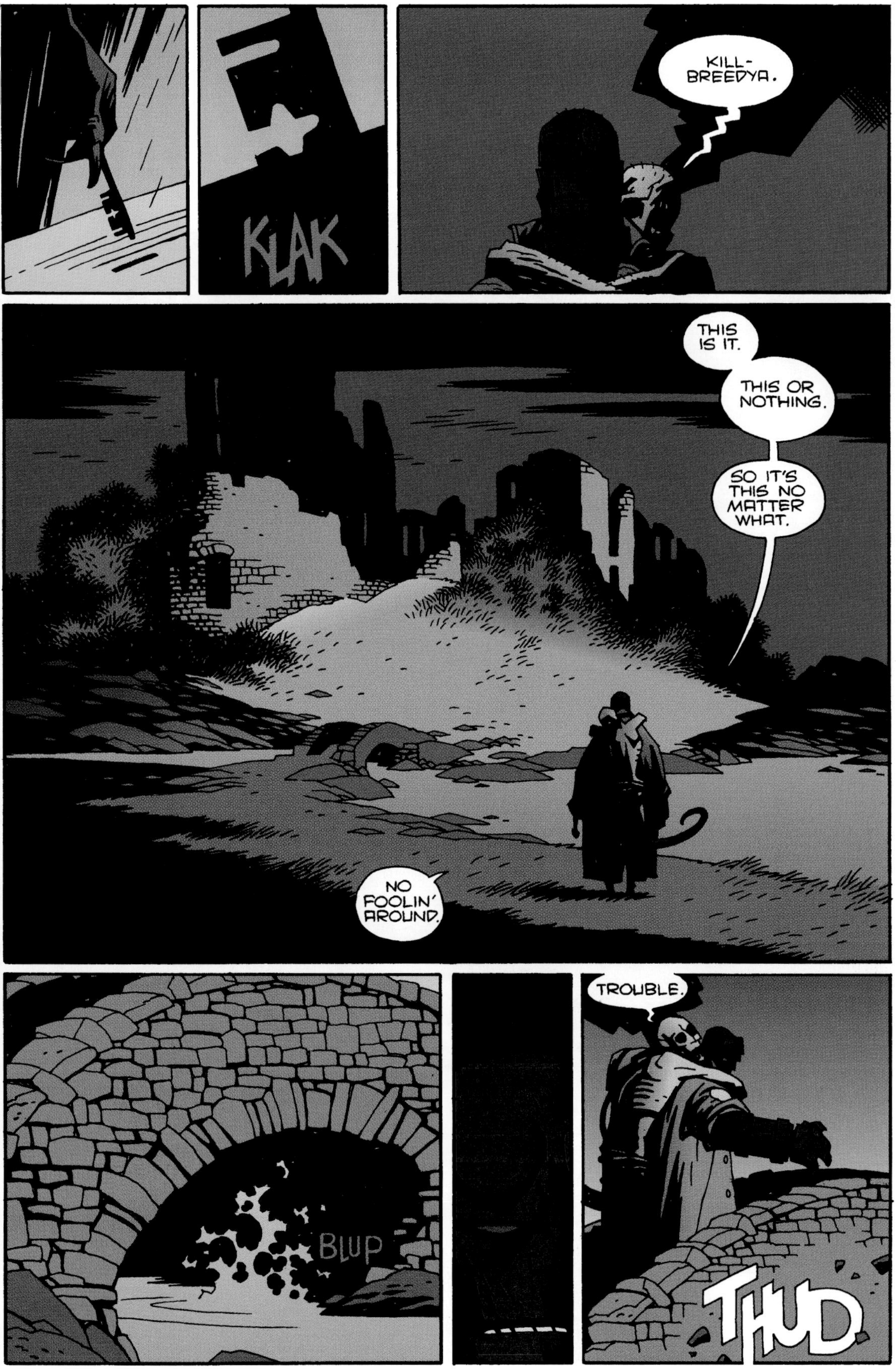
KLAK
KILL-BREEDYA.
THIS IS IT.
THIS OR NOTHING.
SO IT'S THIS NO MATTER WHAT.
NO FOOLIN' AROUND.
BLUP
TROUBLE.
THUD.

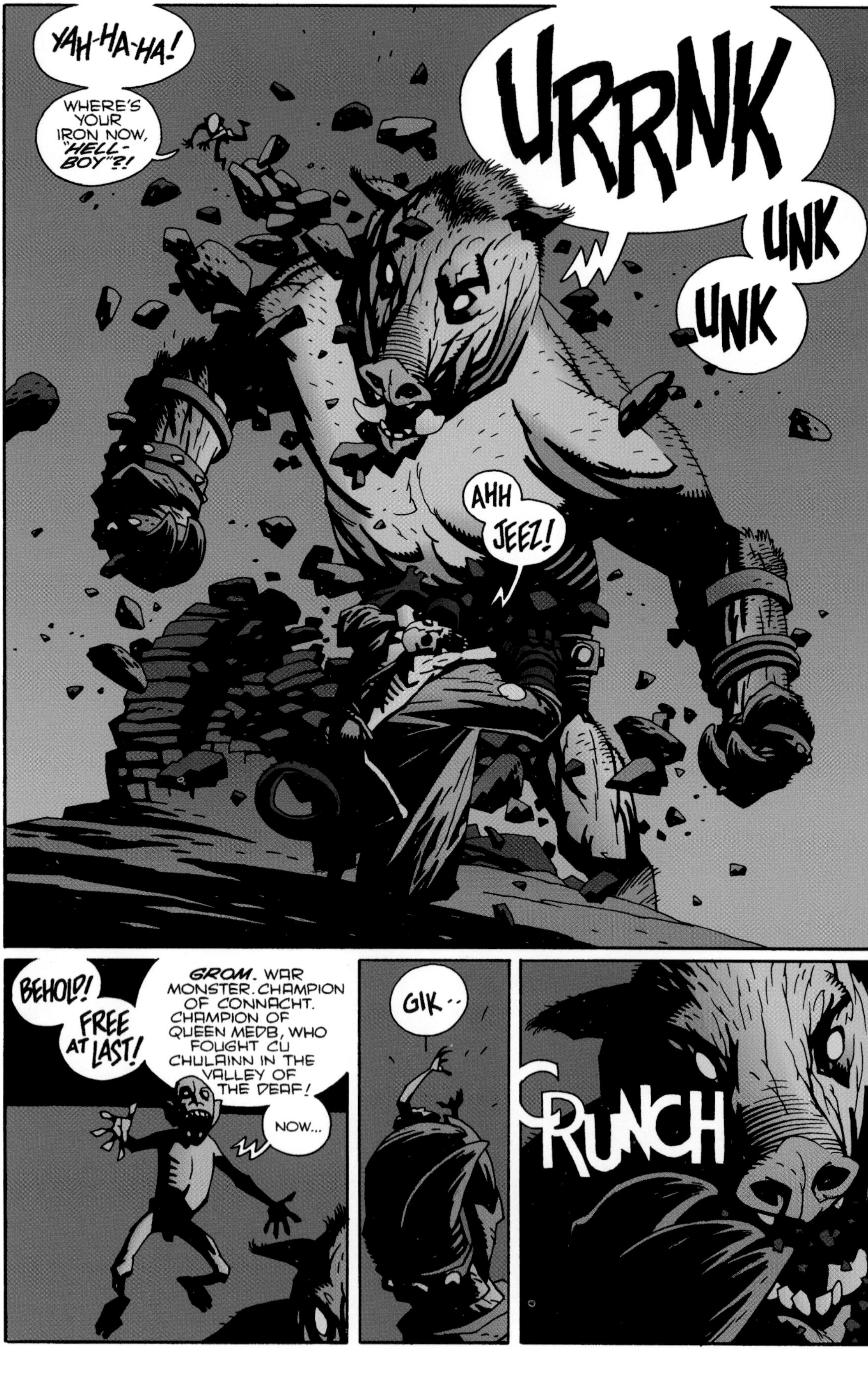
YAH-HA-HA!
WHERE'S YOUR IRON NOW, "HELL-BOY"?!
URRNK
UNK
UNK
AHH JEEZ!
BEHOLD!
FREE AT LAST!
GROM. WAR MONSTER. CHAMPION OF CONNACHT. CHAMPION OF QUEEN MEDB, WHO FOUGHT CU CHULAINN IN THE VALLEY OF THE DEAF!
NOW...
GIK..
CRUNCH

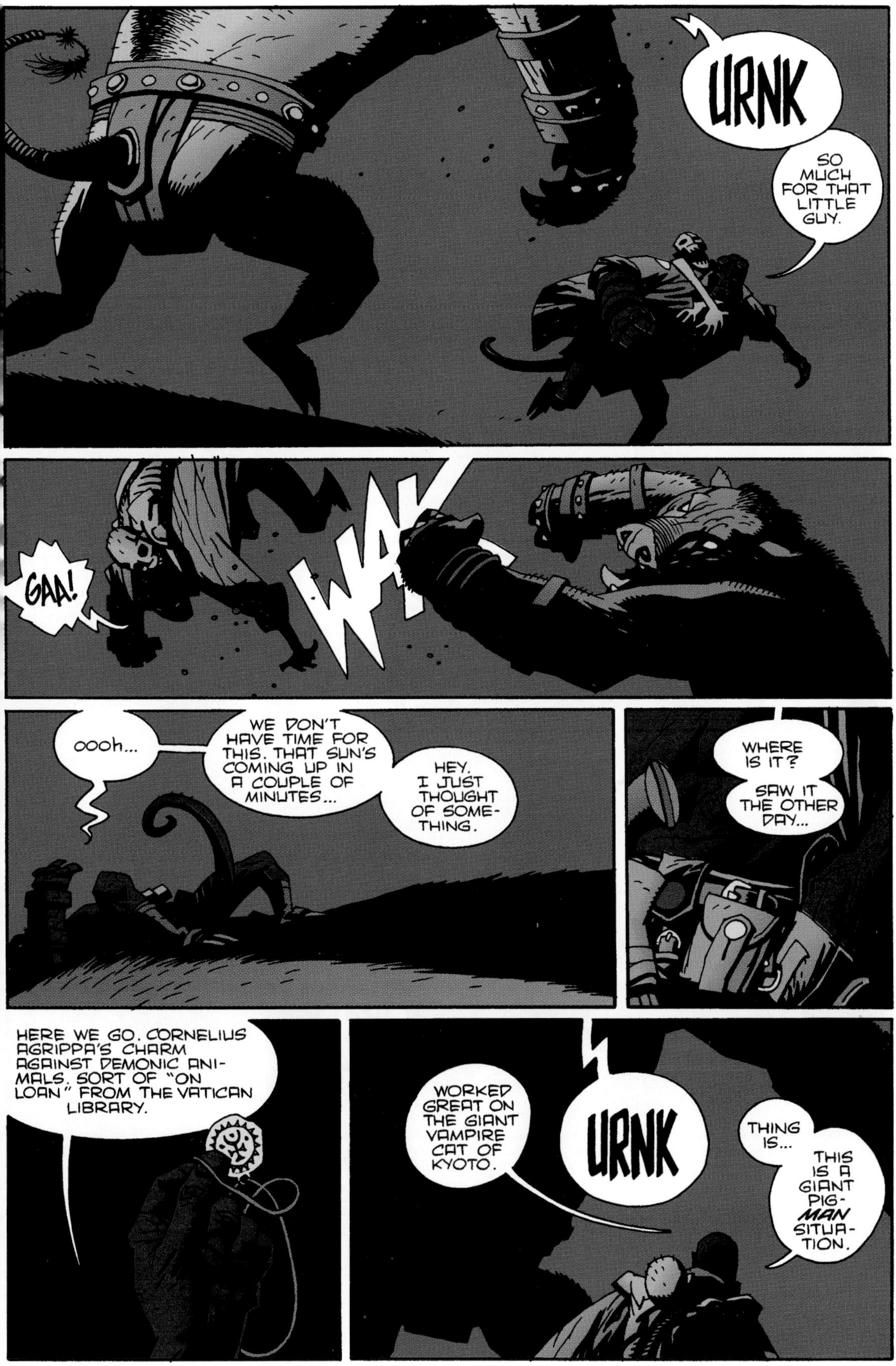
URNK
SO MUCH FOR THAT LITTLE GUY.
GAA!
WAK
oooh...
WE DON'T HAVE TIME FOR THIS. THAT SUN'S COMING UP IN A COUPLE OF MINUTES...
HEY. I JUST THOUGHT OF SOME-THING.
WHERE IS IT?
SAW IT THE OTHER DAY...
HERE WE GO. CORNELIUS AGRIPPA'S CHARM AGAINST DEMONIC ANI-MALS. SORT OF "ON LOAN" FROM THE VATICAN LIBRARY.
WORKED GREAT ON THE GIANT VAMPIRE CAT OF KYOTO.
URNK
THING IS...
THIS IS A GIANT PIG-*MAN* SITUA-TION.

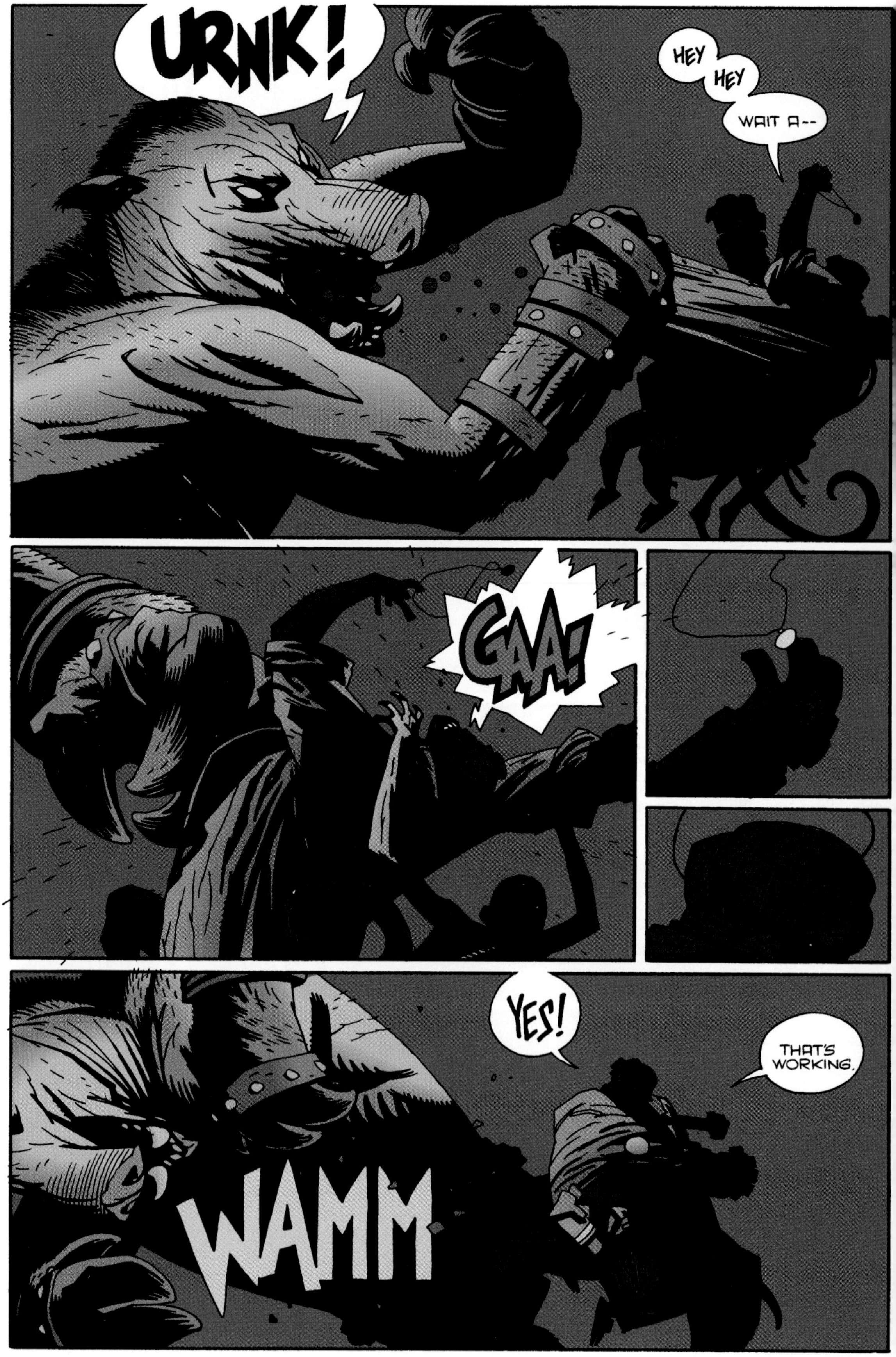
URNK!
HEY
HEY
WAIT A--
GAA!
YES!
THAT'S WORKING.
WAMM

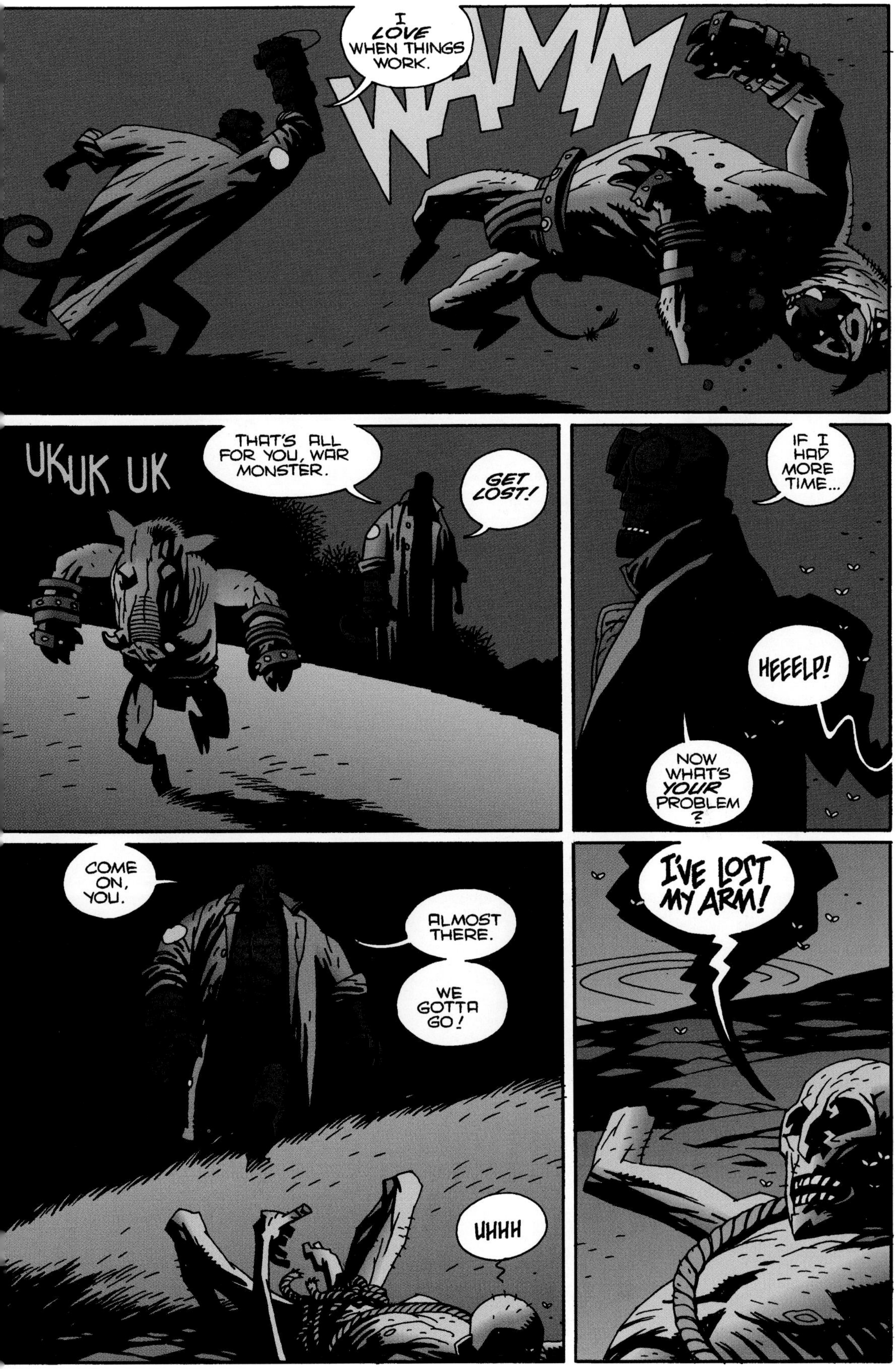
I LOVE WHEN THINGS WORK.
WAMM
UKUK UK
THAT'S ALL FOR YOU, WAR MONSTER.
GET LOST!
IF I HAD MORE TIME...
HEEELP!
NOW WHAT'S YOUR PROBLEM?
COME ON, YOU.
ALMOST THERE.
WE GOTTA GO!
UHHH
I'VE LOST MY ARM!

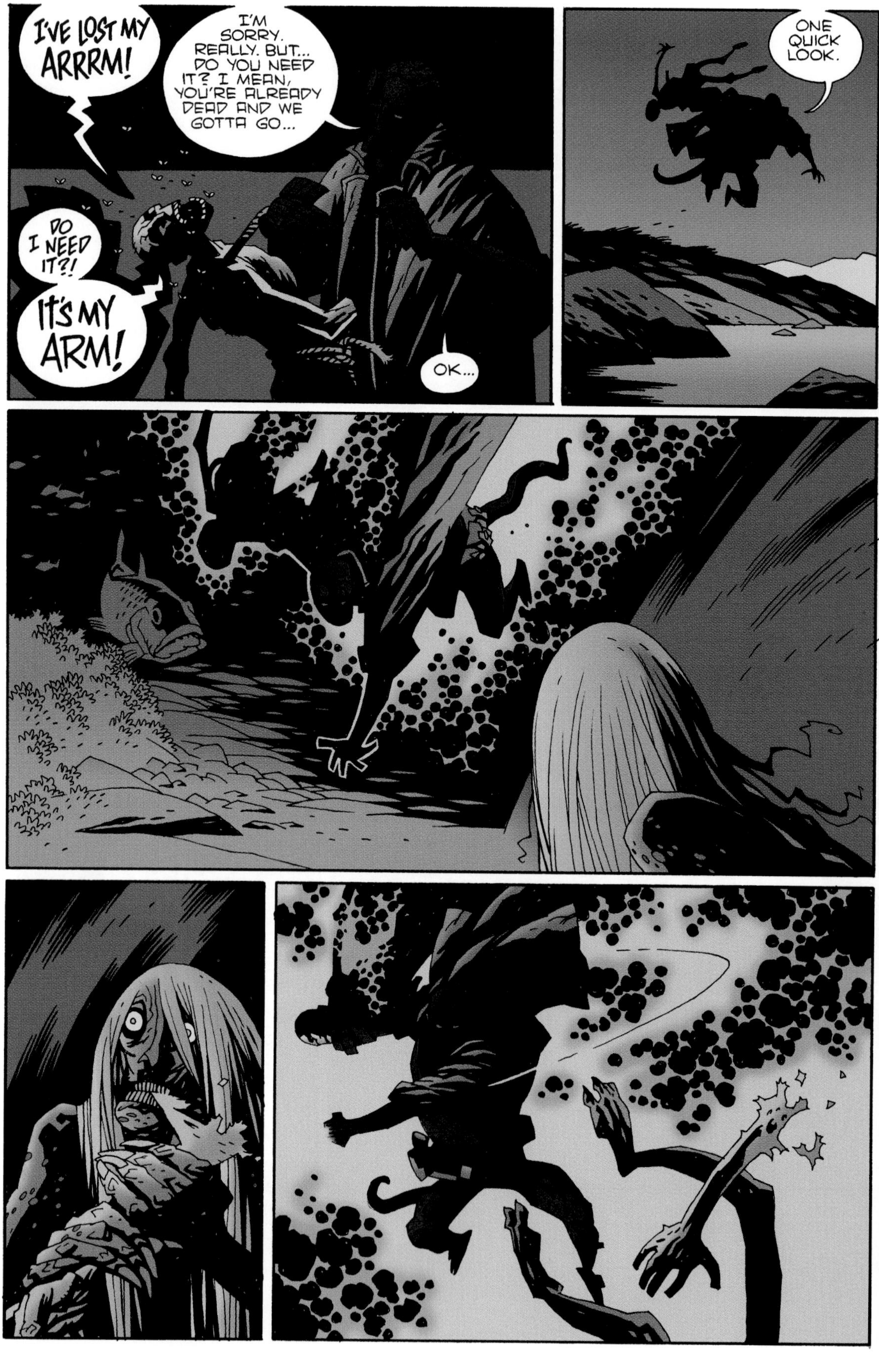
I'VE LOST MY ARRRM!
I'M SORRY. REALLY. BUT... DO YOU NEED IT? I MEAN, YOU'RE ALREADY DEAD AND WE GOTTA GO...
DO I NEED IT?!
IT'S MY ARM!
OK...
ONE QUICK LOOK.

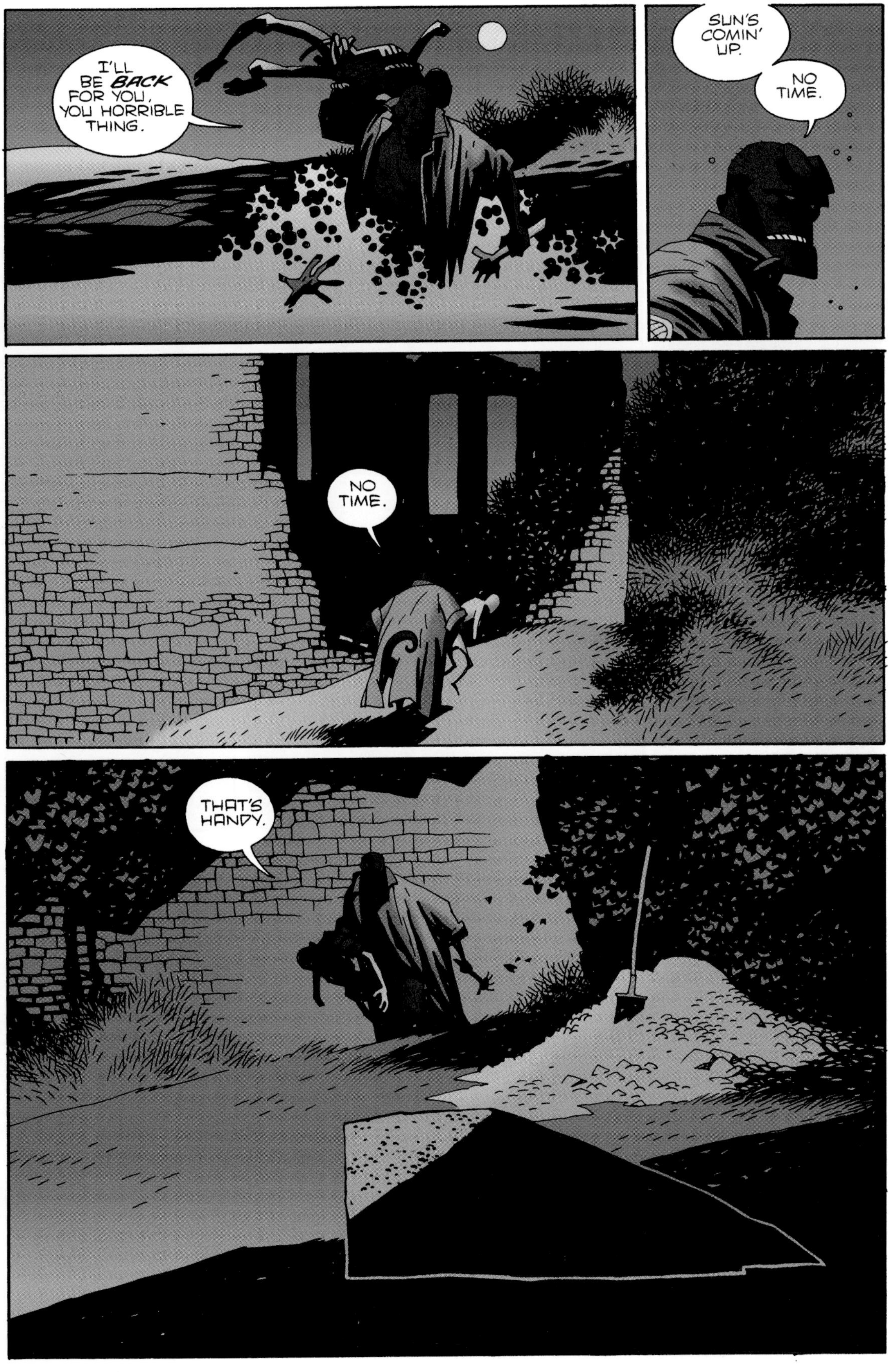

I'LL BE BACK FOR YOU, YOU HORRIBLE THING.
SUN'S COMIN' UP.
NO TIME.
NO TIME.
THAT'S HANDY.

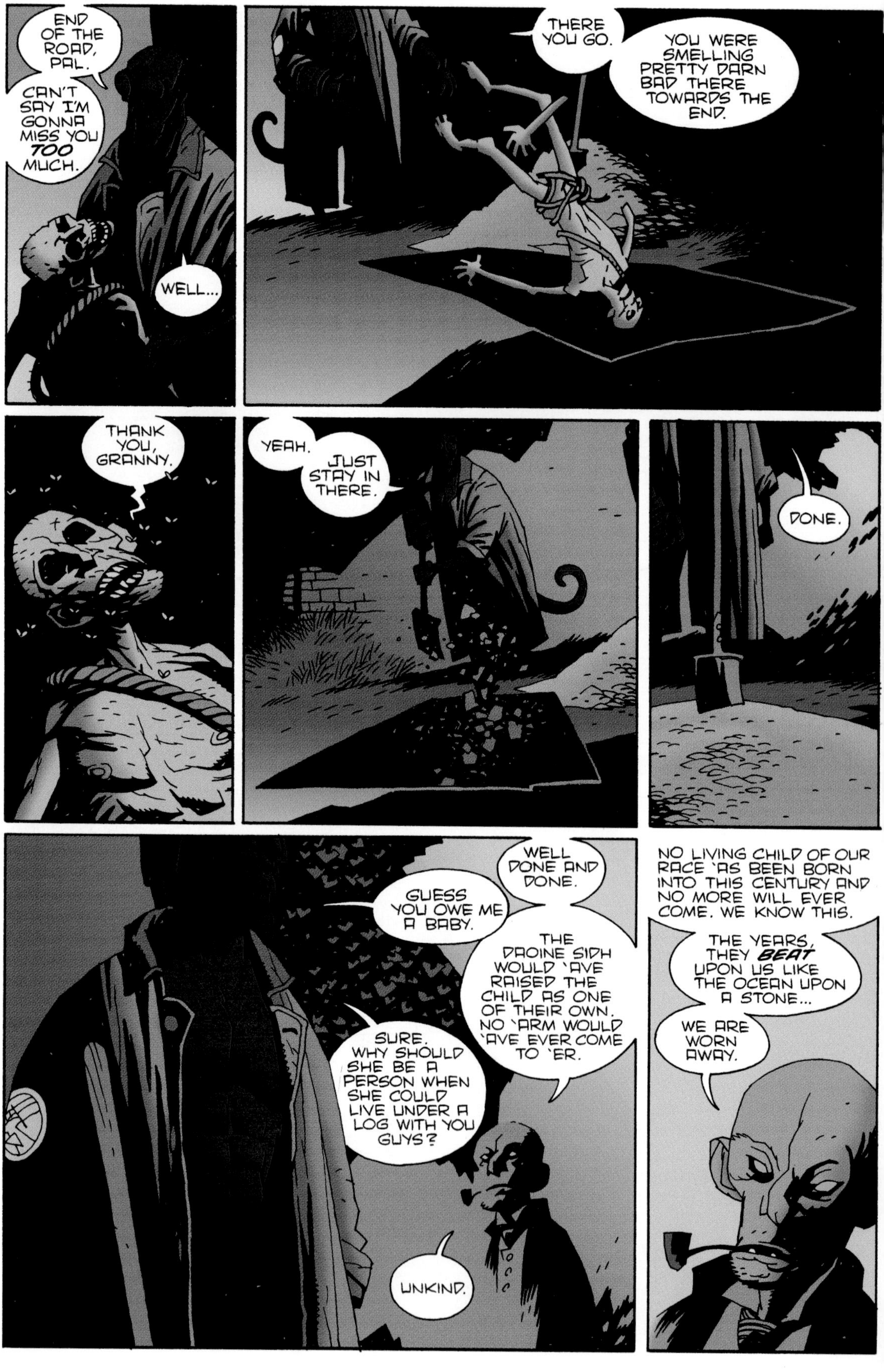

END OF THE ROAD, PAL.
CAN'T SAY I'M GONNA MISS YOU TOO MUCH.
WELL...
THERE YOU GO.
YOU WERE SMELLING PRETTY DARN BAD THERE TOWARDS THE END.
THANK YOU, GRANNY.
YEAH.
JUST STAY IN THERE.
DONE.
WELL DONE AND DONE.
GUESS YOU OWE ME A BABY.
THE DAOINE SIDH WOULD 'AVE RAISED THE CHILD AS ONE OF THEIR OWN. NO 'ARM WOULD 'AVE EVER COME TO 'ER.
SURE. WHY SHOULD SHE BE A PERSON WHEN SHE COULD LIVE UNDER A LOG WITH YOU GUYS?
UNKIND.
NO LIVING CHILD OF OUR RACE 'AS BEEN BORN INTO THIS CENTURY AND NO MORE WILL EVER COME. WE KNOW THIS.
THE YEARS, THEY BEAT UPON US LIKE THE OCEAN UPON A STONE...
WE ARE WORN AWAY.

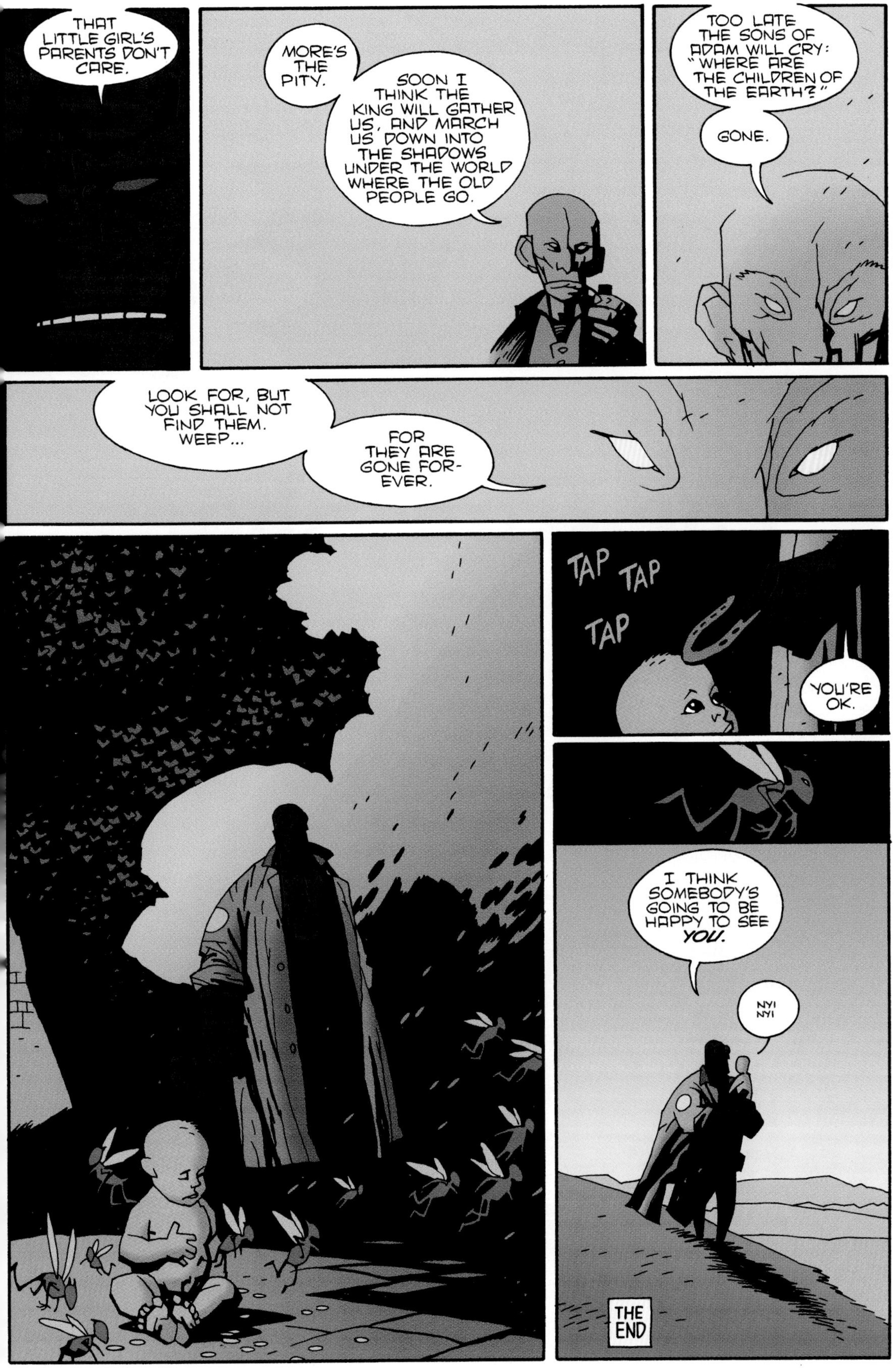
THAT LITTLE GIRL'S PARENTS DON'T CARE.
MORE'S THE PITY.
SOON I THINK THE KING WILL GATHER US, AND MARCH US DOWN INTO THE SHADOWS UNDER THE WORLD WHERE THE OLD PEOPLE GO.
TOO LATE THE SONS OF ADAM WILL CRY: "WHERE ARE THE CHILDREN OF THE EARTH?"
GONE.
LOOK FOR, BUT YOU SHALL NOT FIND THEM. WEEP...
FOR THEY ARE GONE FOR-EVER.
TAP TAP TAP
YOU'RE OK.
I THINK SOMEBODY'S GOING TO BE HAPPY TO SEE *YOU.*
NYI NYI
THE END

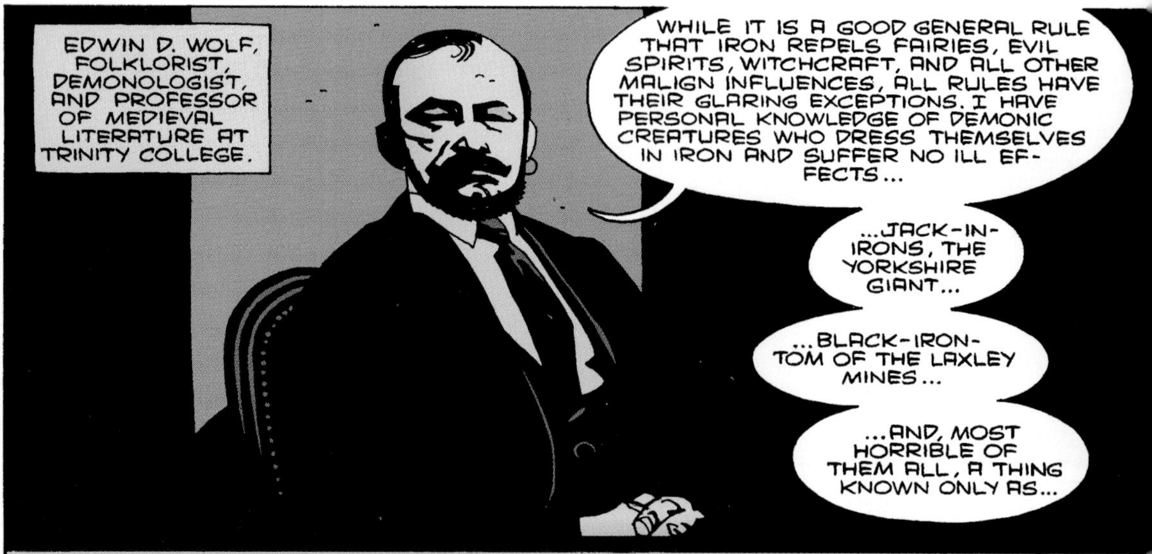
EDWIN D. WOLF, FOLKLORIST, DEMONOLOGIST, AND PROFESSOR OF MEDIEVAL LITERATURE AT TRINITY COLLEGE.
WHILE IT IS A GOOD GENERAL RULE THAT IRON REPELS FAIRIES, EVIL SPIRITS, WITCHCRAFT, AND ALL OTHER MALIGN INFLUENCES, ALL RULES HAVE THEIR GLARING EXCEPTIONS. I HAVE PERSONAL KNOWLEDGE OF DEMONIC CREATURES WHO DRESS THEMSELVES IN IRON AND SUFFER NO ILL EFFECTS...
...JACK-IN-IRONS, THE YORKSHIRE GIANT...
...BLACK-IRON-TOM OF THE LAXLEY MINES...
...AND, MOST HORRIBLE OF THEM ALL, A THING KNOWN ONLY AS...

The Iron Shoes

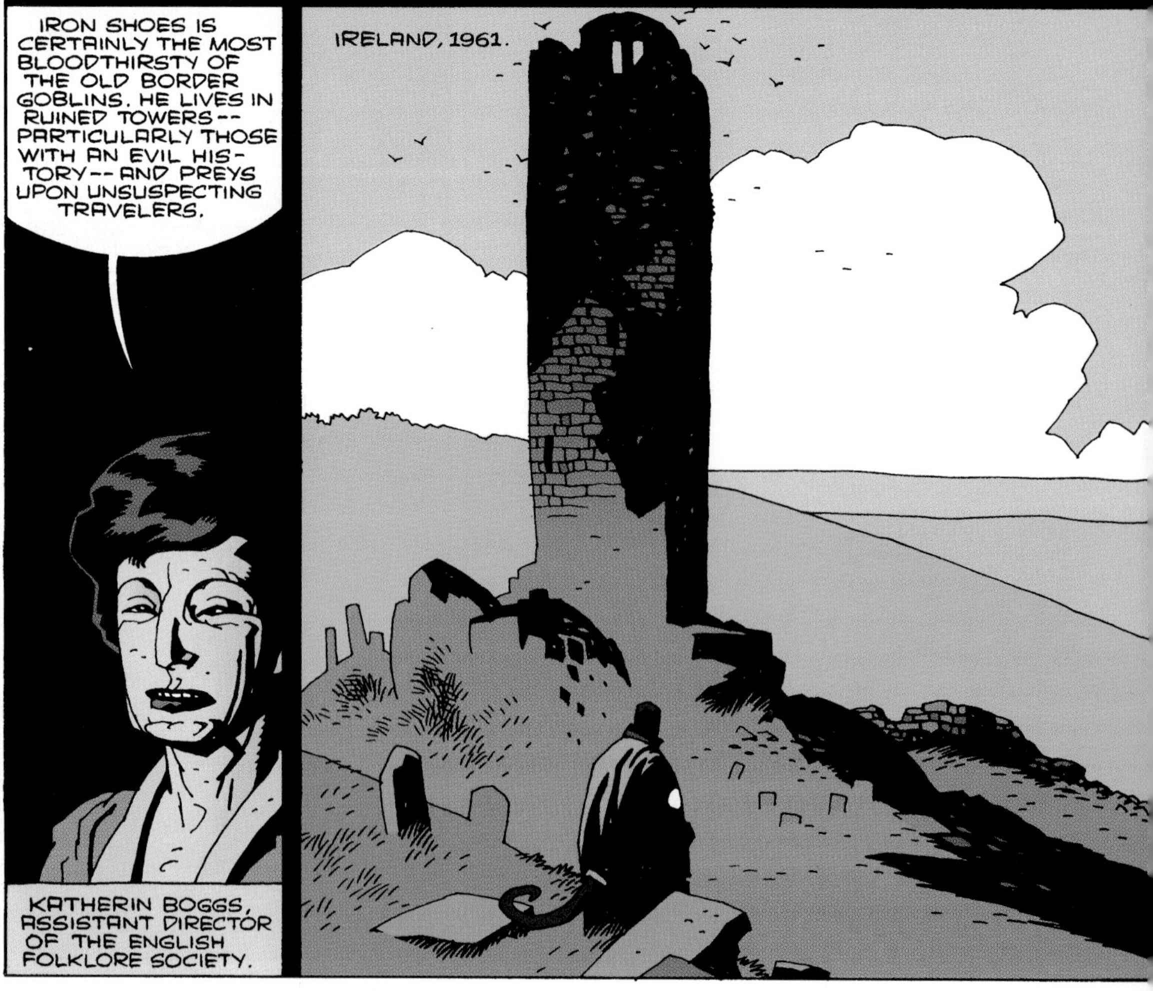
IRON SHOES IS CERTAINLY THE MOST BLOODTHIRSTY OF THE OLD BORDER GOBLINS. HE LIVES IN RUINED TOWERS--PARTICULARLY THOSE WITH AN EVIL HISTORY--AND PREYS UPON UNSUSPECTING TRAVELERS.
KATHERIN BOGGS, ASSISTANT DIRECTOR OF THE ENGLISH FOLKLORE SOCIETY.
IRELAND, 1961.

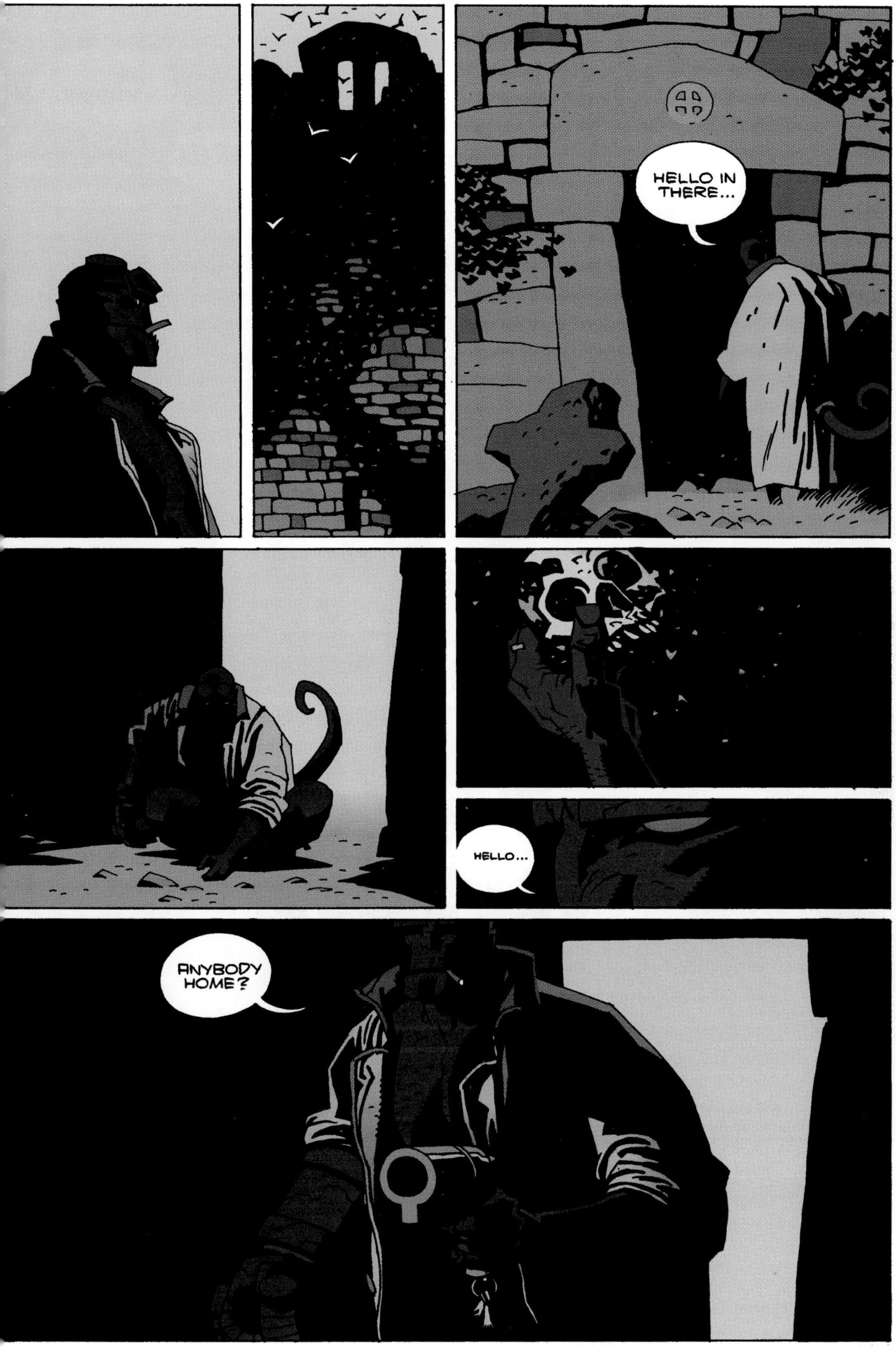
HELLO IN THERE...
HELLO...
ANYBODY HOME?

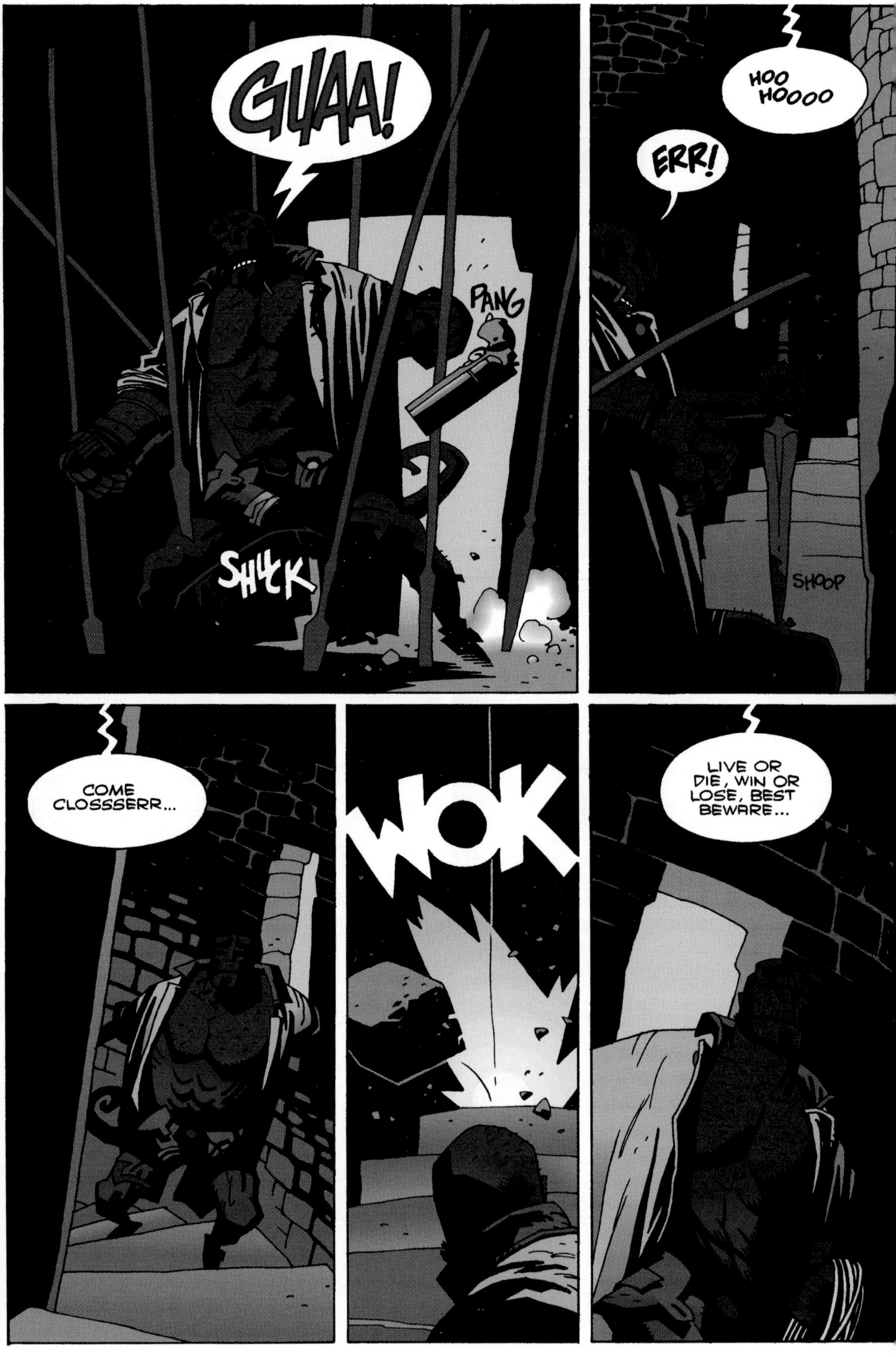
GUAA!
PANG
SHUCK
HOO HOOOO
ERR!
SHOOP
COME CLOSSSERR...
WOK
LIVE OR DIE, WIN OR LOSE, BEST BEWARE...

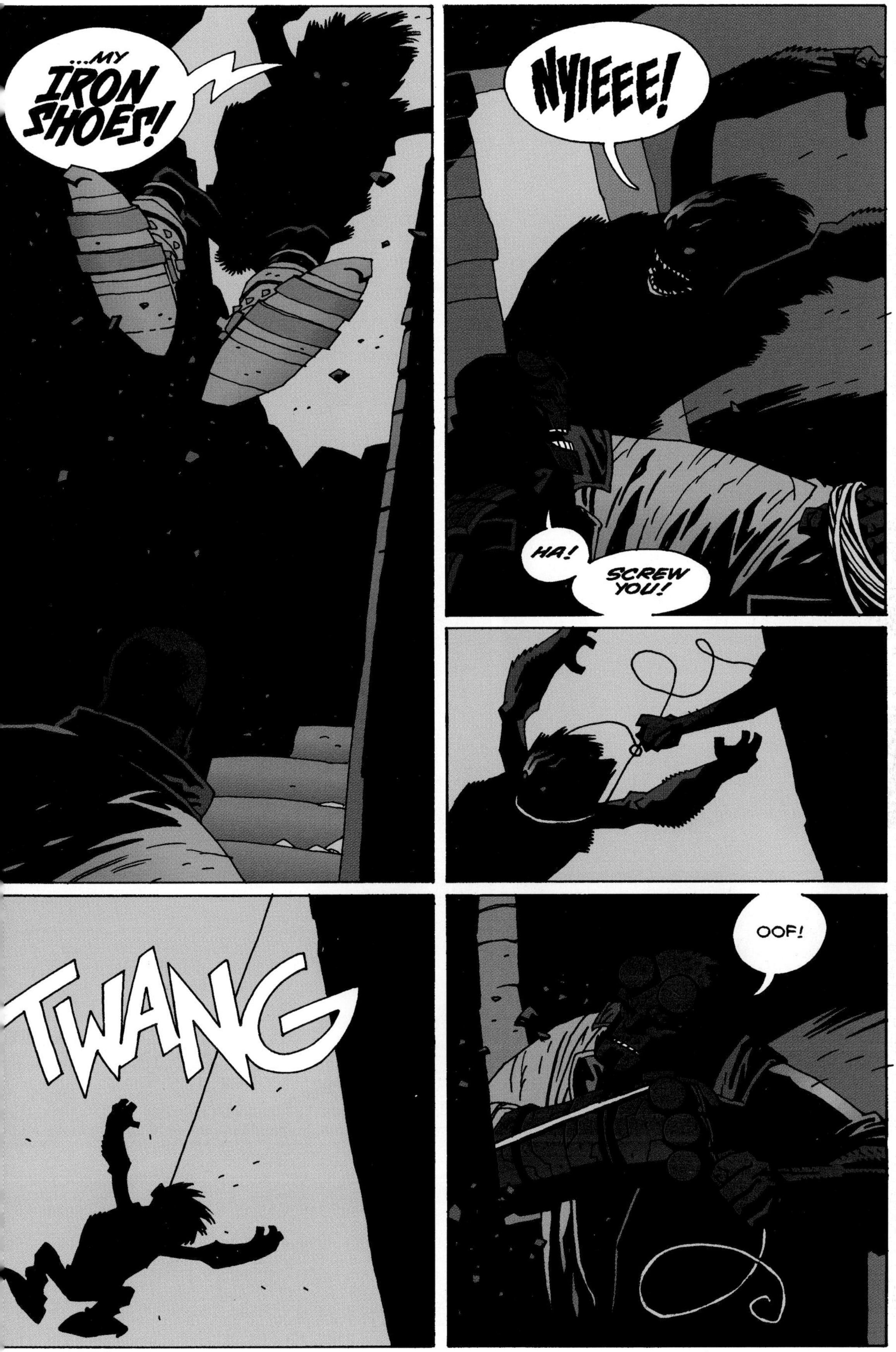
...MY IRON SHOES!
NYIEEE!
HA!
SCREW YOU!
TWANG
OOF!

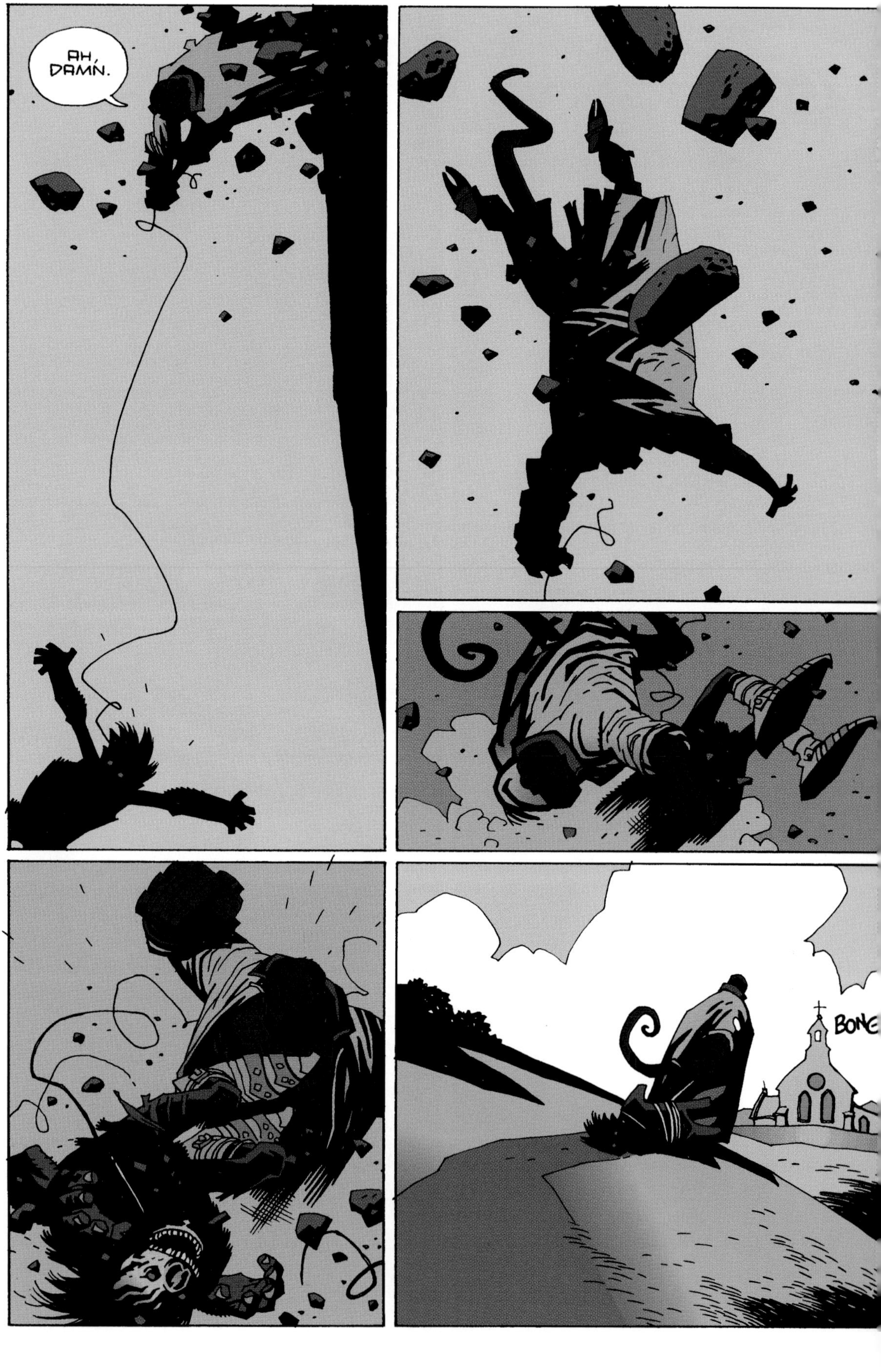
AH, DAMN.
BONG

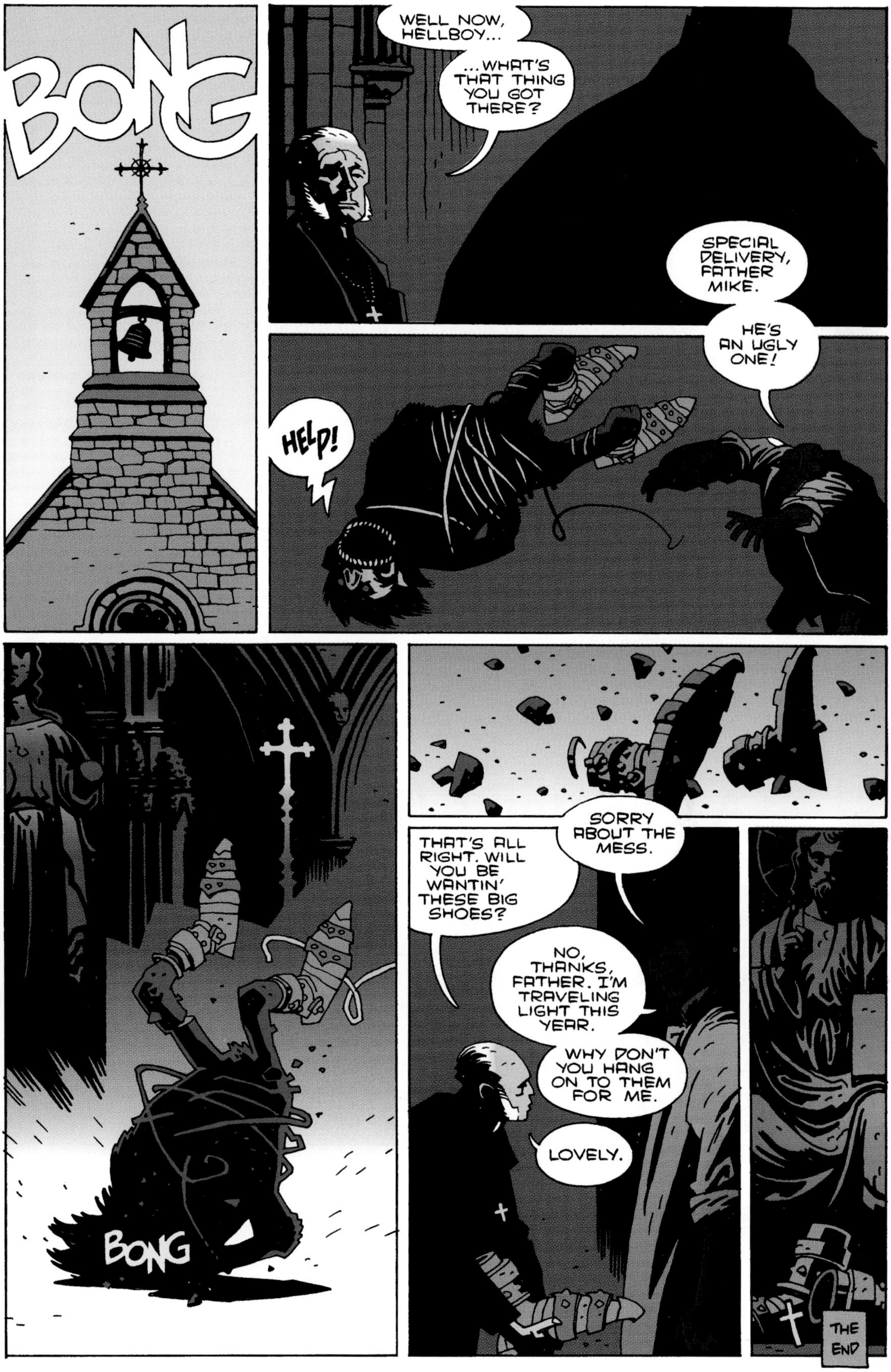
BONG
WELL NOW, HELLBOY...
...WHAT'S THAT THING YOU GOT THERE?
SPECIAL DELIVERY, FATHER MIKE.
HE'S AN UGLY ONE!
HELP!
BONG
THAT'S ALL RIGHT. WILL YOU BE WANTIN' THESE BIG SHOES?
SORRY ABOUT THE MESS.
NO, THANKS, FATHER. I'M TRAVELING LIGHT THIS YEAR.
WHY DON'T YOU HANG ON TO THEM FOR ME.
LOVELY.
THE END

The Baba Yaga

I HAD ORIGINALLY PLANNED to do this story as one of four backup features in Art Adams' *Monkeyman and O'Brien* miniseries. When Art took longer than expected on that series, I went ahead with other projects. Eventually I worked Baba Yaga (the most famous witch in Russian folklore) into *Wake the Devil*, the second Hellboy miniseries. In there I mentioned Hellboy shooting her eye out, but I still really wanted to draw that scene. It's sort of an important moment in Hellboy's history. So here it is, done specifically for this collection.

I made up all the business about counting dead men's fingers, but (believe it or not) the thing about Baba Yaga counting spoons is an actual Russian folktale.

✠

A Christmas Underground

LIKE "THE CORPSE," this one was inspired by a folktale I read years ago. It was an odd thing about a girl who looks under a bush and finds stairs leading down to some kind of palace, where she falls in love with an invisible prince. The stairs underground struck me as a sort of symbolic death/grave thing, turning the prince into a more sinister character. Well, I filed the story away in my head until Gary Gianni and I came up with the idea of doing a Christmas special. I realized I didn't have a Hellboy Christmas story, so I added the Christmas angel to the underground story, which helped it a lot, and there you go.

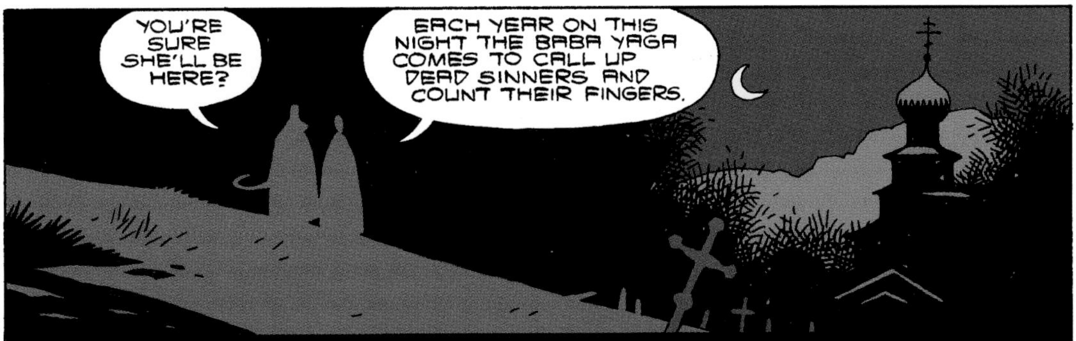
YOU'RE SURE SHE'LL BE HERE?
EACH YEAR ON THIS NIGHT THE BABA YAGA COMES TO CALL UP DEAD SINNERS AND COUNT THEIR FINGERS.

The Baba Yaga

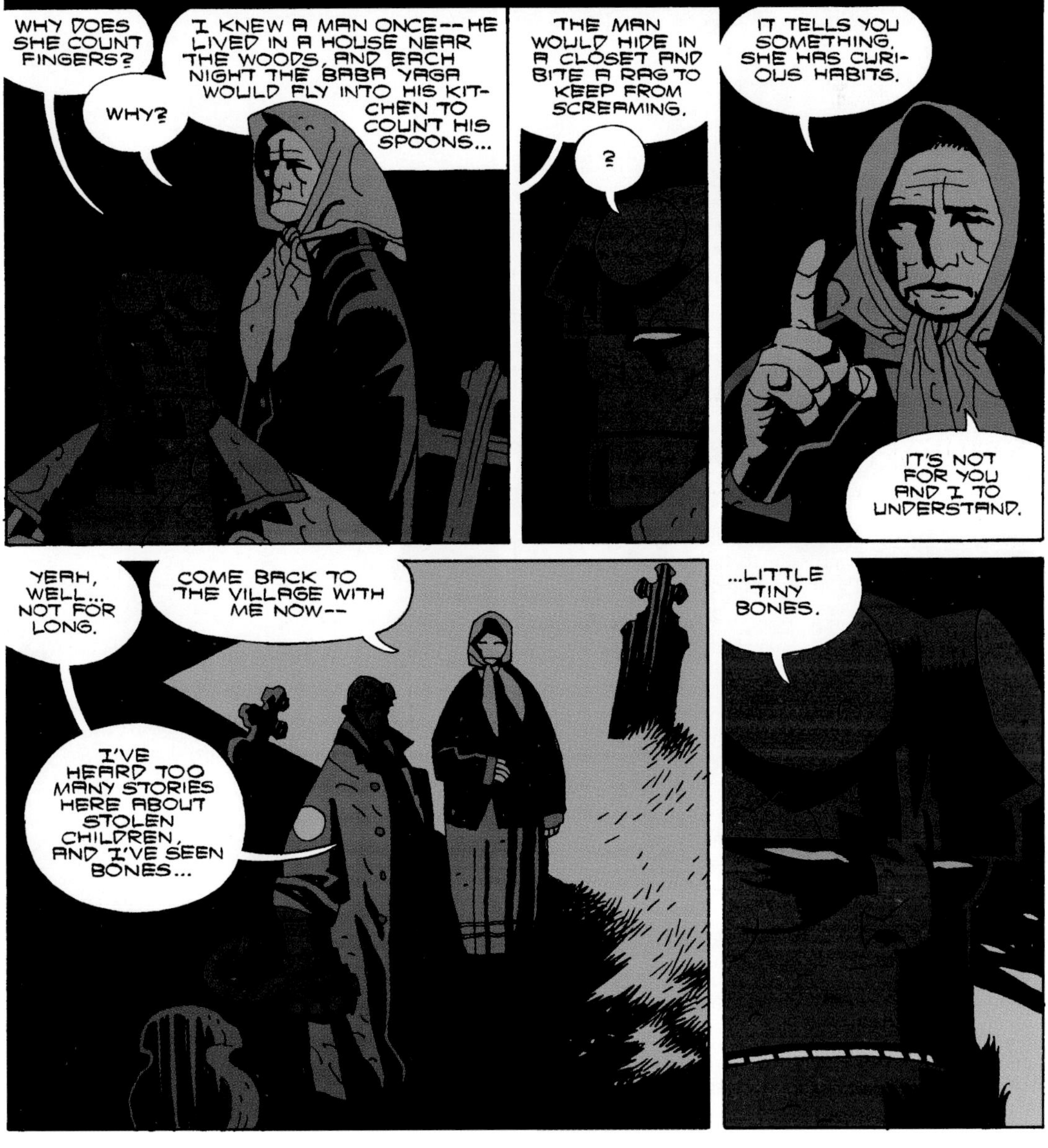
WHY DOES SHE COUNT FINGERS?
I KNEW A MAN ONCE--HE LIVED IN A HOUSE NEAR THE WOODS, AND EACH NIGHT THE BABA YAGA WOULD FLY INTO HIS KITCHEN TO COUNT HIS SPOONS...
WHY?
THE MAN WOULD HIDE IN A CLOSET AND BITE A RAG TO KEEP FROM SCREAMING.
?
IT TELLS YOU SOMETHING. SHE HAS CURIOUS HABITS.
IT'S NOT FOR YOU AND I TO UNDERSTAND.
YEAH, WELL... NOT FOR LONG.
COME BACK TO THE VILLAGE WITH ME NOW--
I'VE HEARD TOO MANY STORIES HERE ABOUT STOLEN CHILDREN, AND I'VE SEEN BONES...
...LITTLE TINY BONES.

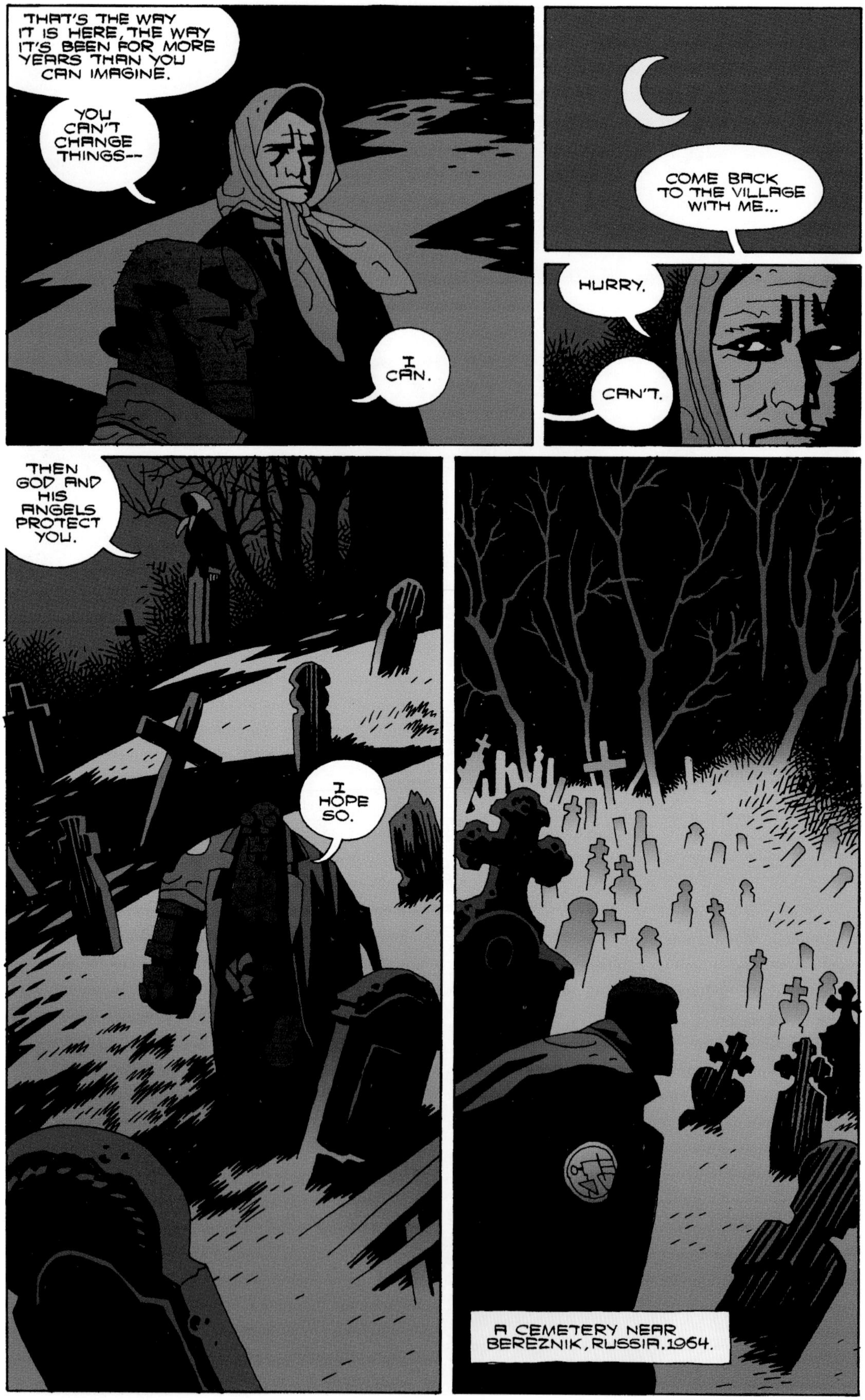
THAT'S THE WAY IT IS HERE, THE WAY IT'S BEEN FOR MORE YEARS THAN YOU CAN IMAGINE.
YOU CAN'T CHANGE THINGS--
I CAN.
COME BACK TO THE VILLAGE WITH ME...
HURRY.
CAN'T.
THEN GOD AND HIS ANGELS PROTECT YOU.
I HOPE SO.
A CEMETERY NEAR BEREZNIK, RUSSIA. 1964.

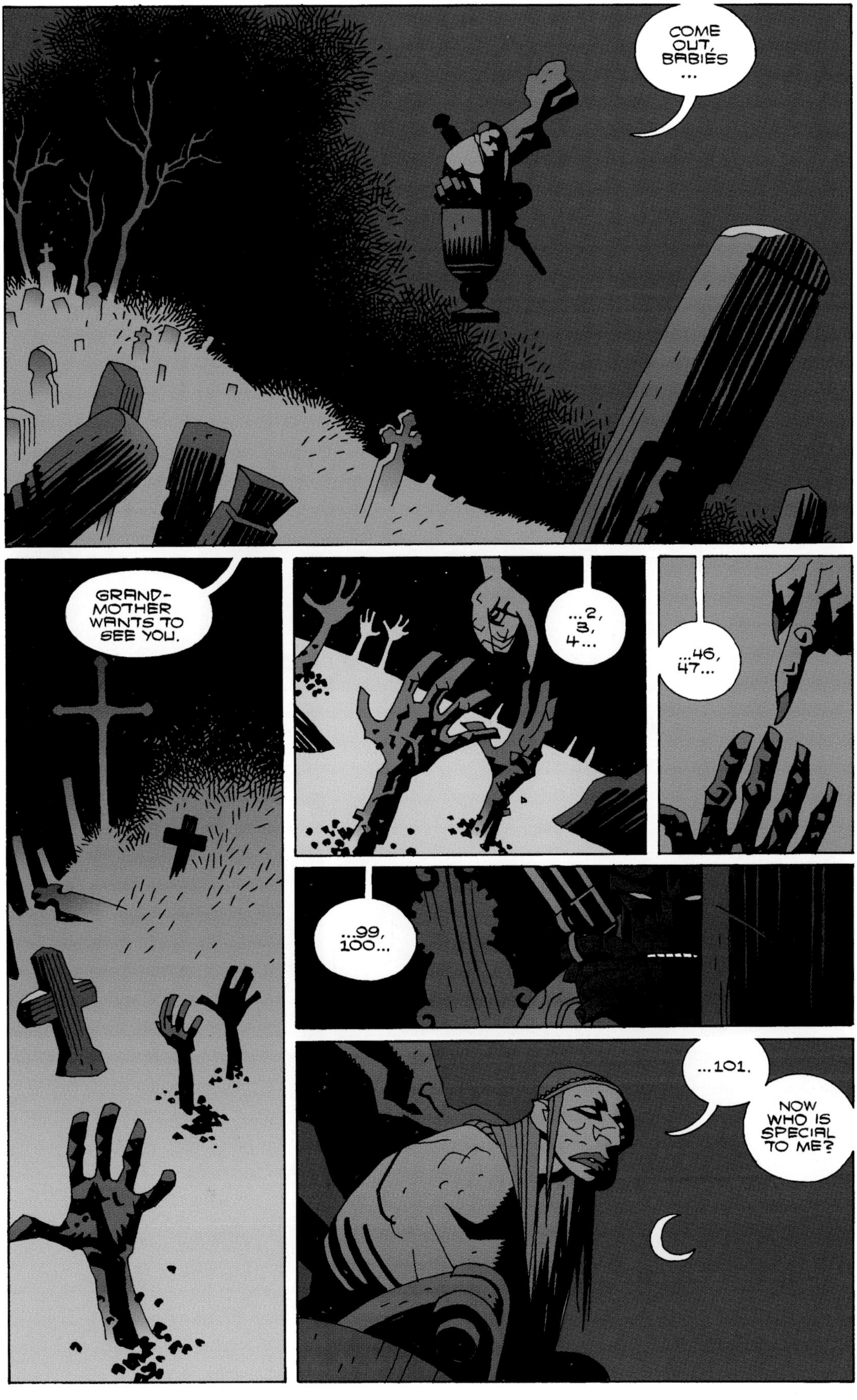
COME OUT, BABIES ...
GRAND-MOTHER WANTS TO SEE YOU.
...2, 3, 4...
...46, 47...
...99, 100...
...101.
NOW WHO IS SPECIAL TO ME?

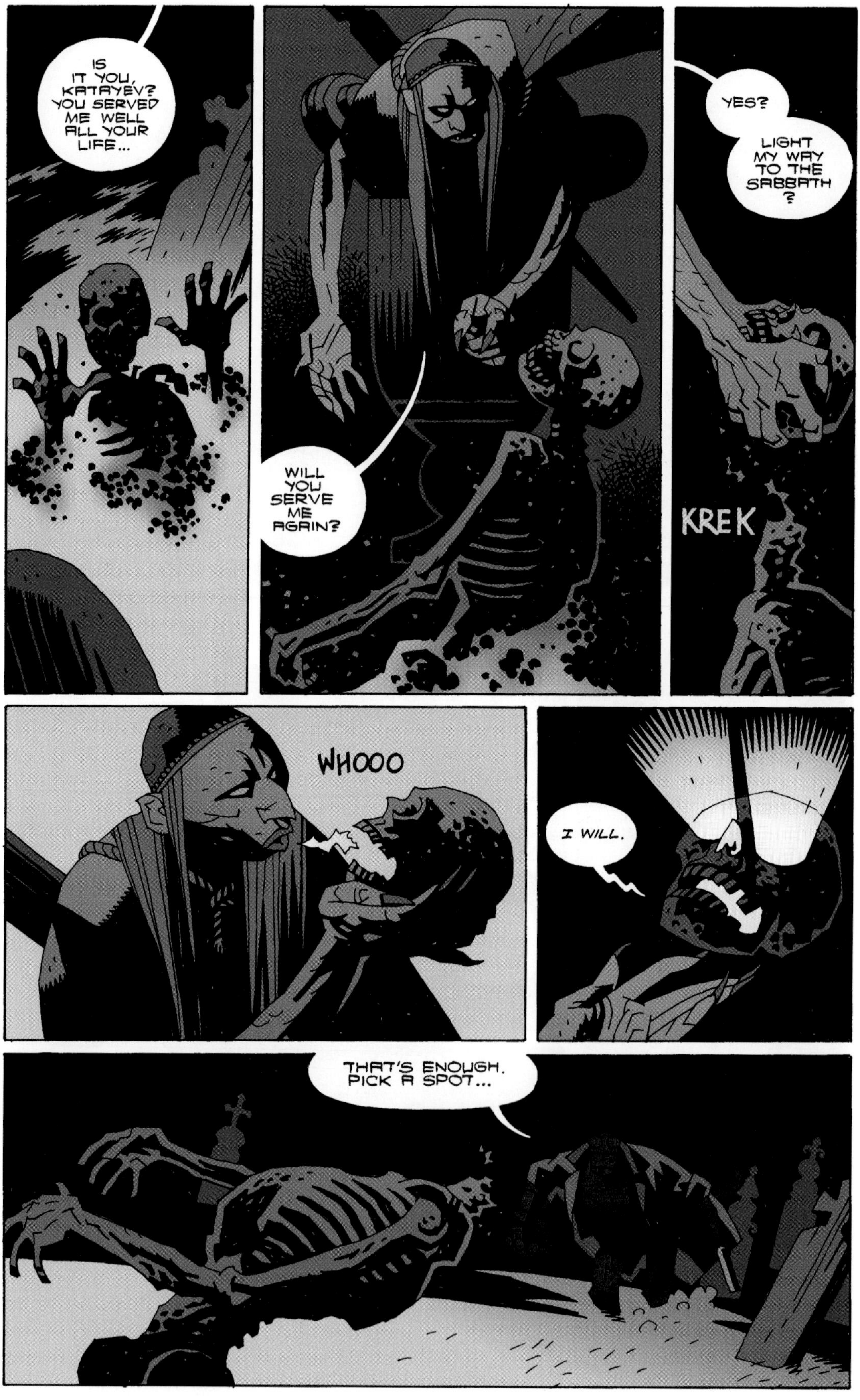
IS IT YOU, KATAYEV? YOU SERVED ME WELL ALL YOUR LIFE...
WILL YOU SERVE ME AGAIN?
YES?
LIGHT MY WAY TO THE SABBATH?
KREK
WHOOO
I WILL.
THAT'S ENOUGH. PICK A SPOT...

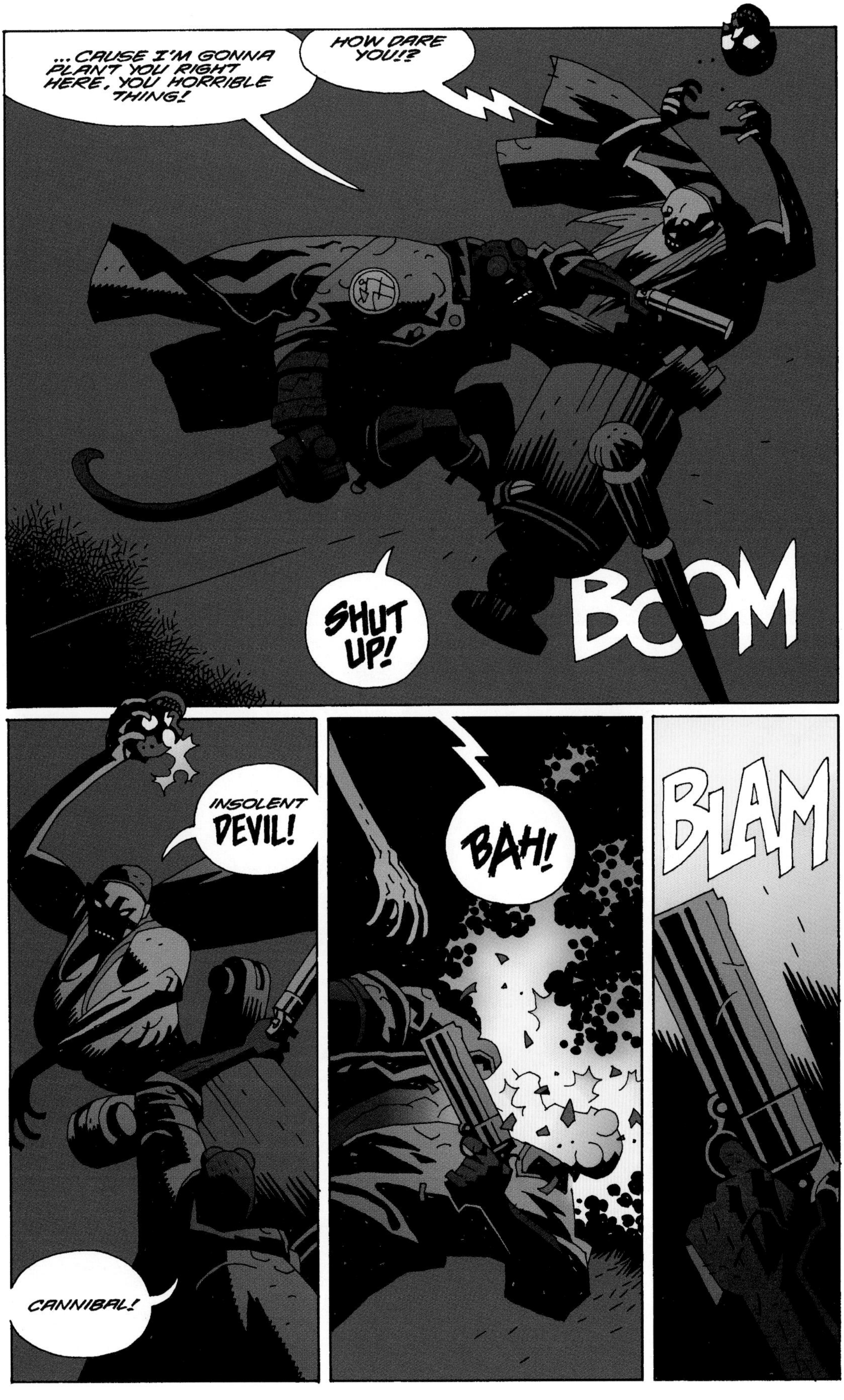
...CAUSE I'M GONNA PLANT YOU RIGHT HERE, YOU HORRIBLE THING!
HOW DARE YOU!?
SHUT UP!
BOOM
INSOLENT DEVIL!
CANNIBAL!
BAH!
BLAM

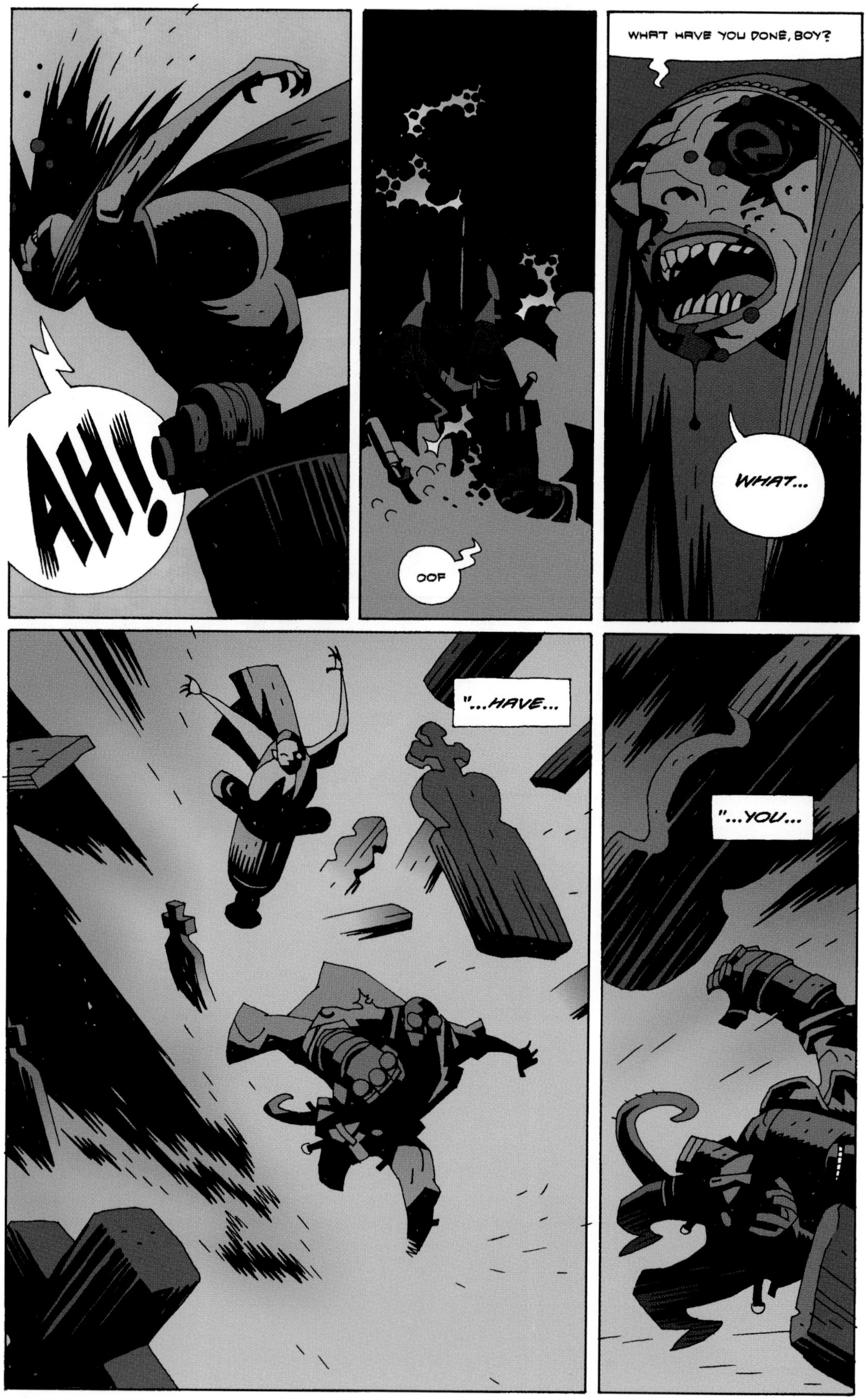
AH!
OOF
WHAT HAVE YOU DONE, BOY?
WHAT...
"...HAVE...
"...YOU...

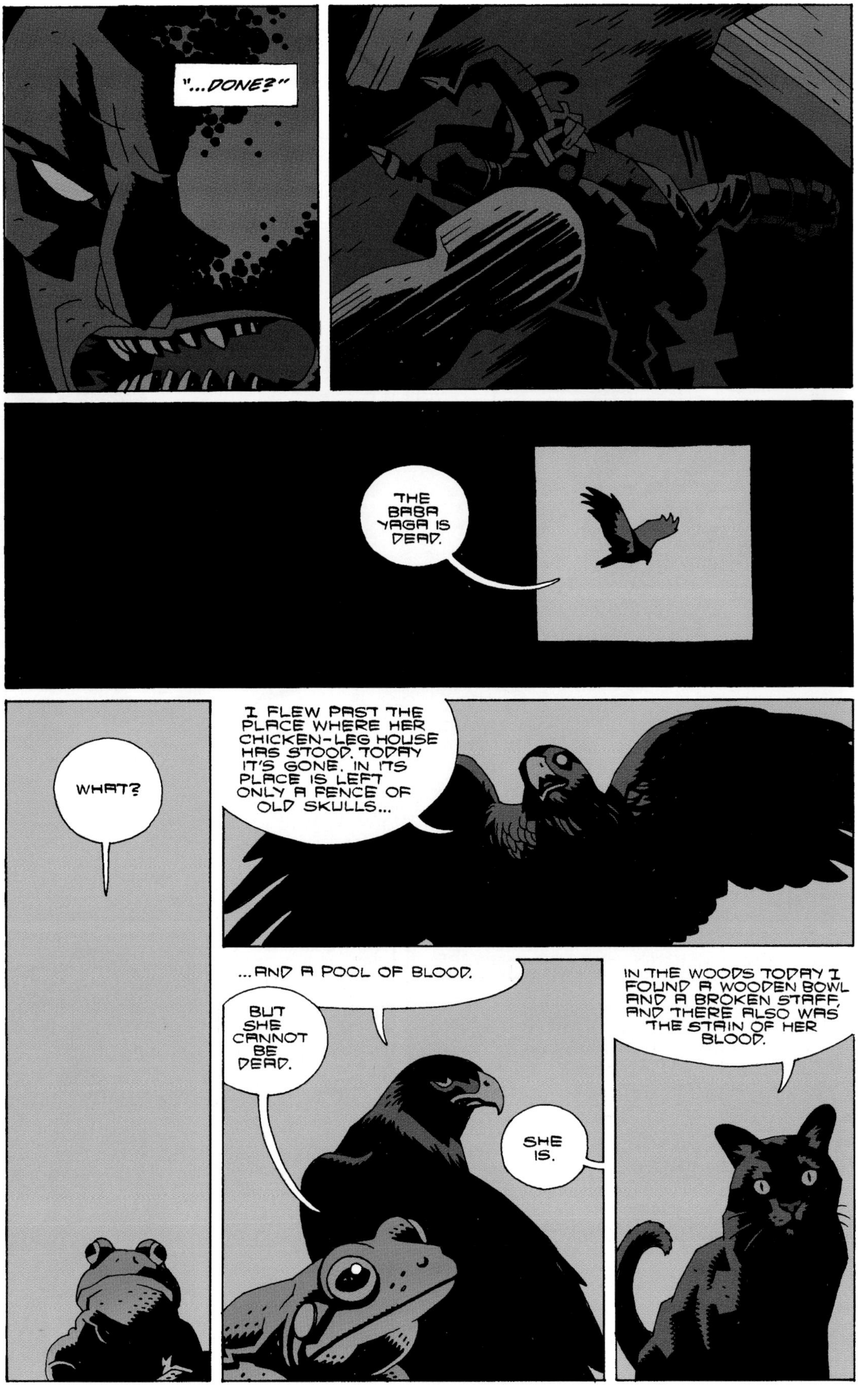
"...DONE?"
THE BABA YAGA IS DEAD.
WHAT?
I FLEW PAST THE PLACE WHERE HER CHICKEN-LEG HOUSE HAS STOOD. TODAY IT'S GONE. IN ITS PLACE IS LEFT ONLY A FENCE OF OLD SKULLS...
...AND A POOL OF BLOOD.
BUT SHE CANNOT BE DEAD.
SHE IS.
IN THE WOODS TODAY I FOUND A WOODEN BOWL AND A BROKEN STAFF, AND THERE ALSO WAS THE STAIN OF HER BLOOD.

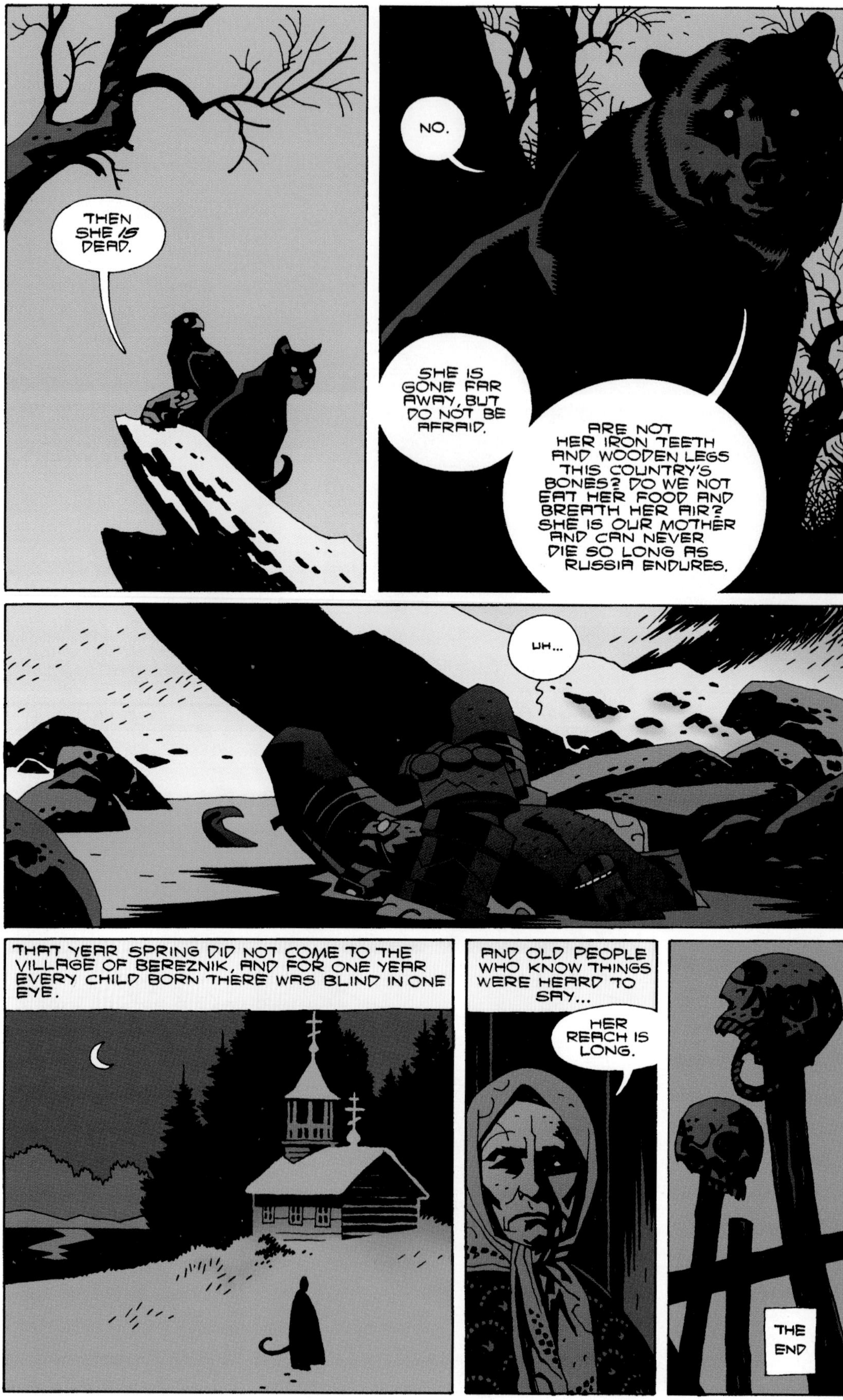

THEN SHE IS DEAD.
NO.
SHE IS GONE FAR AWAY, BUT DO NOT BE AFRAID.
ARE NOT HER IRON TEETH AND WOODEN LEGS THIS COUNTRY'S BONES? DO WE NOT EAT HER FOOD AND BREATH HER AIR? SHE IS OUR MOTHER AND CAN NEVER DIE SO LONG AS RUSSIA ENDURES.
UH...
THAT YEAR SPRING DID NOT COME TO THE VILLAGE OF BEREZNIK, AND FOR ONE YEAR EVERY CHILD BORN THERE WAS BLIND IN ONE EYE.
AND OLD PEOPLE WHO KNOW THINGS WERE HEARD TO SAY...
HER REACH IS LONG.
THE END

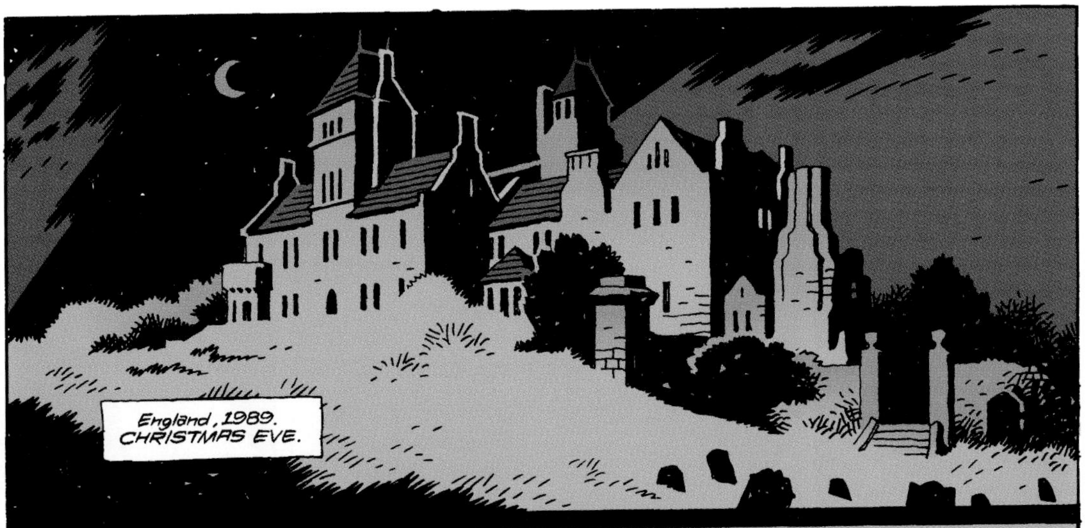
England, 1989.
CHRISTMAS EVE.

A Christmas Underground

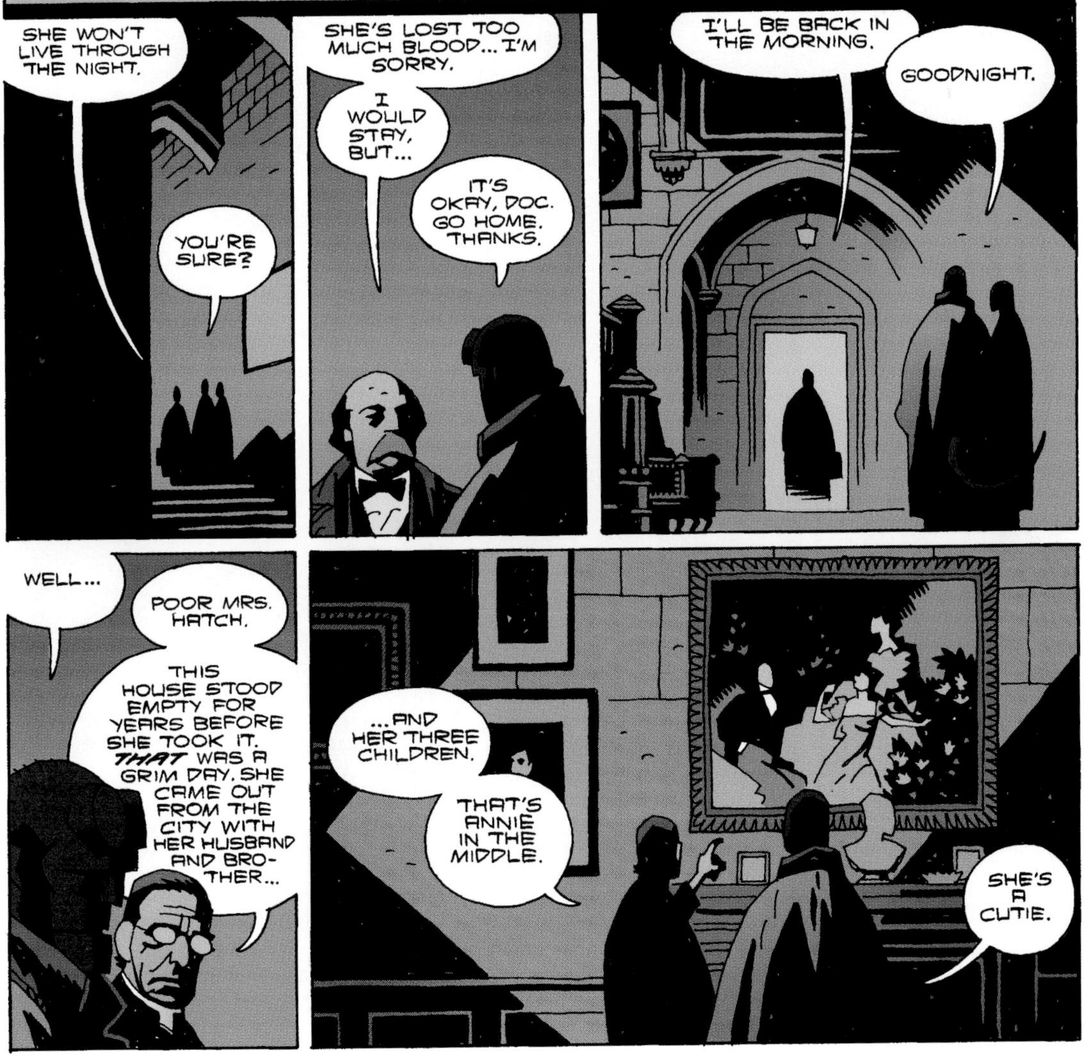
SHE WON'T LIVE THROUGH THE NIGHT.
YOU'RE SURE?
SHE'S LOST TOO MUCH BLOOD... I'M SORRY.
I WOULD STAY, BUT...
IT'S OKAY, DOC. GO HOME. THANKS.
I'LL BE BACK IN THE MORNING.
GOODNIGHT.
WELL...
POOR MRS. HATCH.
THIS HOUSE STOOD EMPTY FOR YEARS BEFORE SHE TOOK IT. THAT WAS A GRIM DAY. SHE CAME OUT FROM THE CITY WITH HER HUSBAND AND BRO-THER...
...AND HER THREE CHILDREN.
THAT'S ANNIE IN THE MIDDLE.
SHE'S A CUTIE.

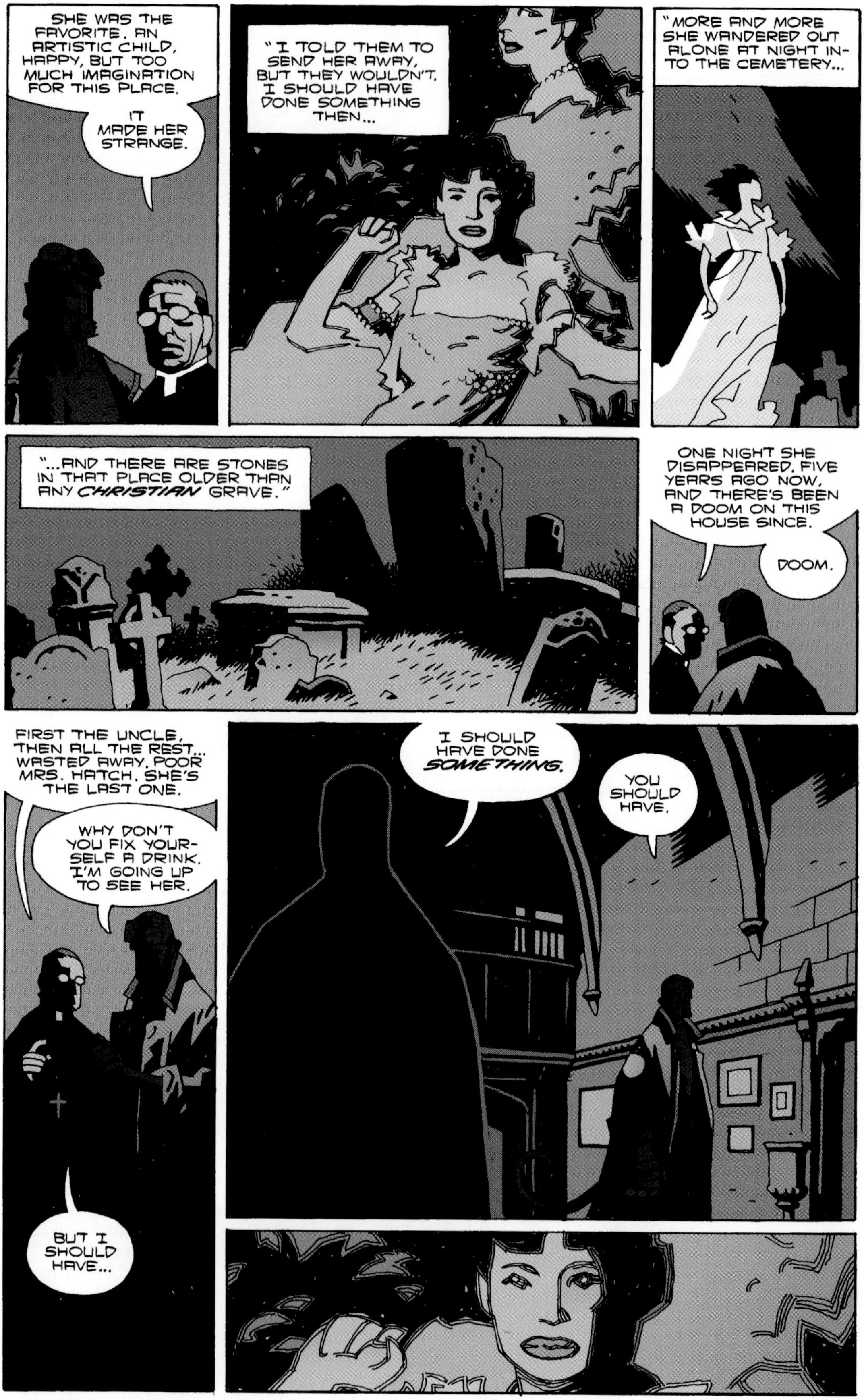
SHE WAS THE FAVORITE. AN ARTISTIC CHILD, HAPPY, BUT TOO MUCH IMAGINATION FOR THIS PLACE.
IT MADE HER STRANGE.
"I TOLD THEM TO SEND HER AWAY, BUT THEY WOULDN'T. I SHOULD HAVE DONE SOMETHING THEN...
"MORE AND MORE SHE WANDERED OUT ALONE AT NIGHT INTO THE CEMETERY...
"...AND THERE ARE STONES IN THAT PLACE OLDER THAN ANY CHRISTIAN GRAVE."
ONE NIGHT SHE DISAPPEARED. FIVE YEARS AGO NOW, AND THERE'S BEEN A DOOM ON THIS HOUSE SINCE.
DOOM.
FIRST THE UNCLE, THEN ALL THE REST... WASTED AWAY. POOR MRS. HATCH. SHE'S THE LAST ONE.
WHY DON'T YOU FIX YOURSELF A DRINK. I'M GOING UP TO SEE HER.
BUT I SHOULD HAVE...
I SHOULD HAVE DONE SOMETHING.
YOU SHOULD HAVE.

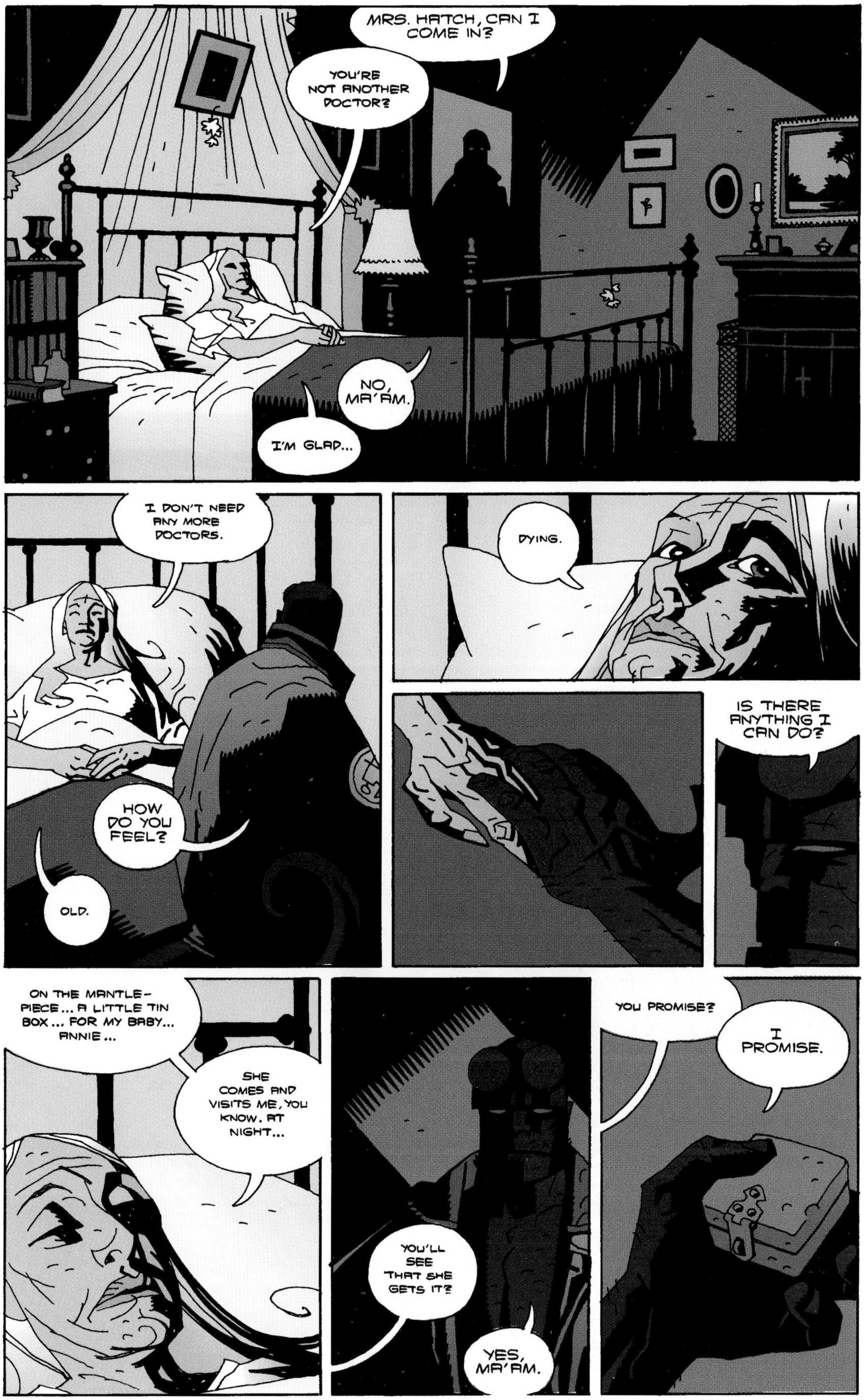
MRS. HATCH, CAN I COME IN?
YOU'RE NOT ANOTHER DOCTOR?
NO, MA'AM.
I'M GLAD...
I DON'T NEED ANY MORE DOCTORS.
HOW DO YOU FEEL?
OLD.
DYING.
IS THERE ANYTHING I CAN DO?
ON THE MANTLE-PIECE... A LITTLE TIN BOX... FOR MY BABY... ANNIE...
SHE COMES AND VISITS ME, YOU KNOW. AT NIGHT...
YOU'LL SEE THAT SHE GETS IT?
YES, MA'AM.
YOU PROMISE?
I PROMISE.

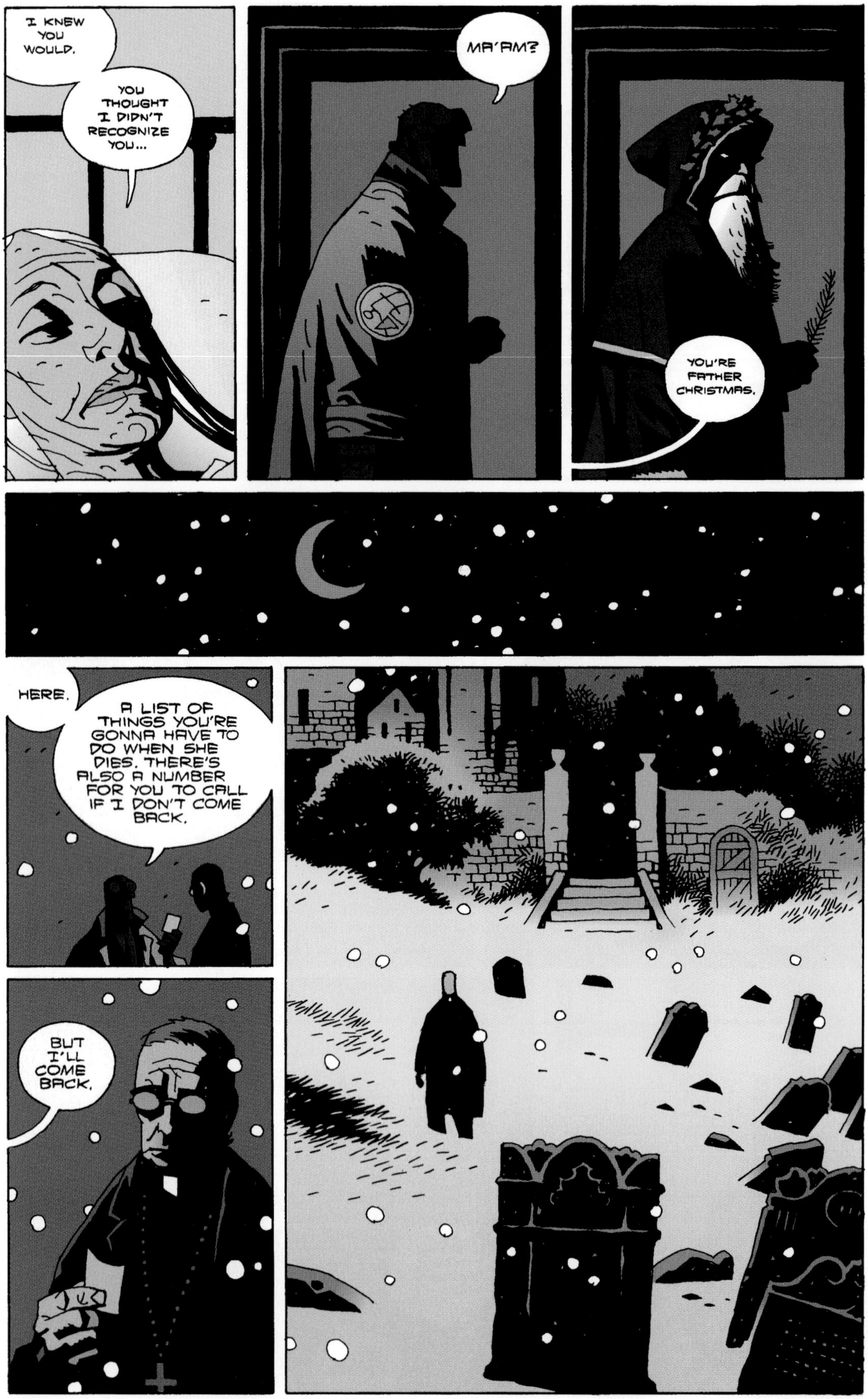
I KNEW YOU WOULD.
YOU THOUGHT I DIDN'T RECOGNIZE YOU...
MA'AM?
YOU'RE FATHER CHRISTMAS.
HERE.
A LIST OF THINGS YOU'RE GONNA HAVE TO DO WHEN SHE DIES. THERE'S ALSO A NUMBER FOR YOU TO CALL IF I DON'T COME BACK.
BUT I'LL COME BACK.

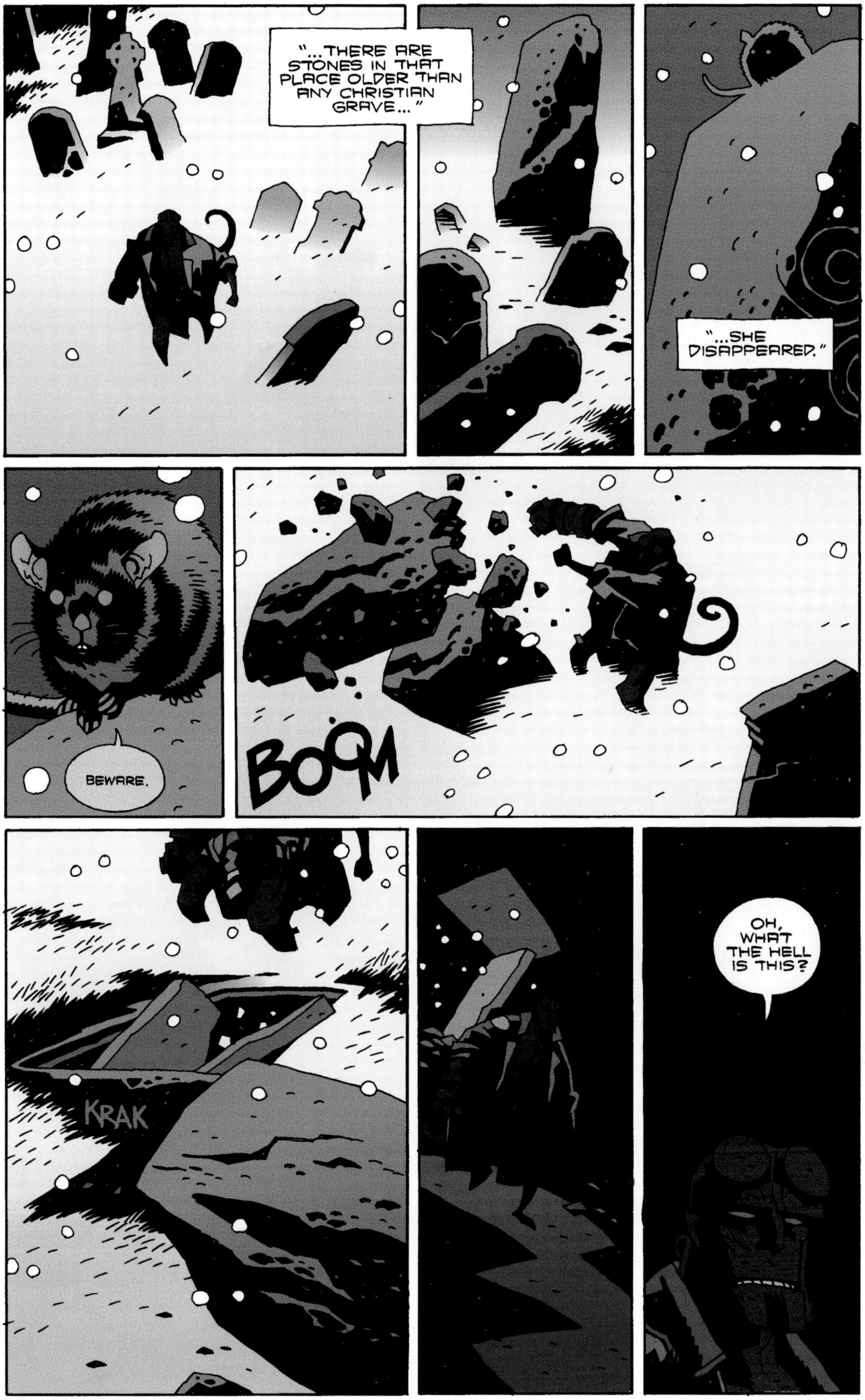
"...THERE ARE STONES IN THAT PLACE OLDER THAN ANY CHRISTIAN GRAVE..."
"...SHE DISAPPEARED."
BEWARE.
BOOM
KRAK
OH, WHAT THE HELL IS THIS?

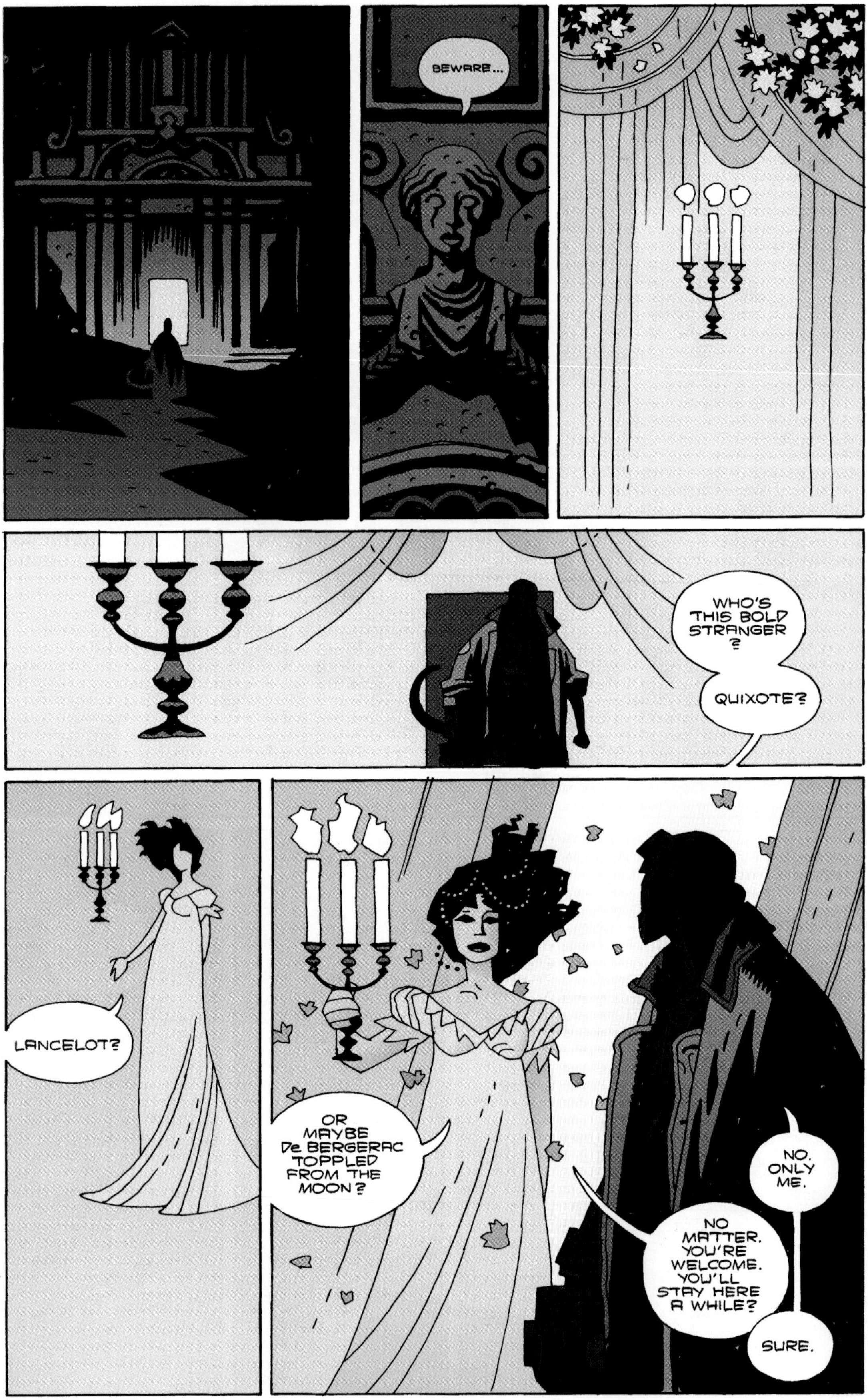
BEWARE...
WHO'S THIS BOLD STRANGER ?
QUIXOTE?
LANCELOT?
OR MAYBE De BERGERAC TOPPLED FROM THE MOON?
NO. ONLY ME.
NO MATTER. YOU'RE WELCOME. YOU'LL STAY HERE A WHILE?
SURE.

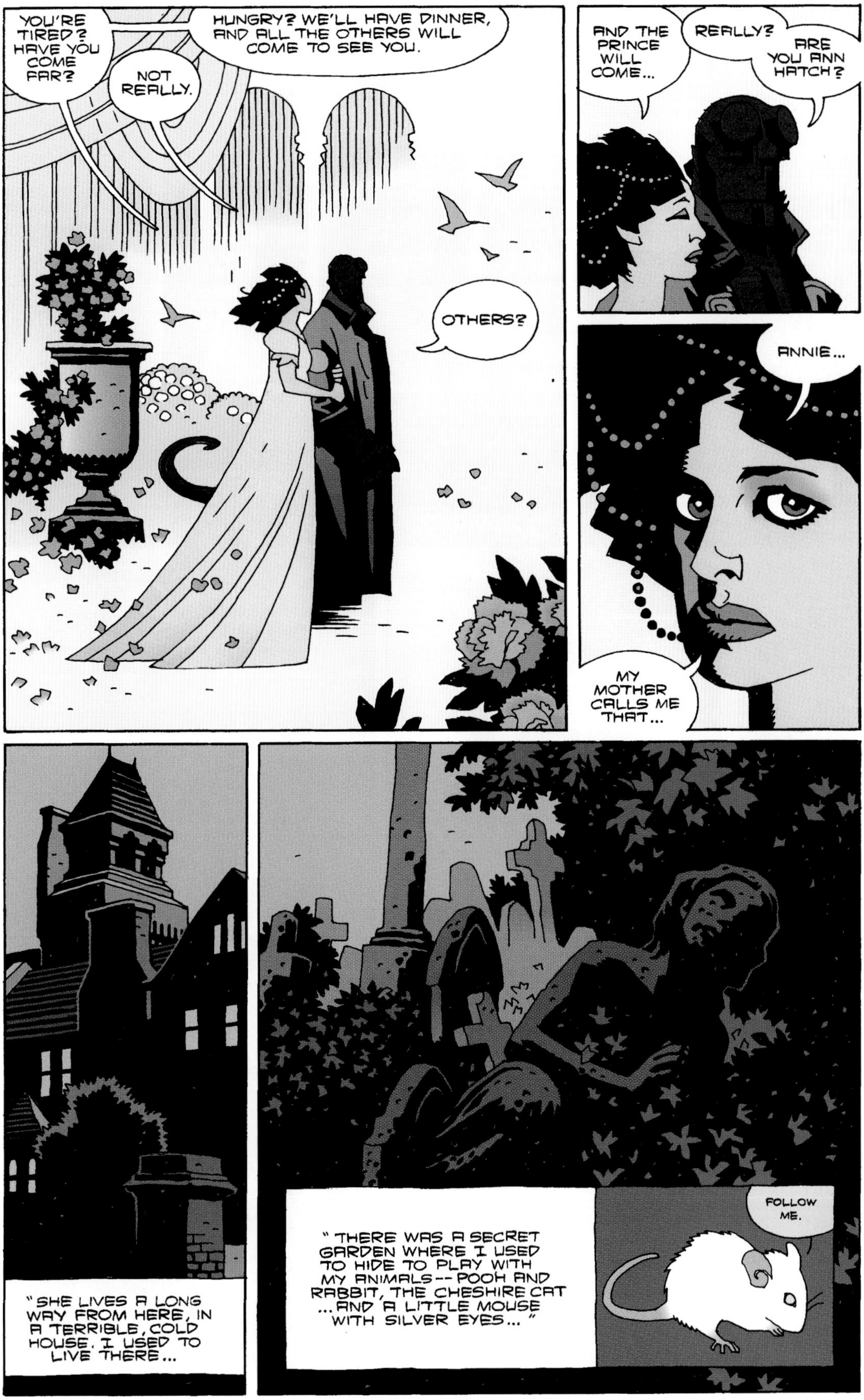
YOU'RE TIRED? HAVE YOU COME FAR?
NOT REALLY.
HUNGRY? WE'LL HAVE DINNER, AND ALL THE OTHERS WILL COME TO SEE YOU.
OTHERS?
AND THE PRINCE WILL COME...
REALLY?
ARE YOU ANN HATCH?
ANNIE...
MY MOTHER CALLS ME THAT...
"SHE LIVES A LONG WAY FROM HERE, IN A TERRIBLE, COLD HOUSE. I USED TO LIVE THERE...
" THERE WAS A SECRET GARDEN WHERE I USED TO HIDE TO PLAY WITH MY ANIMALS-- POOH AND RABBIT, THE CHESHIRE CAT ...AND A LITTLE MOUSE WITH SILVER EYES... "
FOLLOW ME.

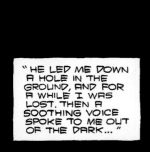

"HE LED ME DOWN A HOLE IN THE GROUND, AND FOR A WHILE I WAS LOST. THEN A SOOTHING VOICE SPOKE TO ME OUT OF THE DARK..."

ABIDE WITH ME AND BE MY BRIDE, AND THOU SHALT HAVE ALL THY HEART'S DESIRES.

WHO ARE YOU?

THE SECOND SON OF A KING.

"AND THAT'S ALL HE WOULD SAY.

"HE TOOK ME TO HIS PALACE AND GAVE ME EVERY- THING I COULD WANT.

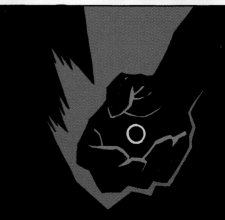

"I BELONG TO HIM."

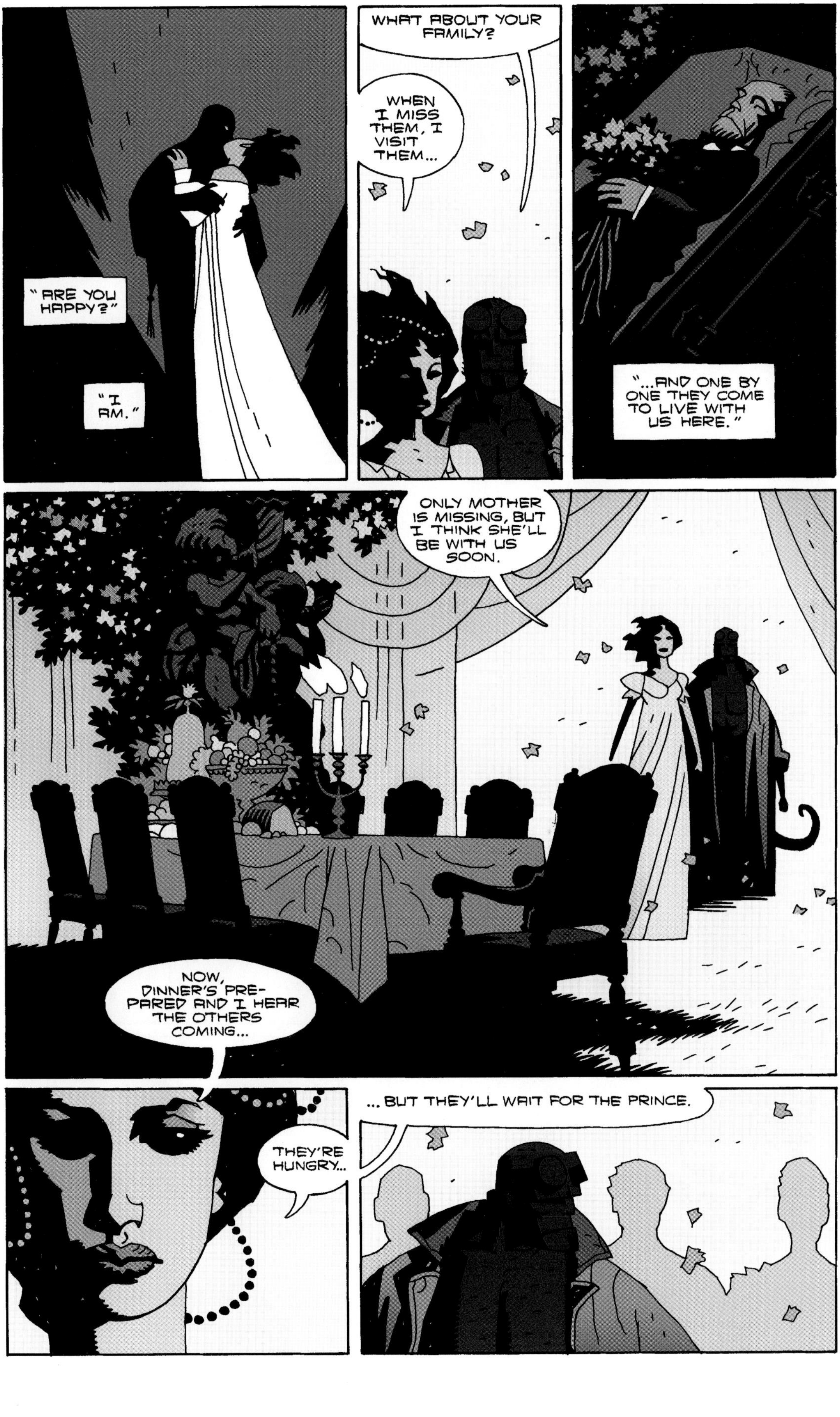
"ARE YOU HAPPY?"
"I AM."
WHAT ABOUT YOUR FAMILY?
WHEN I MISS THEM, I VISIT THEM...
"...AND ONE BY ONE THEY COME TO LIVE WITH US HERE."
ONLY MOTHER IS MISSING, BUT I THINK SHE'LL BE WITH US SOON.
NOW, DINNER'S PRE-PARED AND I HEAR THE OTHERS COMING...
THEY'RE HUNGRY...
... BUT THEY'LL WAIT FOR THE PRINCE.

OKAY, NOW LISTEN TO ME. THIS IS *CHRISTMAS EVE*. DOES THAT RING A BELL?

?

CHRISTMAS EVE. COME ON!

I DON'T...

NO.

I SPOKE TO YOUR MOM TO-NIGHT. SHE SENT ME TO FIND YOU.

SHE WANTED YOU TO HAVE THIS.

IT'S A PRESENT.

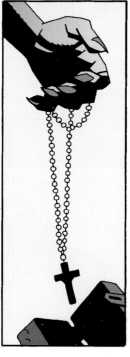

"MERRY CHRISTMAS."

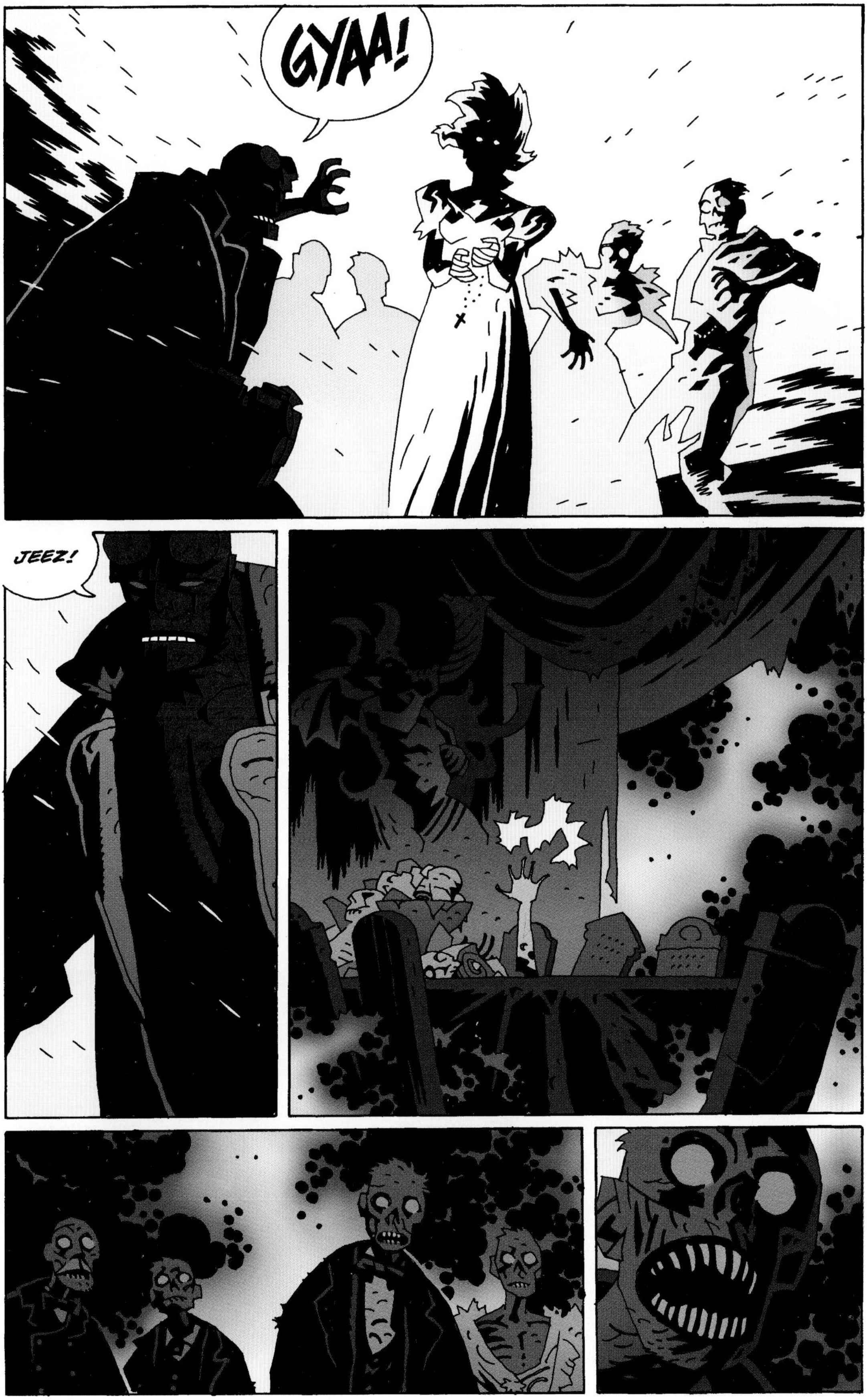
GYAA!
JEEZ!

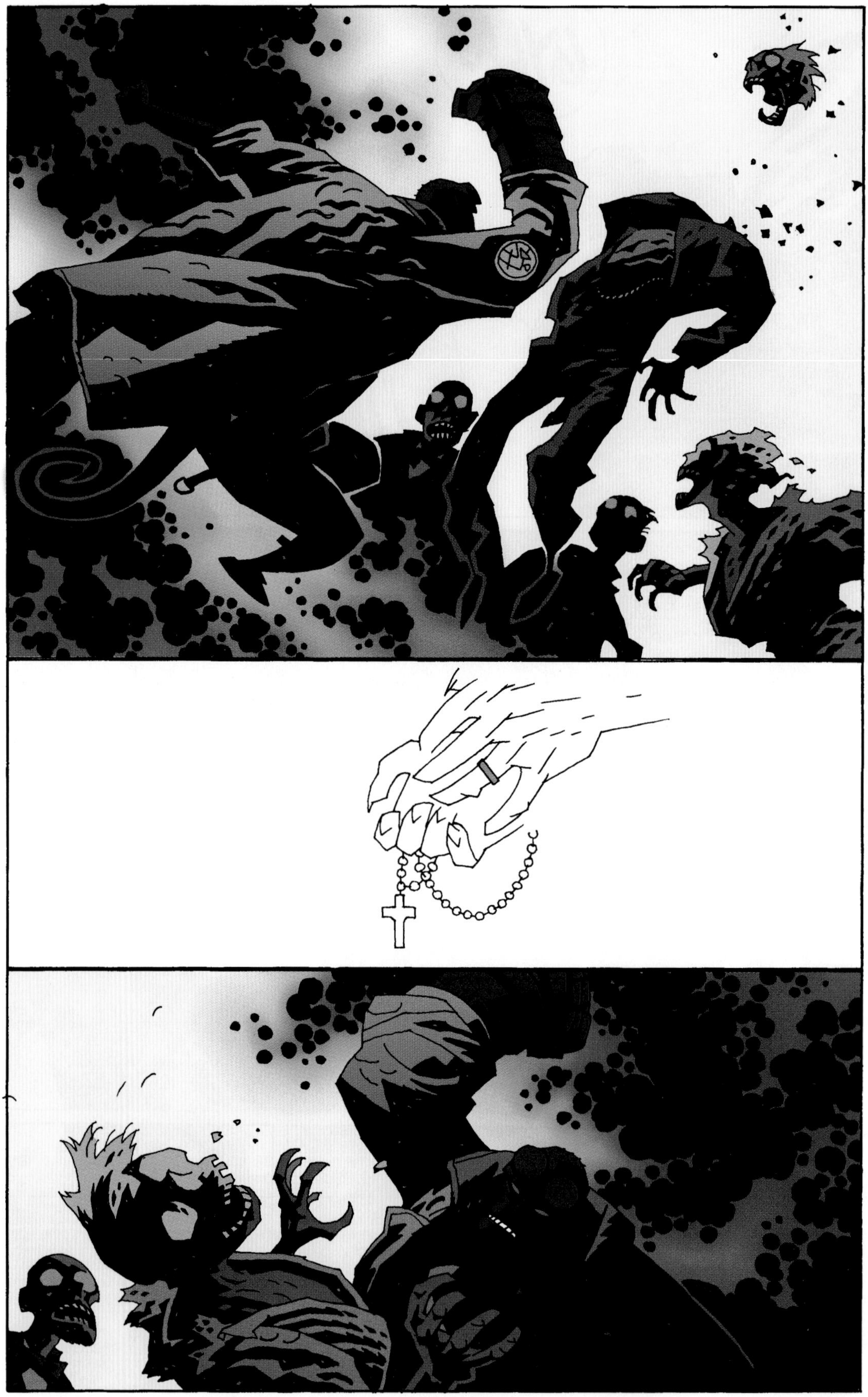

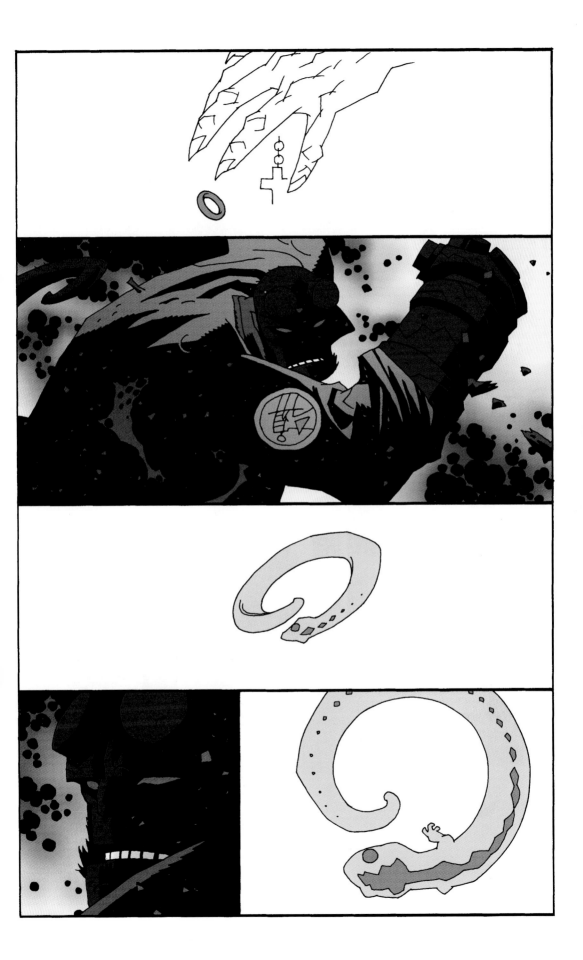

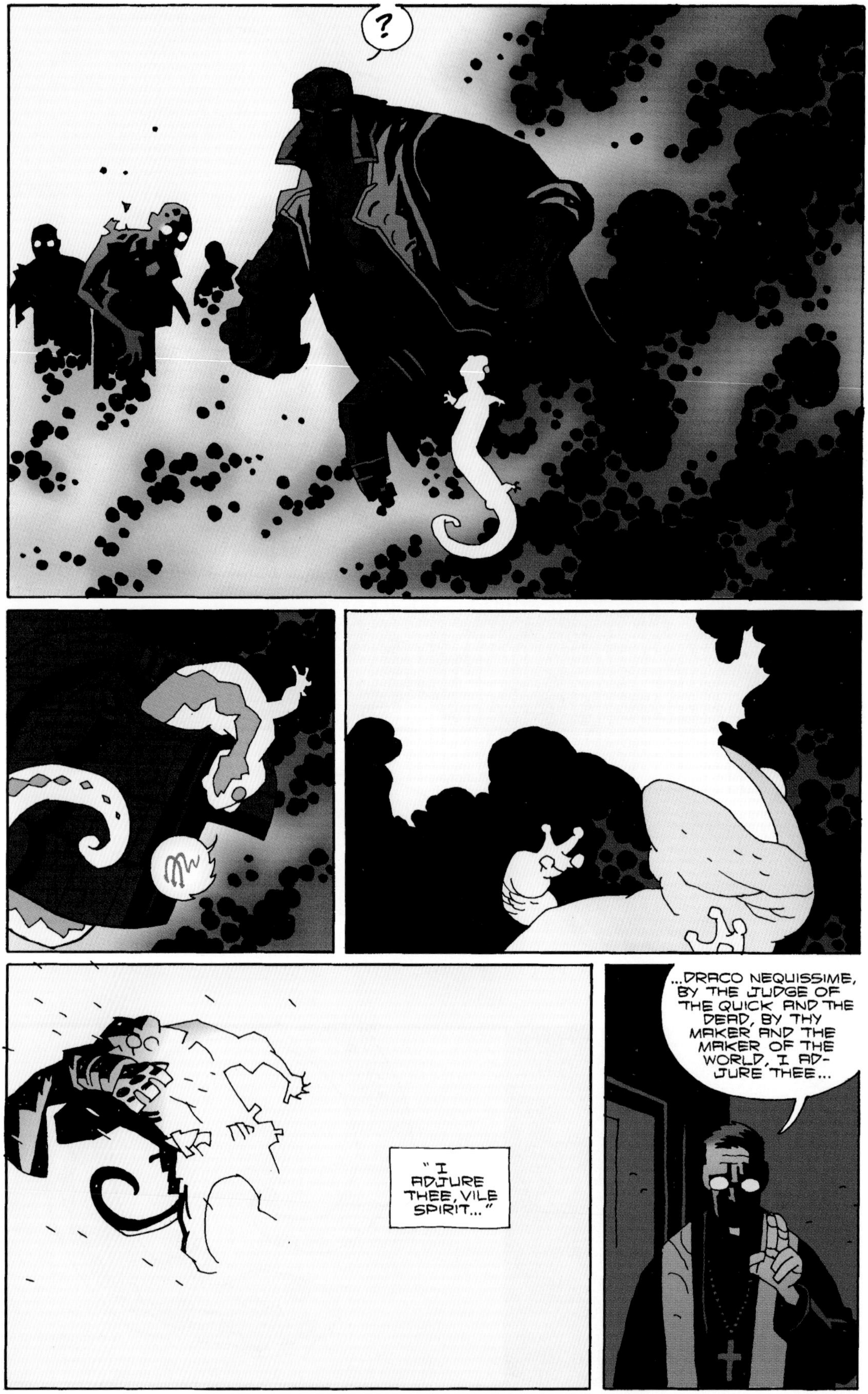
?
"I ADJURE THEE, VILE SPIRIT..."
...DRACO NEQUISSIME, BY THE JUDGE OF THE QUICK AND THE DEAD, BY THY MAKER AND THE MAKER OF THE WORLD, I ADJURE THEE...

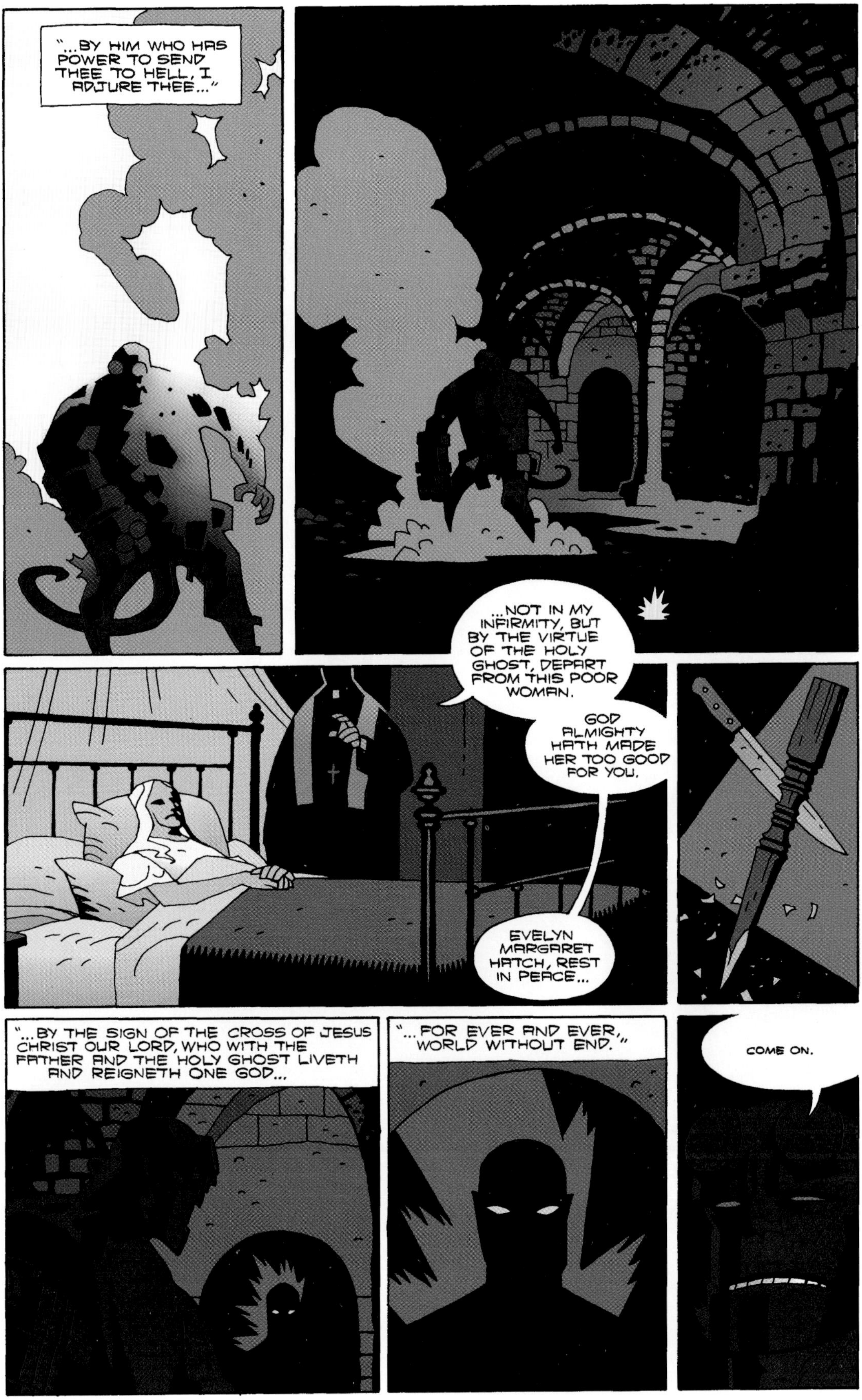
"...BY HIM WHO HAS POWER TO SEND THEE TO HELL, I ADJURE THEE..."
...NOT IN MY INFIRMITY, BUT BY THE VIRTUE OF THE HOLY GHOST, DEPART FROM THIS POOR WOMAN.
GOD ALMIGHTY HATH MADE HER TOO GOOD FOR YOU.
EVELYN MARGARET HATCH, REST IN PEACE...
"...BY THE SIGN OF THE CROSS OF JESUS CHRIST OUR LORD, WHO WITH THE FATHER AND THE HOLY GHOST LIVETH AND REIGNETH ONE GOD...
"...FOR EVER AND EVER, WORLD WITHOUT END."
COME ON.

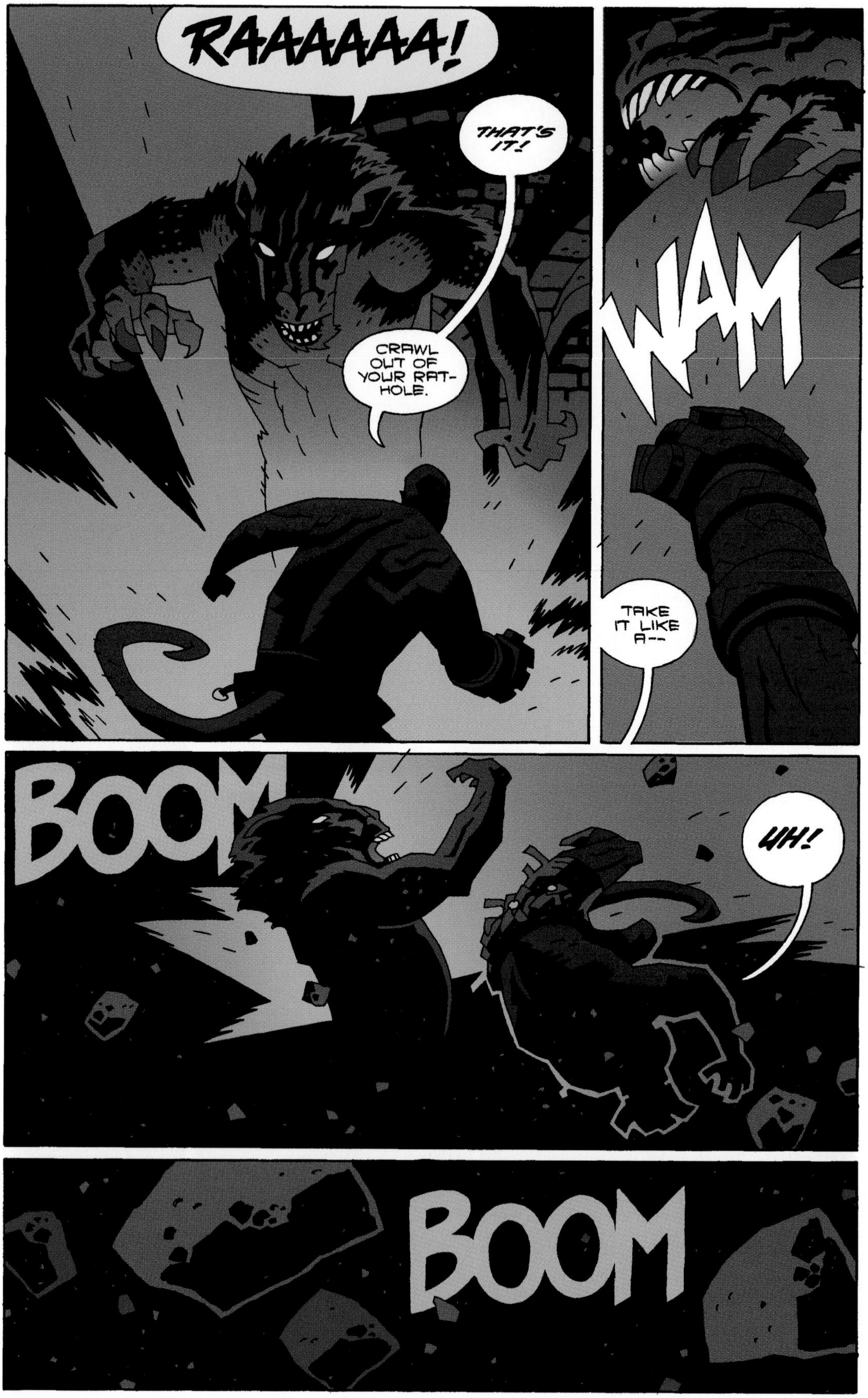
RAAAAAA!
THAT'S IT!
CRAWL OUT OF YOUR RAT-HOLE.
WAM
TAKE IT LIKE A--
BOOM
UH!
BOOM

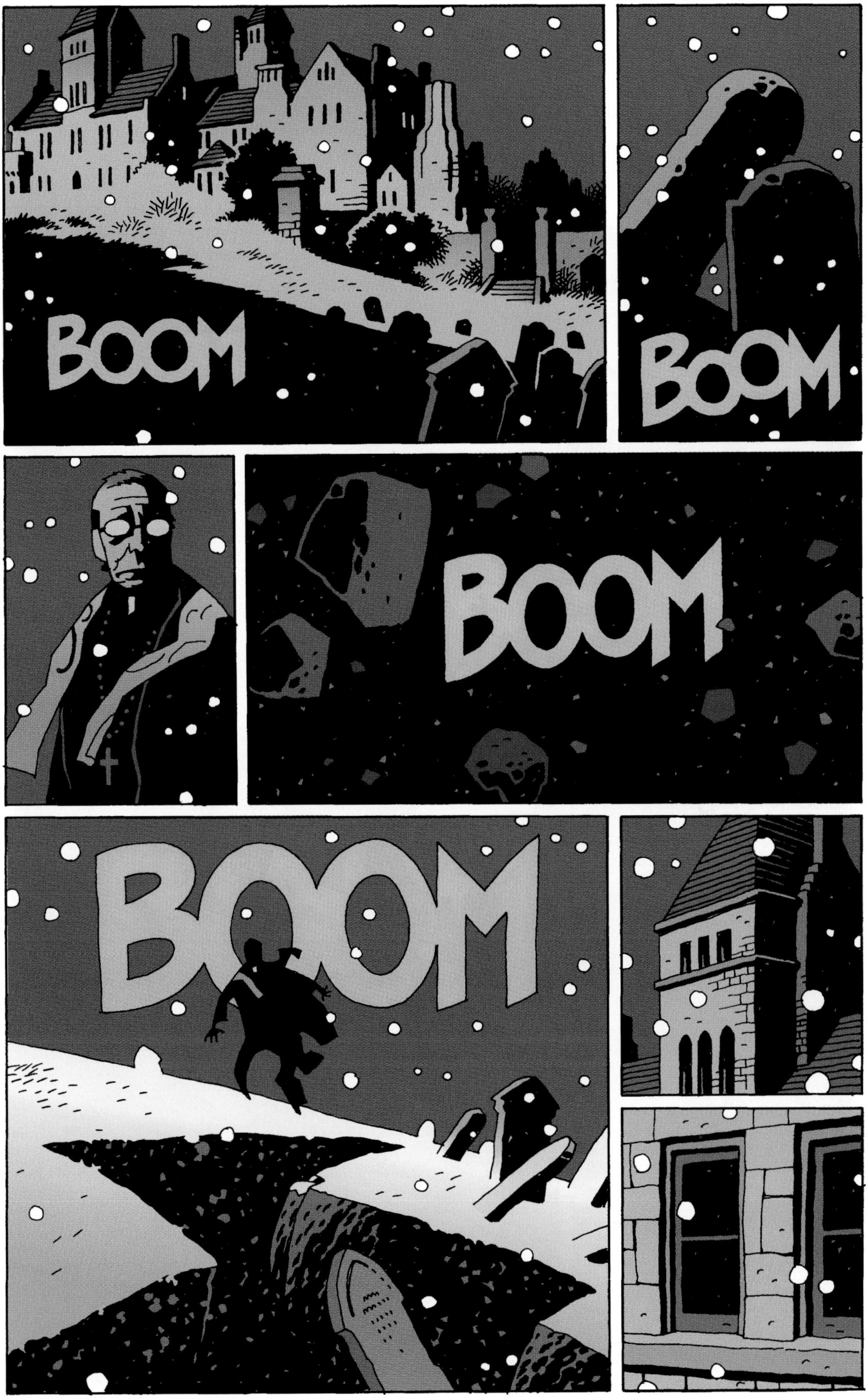
BOOM
BOOM
BOOM
BOOM

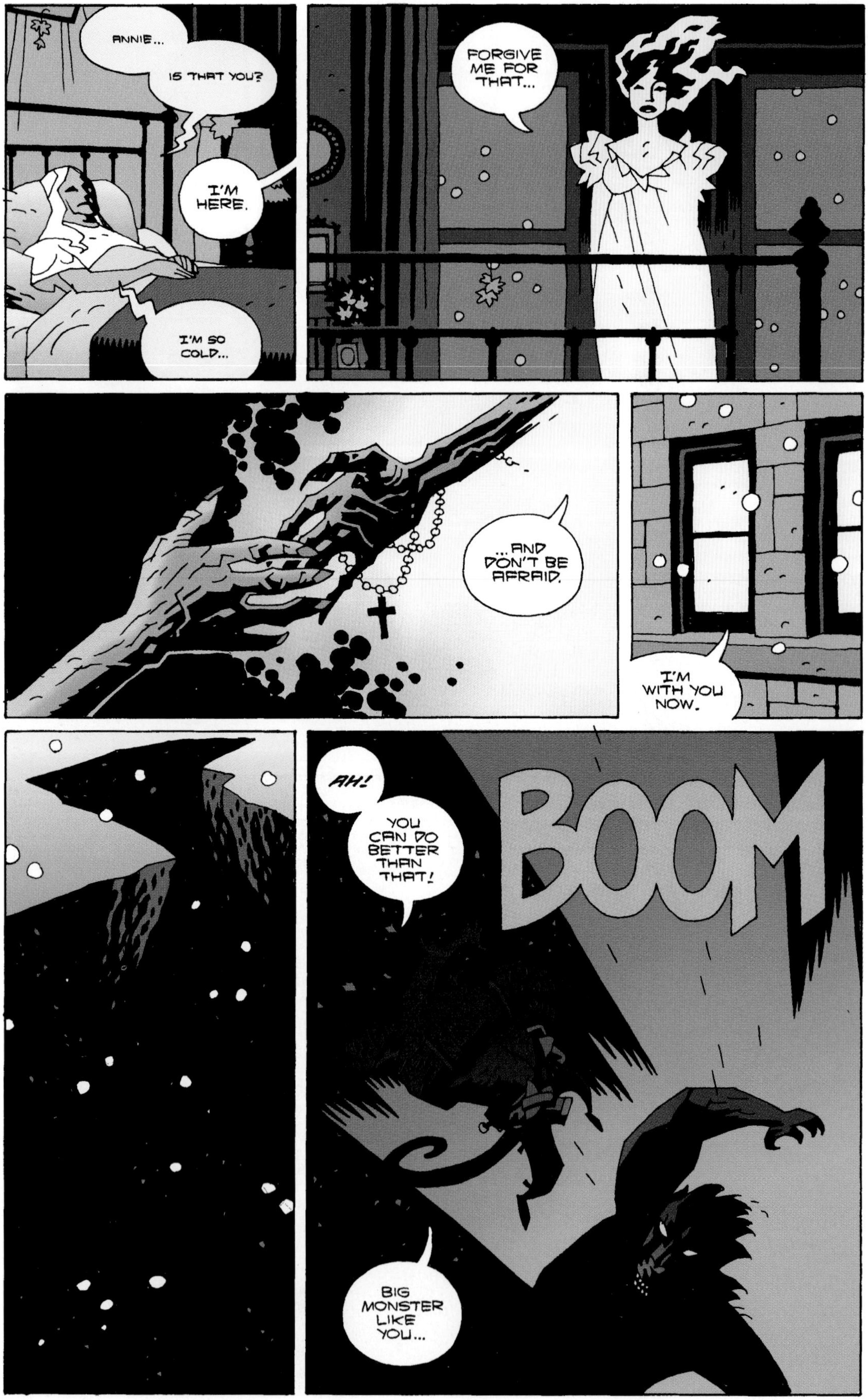
ANNIE...
IS THAT YOU?
I'M HERE.
I'M SO COLD...
FORGIVE ME FOR THAT...
...AND DON'T BE AFRAID.
I'M WITH YOU NOW.
AH!
YOU CAN DO BETTER THAN THAT!
BOOM
BIG MONSTER LIKE YOU...

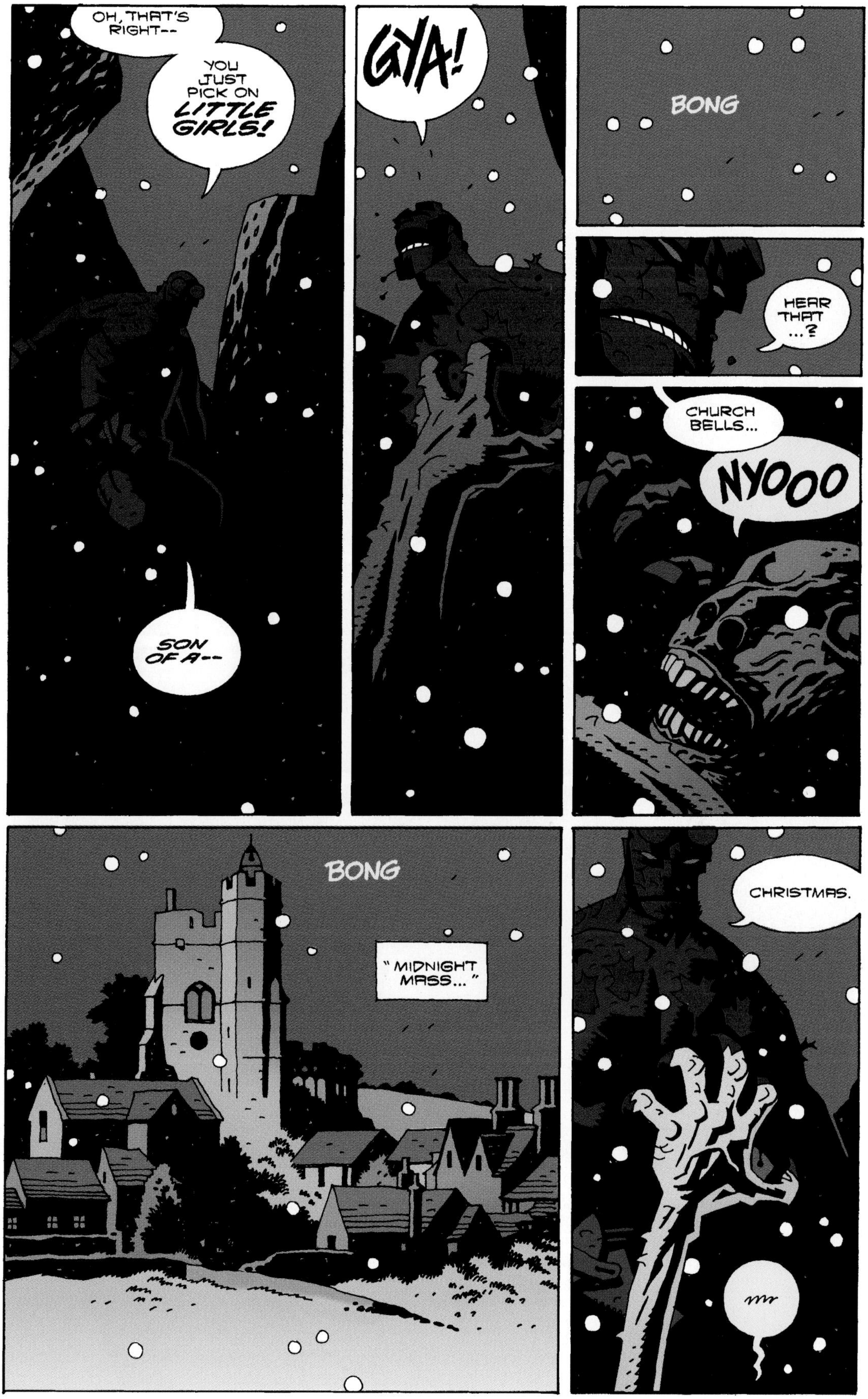

OH, THAT'S RIGHT--
YOU JUST PICK ON LITTLE GIRLS!
SON OF A--
GYA!
BONG
HEAR THAT ...?
CHURCH BELLS...
NYOOO
BONG
"MIDNIGHT MASS..."
CHRISTMAS.

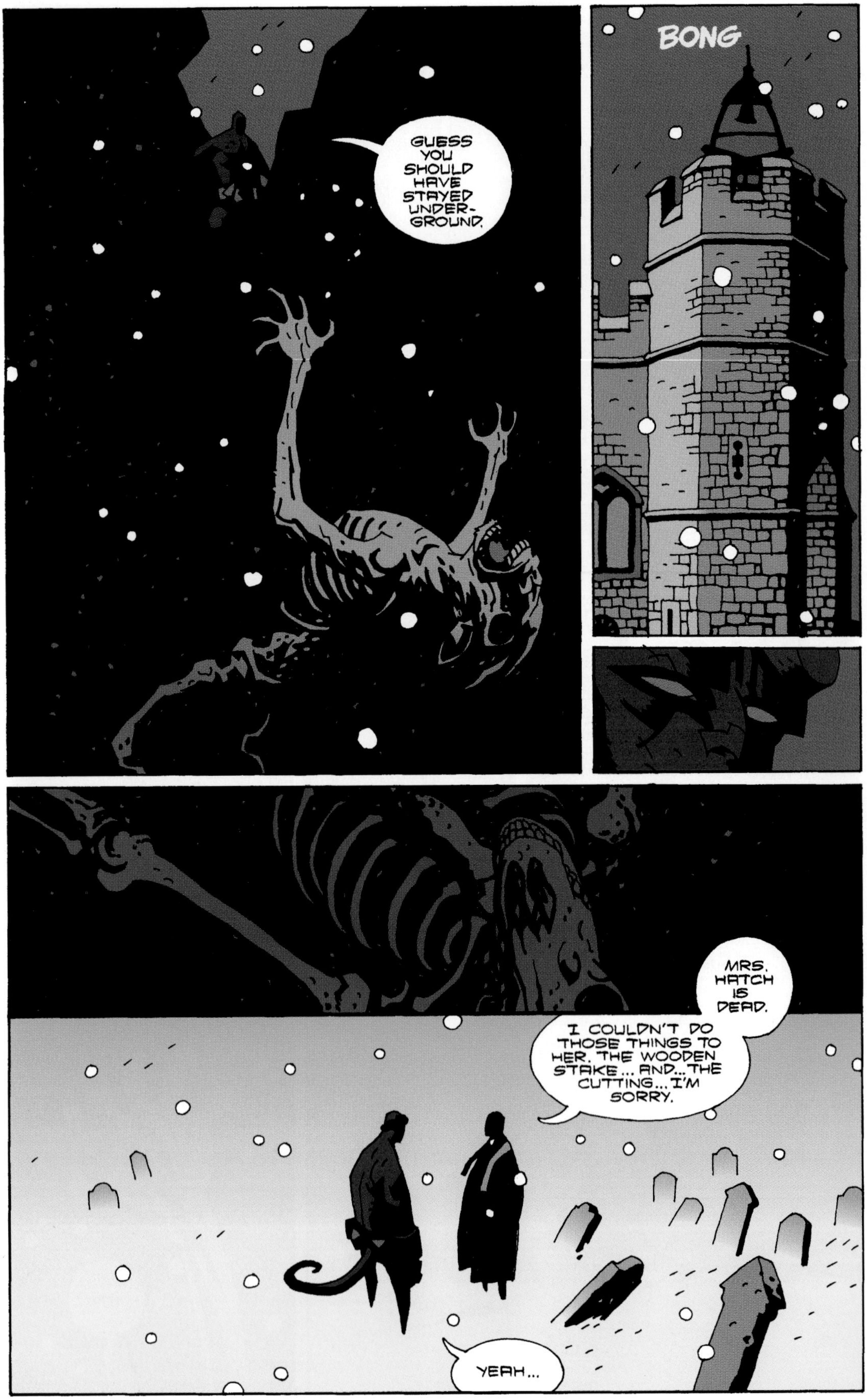
GUESS YOU SHOULD HAVE STAYED UNDER-GROUND.
BONG
MRS. HATCH IS DEAD.
I COULDN'T DO THOSE THINGS TO HER. THE WOODEN STAKE... AND... THE CUTTING... I'M SORRY.
YEAH...

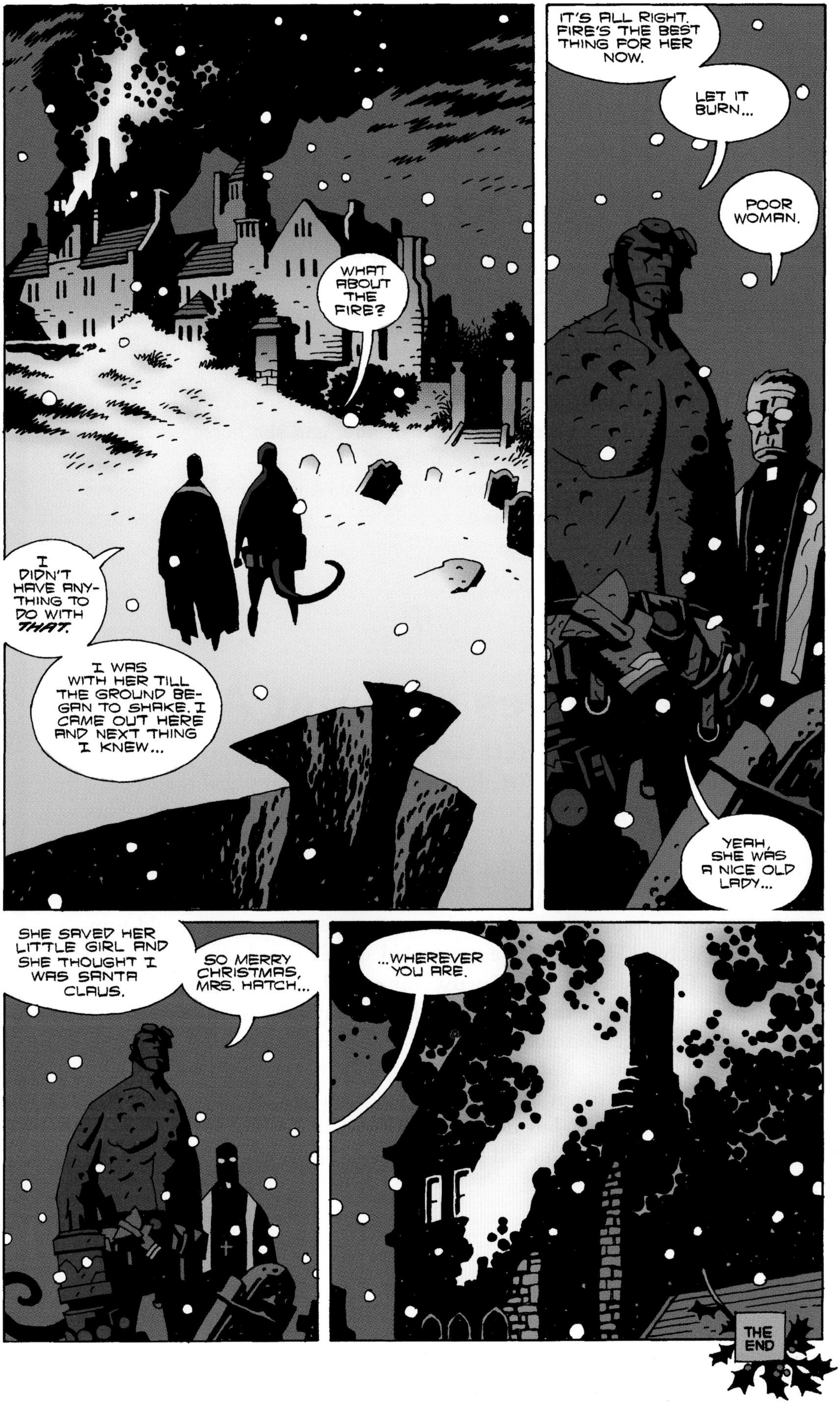
WHAT ABOUT THE FIRE?
I DIDN'T HAVE ANY-THING TO DO WITH *THAT.*
I WAS WITH HER TILL THE GROUND BE-GAN TO SHAKE. I CAME OUT HERE AND NEXT THING I KNEW...
IT'S ALL RIGHT. FIRE'S THE BEST THING FOR HER NOW.
LET IT BURN...
POOR WOMAN.
YEAH, SHE WAS A NICE OLD LADY...
SHE SAVED HER LITTLE GIRL AND SHE THOUGHT I WAS SANTA CLAUS.
SO MERRY CHRISTMAS, MRS. HATCH...
...WHEREVER YOU ARE.
THE END

The Chained Coffin

THIS IS ANOTHER FOLKTALE I'd been thinking about adapting for years. I actually started laying it out once, but somewhere along the way it occurred to me that it would work nicely as a Hellboy origin story. I didn't want to mess up the original English folktale too much, so I kept Hellboy out of the action (a nice change) and kept the whole mother/father angle very vague. The witch's deathbed confession, the chained coffin, the demon, and the horse covered in hooks are all elements from the original folktale.

"The Chained Coffin" was first published in *Dark Horse Presents* 100 Part 2 in 1995. It appears here in color for the first time, with a slightly different first page.

✠

The Wolves of Saint August

WHEN I FINISHED the first Hellboy miniseries, *Seed of Destruction*, my editor (at the time Barbara Kesel) urged me to do a Hellboy story that would be serialized in *Dark Horse Presents*. This would be a fast way to show my audience that I was serious about doing more Hellboy stories. Good idea. I decided to do a werewolf story. I dug around until I found an Irish legend about St. Patrick cursing a group of pagans so that every seven years they would turn into wolves. The rest of the story cobbled itself together around that.

"The Wolves of Saint August" ran as eight-page chapters in *DHP* numbers 88 to 91 in 1994. A year later it was collected into one book with new pages to smooth out some of the rough spots.

John Byrne had scripted the first Hellboy miniseries, so "Wolves" was my first attempt at handling a full writing job. There are plenty of parts I wince at, but there are a few things (like the little girl with the wolf head) that I'm still pretty happy with.

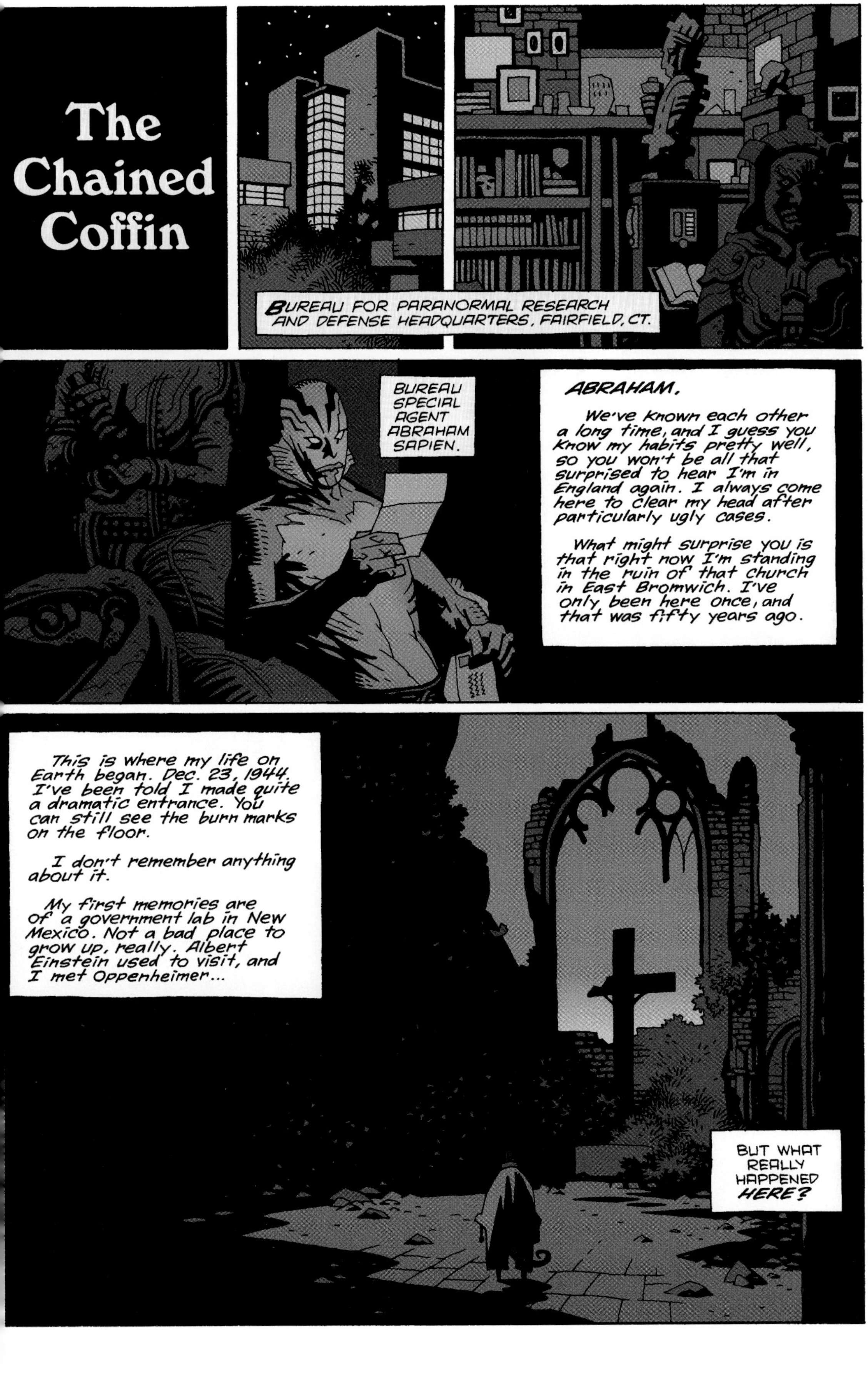

The Chained Coffin
BUREAU FOR PARANORMAL RESEARCH AND DEFENSE HEADQUARTERS, FAIRFIELD, CT.
BUREAU SPECIAL AGENT ABRAHAM SAPIEN.
ABRAHAM,
We've known each other a long time, and I guess you know my habits pretty well, so you won't be all that surprised to hear I'm in England again. I always come here to clear my head after particularly ugly cases.
What might surprise you is that right now I'm standing in the ruin of that church in East Bromwich. I've only been here once, and that was fifty years ago.
This is where my life on Earth began. Dec. 23, 1944. I've been told I made quite a dramatic entrance. You can still see the burn marks on the floor.
I don't remember anything about it.
My first memories are of a government lab in New Mexico. Not a bad place to grow up, really. Albert Einstein used to visit, and I met Oppenheimer...
BUT WHAT REALLY HAPPENED HERE?

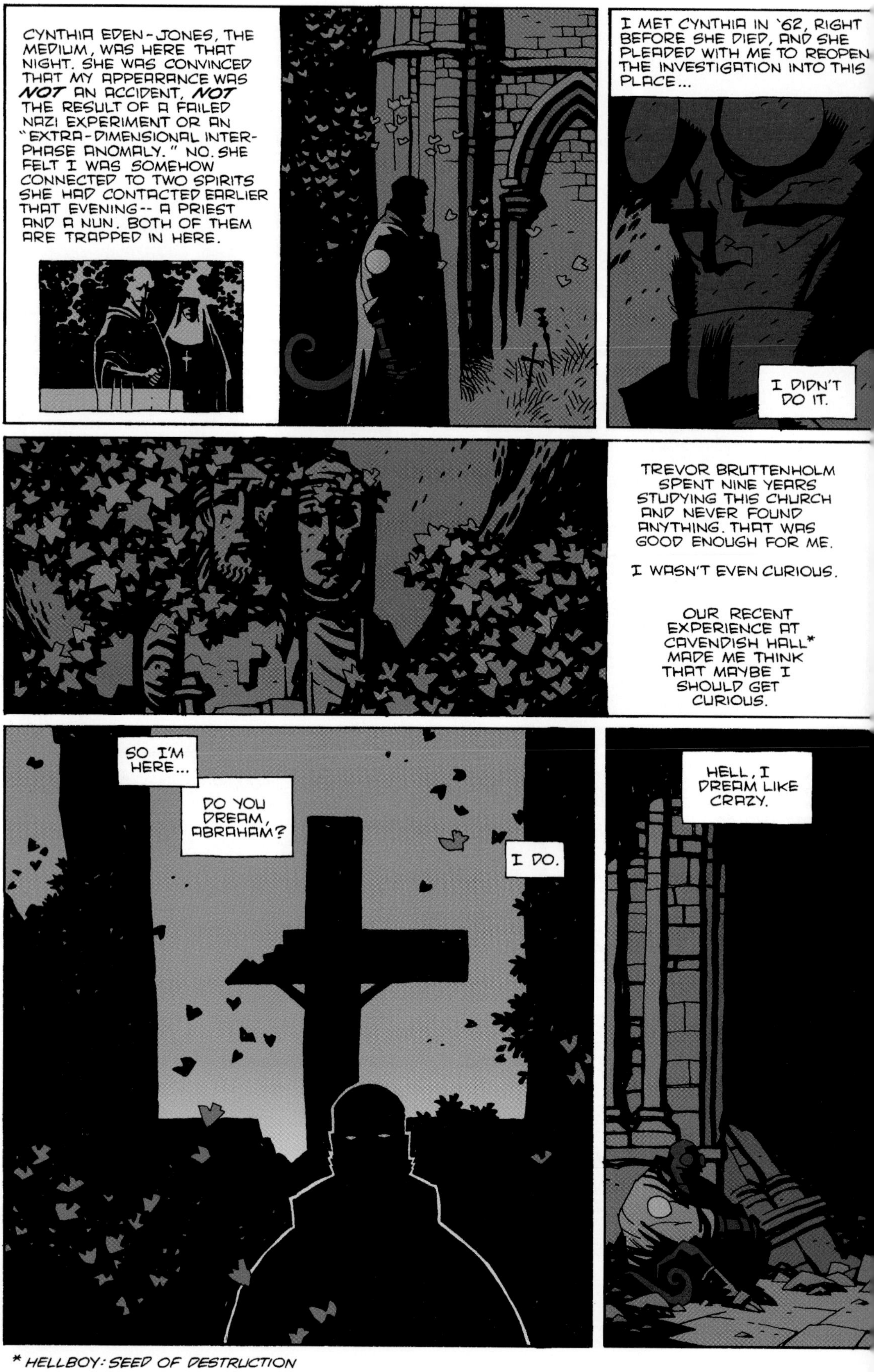
CYNTHIA EDEN-JONES, THE MEDIUM, WAS HERE THAT NIGHT. SHE WAS CONVINCED THAT MY APPEARANCE WAS ***NOT*** AN ACCIDENT, ***NOT*** THE RESULT OF A FAILED NAZI EXPERIMENT OR AN "EXTRA-DIMENSIONAL INTER-PHASE ANOMALY." NO. SHE FELT I WAS SOMEHOW CONNECTED TO TWO SPIRITS SHE HAD CONTACTED EARLIER THAT EVENING-- A PRIEST AND A NUN. BOTH OF THEM ARE TRAPPED IN HERE.
I MET CYNTHIA IN '62, RIGHT BEFORE SHE DIED, AND SHE PLEADED WITH ME TO REOPEN THE INVESTIGATION INTO THIS PLACE...
I DIDN'T DO IT.
TREVOR BRUTTENHOLM SPENT NINE YEARS STUDYING THIS CHURCH AND NEVER FOUND ANYTHING. THAT WAS GOOD ENOUGH FOR ME.
I WASN'T EVEN CURIOUS.
OUR RECENT EXPERIENCE AT CAVENDISH HALL* MADE ME THINK THAT MAYBE I SHOULD GET CURIOUS.
SO I'M HERE...
DO YOU DREAM, ABRAHAM?
I DO.
HELL, I DREAM LIKE CRAZY.

* *HELLBOY: SEED OF DESTRUCTION*

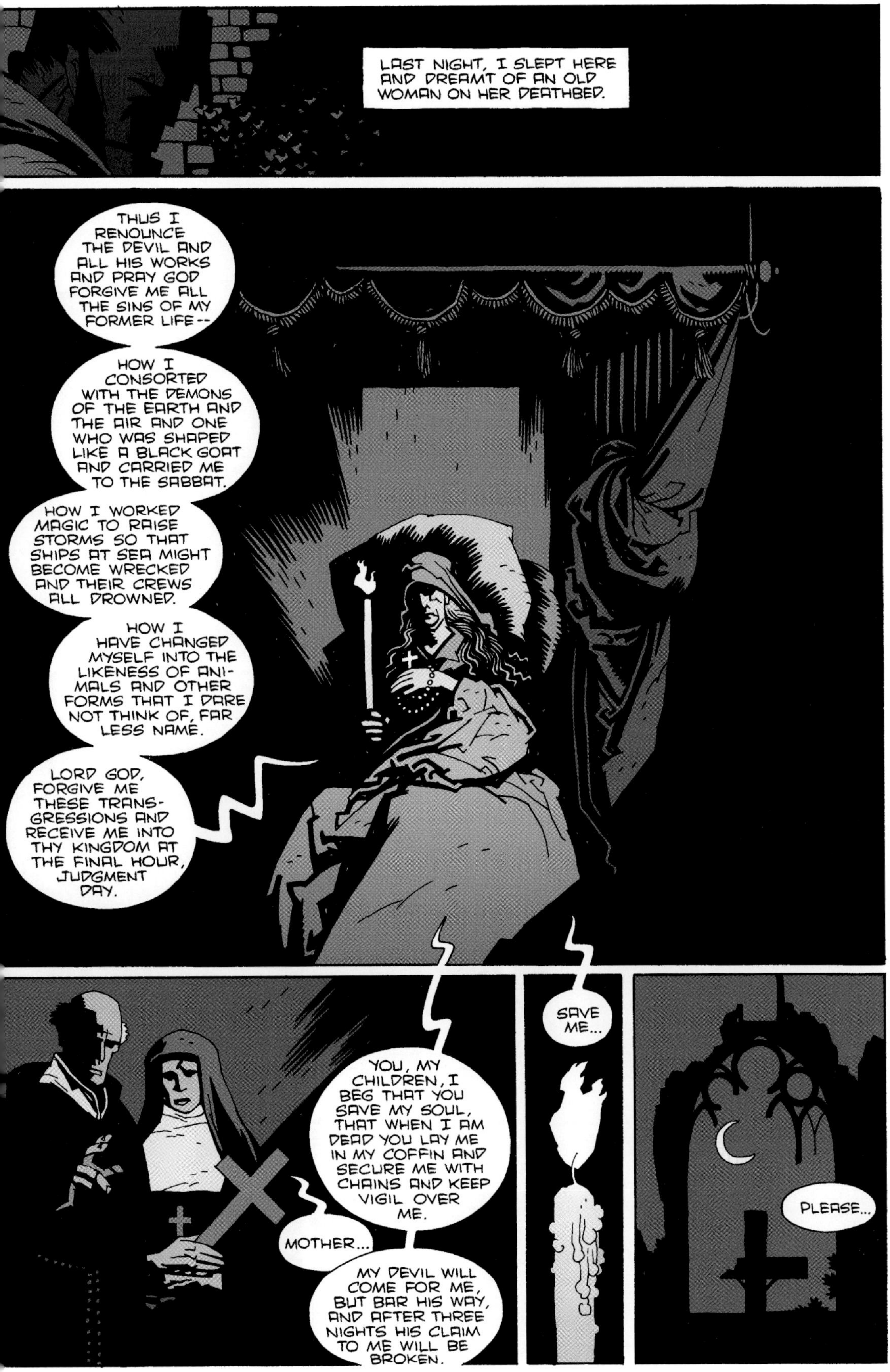

LAST NIGHT, I SLEPT HERE AND DREAMT OF AN OLD WOMAN ON HER DEATHBED.
THUS I RENOUNCE THE DEVIL AND ALL HIS WORKS AND PRAY GOD FORGIVE ME ALL THE SINS OF MY FORMER LIFE--
HOW I CONSORTED WITH THE DEMONS OF THE EARTH AND THE AIR AND ONE WHO WAS SHAPED LIKE A BLACK GOAT AND CARRIED ME TO THE SABBAT.
HOW I WORKED MAGIC TO RAISE STORMS SO THAT SHIPS AT SEA MIGHT BECOME WRECKED AND THEIR CREWS ALL DROWNED.
HOW I HAVE CHANGED MYSELF INTO THE LIKENESS OF ANIMALS AND OTHER FORMS THAT I DARE NOT THINK OF, FAR LESS NAME.
LORD GOD, FORGIVE ME THESE TRANSGRESSIONS AND RECEIVE ME INTO THY KINGDOM AT THE FINAL HOUR, JUDGMENT DAY.
YOU, MY CHILDREN, I BEG THAT YOU SAVE MY SOUL, THAT WHEN I AM DEAD YOU LAY ME IN MY COFFIN AND SECURE ME WITH CHAINS AND KEEP VIGIL OVER ME.
MOTHER...
MY DEVIL WILL COME FOR ME, BUT BAR HIS WAY, AND AFTER THREE NIGHTS HIS CLAIM TO ME WILL BE BROKEN.
SAVE ME...
PLEASE...

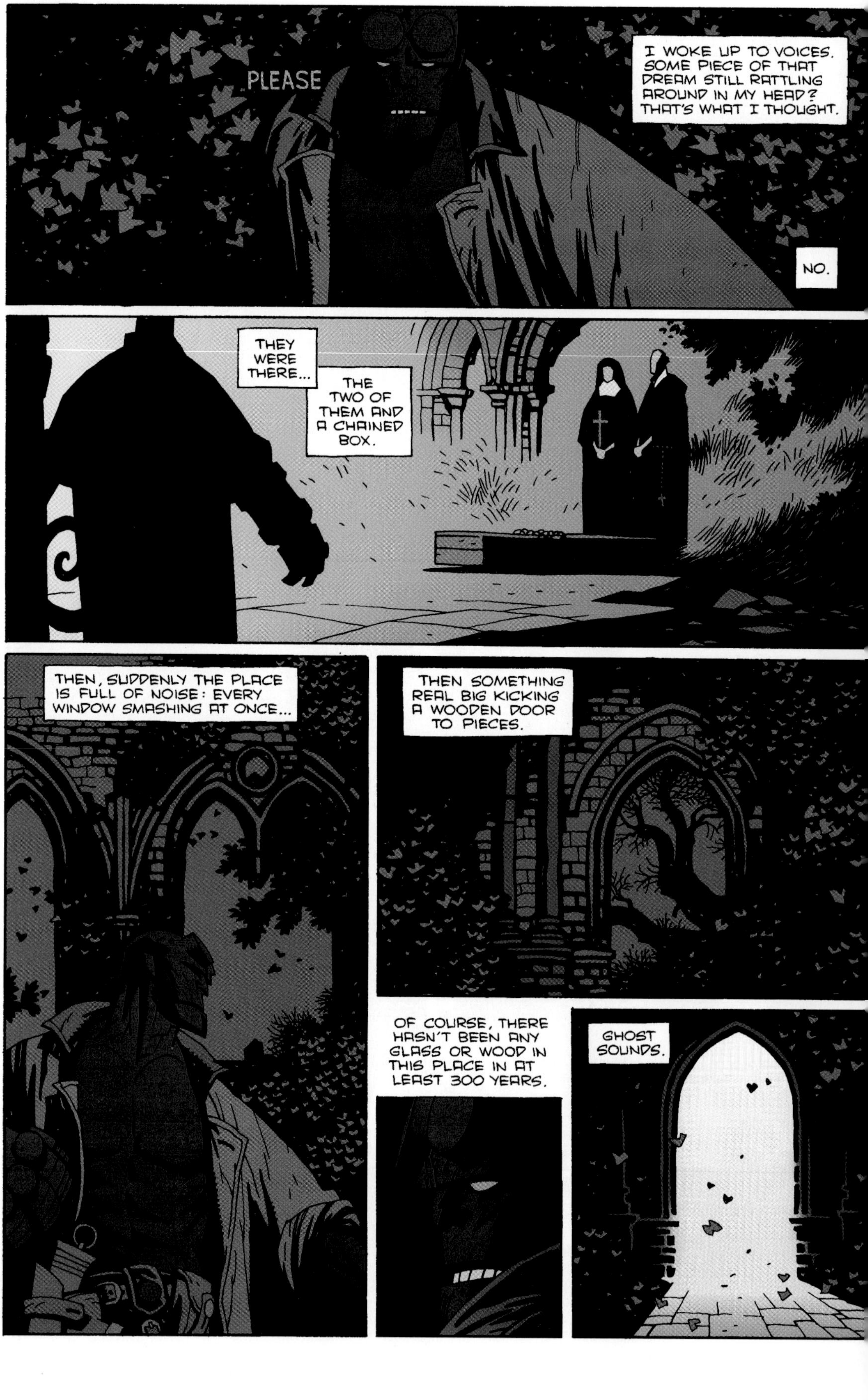
PLEASE
I WOKE UP TO VOICES. SOME PIECE OF THAT DREAM STILL RATTLING AROUND IN MY HEAD? THAT'S WHAT I THOUGHT.
NO.
THEY WERE THERE...
THE TWO OF THEM AND A CHAINED BOX.
THEN, SUDDENLY THE PLACE IS FULL OF NOISE: EVERY WINDOW SMASHING AT ONCE...
THEN SOMETHING REAL BIG KICKING A WOODEN DOOR TO PIECES.
OF COURSE, THERE HASN'T BEEN ANY GLASS OR WOOD IN THIS PLACE IN AT LEAST 300 YEARS.
GHOST SOUNDS.

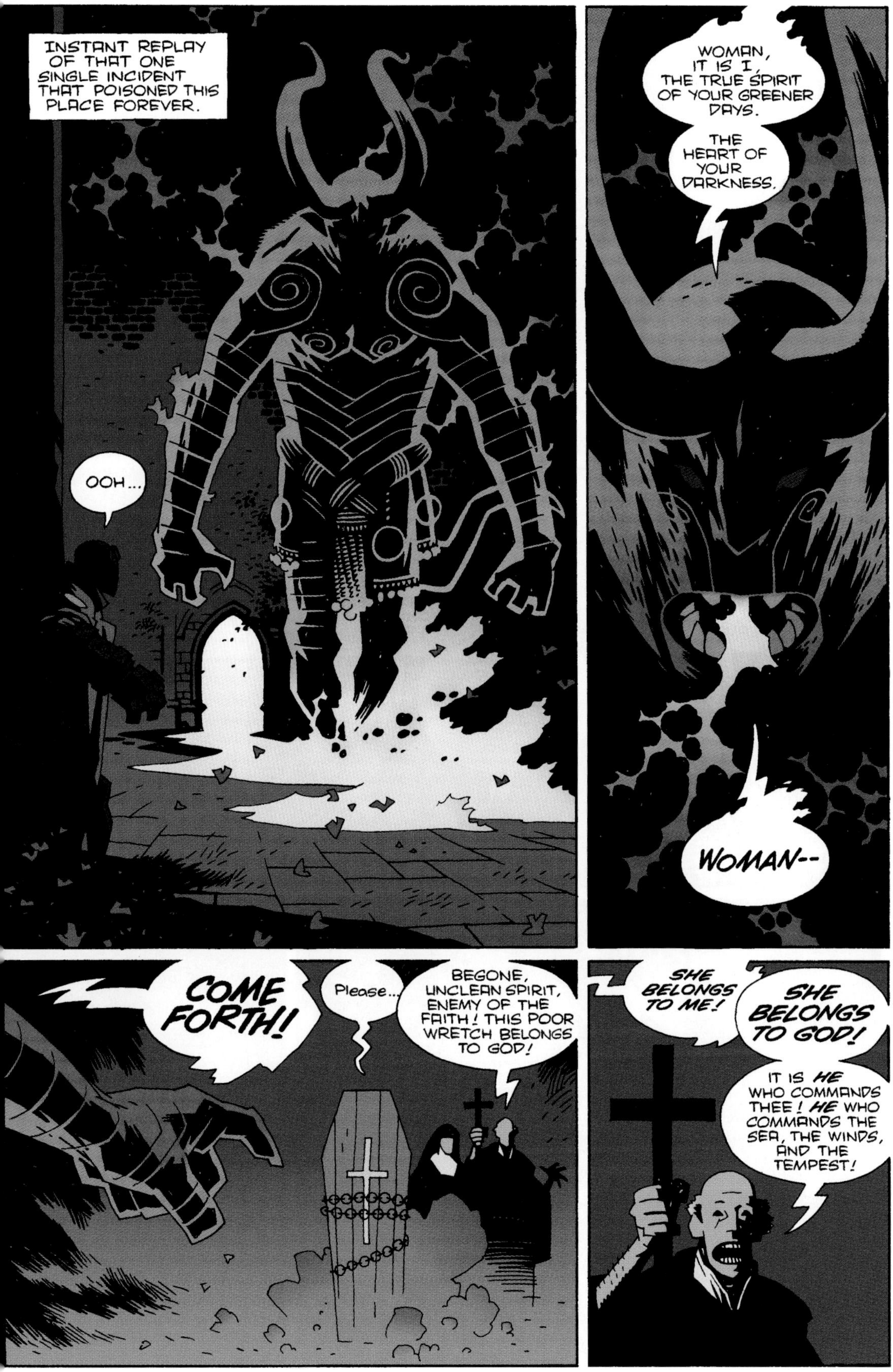
INSTANT REPLAY OF THAT ONE SINGLE INCIDENT THAT POISONED THIS PLACE FOREVER.
OOH...
WOMAN, IT IS I, THE TRUE SPIRIT OF YOUR GREENER DAYS.
THE HEART OF YOUR DARKNESS.
WOMAN--
COME FORTH!
Please...
BEGONE, UNCLEAN SPIRIT, ENEMY OF THE FAITH! THIS POOR WRETCH BELONGS TO GOD!
SHE BELONGS TO ME!
SHE BELONGS TO GOD!
IT IS HE WHO COMMANDS THEE! HE WHO COMMANDS THE SEA, THE WINDS, AND THE TEMPEST!

WOMAN, YOU ARE MINE. **COME FORTH!**

YOU STRUCK YOUR OWN NAME OUT OF THE BOOK OF LIFE.

YOU TURNED YOUR BACK ON THE LIGHT OF DAY TO WALK IN SHADOWS WITH **ME.**

PLEASE. MERCY.

IF HE WILL FORGIVE ME, LET ME GO TO GOD.

GOD!?

WAS **I** NOT GOD IN OLD BABYLON?

WAS **I** NOT GOD TO THE WOMEN OF EAST BROMWICH, LANCASHIRE, AND FAVERSHAM?

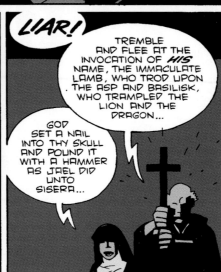

LIAR!

TREMBLE AND FLEE AT THE INVOCATION OF **HIS** NAME, THE IMMACULATE LAMB, WHO TROD UPON THE ASP AND BASILISK, WHO TRAMPLED THE LION AND THE DRAGON...

GOD SET A NAIL INTO THY SKULL AND POUND IT WITH A HAMMER AS JAEL DID UNTO SISERA...

ENOUGH!

THE WORD MADE FLESH COMMANDS THEE...

GUAAA...

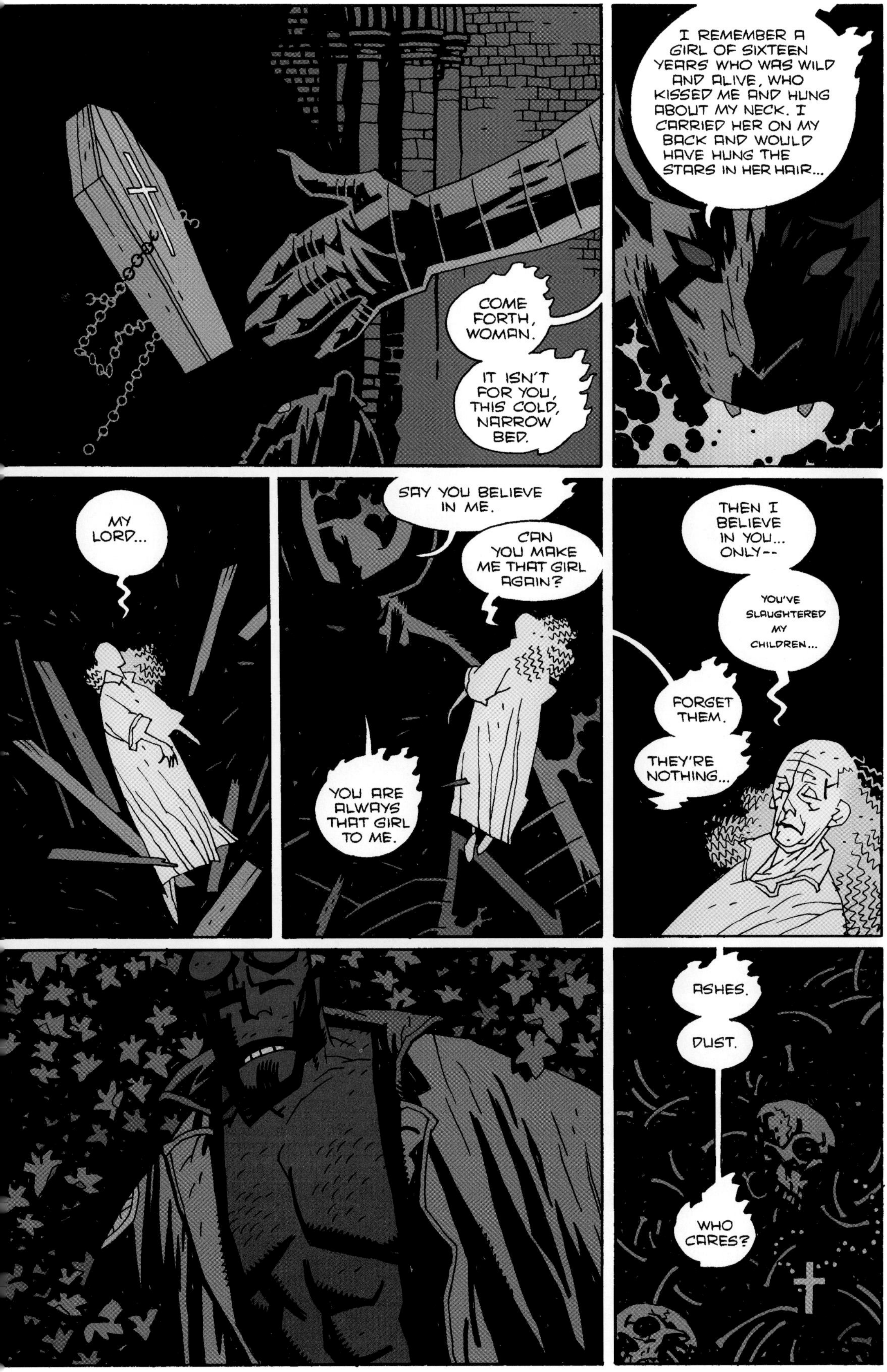

COME FORTH, WOMAN.
IT ISN'T FOR YOU, THIS COLD, NARROW BED.
I REMEMBER A GIRL OF SIXTEEN YEARS WHO WAS WILD AND ALIVE, WHO KISSED ME AND HUNG ABOUT MY NECK. I CARRIED HER ON MY BACK AND WOULD HAVE HUNG THE STARS IN HER HAIR...
MY LORD...
SAY YOU BELIEVE IN ME.
CAN YOU MAKE ME THAT GIRL AGAIN?
YOU ARE ALWAYS THAT GIRL TO ME.
THEN I BELIEVE IN YOU... ONLY--
YOU'VE SLAUGHTERED MY CHILDREN...
FORGET THEM.
THEY'RE NOTHING...
ASHES.
DUST.
WHO CARES?

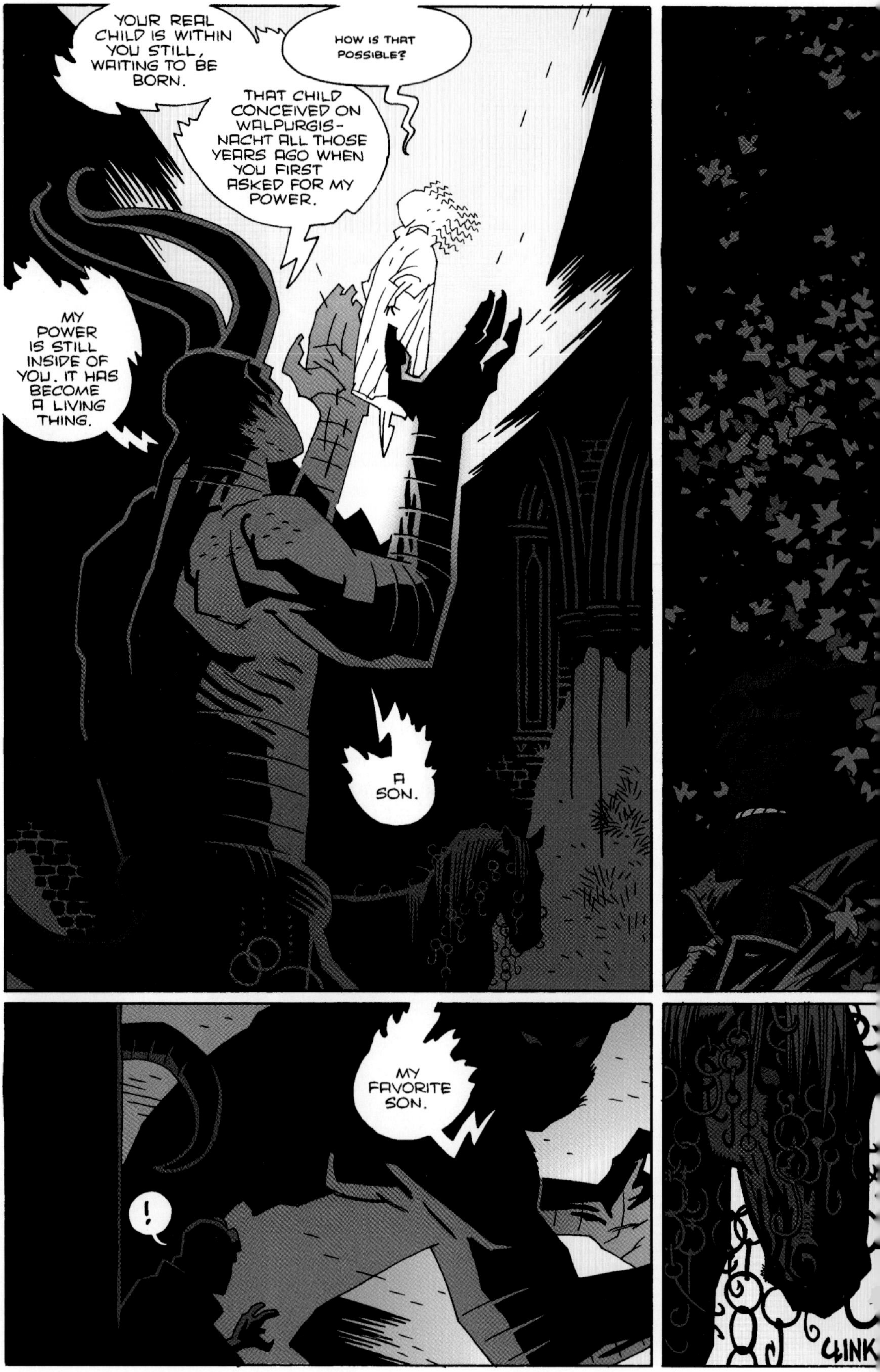
YOUR REAL CHILD IS WITHIN YOU STILL, WAITING TO BE BORN.
HOW IS THAT POSSIBLE?
THAT CHILD CONCEIVED ON WALPURGIS-NACHT ALL THOSE YEARS AGO WHEN YOU FIRST ASKED FOR MY POWER.
MY POWER IS STILL INSIDE OF YOU. IT HAS BECOME A LIVING THING.
A SON.
MY FAVORITE SON.
!
CLINK

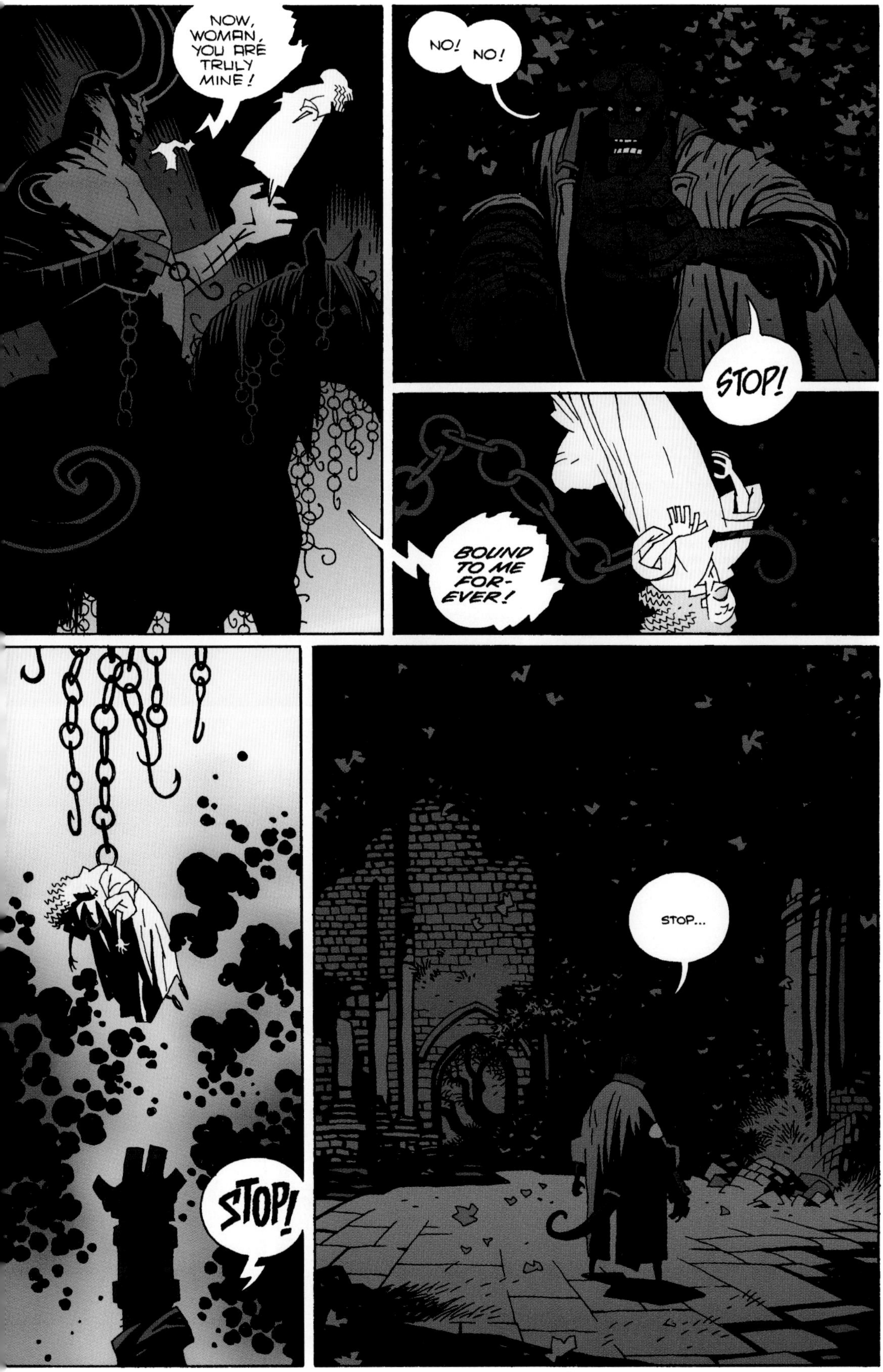
NOW, WOMAN, YOU ARE TRULY MINE!
NO!
NO!
STOP!
BOUND TO ME FOR-EVER!
STOP!
STOP...

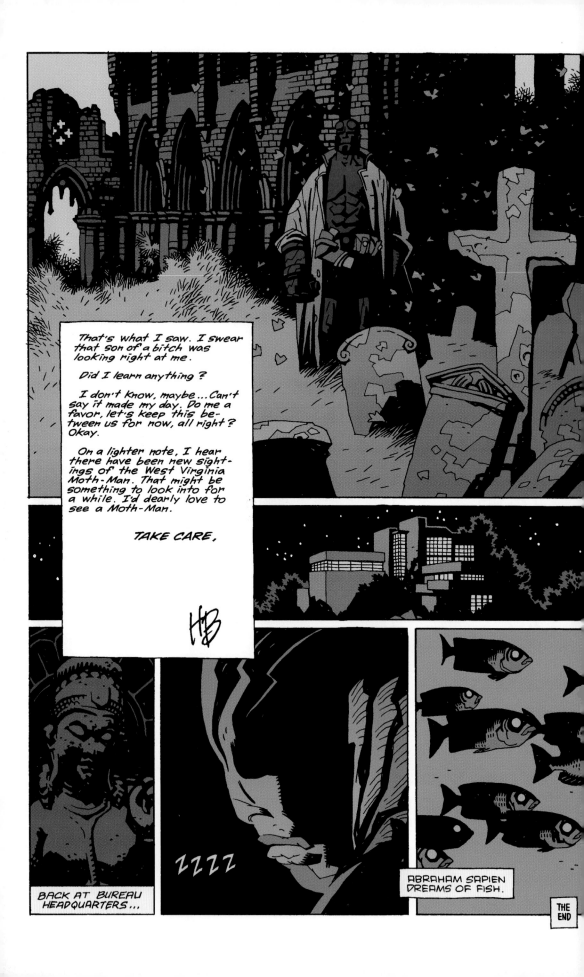

That's what I saw. I swear that son of a bitch was looking right at me.

Did I learn anything?

I don't know, maybe...Can't say it made my day. Do me a favor, let's keep this between us for now, all right? Okay.

On a lighter note, I hear there have been new sightings of the West Virginia Moth-Man. That might be something to look into for a while. I'd dearly love to see a Moth-Man.

TAKE CARE,

HB

ZZZZ

BACK AT BUREAU HEADQUARTERS...

ABRAHAM SAPIEN DREAMS OF FISH.

THE END

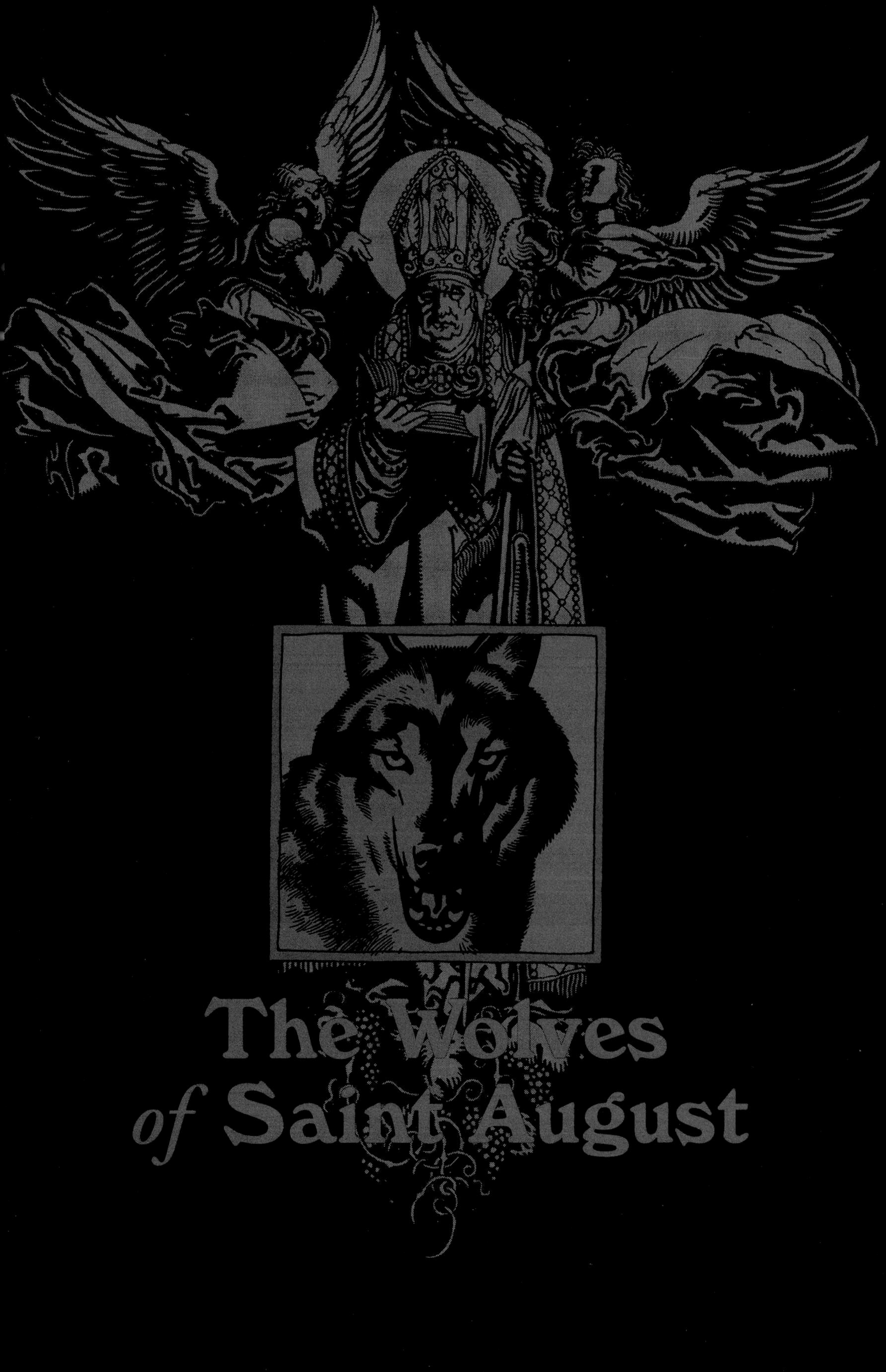
The Wolves
of Saint August

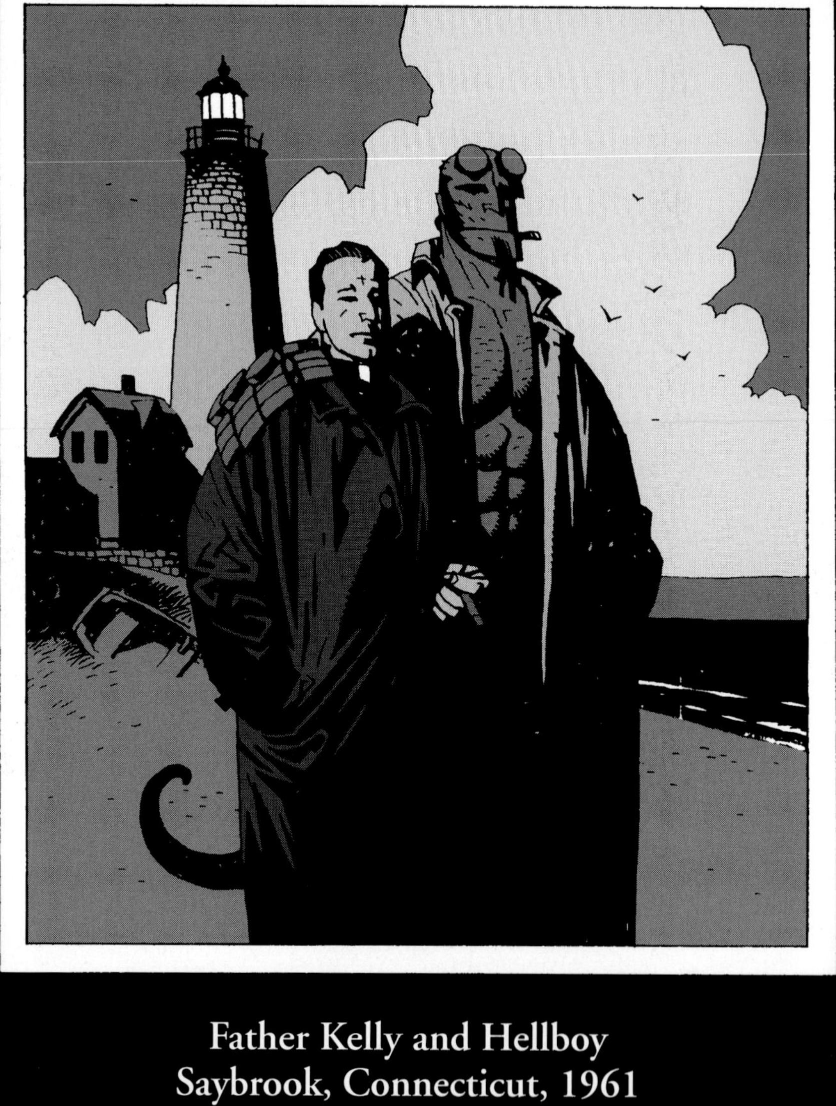

Father Kelly and Hellboy
Saybrook, Connecticut, 1961

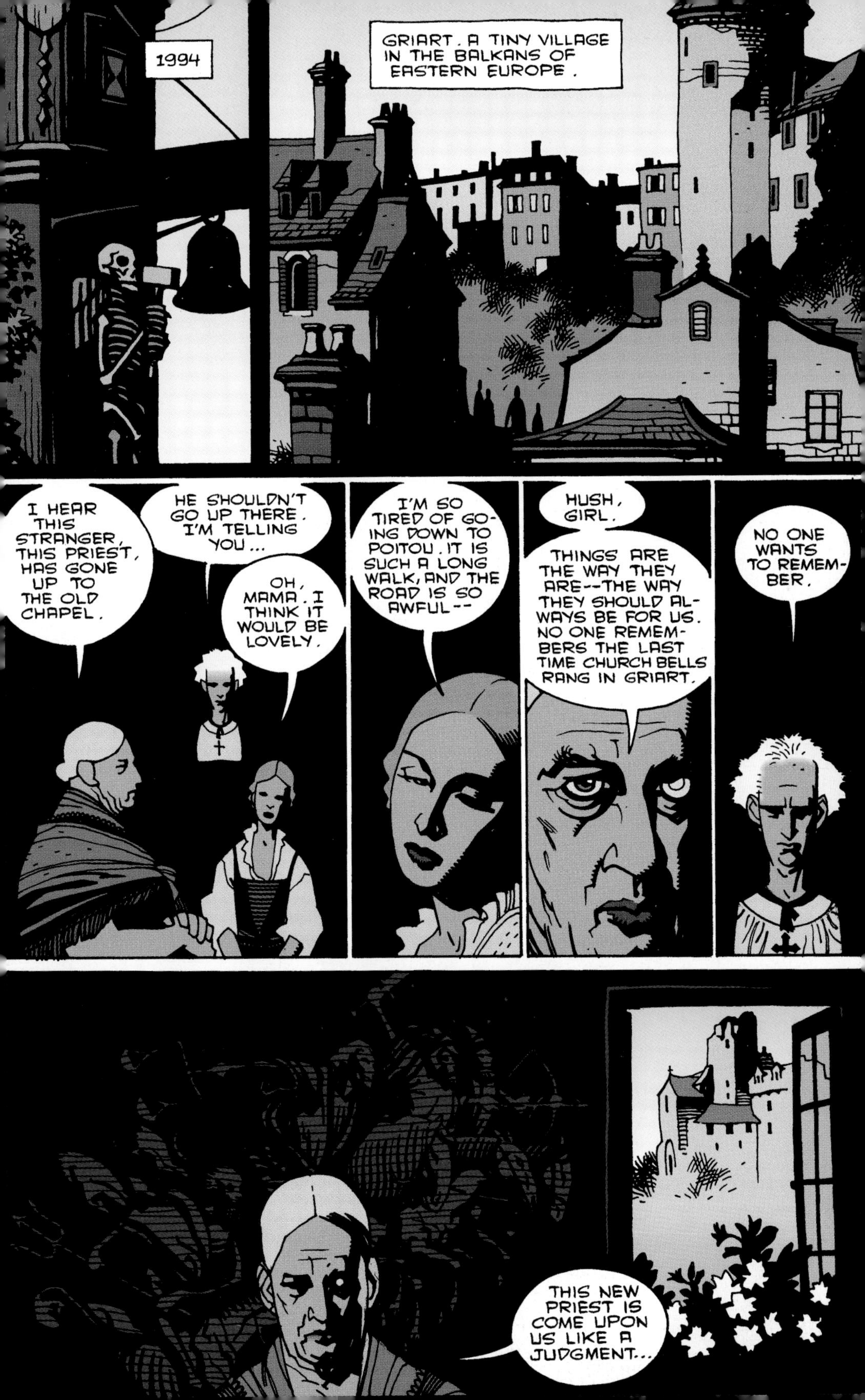
1994
GRIART. A TINY VILLAGE IN THE BALKANS OF EASTERN EUROPE.
I HEAR THIS STRANGER, THIS PRIEST, HAS GONE UP TO THE OLD CHAPEL.
HE SHOULDN'T GO UP THERE. I'M TELLING YOU...
OH, MAMA. I THINK IT WOULD BE LOVELY.
I'M SO TIRED OF GOING DOWN TO POITOU. IT IS SUCH A LONG WALK, AND THE ROAD IS SO AWFUL--
HUSH, GIRL.
THINGS ARE THE WAY THEY ARE--THE WAY THEY SHOULD ALWAYS BE FOR US. NO ONE REMEMBERS THE LAST TIME CHURCH BELLS RANG IN GRIART.
NO ONE WANTS TO REMEMBER.
THIS NEW PRIEST IS COME UPON US LIKE A JUDGMENT...

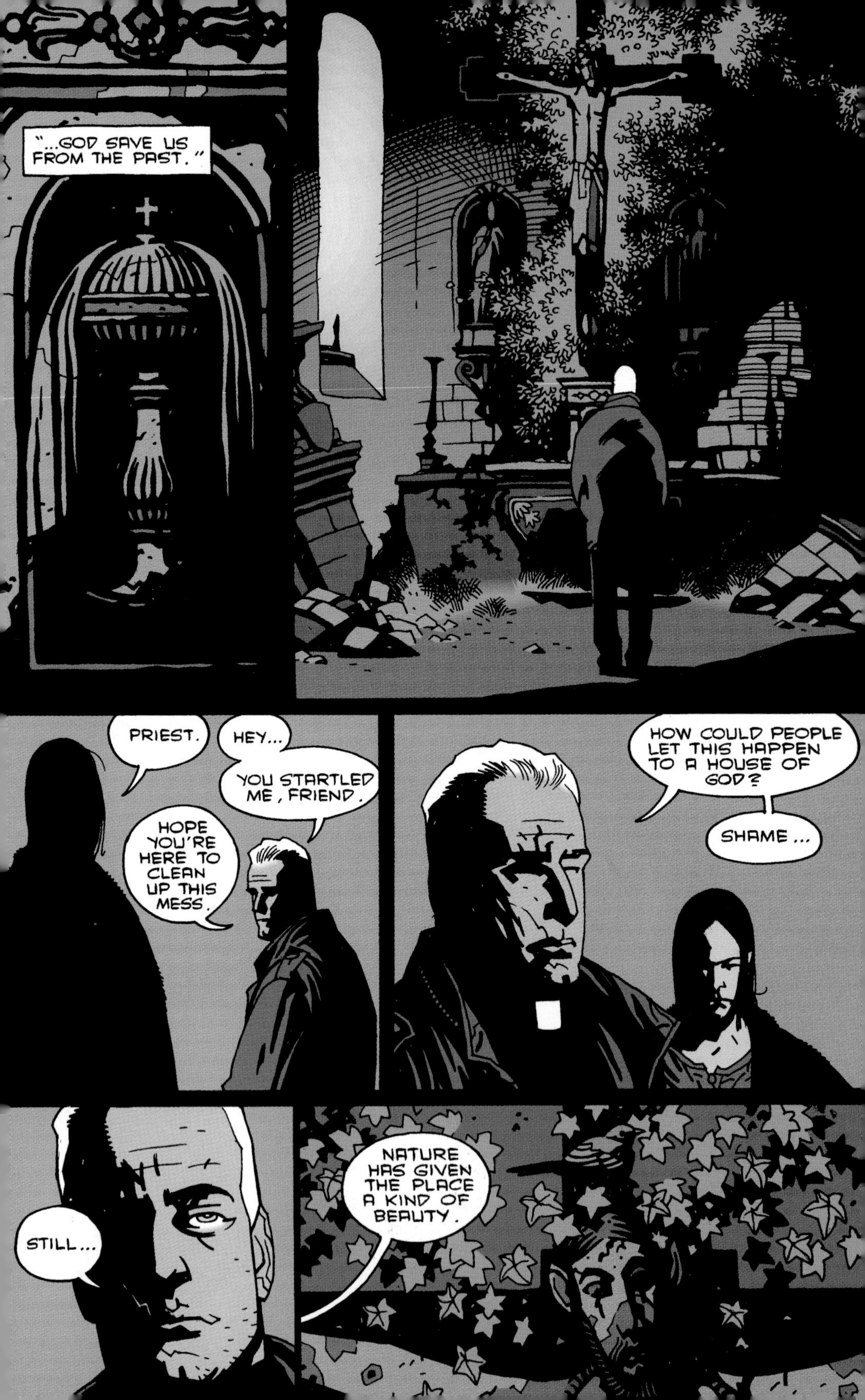
"...GOD SAVE US FROM THE PAST."
PRIEST.
HEY...
YOU STARTLED ME, FRIEND.
HOPE YOU'RE HERE TO CLEAN UP THIS MESS.
HOW COULD PEOPLE LET THIS HAPPEN TO A HOUSE OF GOD?
SHAME...
STILL...
NATURE HAS GIVEN THE PLACE A KIND OF BEAUTY.

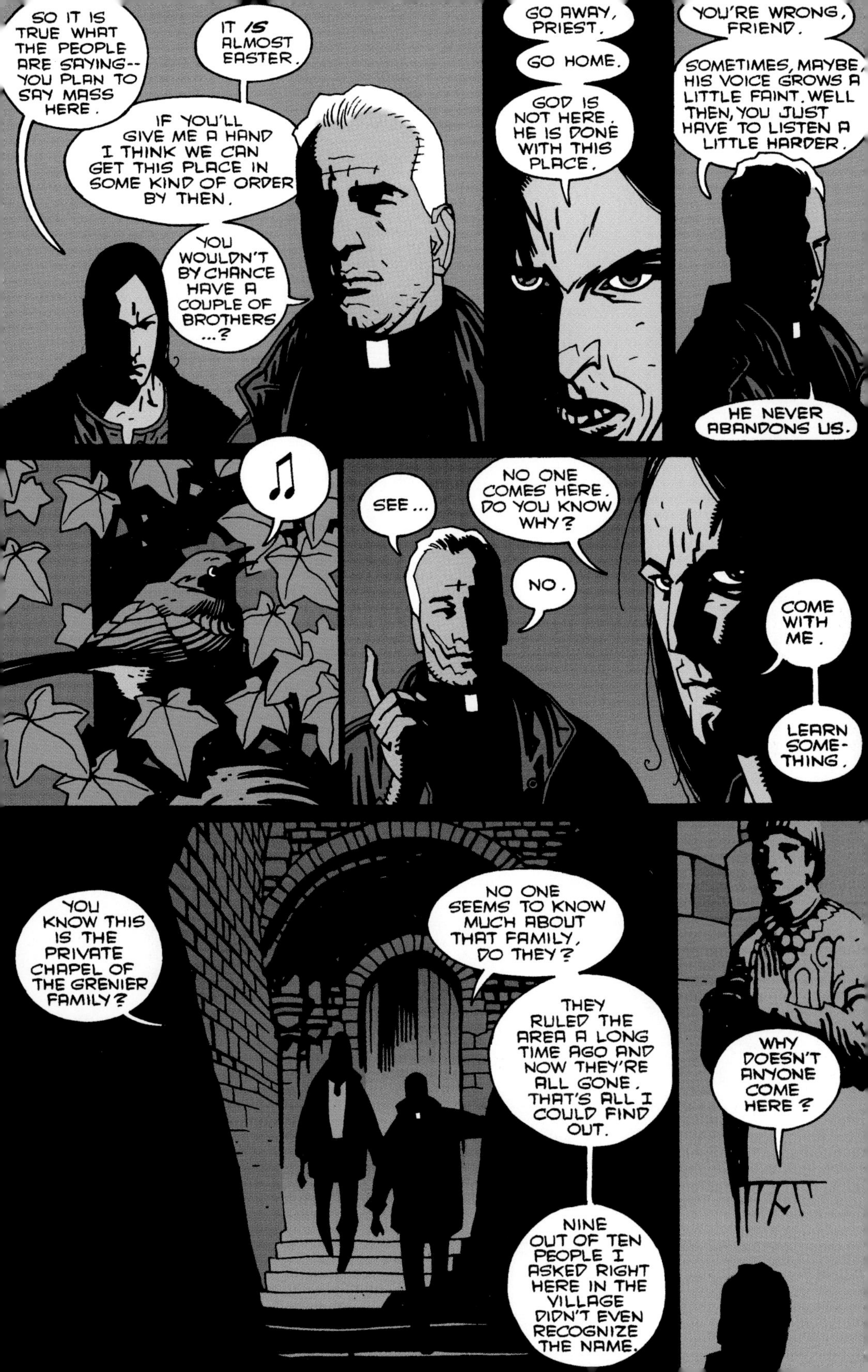
SO IT IS TRUE WHAT THE PEOPLE ARE SAYING-- YOU PLAN TO SAY MASS HERE.
IT IS ALMOST EASTER.
IF YOU'LL GIVE ME A HAND I THINK WE CAN GET THIS PLACE IN SOME KIND OF ORDER BY THEN.
YOU WOULDN'T BY CHANCE HAVE A COUPLE OF BROTHERS ...?
GO AWAY, PRIEST.
GO HOME.
GOD IS NOT HERE. HE IS DONE WITH THIS PLACE.
YOU'RE WRONG, FRIEND.
SOMETIMES, MAYBE, HIS VOICE GROWS A LITTLE FAINT. WELL THEN, YOU JUST HAVE TO LISTEN A LITTLE HARDER.
HE NEVER ABANDONS US.
♫
SEE...
NO ONE COMES HERE. DO YOU KNOW WHY?
NO.
COME WITH ME.
LEARN SOME-THING.
YOU KNOW THIS IS THE PRIVATE CHAPEL OF THE GRENIER FAMILY?
NO ONE SEEMS TO KNOW MUCH ABOUT THAT FAMILY, DO THEY?
THEY RULED THE AREA A LONG TIME AGO AND NOW THEY'RE ALL GONE. THAT'S ALL I COULD FIND OUT.
NINE OUT OF TEN PEOPLE I ASKED RIGHT HERE IN THE VILLAGE DIDN'T EVEN RECOGNIZE THE NAME.
WHY DOESN'T ANYONE COME HERE?

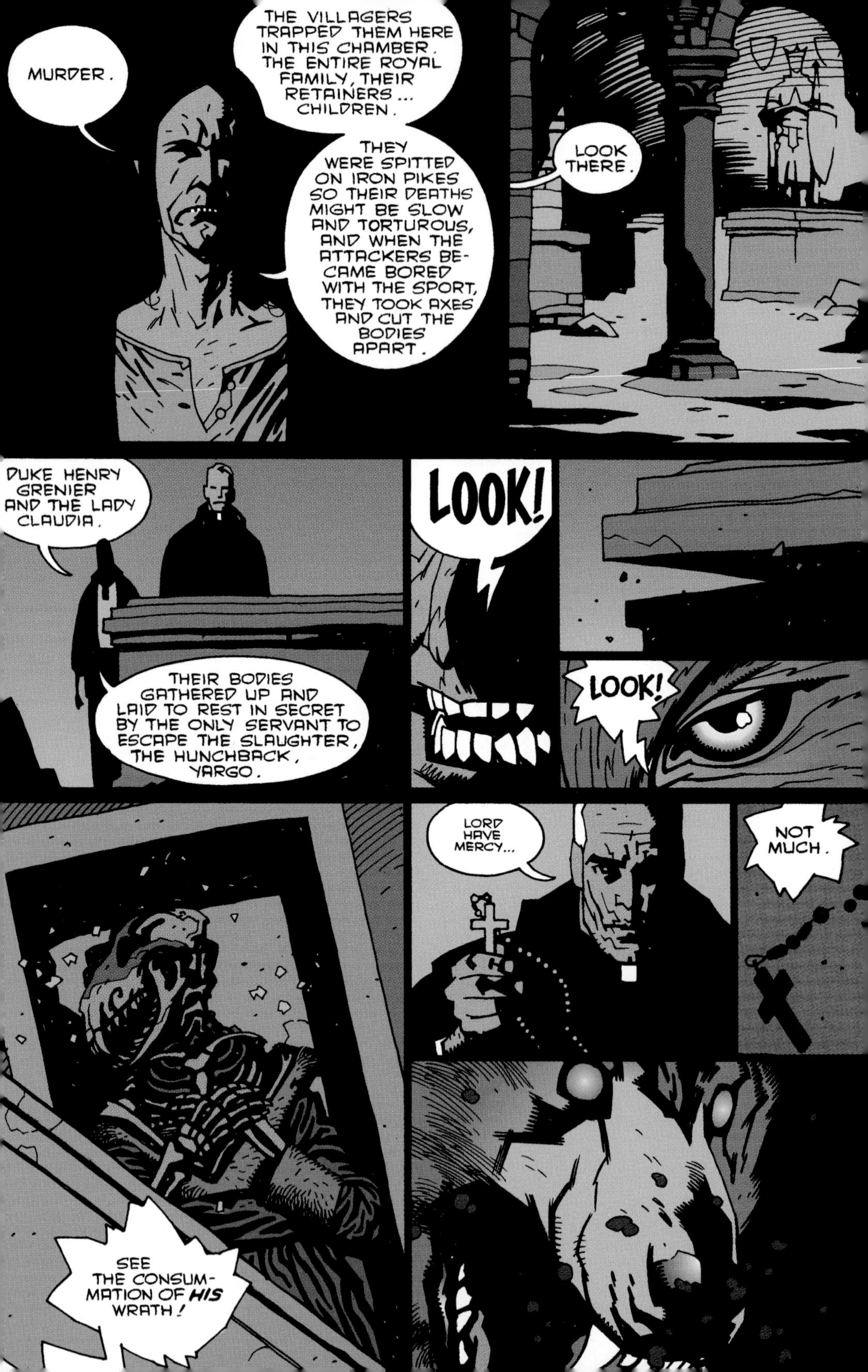
MURDER.
THE VILLAGERS TRAPPED THEM HERE IN THIS CHAMBER. THE ENTIRE ROYAL FAMILY, THEIR RETAINERS... CHILDREN.
THEY WERE SPITTED ON IRON PIKES SO THEIR DEATHS MIGHT BE SLOW AND TORTUROUS, AND WHEN THE ATTACKERS BE-CAME BORED WITH THE SPORT, THEY TOOK AXES AND CUT THE BODIES APART.
LOOK THERE.
DUKE HENRY GRENIER AND THE LADY CLAUDIA.
THEIR BODIES GATHERED UP AND LAID TO REST IN SECRET BY THE ONLY SERVANT TO ESCAPE THE SLAUGHTER, THE HUNCHBACK, YARGO.
LOOK!
LOOK!
SEE THE CONSUM-MATION OF **HIS** WRATH!
LORD HAVE MERCY...
NOT MUCH.

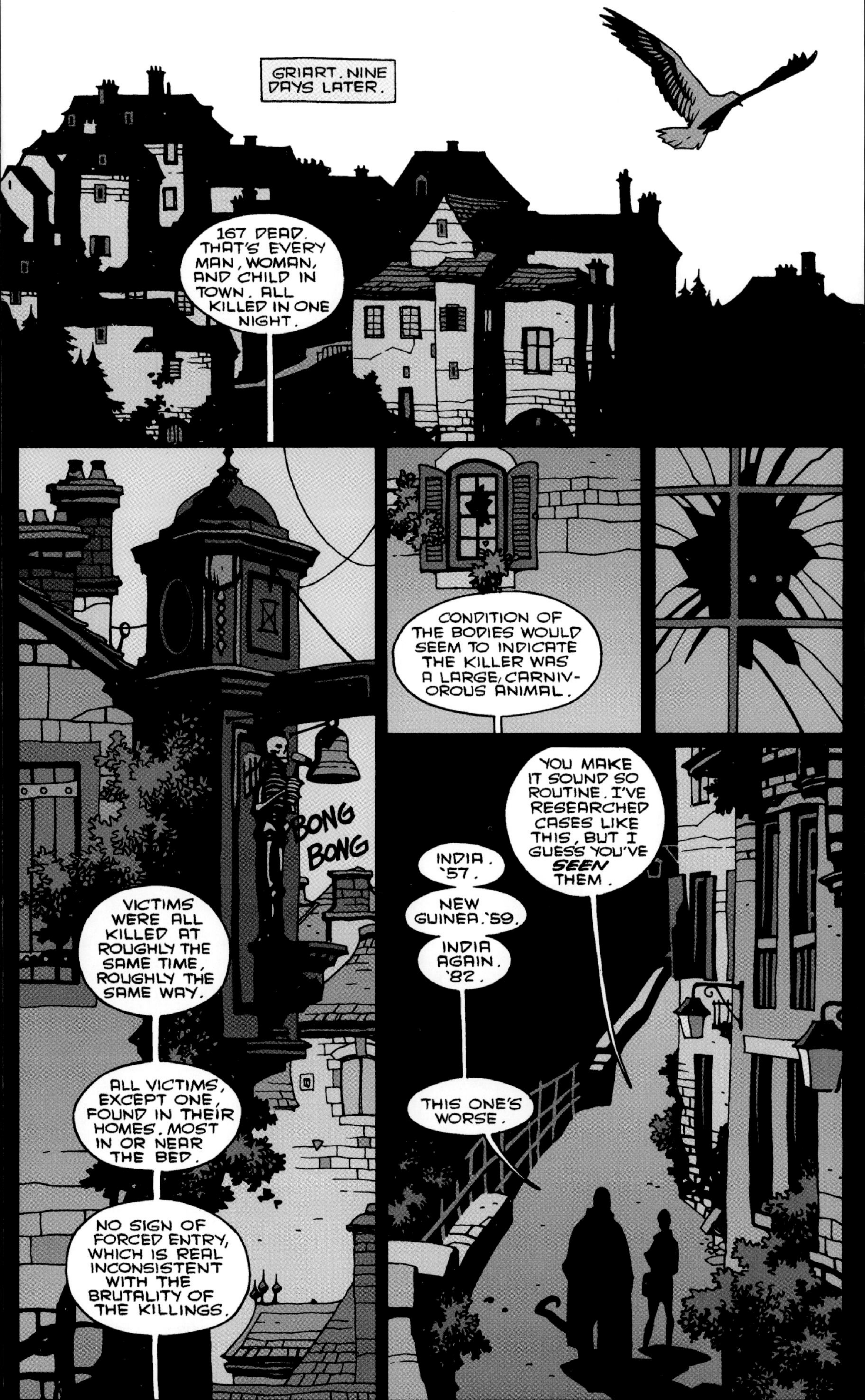

GRIART. NINE DAYS LATER.
167 DEAD. THAT'S EVERY MAN, WOMAN, AND CHILD IN TOWN. ALL KILLED IN ONE NIGHT.
BONG BONG
VICTIMS WERE ALL KILLED AT ROUGHLY THE SAME TIME, ROUGHLY THE SAME WAY.
ALL VICTIMS, EXCEPT ONE, FOUND IN THEIR HOMES. MOST IN OR NEAR THE BED.
NO SIGN OF FORCED ENTRY, WHICH IS REAL INCONSISTENT WITH THE BRUTALITY OF THE KILLINGS.
CONDITION OF THE BODIES WOULD SEEM TO INDICATE THE KILLER WAS A LARGE, CARNIVOROUS ANIMAL.
YOU MAKE IT SOUND SO ROUTINE. I'VE RESEARCHED CASES LIKE THIS, BUT I GUESS YOU'VE *SEEN* THEM.
INDIA. '57.
NEW GUINEA. '59.
INDIA AGAIN. '82.
THIS ONE'S WORSE.

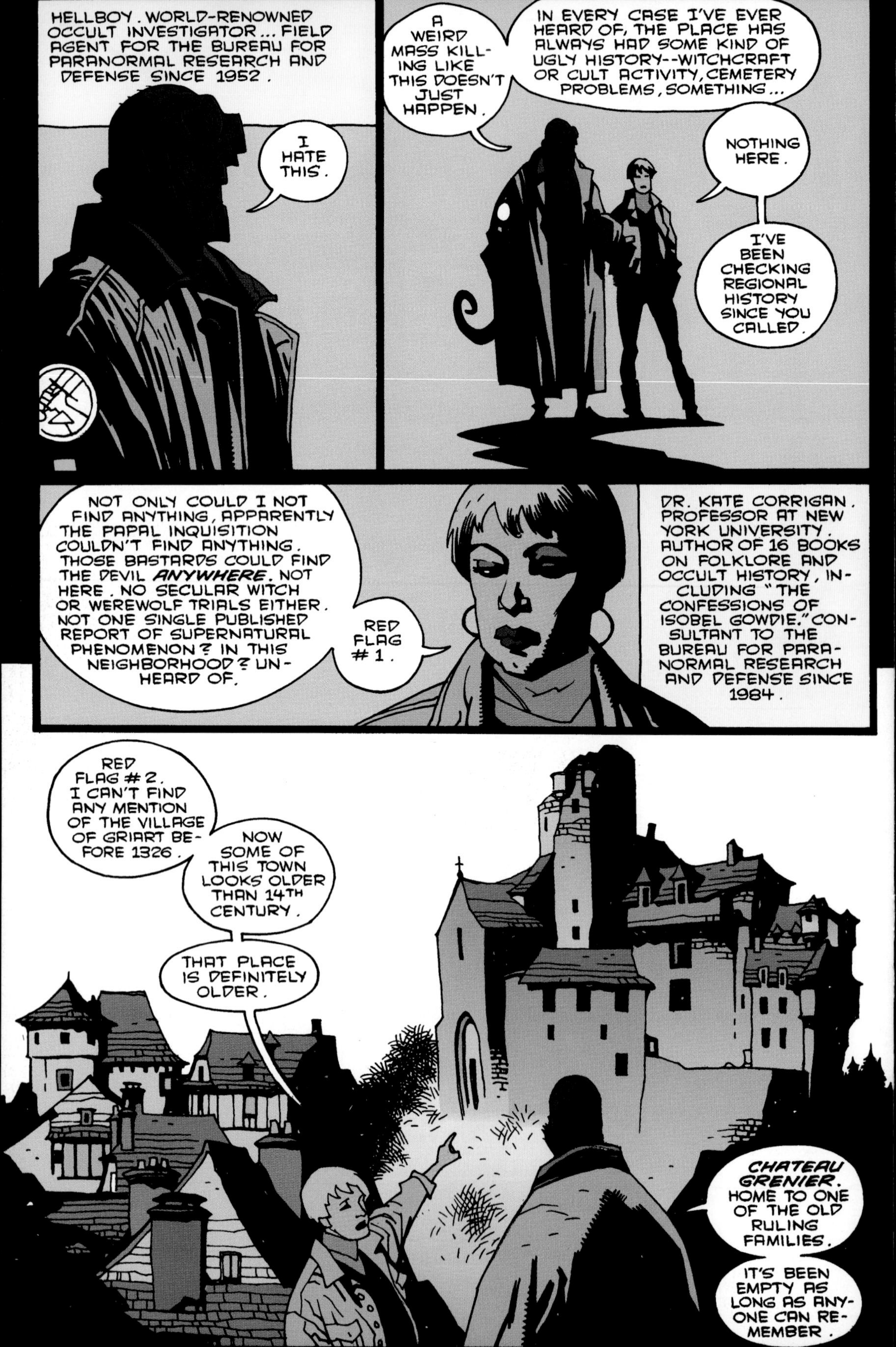

HELLBOY. WORLD-RENOWNED OCCULT INVESTIGATOR... FIELD AGENT FOR THE BUREAU FOR PARANORMAL RESEARCH AND DEFENSE SINCE 1952.
I HATE THIS.
A WEIRD MASS KILLING LIKE THIS DOESN'T JUST HAPPEN.
IN EVERY CASE I'VE EVER HEARD OF, THE PLACE HAS ALWAYS HAD SOME KIND OF UGLY HISTORY--WITCHCRAFT OR CULT ACTIVITY, CEMETERY PROBLEMS, SOMETHING...
NOTHING HERE.
I'VE BEEN CHECKING REGIONAL HISTORY SINCE YOU CALLED.
NOT ONLY COULD I NOT FIND ANYTHING, APPARENTLY THE PAPAL INQUISITION COULDN'T FIND ANYTHING. THOSE BASTARDS COULD FIND THE DEVIL *ANYWHERE*. NOT HERE. NO SECULAR WITCH OR WEREWOLF TRIALS EITHER. NOT ONE SINGLE PUBLISHED REPORT OF SUPERNATURAL PHENOMENON? IN THIS NEIGHBORHOOD? UNHEARD OF.
RED FLAG #1.
DR. KATE CORRIGAN. PROFESSOR AT NEW YORK UNIVERSITY. AUTHOR OF 16 BOOKS ON FOLKLORE AND OCCULT HISTORY, INCLUDING "THE CONFESSIONS OF ISOBEL GOWDIE." CONSULTANT TO THE BUREAU FOR PARANORMAL RESEARCH AND DEFENSE SINCE 1984.
RED FLAG #2. I CAN'T FIND ANY MENTION OF THE VILLAGE OF GRIART BEFORE 1326.
NOW SOME OF THIS TOWN LOOKS OLDER THAN 14TH CENTURY.
THAT PLACE IS DEFINITELY OLDER.
CHATEAU GRENIER. HOME TO ONE OF THE OLD RULING FAMILIES.
IT'S BEEN EMPTY AS LONG AS ANYONE CAN REMEMBER.

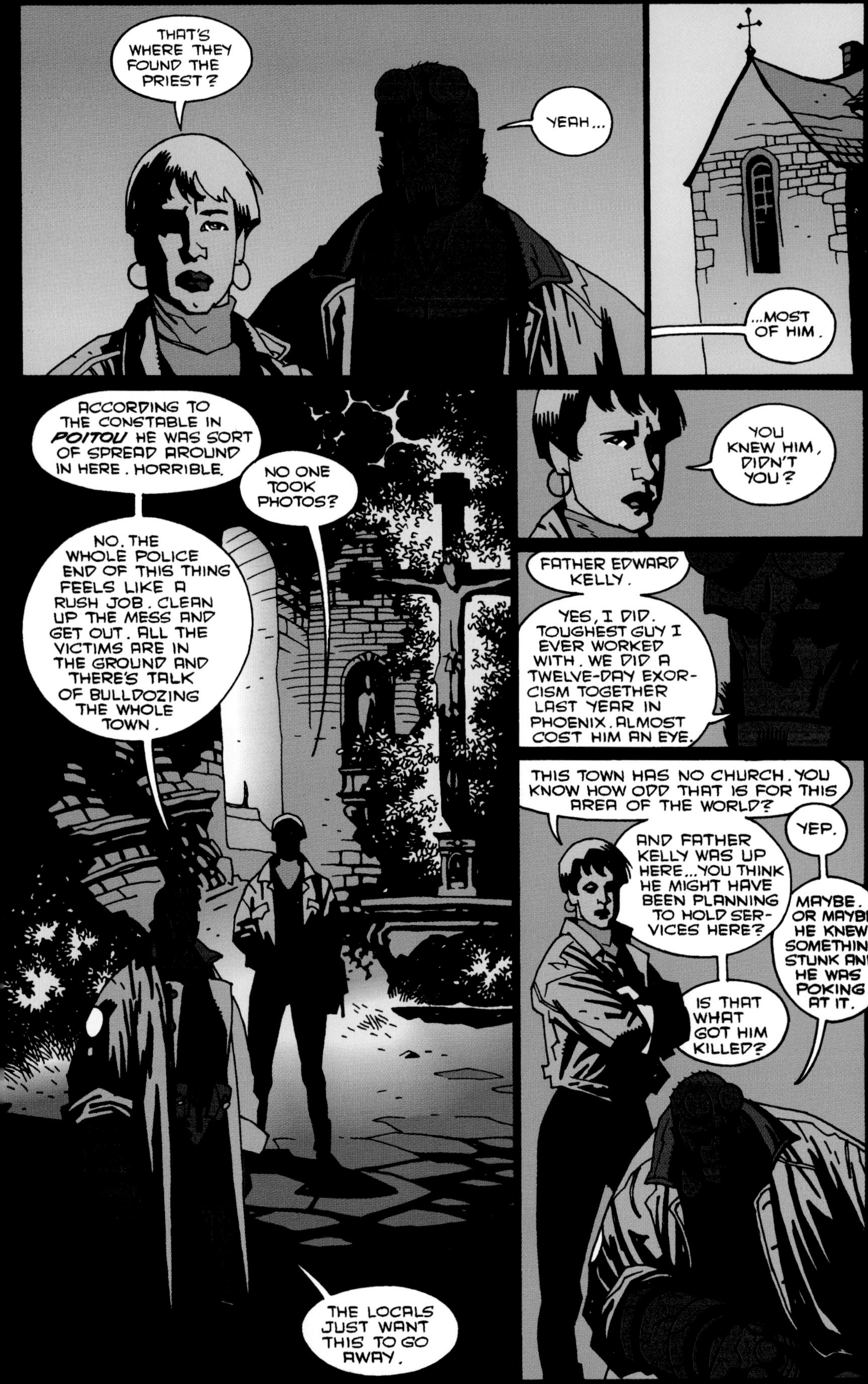
THAT'S WHERE THEY FOUND THE PRIEST?
YEAH...
...MOST OF HIM.
ACCORDING TO THE CONSTABLE IN POITOU HE WAS SORT OF SPREAD AROUND IN HERE. HORRIBLE.
NO ONE TOOK PHOTOS?
NO. THE WHOLE POLICE END OF THIS THING FEELS LIKE A RUSH JOB. CLEAN UP THE MESS AND GET OUT. ALL THE VICTIMS ARE IN THE GROUND AND THERE'S TALK OF BULLDOZING THE WHOLE TOWN.
THE LOCALS JUST WANT THIS TO GO AWAY.
YOU KNEW HIM, DIDN'T YOU?
FATHER EDWARD KELLY.
YES, I DID. TOUGHEST GUY I EVER WORKED WITH. WE DID A TWELVE-DAY EXORCISM TOGETHER LAST YEAR IN PHOENIX. ALMOST COST HIM AN EYE.
THIS TOWN HAS NO CHURCH. YOU KNOW HOW ODD THAT IS FOR THIS AREA OF THE WORLD?
YEP.
AND FATHER KELLY WAS UP HERE... YOU THINK HE MIGHT HAVE BEEN PLANNING TO HOLD SERVICES HERE?
MAYBE. OR MAYBE HE KNEW SOMETHING STUNK AND HE WAS POKING AT IT.
IS THAT WHAT GOT HIM KILLED?

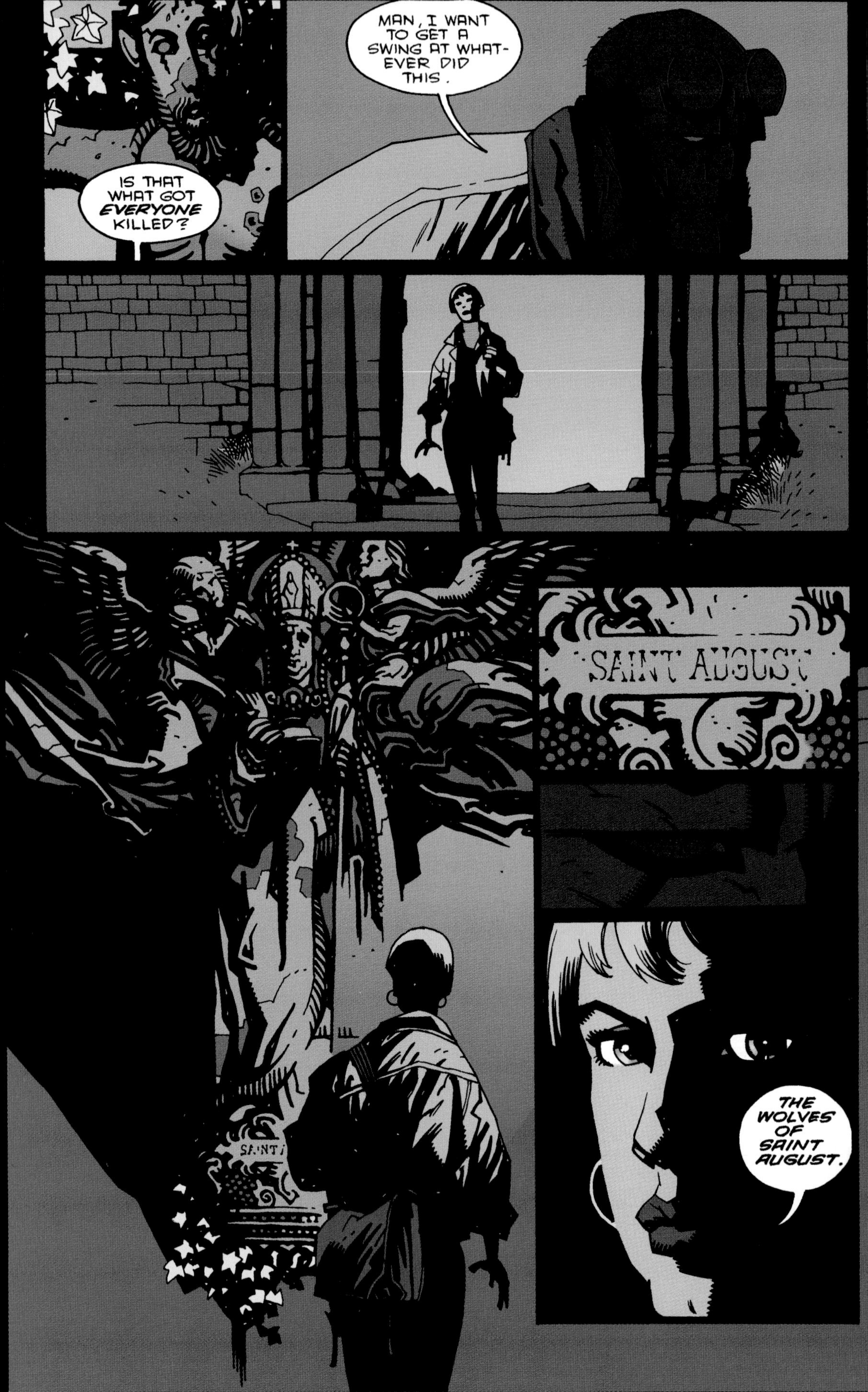
IS THAT WHAT GOT EVERYONE KILLED?
MAN, I WANT TO GET A SWING AT WHAT-EVER DID THIS.
SAINT AUGUST
SAINT
THE WOLVES OF SAINT AUGUST.

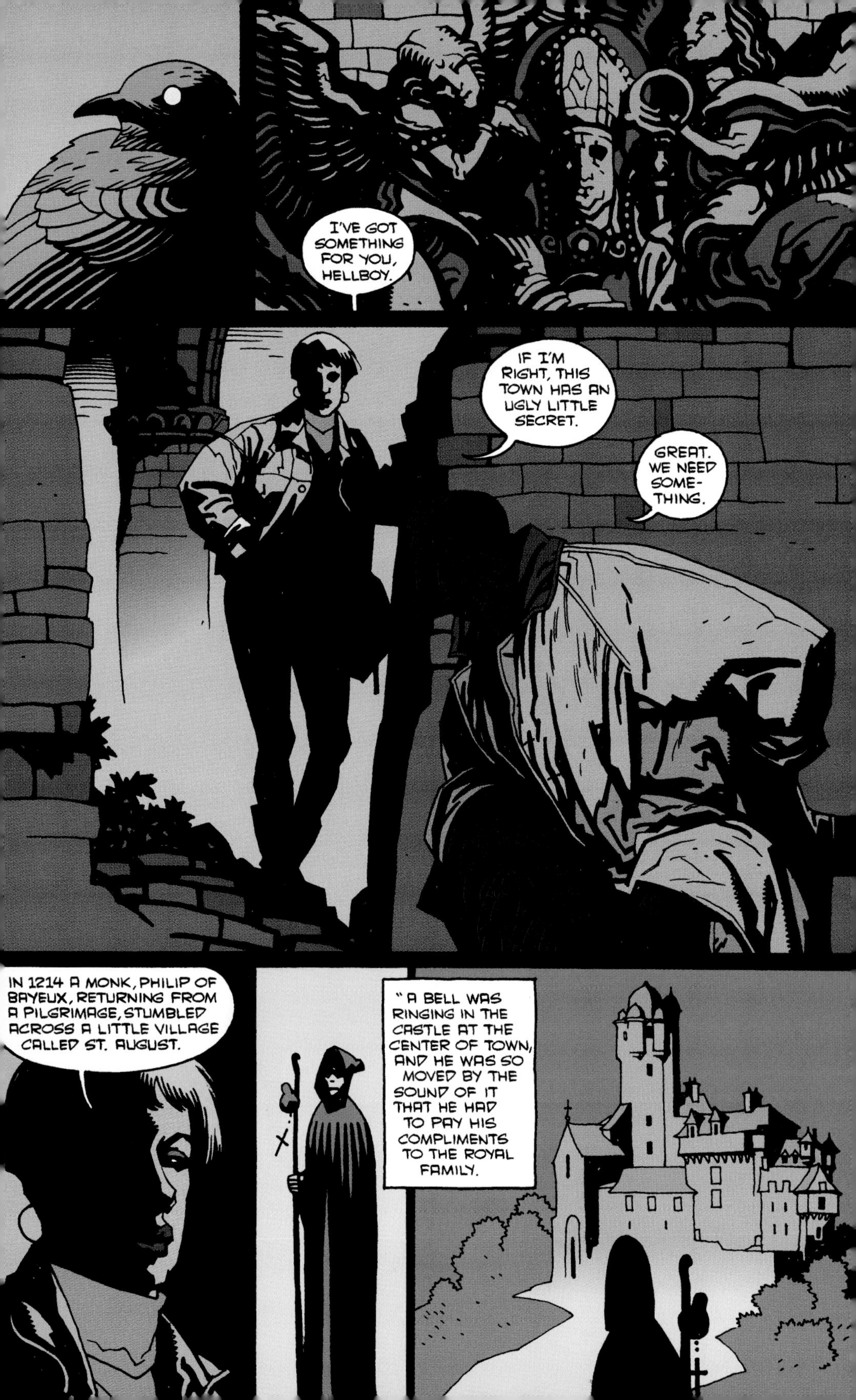
I'VE GOT SOMETHING FOR YOU, HELLBOY.
IF I'M RIGHT, THIS TOWN HAS AN UGLY LITTLE SECRET.
GREAT. WE NEED SOME-THING.
IN 1214 A MONK, PHILIP OF BAYEUX, RETURNING FROM A PILGRIMAGE, STUMBLED ACROSS A LITTLE VILLAGE CALLED ST. AUGUST.
"A BELL WAS RINGING IN THE CASTLE AT THE CENTER OF TOWN, AND HE WAS SO MOVED BY THE SOUND OF IT THAT HE HAD TO PAY HIS COMPLIMENTS TO THE ROYAL FAMILY.

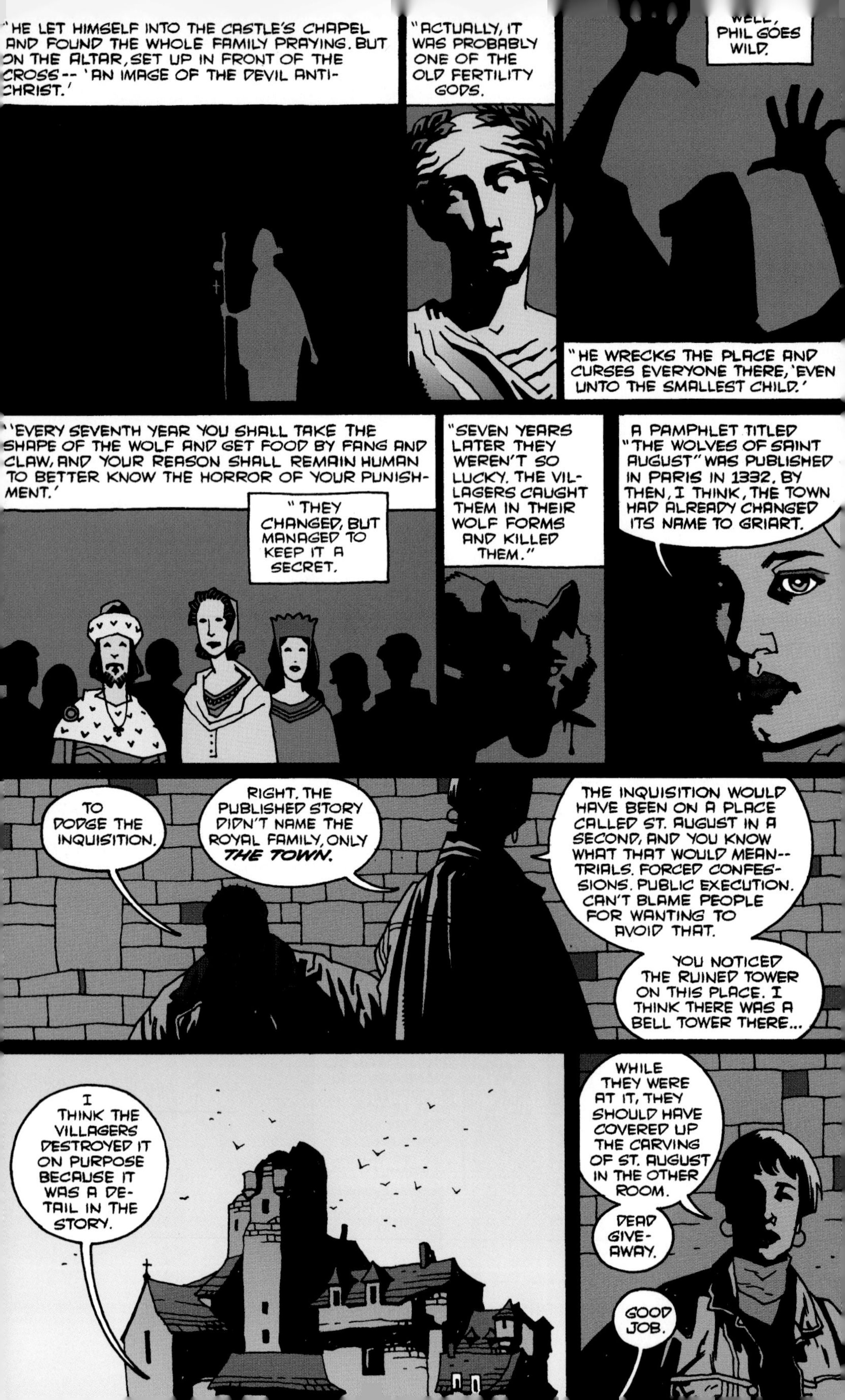
"HE LET HIMSELF INTO THE CASTLE'S CHAPEL AND FOUND THE WHOLE FAMILY PRAYING. BUT ON THE ALTAR, SET UP IN FRONT OF THE CROSS-- 'AN IMAGE OF THE DEVIL ANTI-CHRIST.'
"ACTUALLY, IT WAS PROBABLY ONE OF THE OLD FERTILITY GODS.
WELL, PHIL GOES WILD.
"HE WRECKS THE PLACE AND CURSES EVERYONE THERE, 'EVEN UNTO THE SMALLEST CHILD.'
"'EVERY SEVENTH YEAR YOU SHALL TAKE THE SHAPE OF THE WOLF AND GET FOOD BY FANG AND CLAW, AND YOUR REASON SHALL REMAIN HUMAN TO BETTER KNOW THE HORROR OF YOUR PUNISHMENT.'
"THEY CHANGED, BUT MANAGED TO KEEP IT A SECRET.
"SEVEN YEARS LATER THEY WEREN'T SO LUCKY. THE VILLAGERS CAUGHT THEM IN THEIR WOLF FORMS AND KILLED THEM."
A PAMPHLET TITLED "THE WOLVES OF SAINT AUGUST" WAS PUBLISHED IN PARIS IN 1332. BY THEN, I THINK, THE TOWN HAD ALREADY CHANGED ITS NAME TO GRIART.
TO DODGE THE INQUISITION.
RIGHT. THE PUBLISHED STORY DIDN'T NAME THE ROYAL FAMILY, ONLY *THE TOWN.*
THE INQUISITION WOULD HAVE BEEN ON A PLACE CALLED ST. AUGUST IN A SECOND, AND YOU KNOW WHAT THAT WOULD MEAN-- TRIALS. FORCED CONFESSIONS. PUBLIC EXECUTION. CAN'T BLAME PEOPLE FOR WANTING TO AVOID THAT.
YOU NOTICED THE RUINED TOWER ON THIS PLACE. I THINK THERE WAS A BELL TOWER THERE...
I THINK THE VILLAGERS DESTROYED IT ON PURPOSE BECAUSE IT WAS A DETAIL IN THE STORY.
WHILE THEY WERE AT IT, THEY SHOULD HAVE COVERED UP THE CARVING OF ST. AUGUST IN THE OTHER ROOM.
DEAD GIVEAWAY.
GOOD JOB.

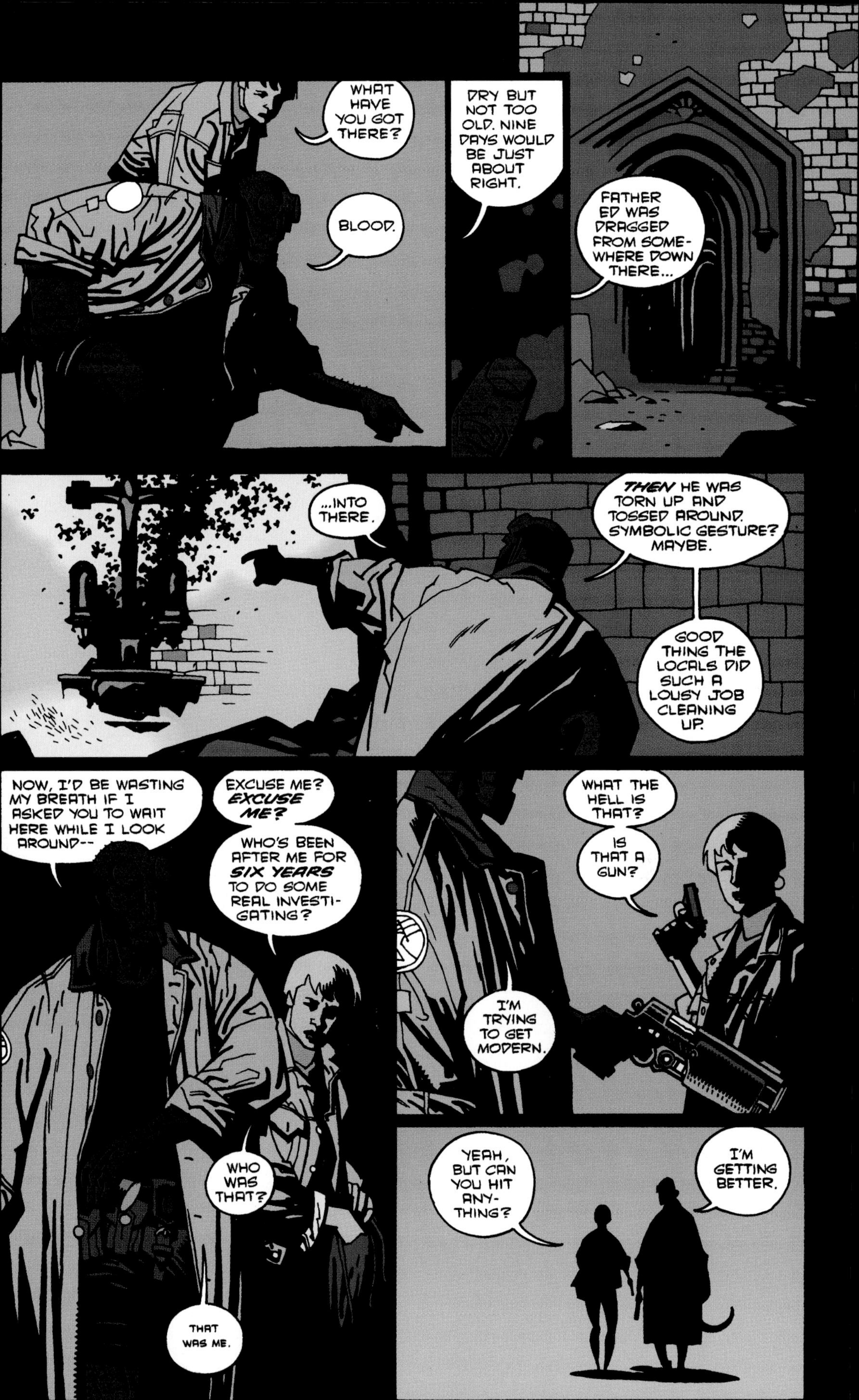
WHAT HAVE YOU GOT THERE?
BLOOD.
DRY BUT NOT TOO OLD. NINE DAYS WOULD BE JUST ABOUT RIGHT.
FATHER ED WAS DRAGGED FROM SOME-WHERE DOWN THERE...
...INTO THERE.
THEN HE WAS TORN UP AND TOSSED AROUND. SYMBOLIC GESTURE? MAYBE.
GOOD THING THE LOCALS DID SUCH A LOUSY JOB CLEANING UP.
NOW, I'D BE WASTING MY BREATH IF I ASKED YOU TO WAIT HERE WHILE I LOOK AROUND--
EXCUSE ME? EXCUSE ME?
WHO'S BEEN AFTER ME FOR SIX YEARS TO DO SOME REAL INVESTI-GATING?
WHO WAS THAT?
THAT WAS ME.
WHAT THE HELL IS THAT?
IS THAT A GUN?
I'M TRYING TO GET MODERN.
YEAH, BUT CAN YOU HIT ANY-THING?
I'M GETTING BETTER.

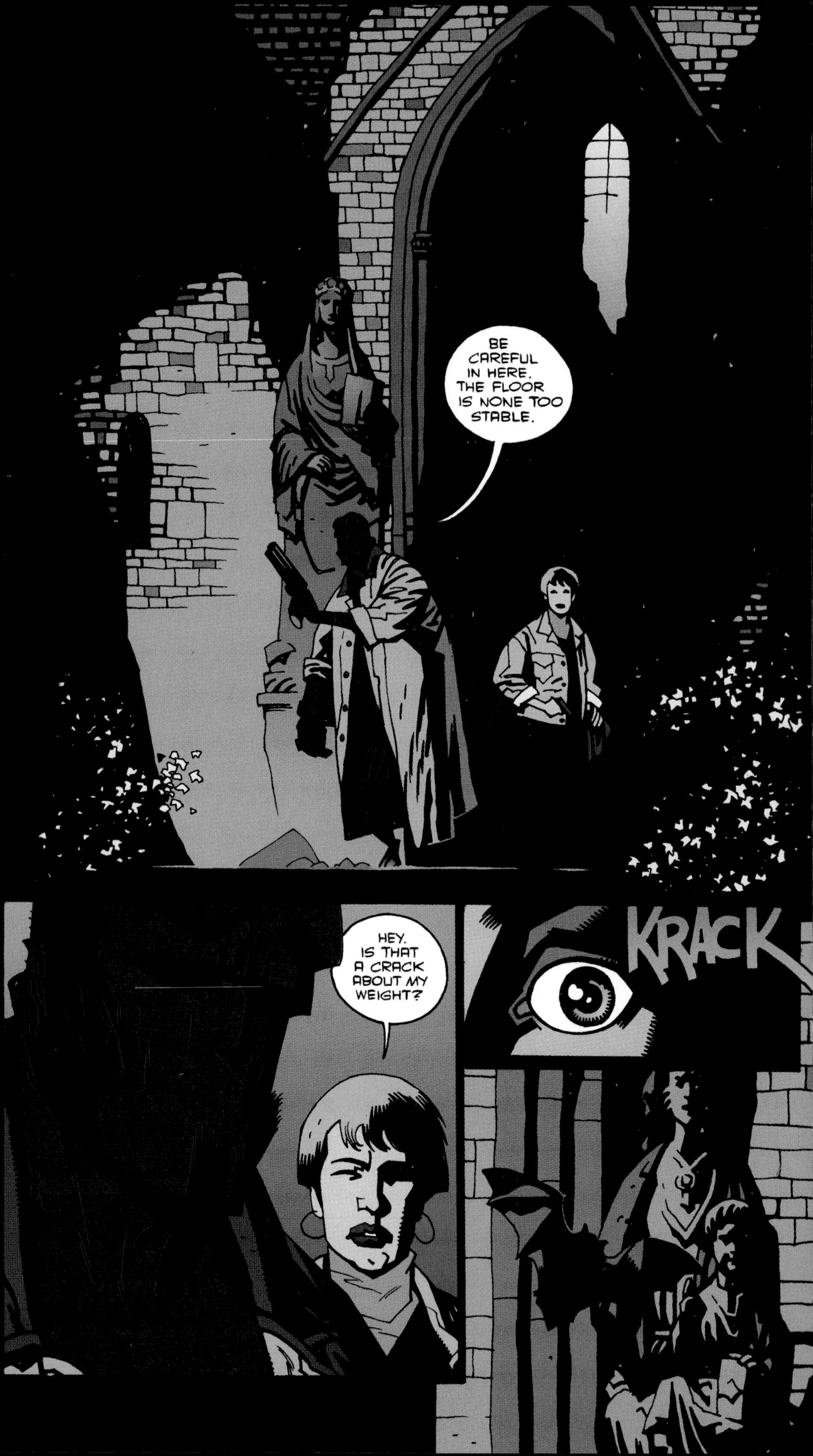
BE CAREFUL IN HERE. THE FLOOR IS NONE TOO STABLE.
HEY. IS THAT A CRACK ABOUT MY WEIGHT?
KRACK

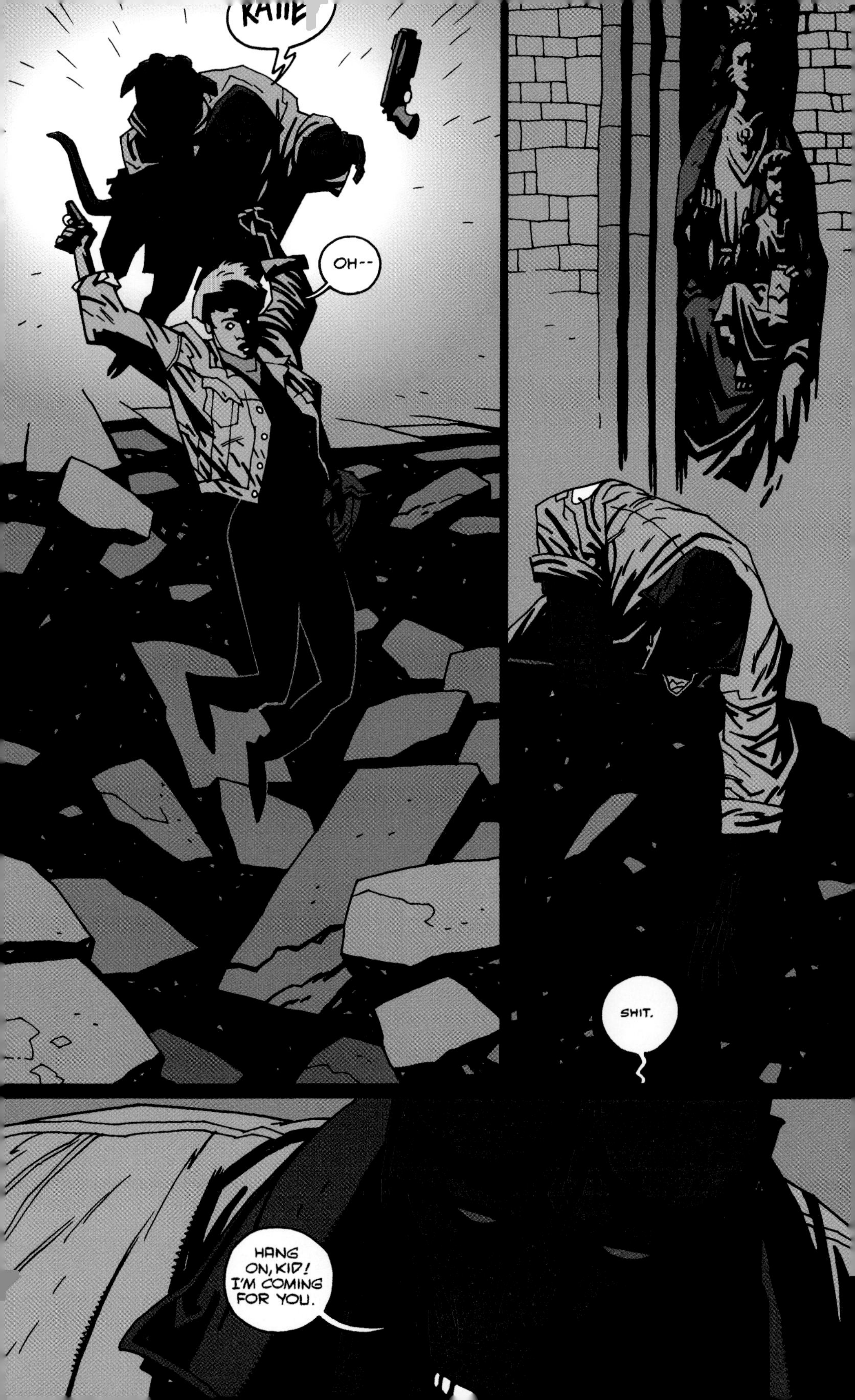
KATIE
OH--
SHIT.
HANG ON, KID! I'M COMING FOR YOU.

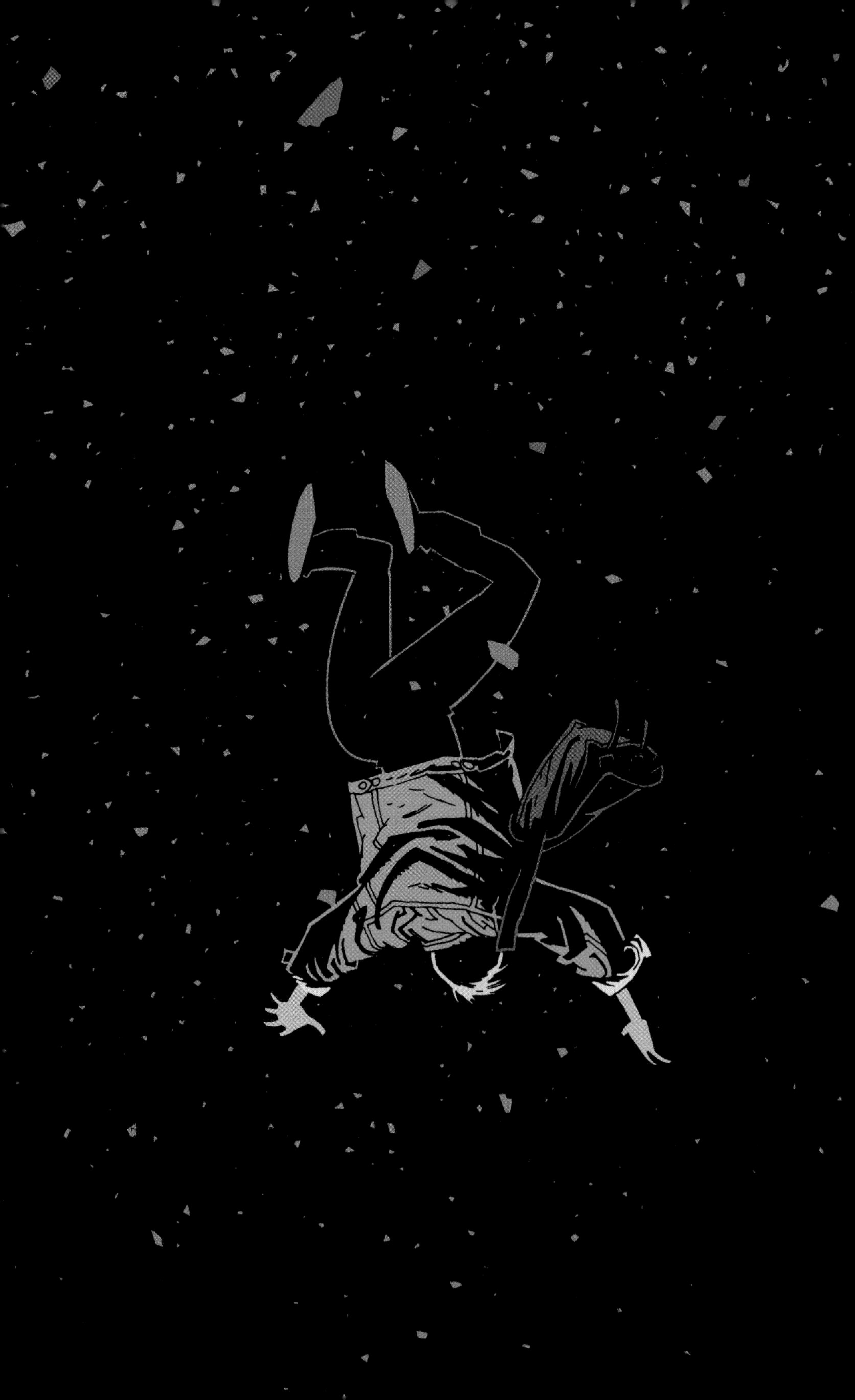

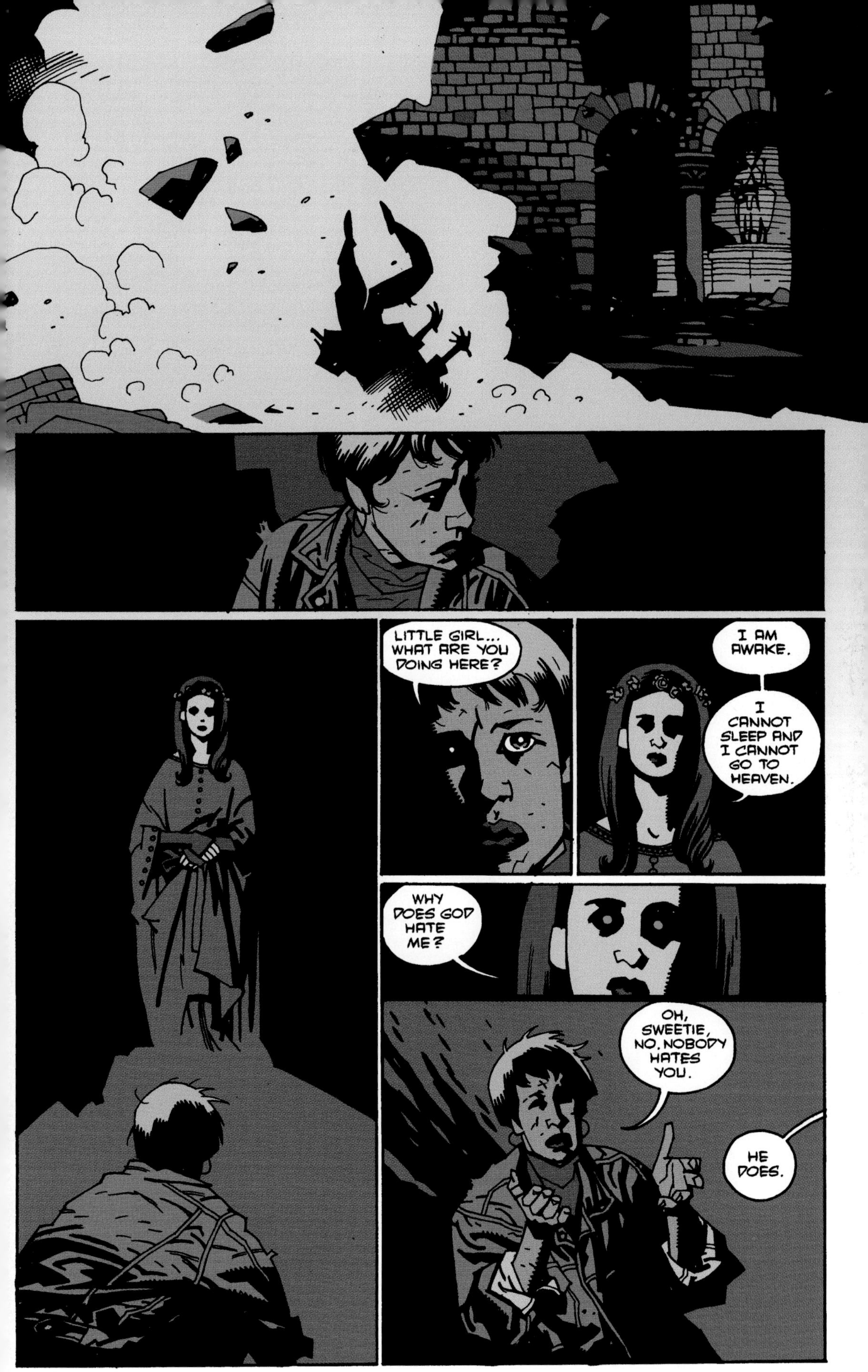
LITTLE GIRL... WHAT ARE YOU DOING HERE?
I AM AWAKE.
I CANNOT SLEEP AND I CANNOT GO TO HEAVEN.
WHY DOES GOD HATE ME?
OH, SWEETIE, NO. NOBODY HATES YOU.
HE DOES.

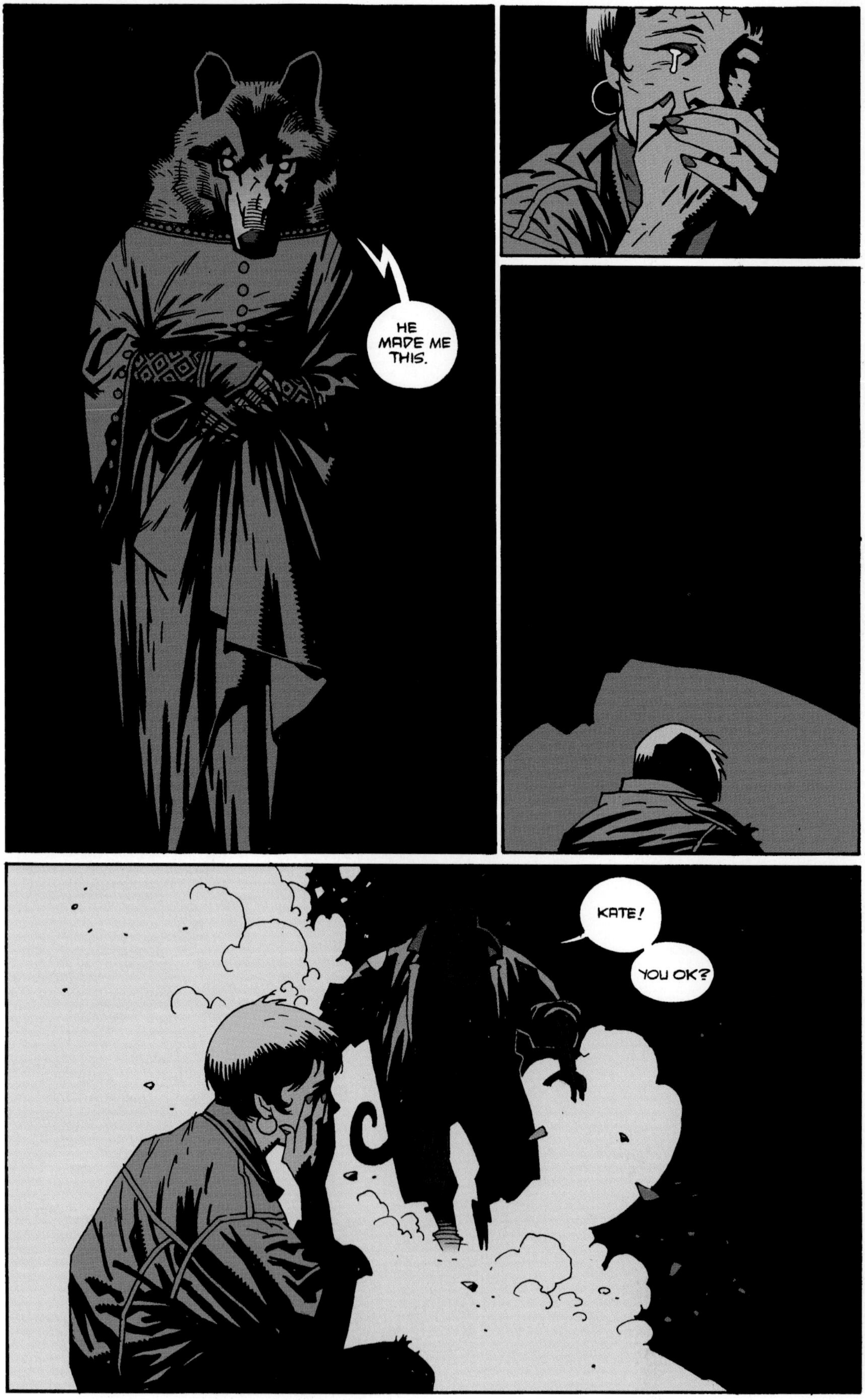
HE MADE ME THIS.
KATE!
YOU OK?

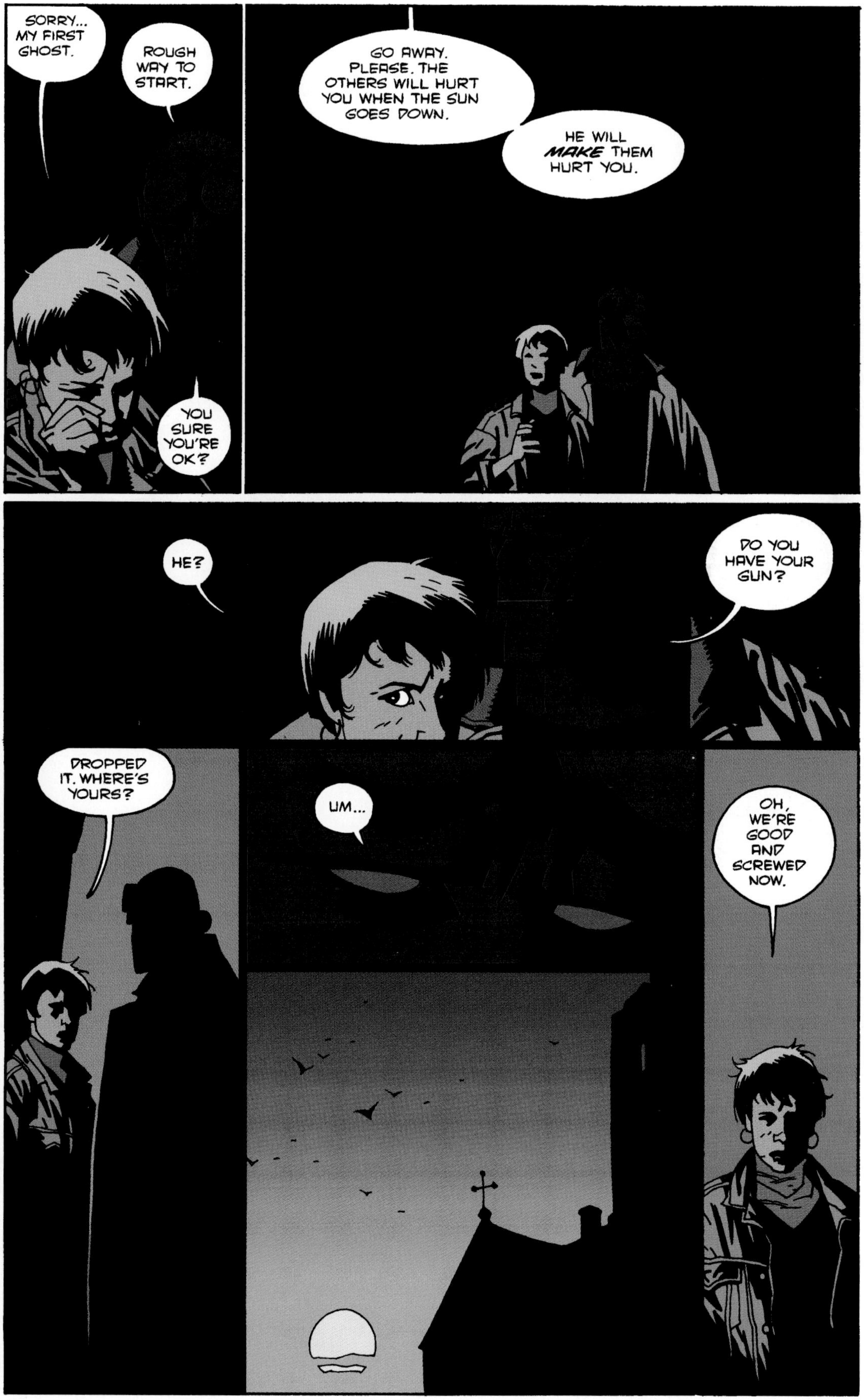
SORRY... MY FIRST GHOST.
ROUGH WAY TO START.
YOU SURE YOU'RE OK?
GO AWAY. PLEASE. THE OTHERS WILL HURT YOU WHEN THE SUN GOES DOWN.
HE WILL *MAKE* THEM HURT YOU.
HE?
DO YOU HAVE YOUR GUN?
DROPPED IT. WHERE'S YOURS?
UM...
OH, WE'RE GOOD AND SCREWED NOW.

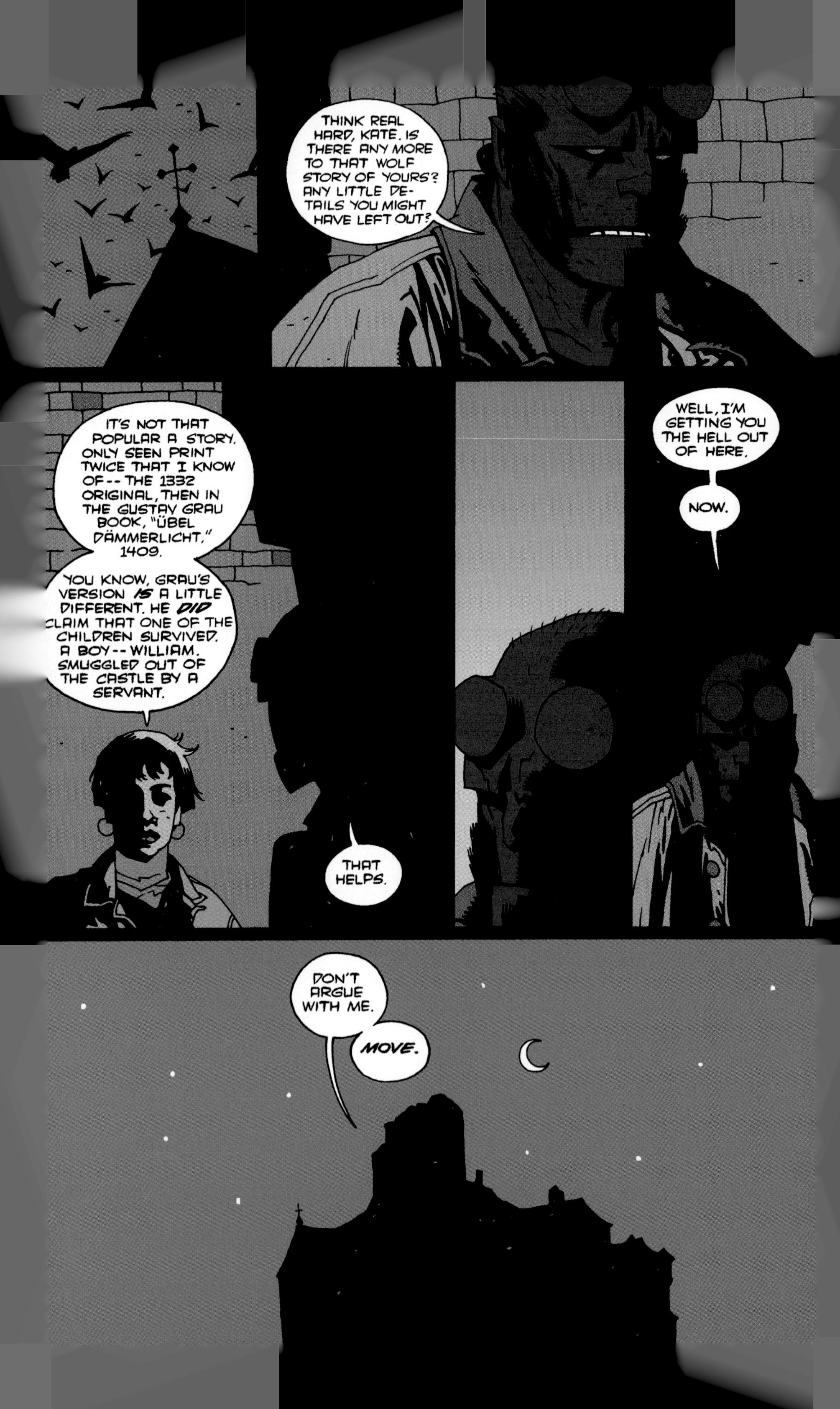
THINK REAL HARD, KATE. IS THERE ANY MORE TO THAT WOLF STORY OF YOURS? ANY LITTLE DETAILS YOU MIGHT HAVE LEFT OUT?
IT'S NOT THAT POPULAR A STORY. ONLY SEEN PRINT TWICE THAT I KNOW OF -- THE 1332 ORIGINAL, THEN IN THE GUSTAV GRAU BOOK, "ÜBEL DÄMMERLICHT," 1409.
YOU KNOW, GRAU'S VERSION IS A LITTLE DIFFERENT. HE DID CLAIM THAT ONE OF THE CHILDREN SURVIVED. A BOY -- WILLIAM. SMUGGLED OUT OF THE CASTLE BY A SERVANT.
THAT HELPS.
WELL, I'M GETTING YOU THE HELL OUT OF HERE.
NOW.
DON'T ARGUE WITH ME.
MOVE.

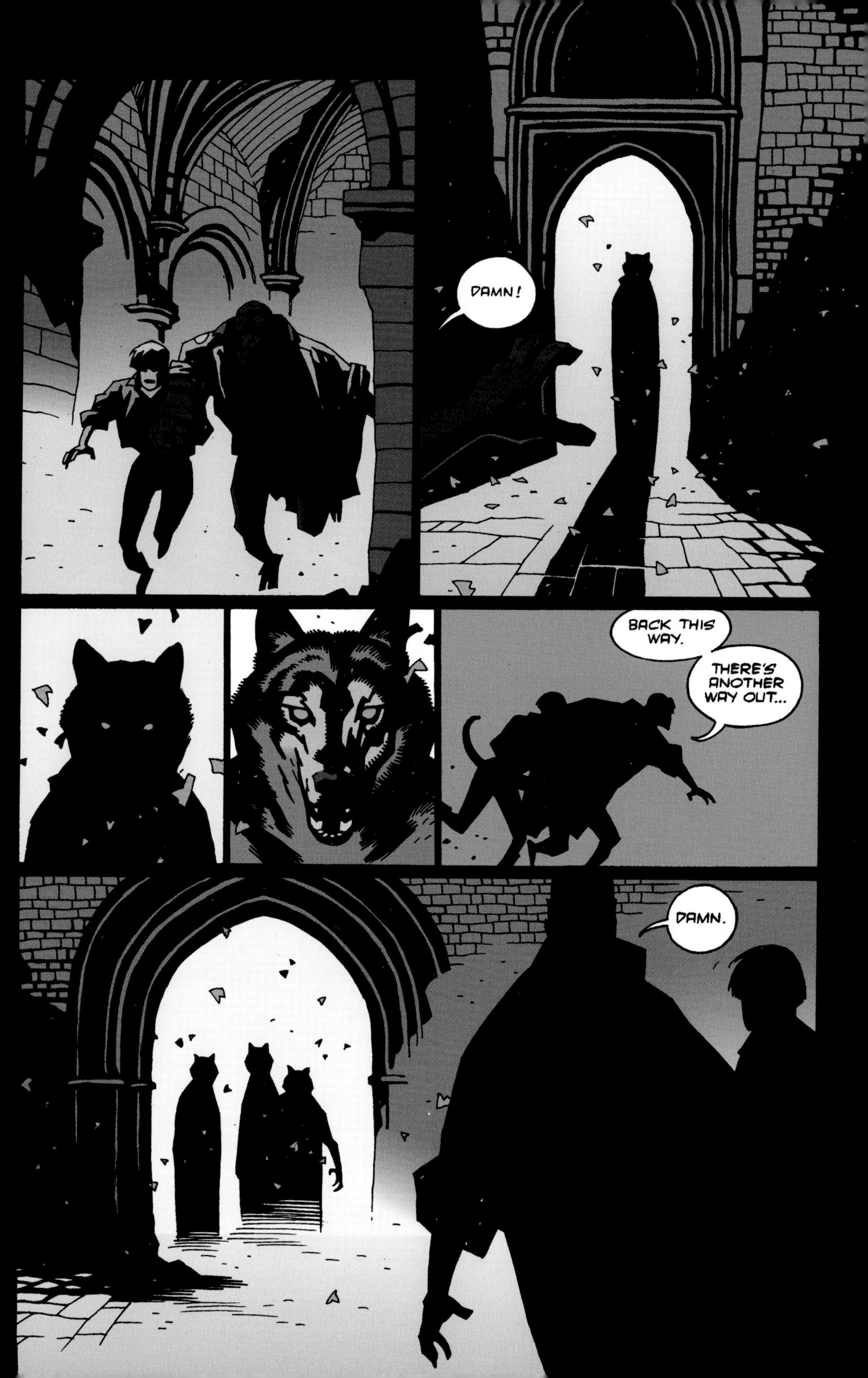
DAMN!
BACK THIS WAY.
THERE'S ANOTHER WAY OUT...
DAMN.

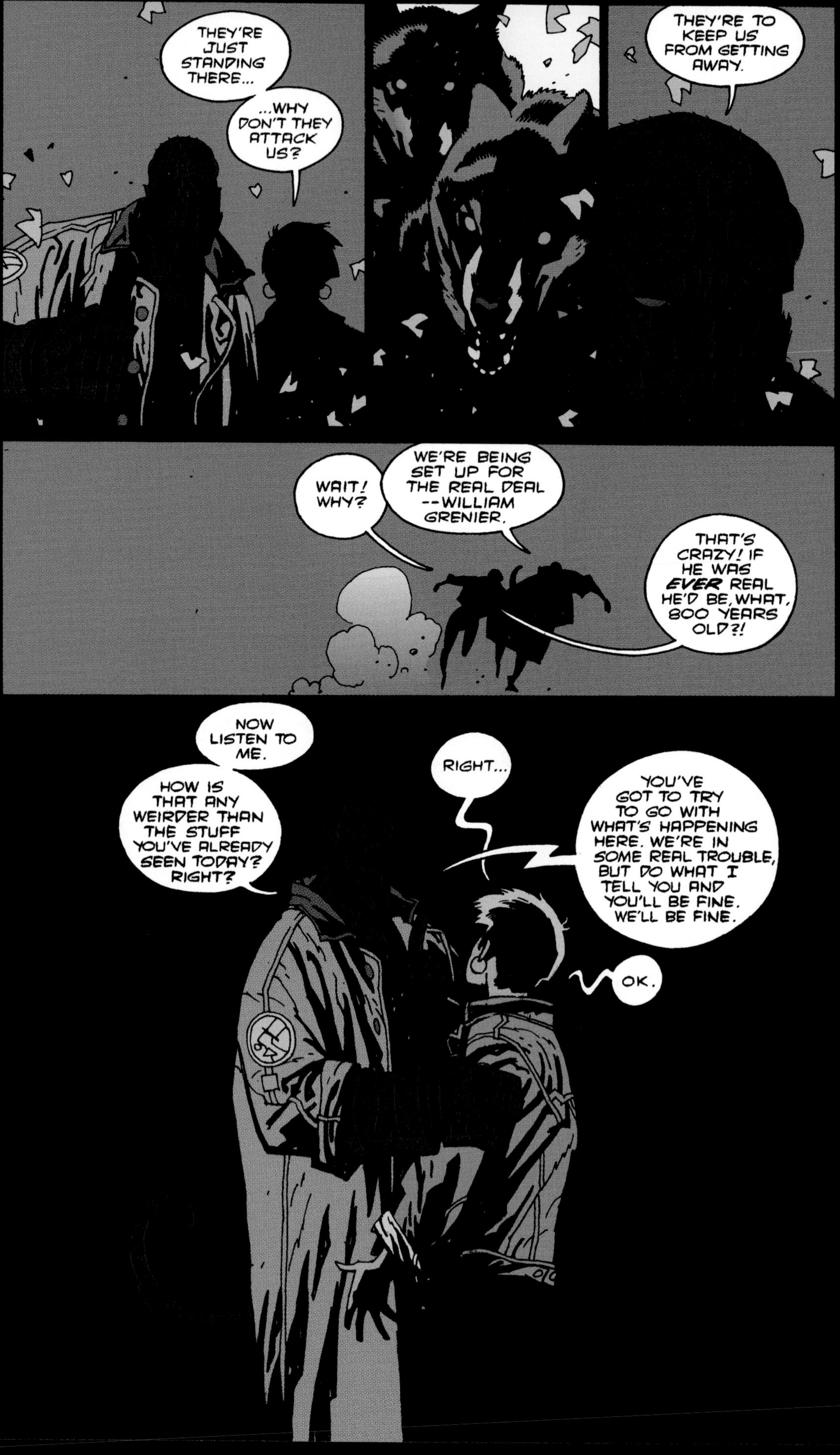
THEY'RE JUST STANDING THERE...
...WHY DON'T THEY ATTACK US?
THEY'RE TO KEEP US FROM GETTING AWAY.
WAIT! WHY?
WE'RE BEING SET UP FOR THE REAL DEAL --WILLIAM GRENIER.
THAT'S CRAZY! IF HE WAS EVER REAL HE'D BE, WHAT, 800 YEARS OLD?!
NOW LISTEN TO ME.
HOW IS THAT ANY WEIRDER THAN THE STUFF YOU'VE ALREADY SEEN TODAY? RIGHT?
RIGHT...
YOU'VE GOT TO TRY TO GO WITH WHAT'S HAPPENING HERE. WE'RE IN SOME REAL TROUBLE, BUT DO WHAT I TELL YOU AND YOU'LL BE FINE. WE'LL BE FINE.
OK.

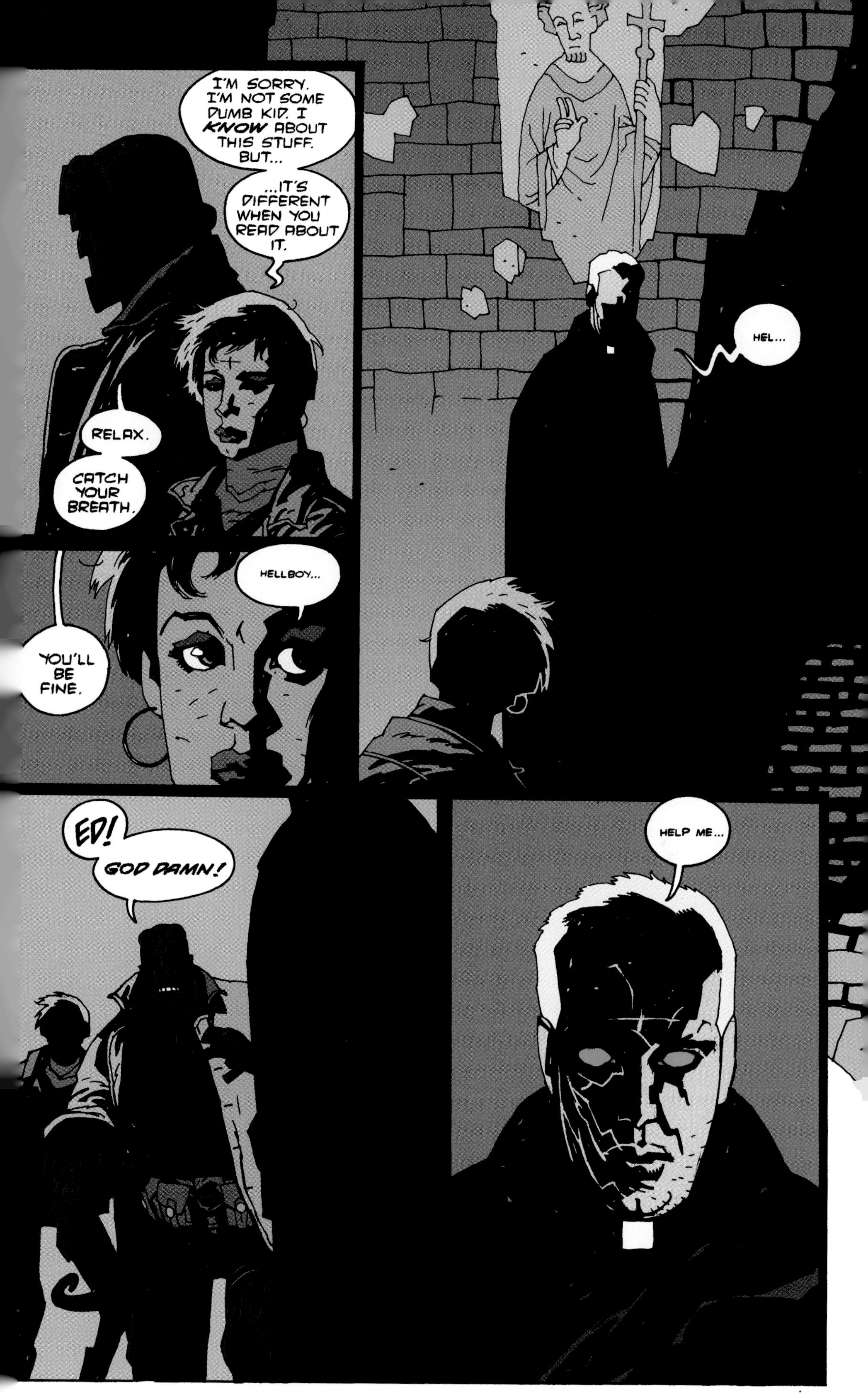
I'M SORRY. I'M NOT SOME DUMB KID. I *KNOW* ABOUT THIS STUFF. BUT...
...IT'S DIFFERENT WHEN YOU READ ABOUT IT.
RELAX.
CATCH YOUR BREATH.
HEL...
HELLBOY...
YOU'LL BE FINE.
ED!
GOD DAMN!
HELP ME...

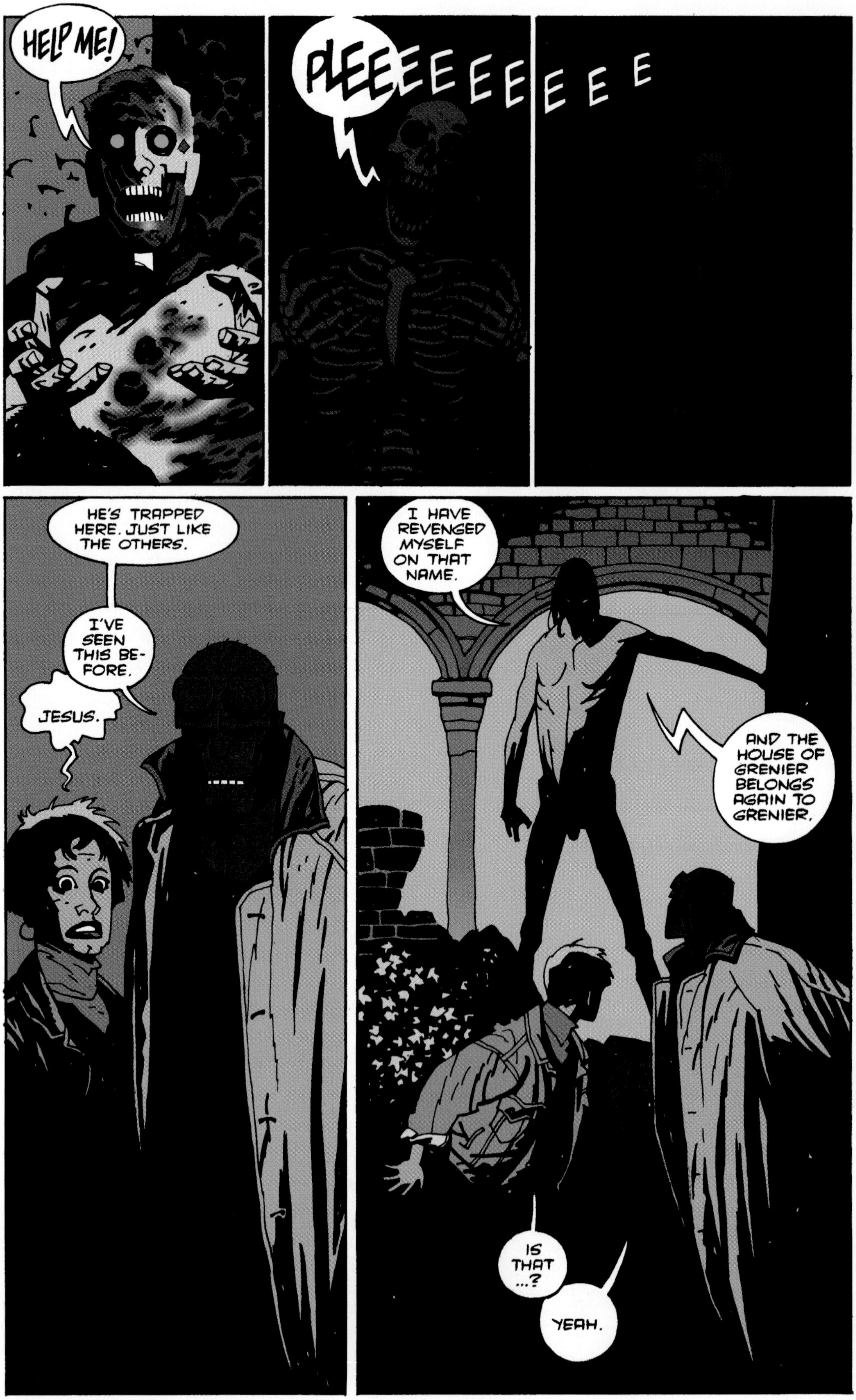
HELP ME!
PLEEEEEEEEEE
HE'S TRAPPED HERE. JUST LIKE THE OTHERS.
I'VE SEEN THIS BE- FORE.
JESUS.
I HAVE REVENGED MYSELF ON THAT NAME.
AND THE HOUSE OF GRENIER BELONGS AGAIN TO GRENIER.
IS THAT ...?
YEAH.

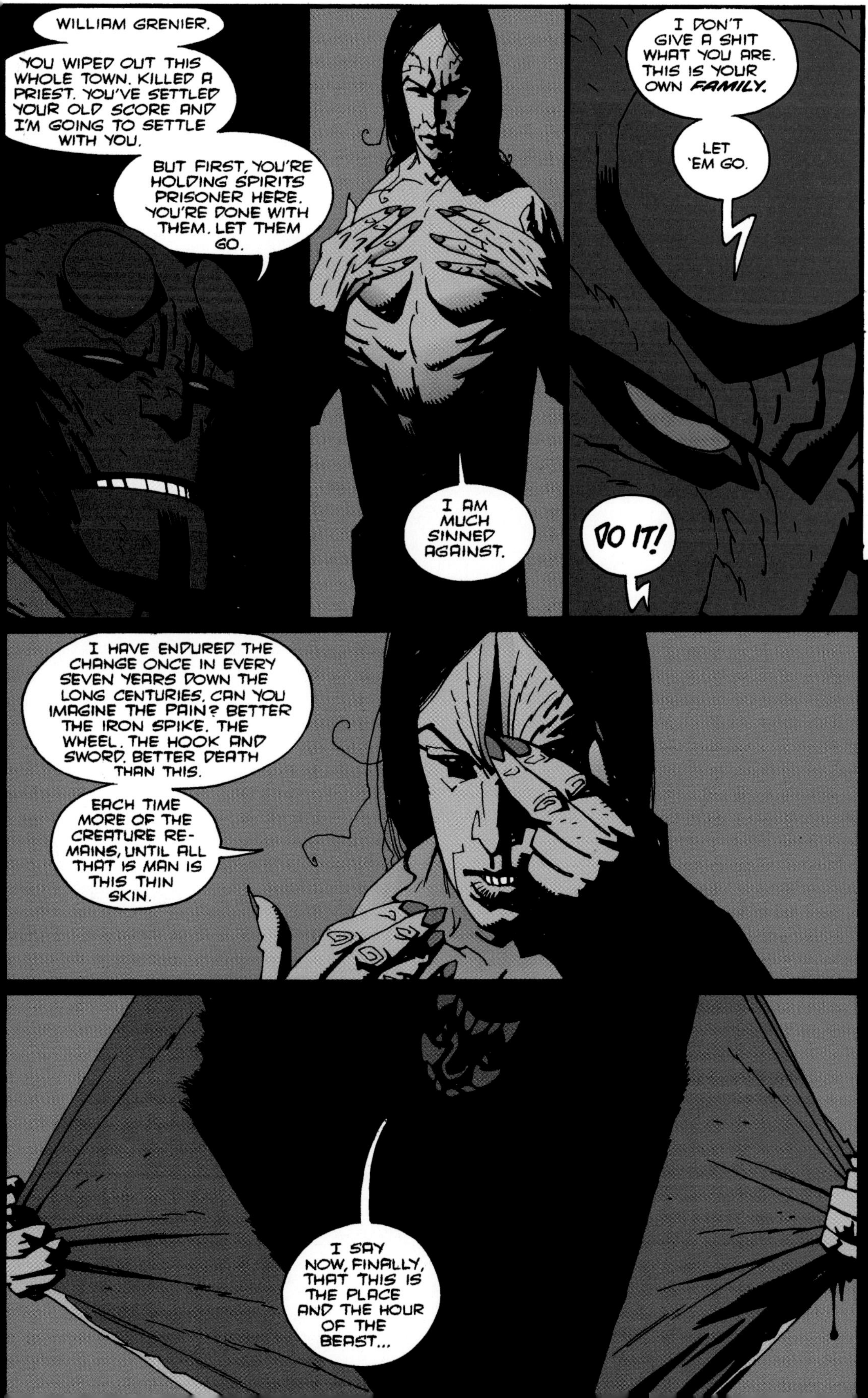
WILLIAM GRENIER.
YOU WIPED OUT THIS WHOLE TOWN. KILLED A PRIEST. YOU'VE SETTLED YOUR OLD SCORE AND I'M GOING TO SETTLE WITH YOU.
BUT FIRST, YOU'RE HOLDING SPIRITS PRISONER HERE. YOU'RE DONE WITH THEM. LET THEM GO.
I AM MUCH SINNED AGAINST.
I DON'T GIVE A SHIT WHAT YOU ARE. THIS IS YOUR OWN FAMILY.
LET 'EM GO.
DO IT!
I HAVE ENDURED THE CHANGE ONCE IN EVERY SEVEN YEARS DOWN THE LONG CENTURIES. CAN YOU IMAGINE THE PAIN? BETTER THE IRON SPIKE. THE WHEEL. THE HOOK AND SWORD. BETTER DEATH THAN THIS.
EACH TIME MORE OF THE CREATURE RE-MAINS, UNTIL ALL THAT IS MAN IS THIS THIN SKIN.
I SAY NOW, FINALLY, THAT THIS IS THE PLACE AND THE HOUR OF THE BEAST...

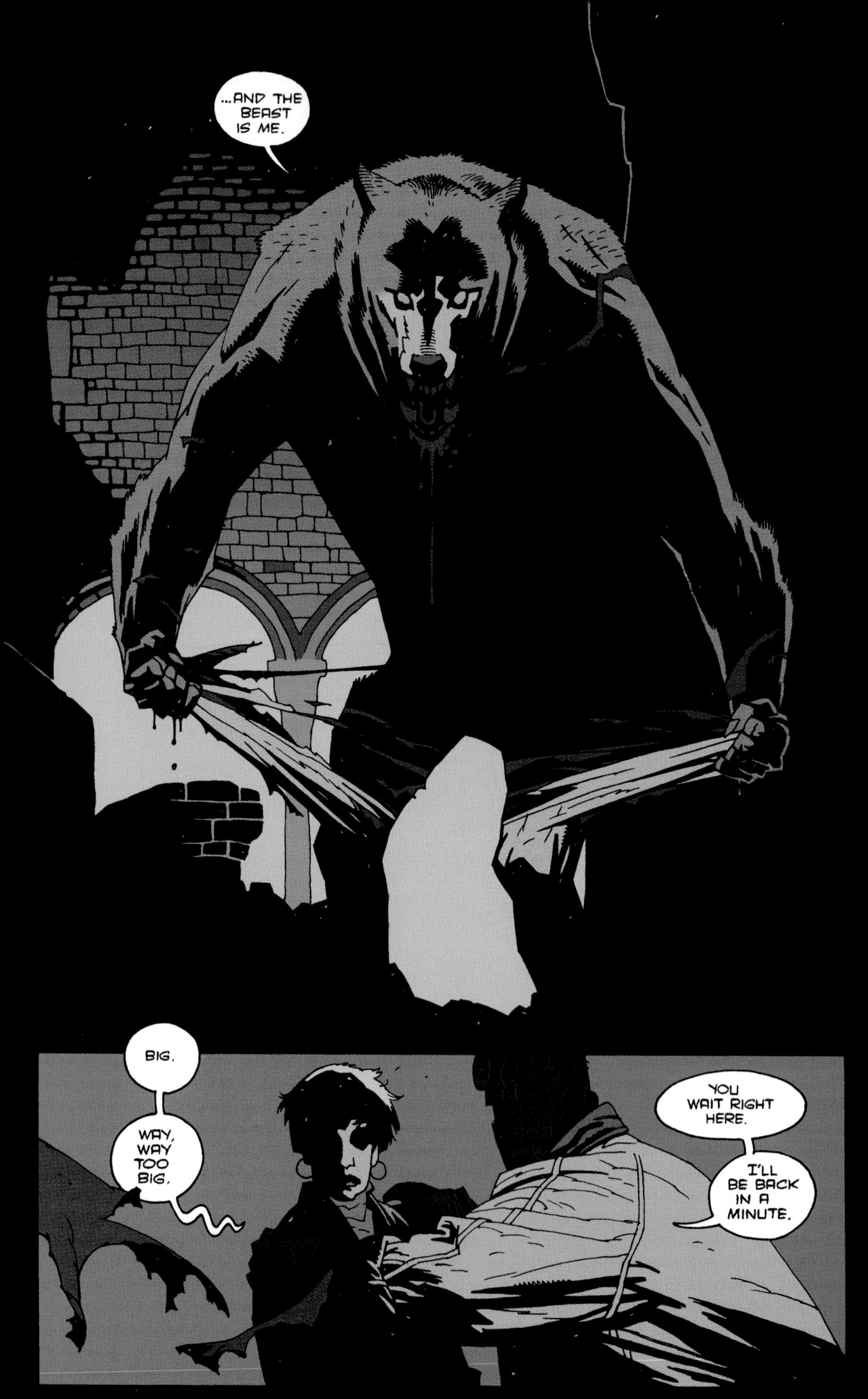
...AND THE BEAST IS ME.
BIG.
WAY, WAY TOO BIG.
YOU WAIT RIGHT HERE.
I'LL BE BACK IN A MINUTE.

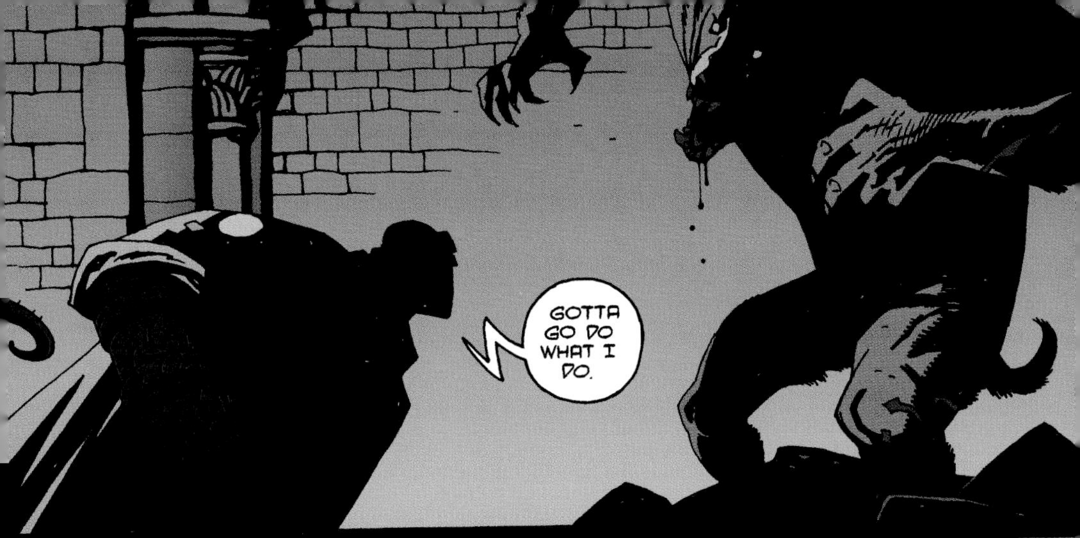
GOTTA GO DO WHAT I DO.

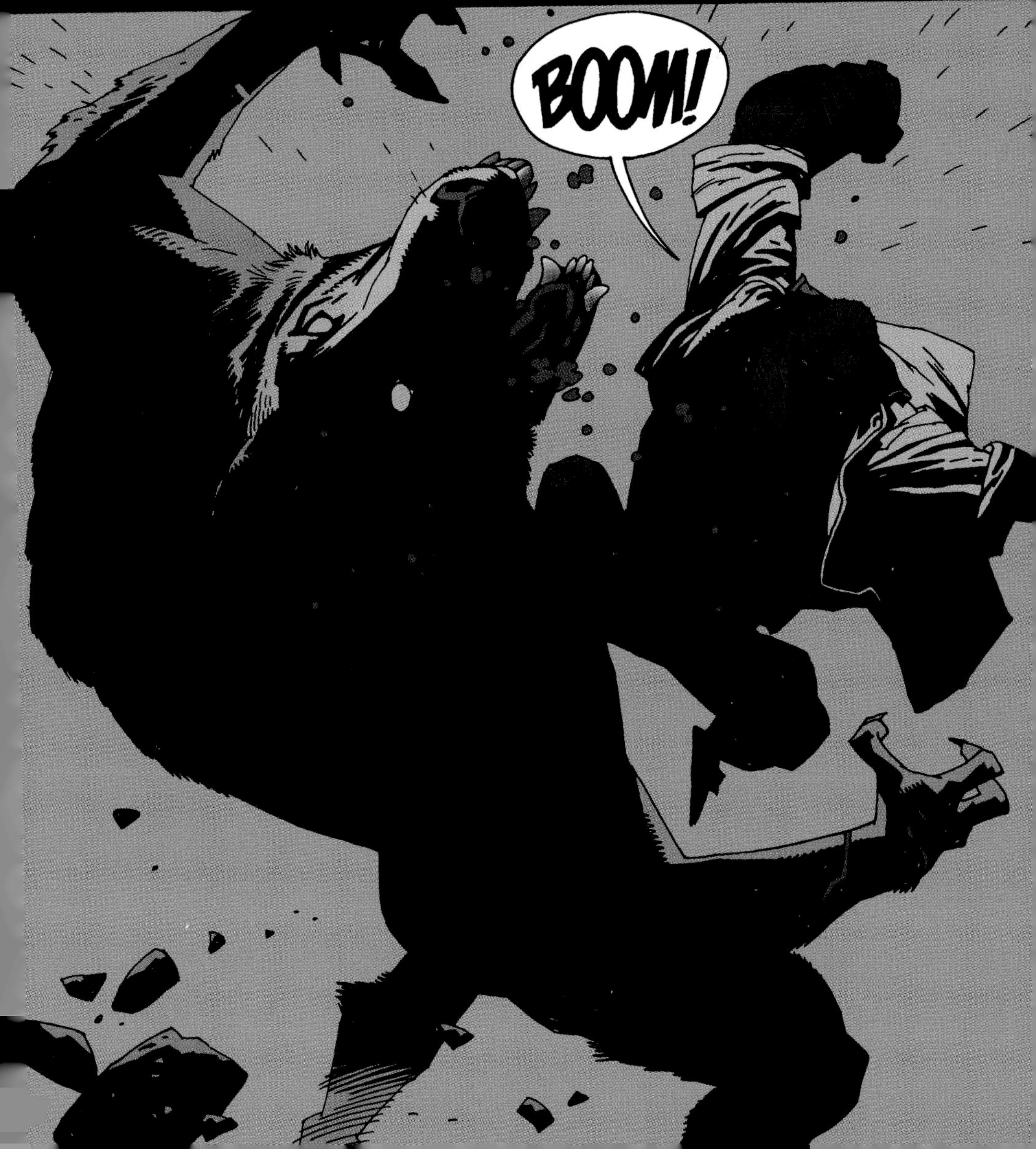
BOOM!

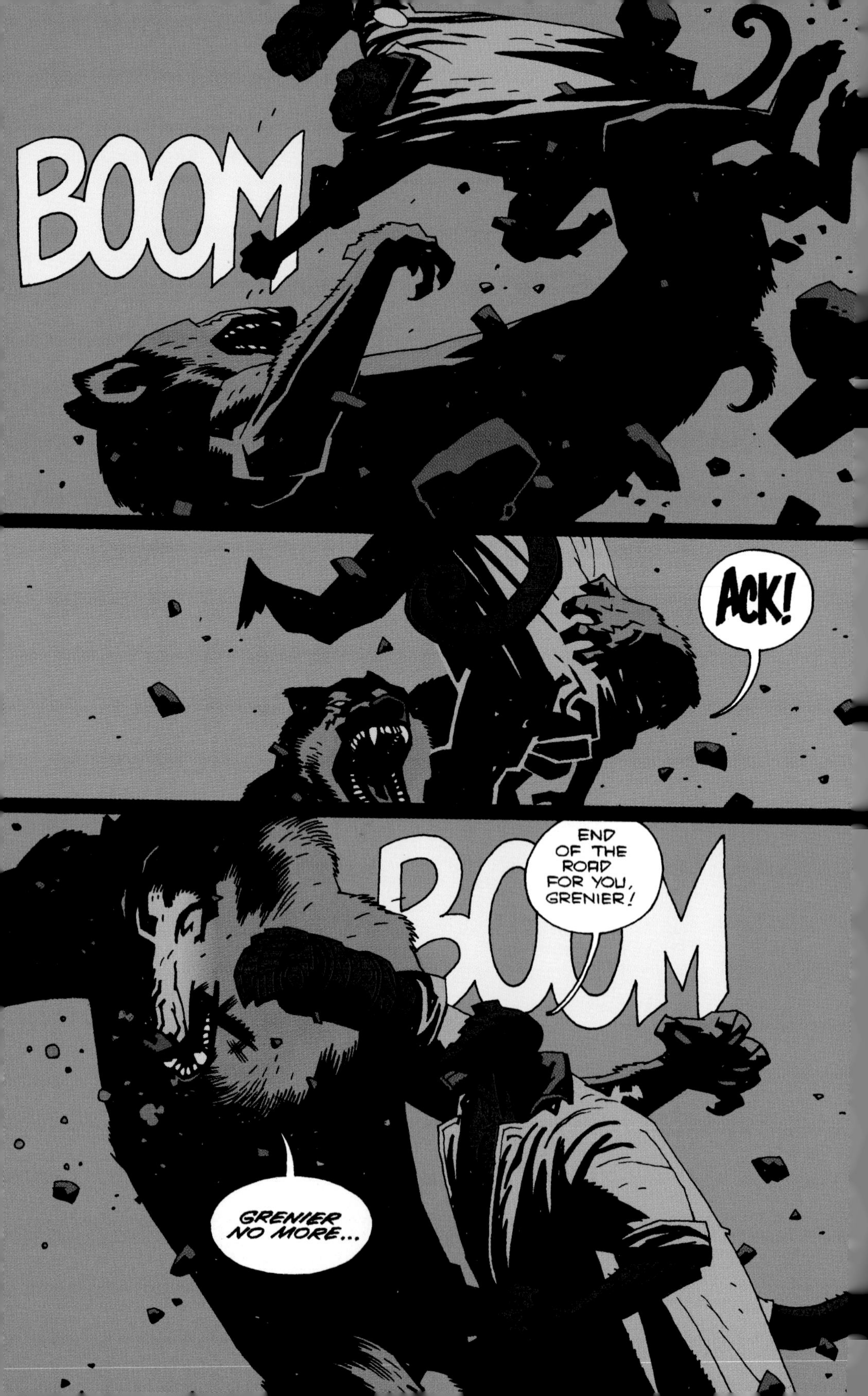
BOOM
ACK!
BOOM
END OF THE ROAD FOR YOU, GRENIER!
GRENIER NO MORE...

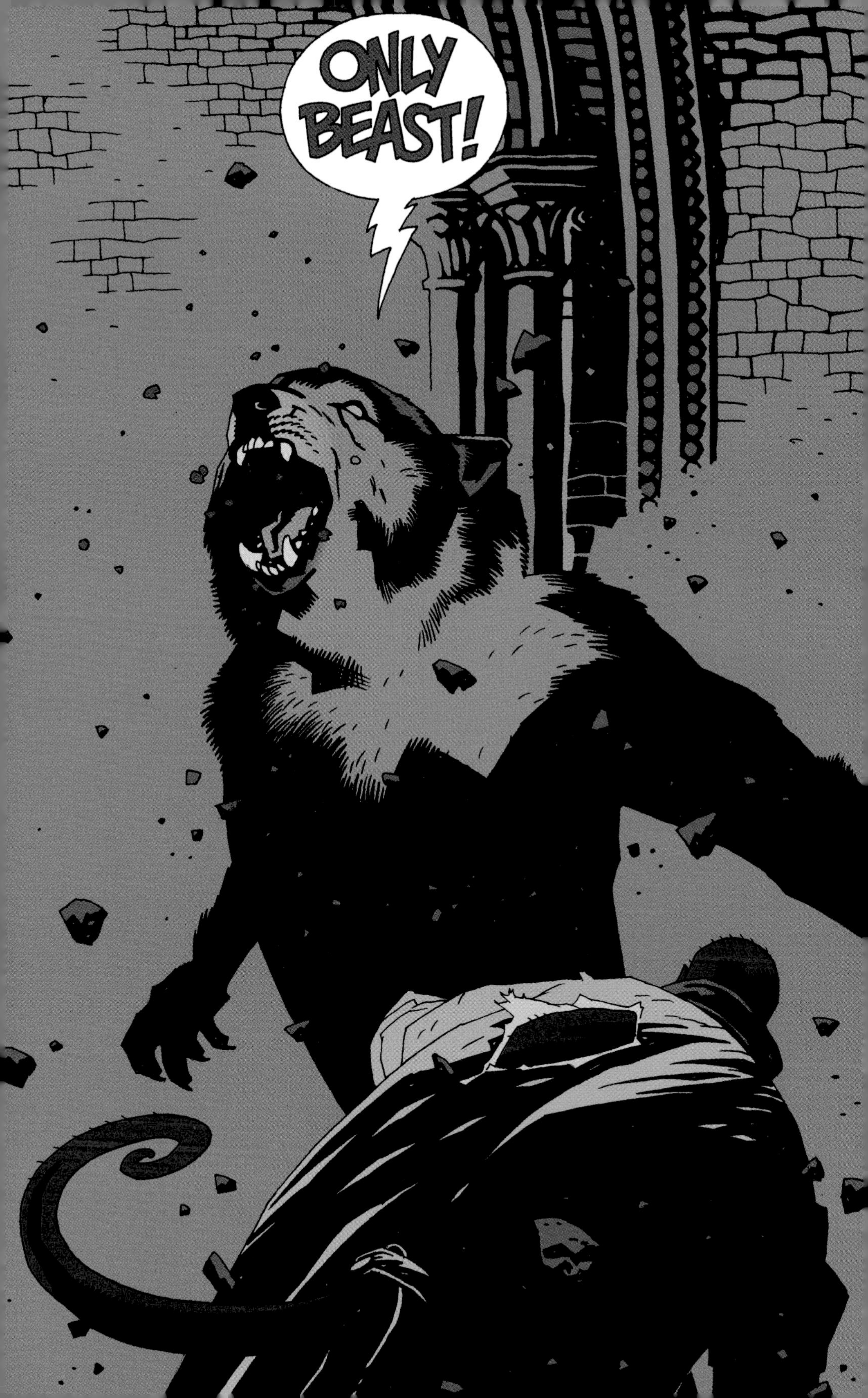
ONLY BEAST!

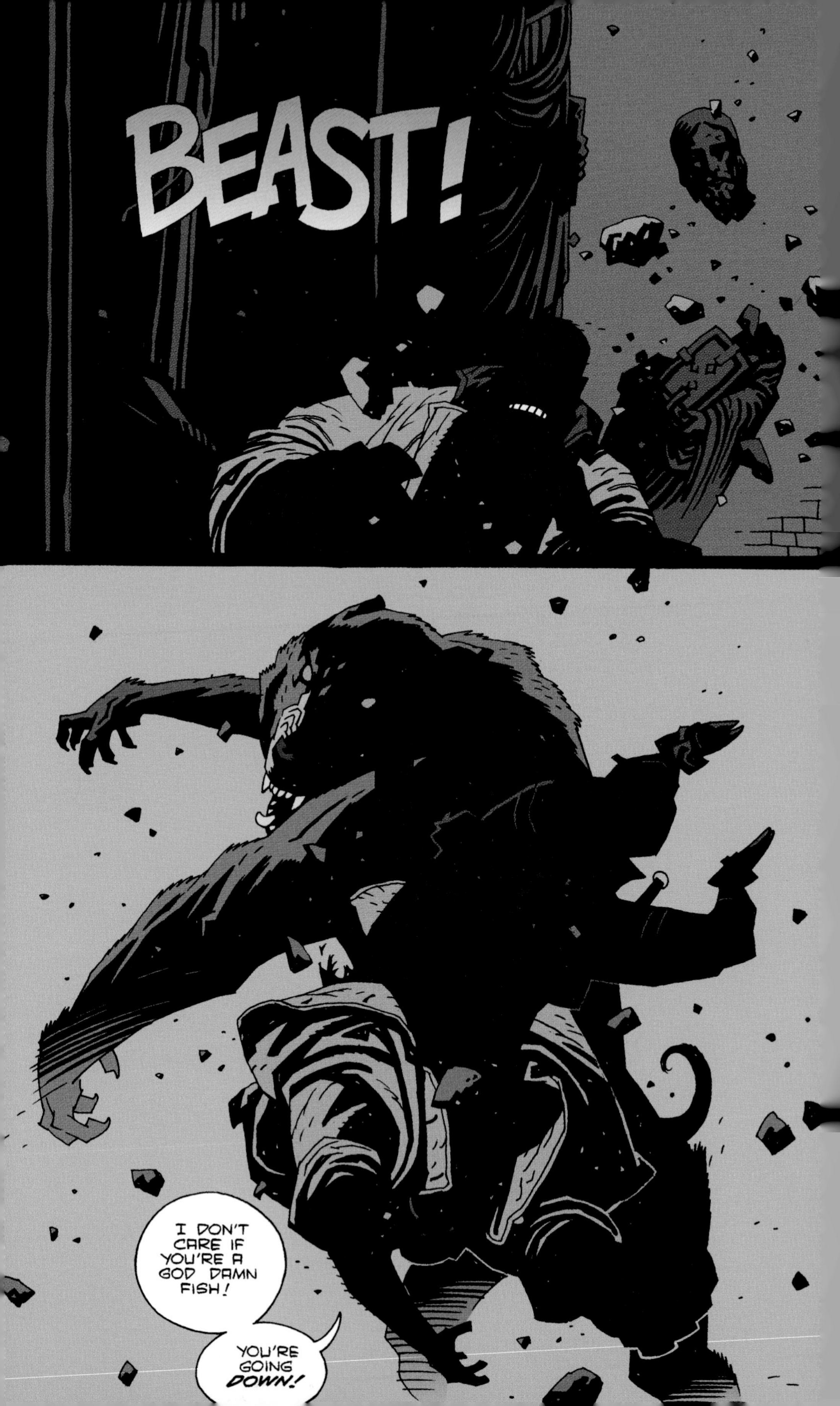
BEAST!
I DON'T CARE IF YOU'RE A GOD DAMN FISH!
YOU'RE GOING DOWN!

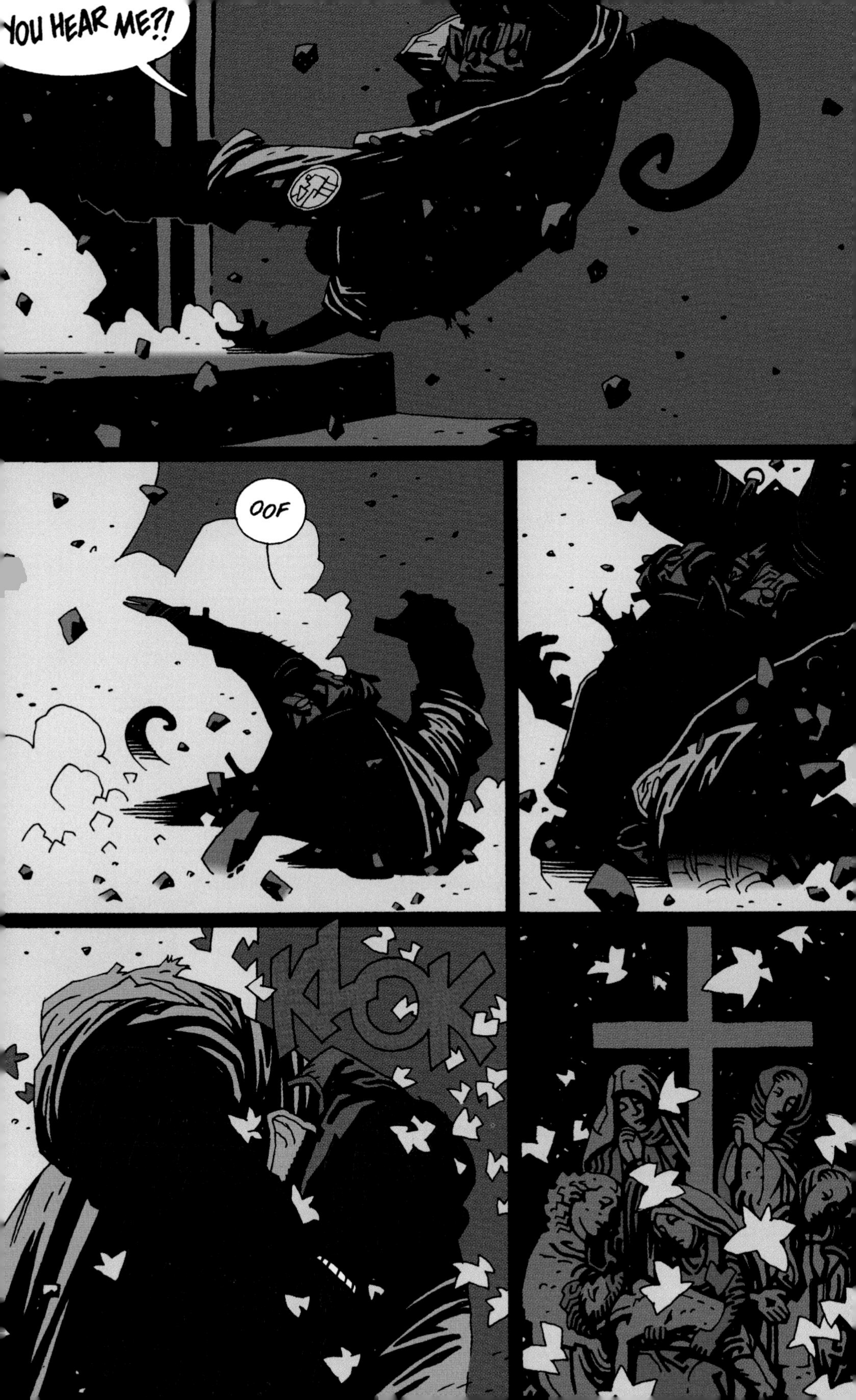
YOU HEAR ME?!
OOF
KLOK

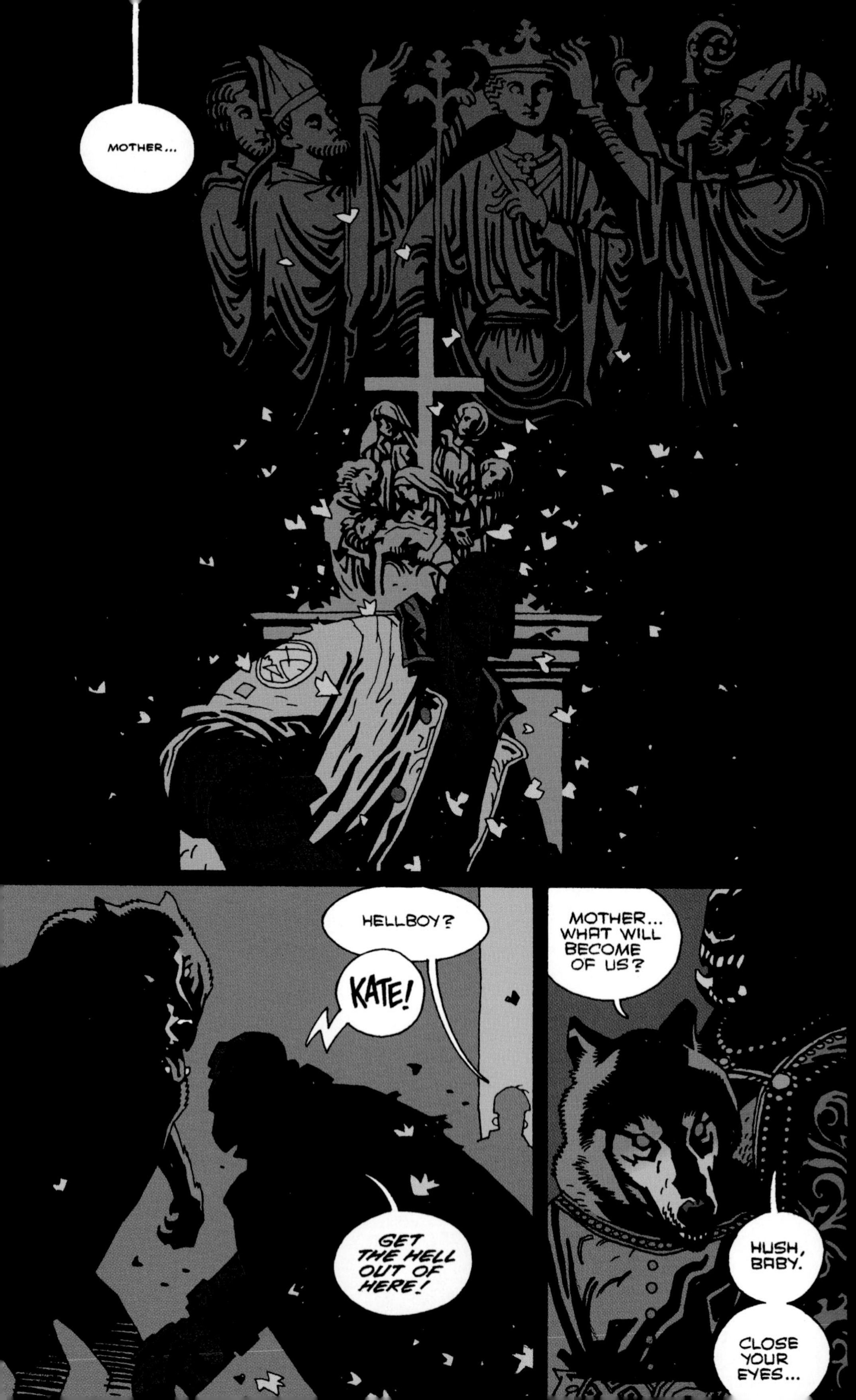

MOTHER...
HELLBOY?
KATE!
GET THE HELL OUT OF HERE!
MOTHER... WHAT WILL BECOME OF US?
HUSH, BABY.
CLOSE YOUR EYES...

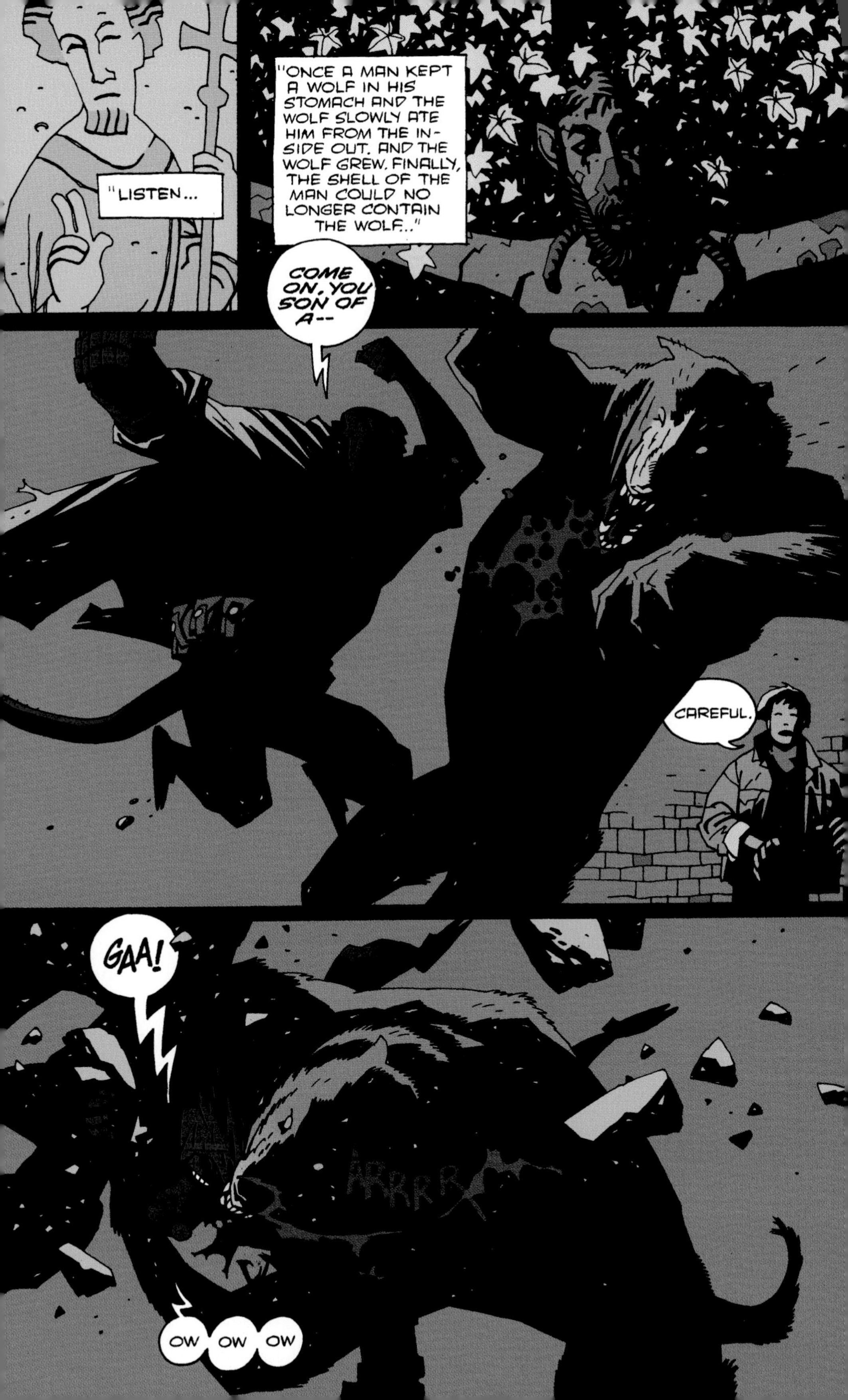
"LISTEN...
"ONCE A MAN KEPT A WOLF IN HIS STOMACH AND THE WOLF SLOWLY ATE HIM FROM THE INSIDE OUT. AND THE WOLF GREW. FINALLY, THE SHELL OF THE MAN COULD NO LONGER CONTAIN THE WOLF.."
COME ON, YOU SON OF A--
CAREFUL.
GAA!
OW
OW
OW

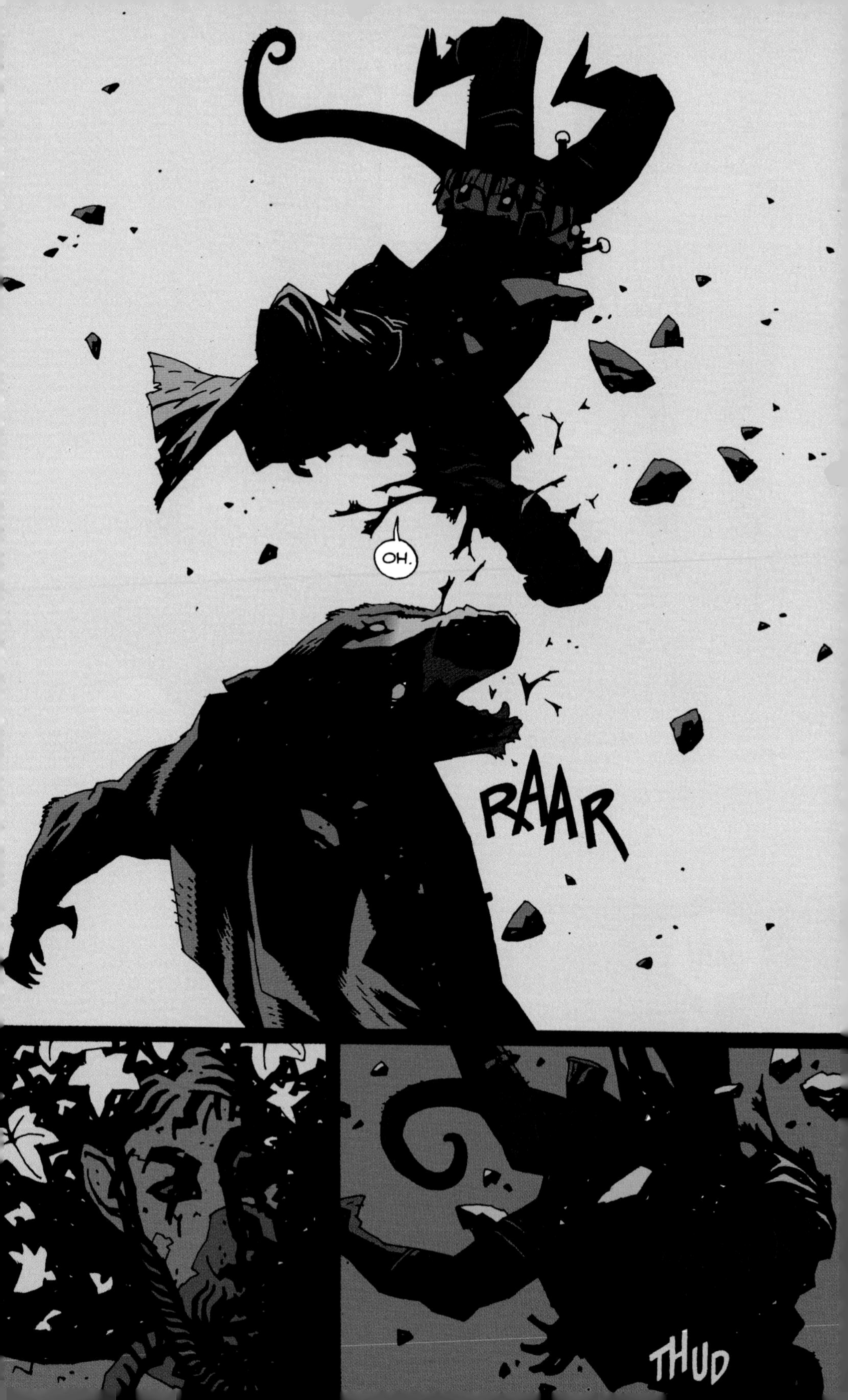
OH.
RAAR
THUD

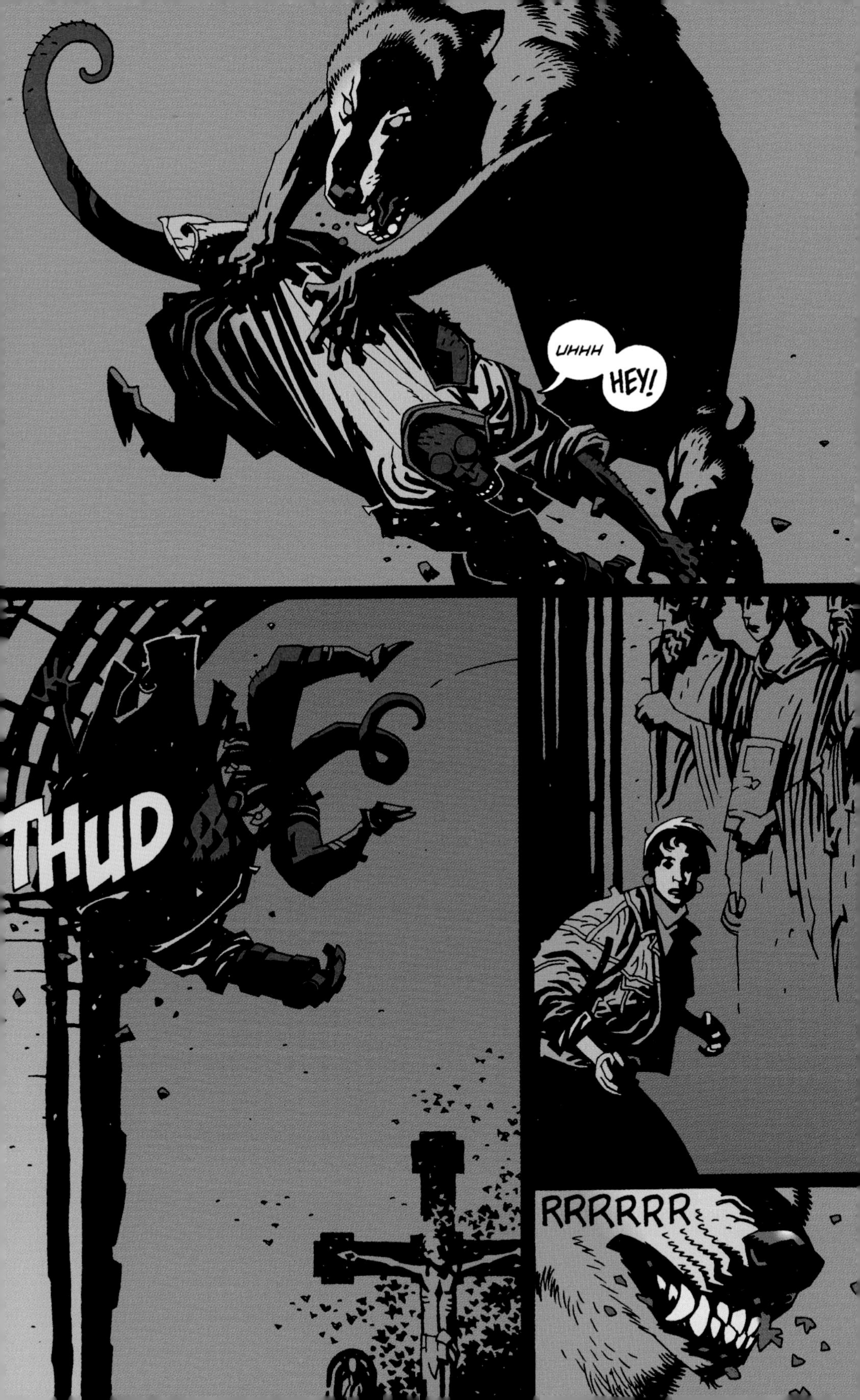
UHHH
HEY!
THUD
RRRRRR

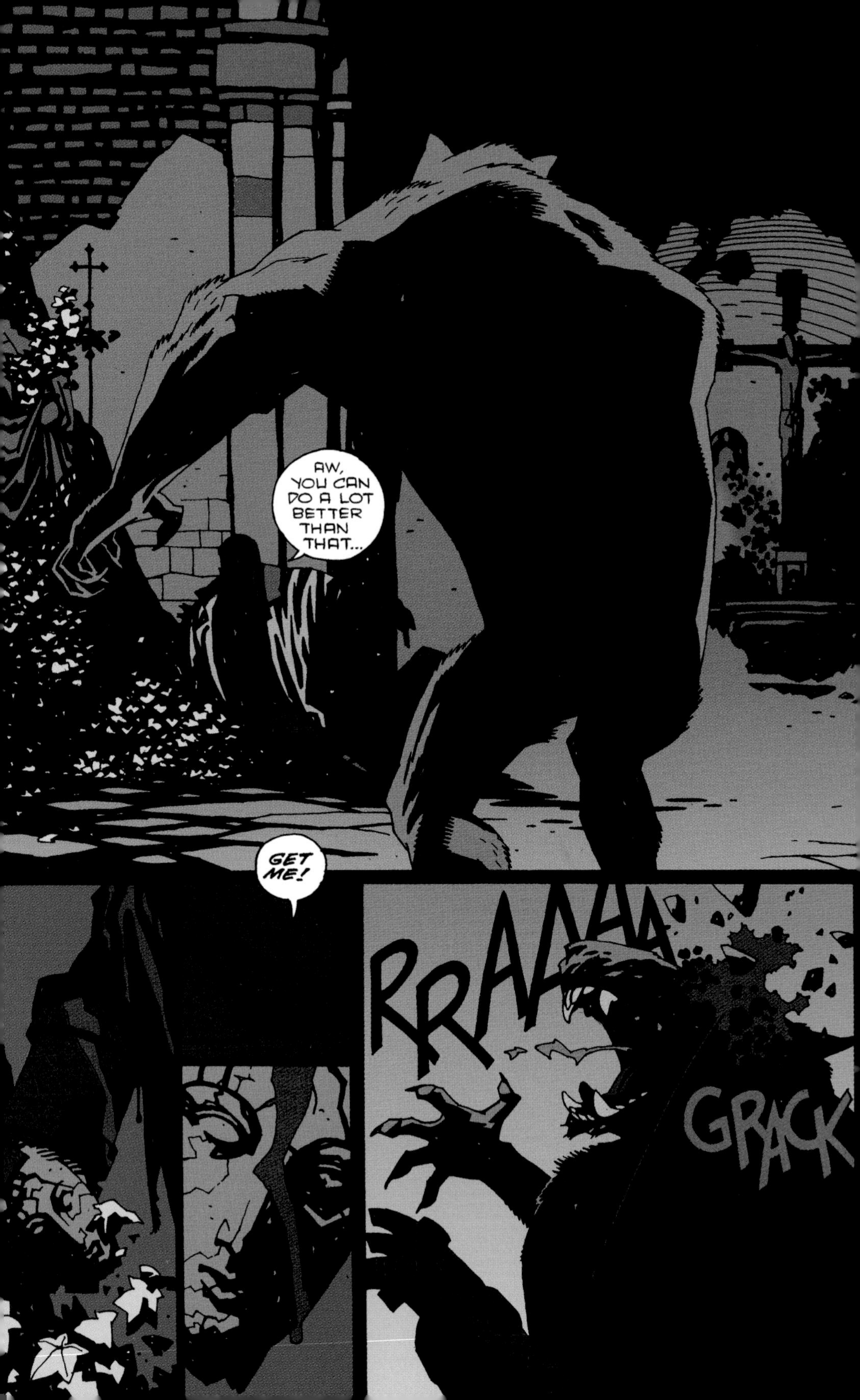

AW, YOU CAN DO A LOT BETTER THAN THAT...
GET ME!
RRAAAA
GRACK

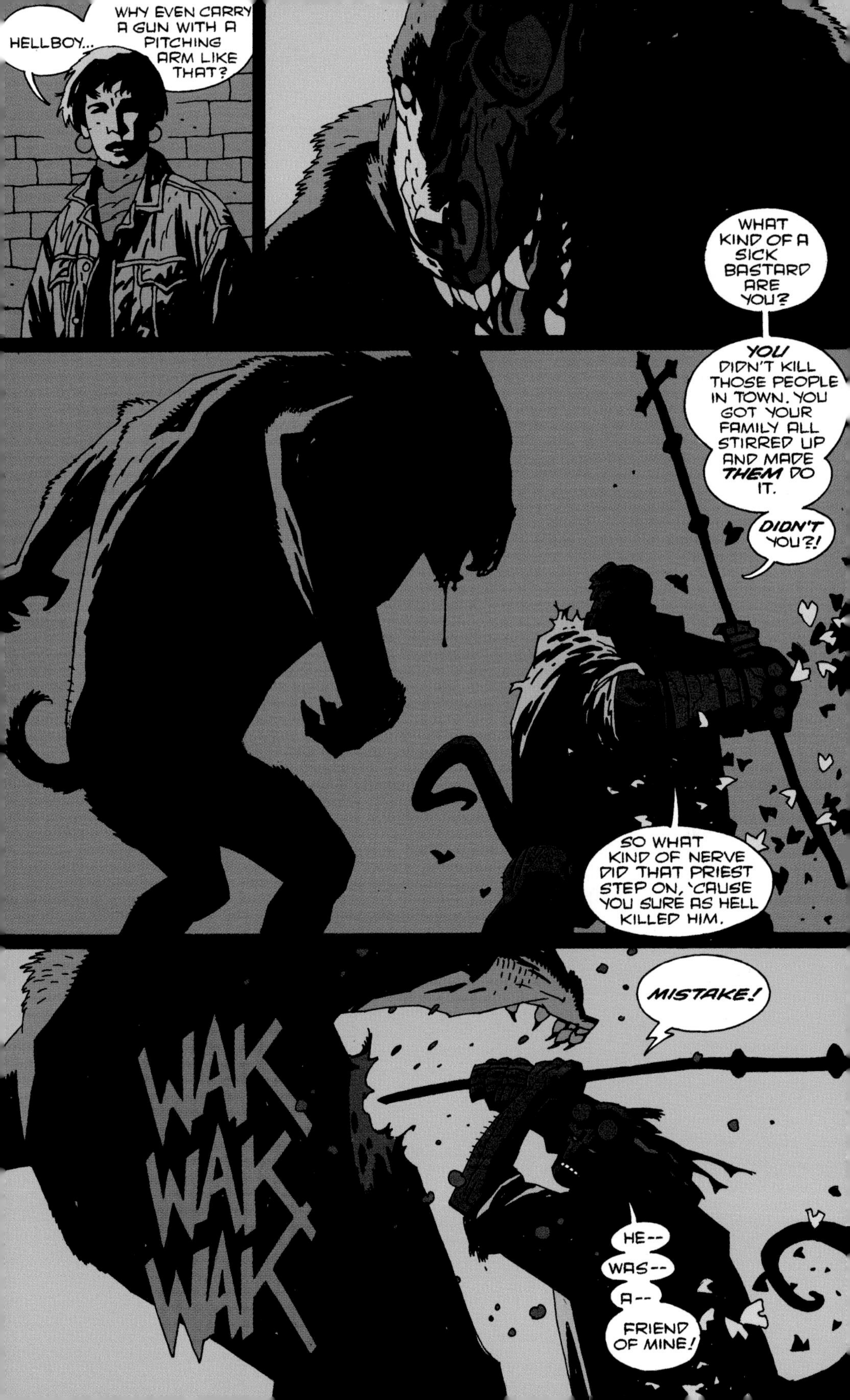
HELLBOY...
WHY EVEN CARRY A GUN WITH A PITCHING ARM LIKE THAT?
WHAT KIND OF A SICK BASTARD ARE YOU?
YOU DIDN'T KILL THOSE PEOPLE IN TOWN. YOU GOT YOUR FAMILY ALL STIRRED UP AND MADE THEM DO IT.
DIDN'T YOU?!
SO WHAT KIND OF NERVE DID THAT PRIEST STEP ON, 'CAUSE YOU SURE AS HELL KILLED HIM.
MISTAKE!
WAK WAK WAK
HE--
WAS--
A--
FRIEND OF MINE!

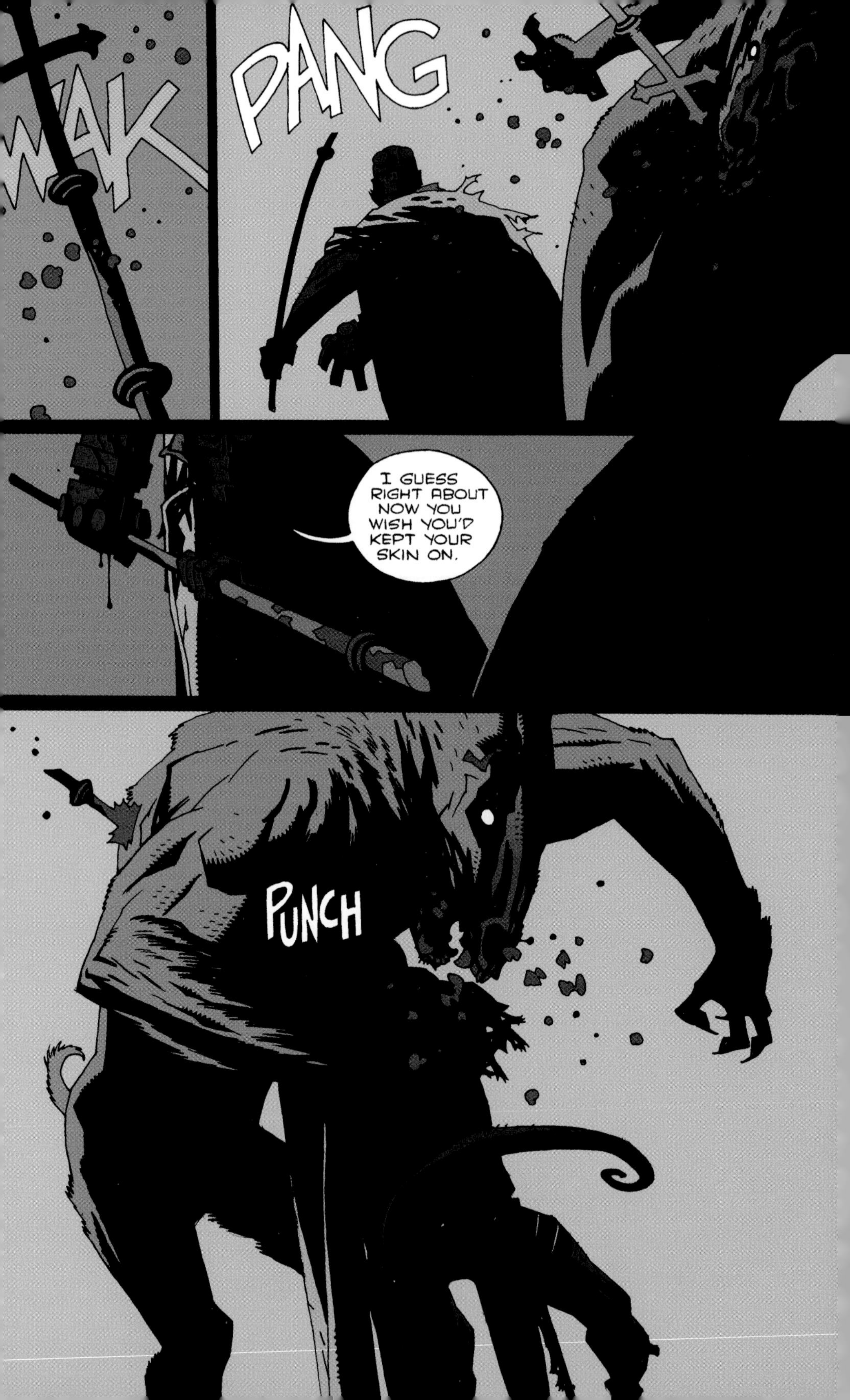
WAK
PANG
I GUESS RIGHT ABOUT NOW YOU WISH YOU'D KEPT YOUR SKIN ON.
PUNCH

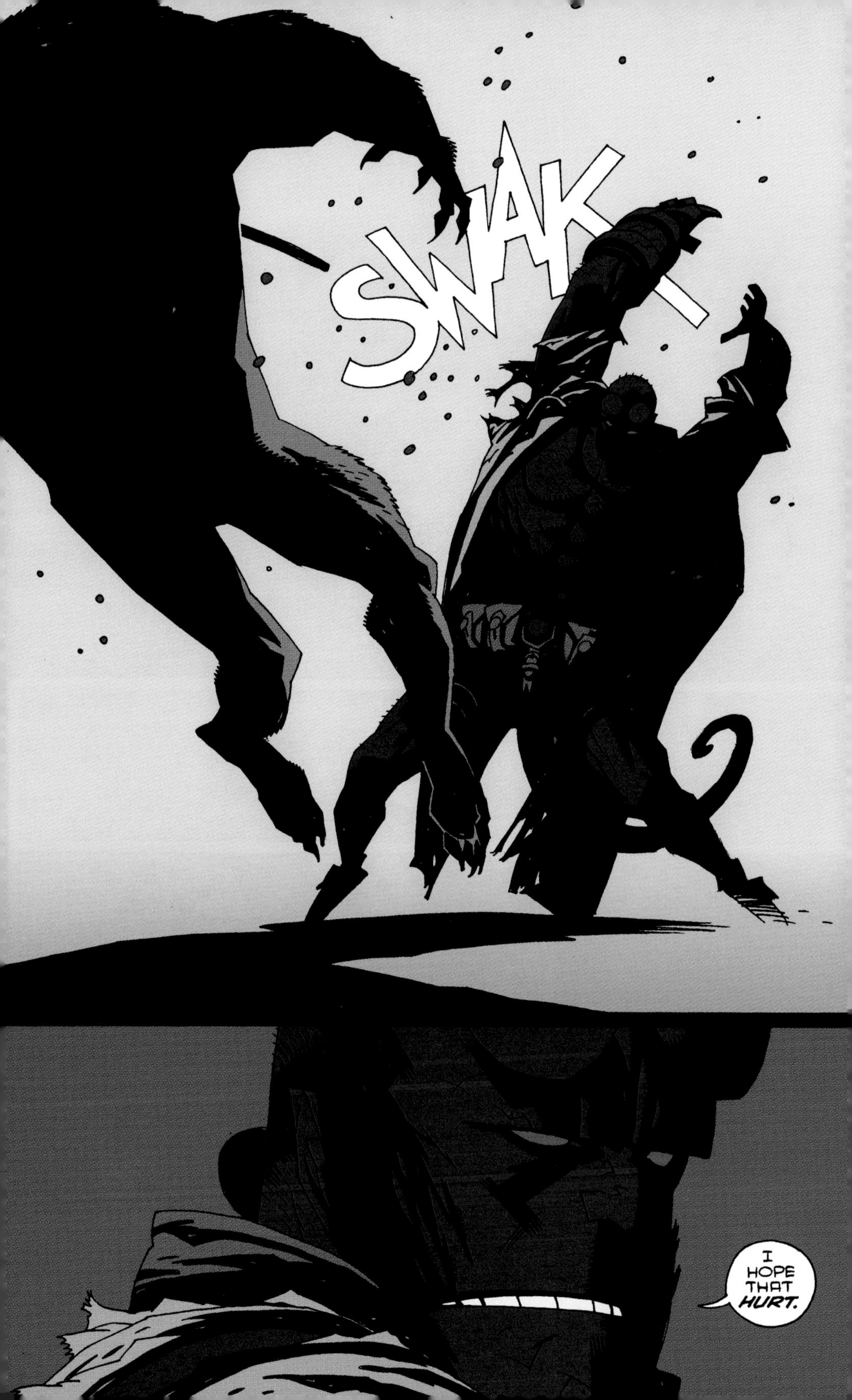
SWAK
I HOPE THAT *HURT.*

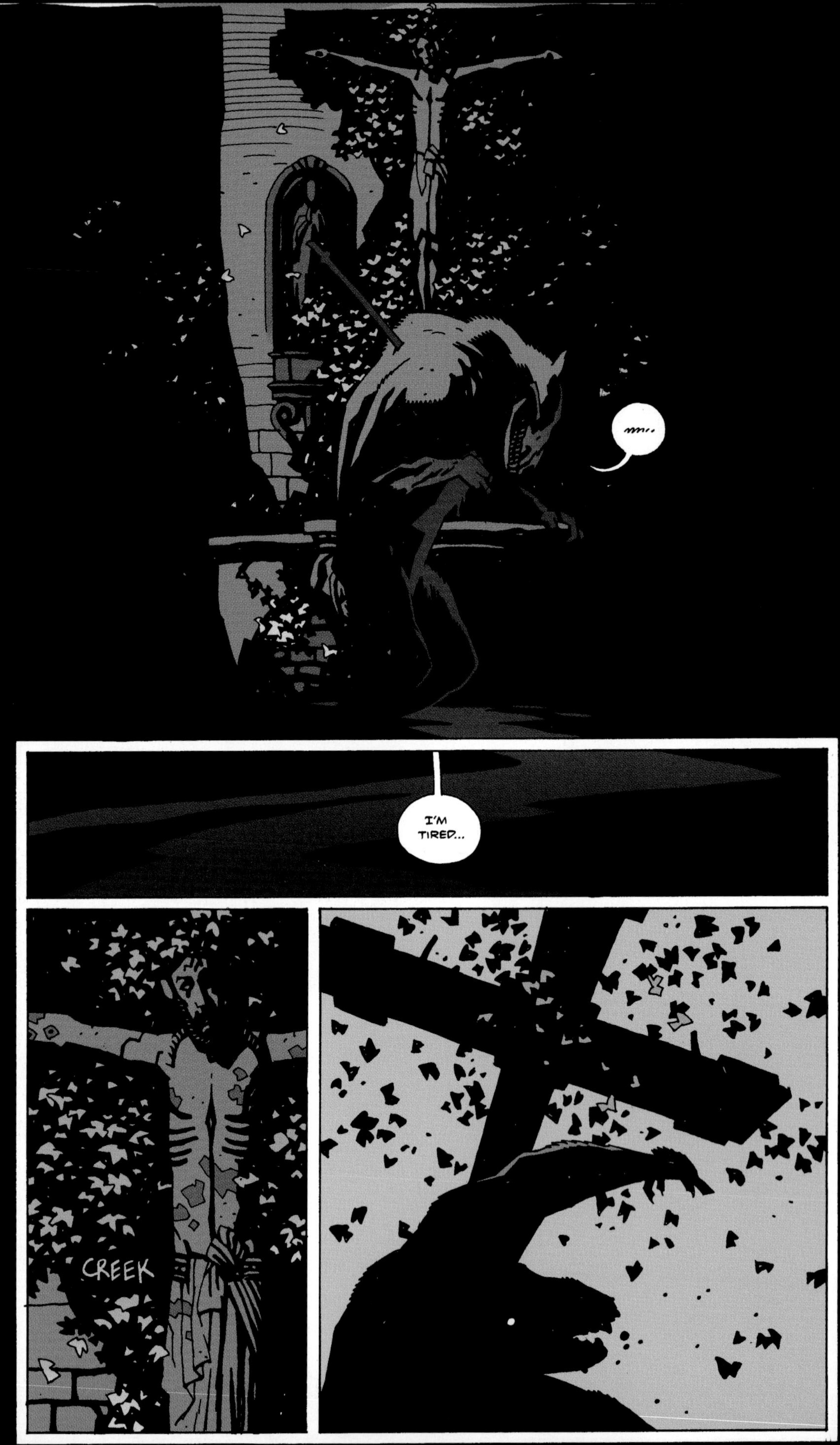
mm..
I'M TIRED...
CREEK

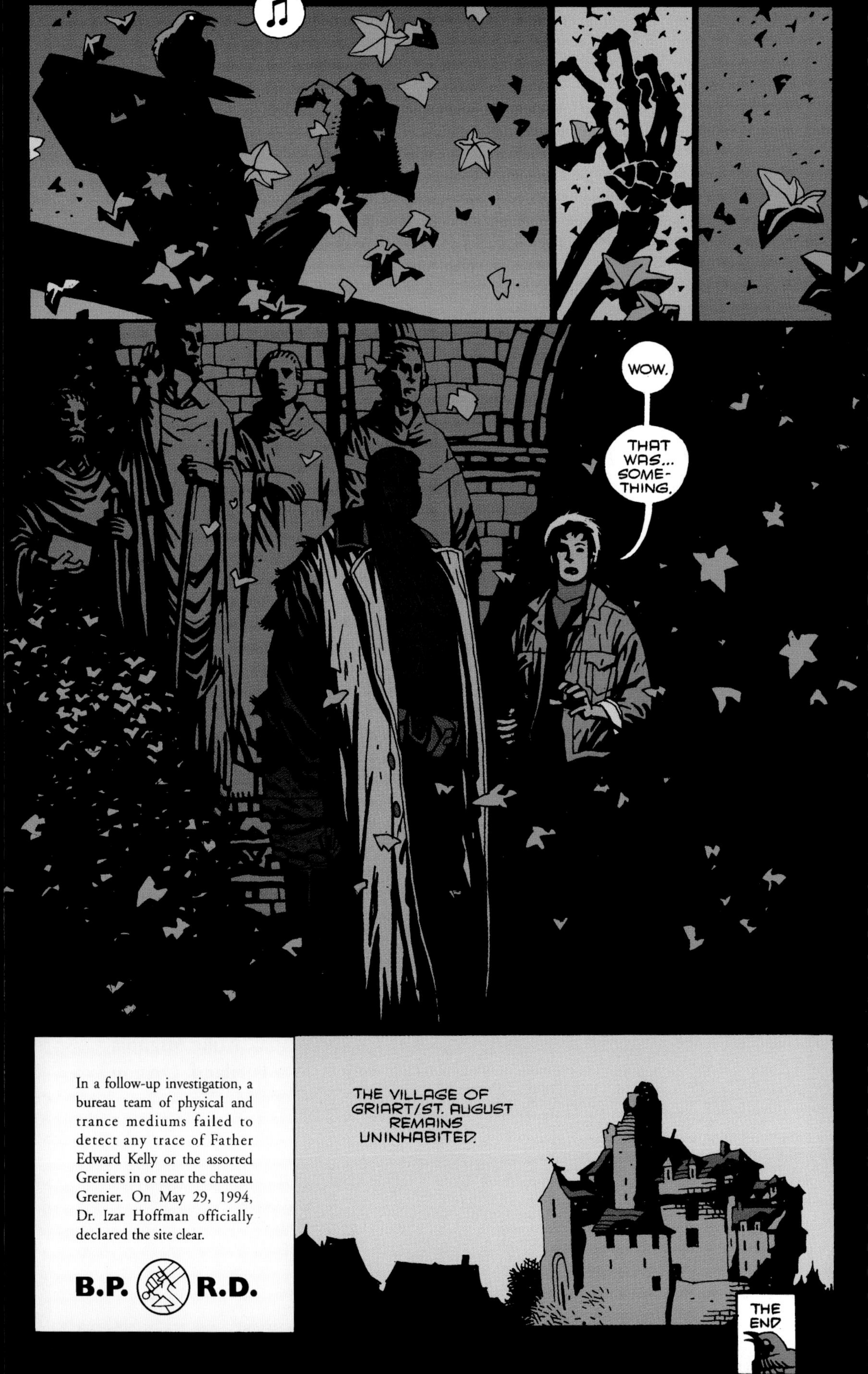
♫
WOW.
THAT WAS... SOME-THING.
In a follow-up investigation, a bureau team of physical and trance mediums failed to detect any trace of Father Edward Kelly or the assorted Greniers in or near the chateau Grenier. On May 29, 1994, Dr. Izar Hoffman officially declared the site clear.
B.P.R.D.
THE VILLAGE OF GRIART/ST. AUGUST REMAINS UNINHABITED.
THE END

Almost Colossus

IN 1996 I INTRODUCED my homunculus character in the *Wake the Devil* miniseries. "Almost Colossus" is sort of a sequel in that it ties up loose ends from that series, but I did everything I could to make it stand on its own. I think it holds up fine by itself. It was inspired by a wonderful story called "The Colossus of Ylourgne," by Clark Ashton Smith, one of my favorite writers from the old *Weird Tales* pulp magazine. The scene in the mountains with the cross and the lightning is my obvious tribute to those wonderful old James Whale *Frankenstein* movies.

Originally Liz Sherman was not going to survive the story. I've never had any real idea what to do with her, so I thought I'd get rid of her. Lazy me. It was Glen Murakami, super-genius art director of the current animated *Superman* show, who saved her. He was so horrified when I mentioned that I was going to kill her off that I was shamed into saving her. It worked out well. It made the story better and now Glen's obligated to draw a solo Liz Sherman story. Cool!

"Almost Colossus" was published as a two-issue miniseries in 1997. For this collection I've added three new story pages to slow down the pacing in a few places.

Well, that's it.

Good night.

MIKE MIGNOLA

Mike Mignola
Portland, Oregon

Almost
Colossus

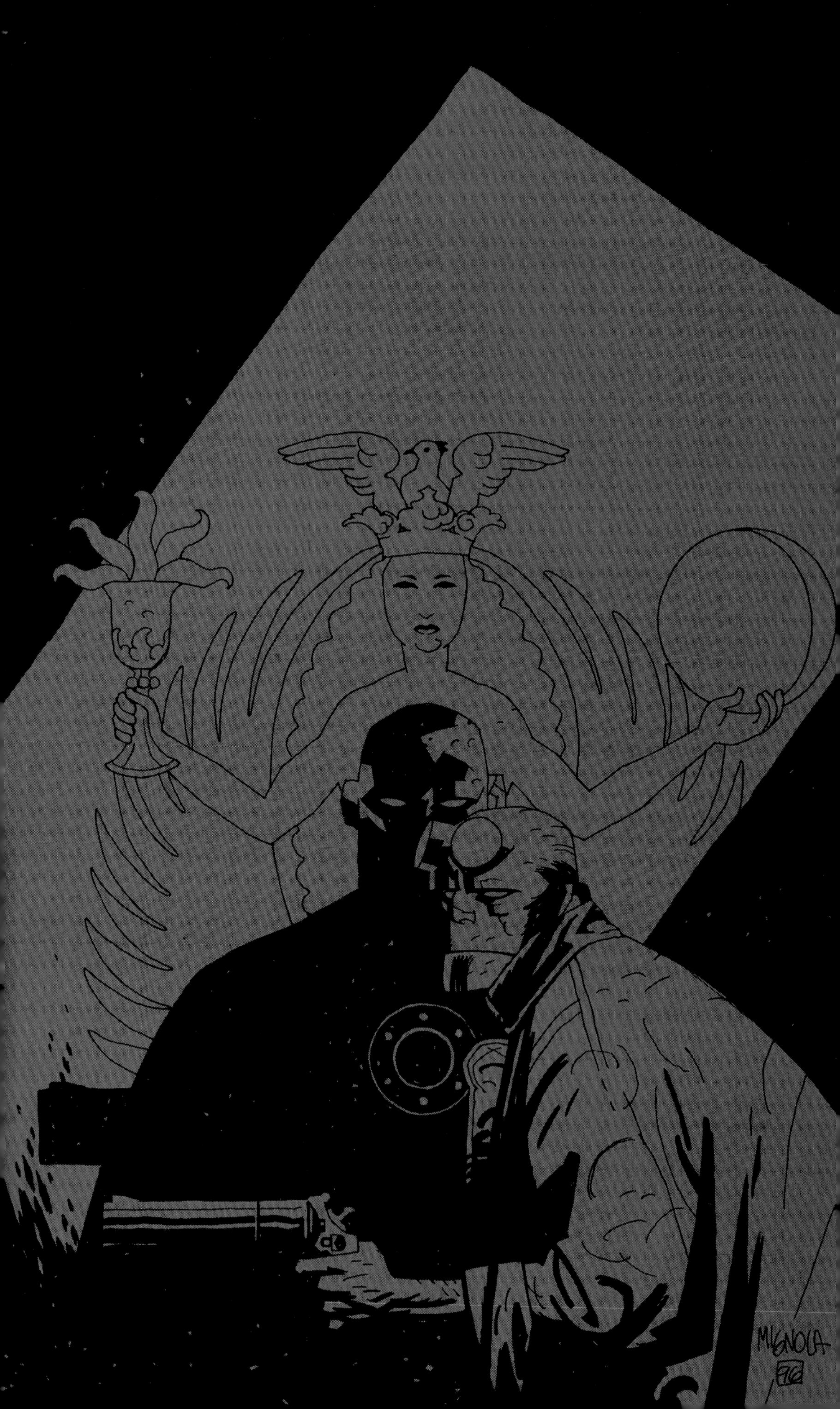
MIGNOLA

THE WAUER INSTITUTE, TIRGOVISTE, ROMANIA.

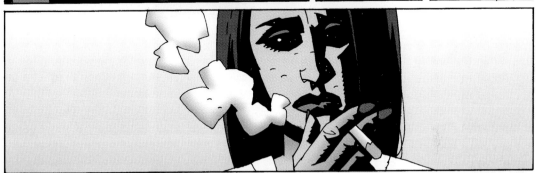

SHE DOESN'T LOOK TOO GOOD.

DOCTOR OLASZ?

WELL... SHE IS *NOT* VERY GOOD.

SHE SHOULD BE. HER GUNSHOT INJURY IS NOT TOO VERY SERIOUS. SHE HAS NO OTHER INJURIES, NO DISEASE... NO, IN EVERY WAY SHE IS LIKE HEALTHY, YOUNG GIRL, BUT I THINK SHE IS GOING AWAY FROM US.

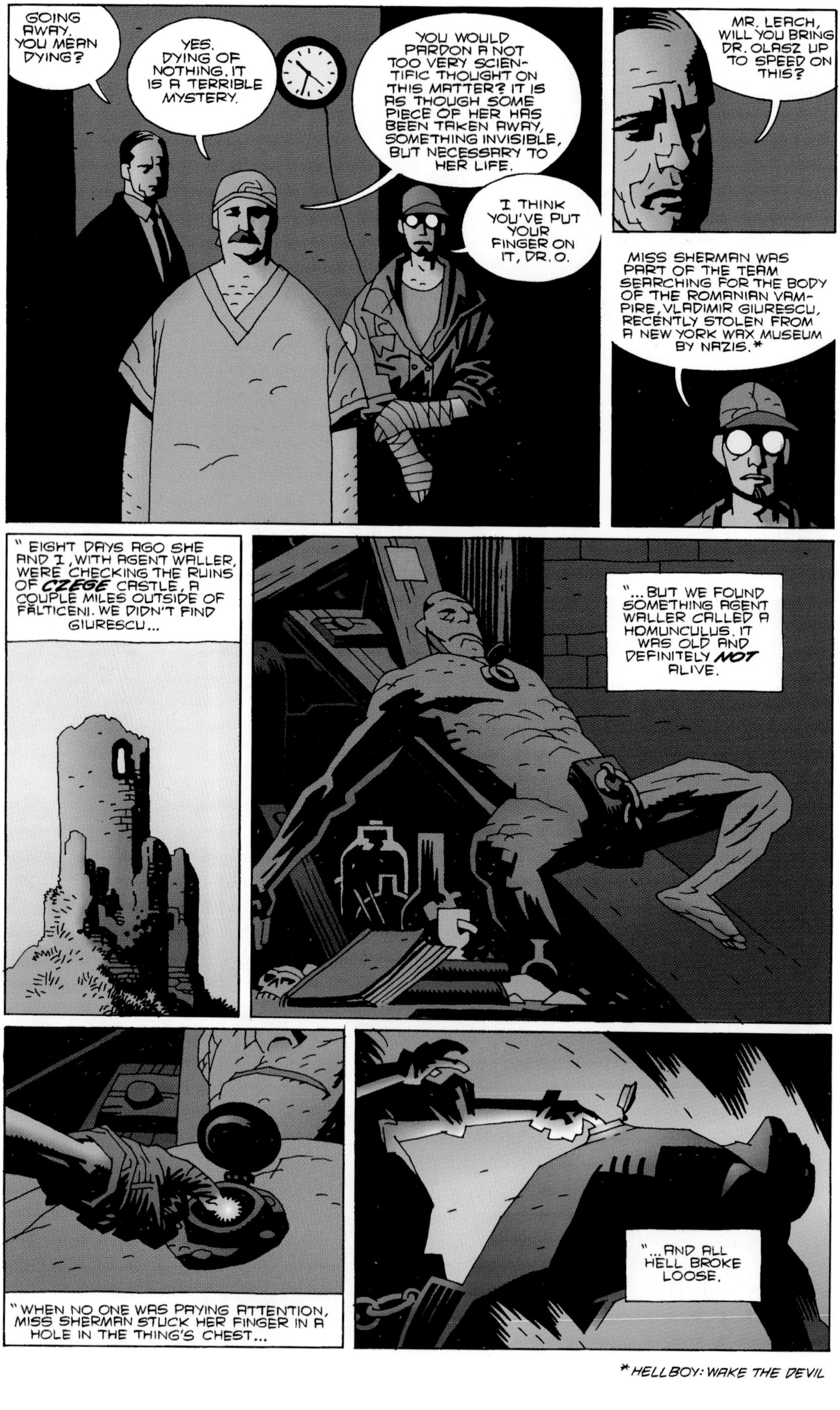
GOING AWAY. YOU MEAN DYING?
YES. DYING OF NOTHING. IT IS A TERRIBLE MYSTERY.
YOU WOULD PARDON A NOT TOO VERY SCIENTIFIC THOUGHT ON THIS MATTER? IT IS AS THOUGH SOME PIECE OF HER HAS BEEN TAKEN AWAY, SOMETHING INVISIBLE, BUT NECESSARY TO HER LIFE.
I THINK YOU'VE PUT YOUR FINGER ON IT, DR. O.
MR. LEACH, WILL YOU BRING DR. OLASZ UP TO SPEED ON THIS?
MISS SHERMAN WAS PART OF THE TEAM SEARCHING FOR THE BODY OF THE ROMANIAN VAMPIRE, VLADIMIR GIURESCU, RECENTLY STOLEN FROM A NEW YORK WAX MUSEUM BY NAZIS.*
"EIGHT DAYS AGO SHE AND I, WITH AGENT WALLER, WERE CHECKING THE RUINS OF CZEGE CASTLE, A COUPLE MILES OUTSIDE OF FALTICENI. WE DIDN'T FIND GIURESCU...
"...BUT WE FOUND SOMETHING AGENT WALLER CALLED A HOMUNCULUS. IT WAS OLD AND DEFINITELY NOT ALIVE.
"WHEN NO ONE WAS PAYING ATTENTION, MISS SHERMAN STUCK HER FINGER IN A HOLE IN THE THING'S CHEST...
"...AND ALL HELL BROKE LOOSE.

*HELLBOY: WAKE THE DEVIL

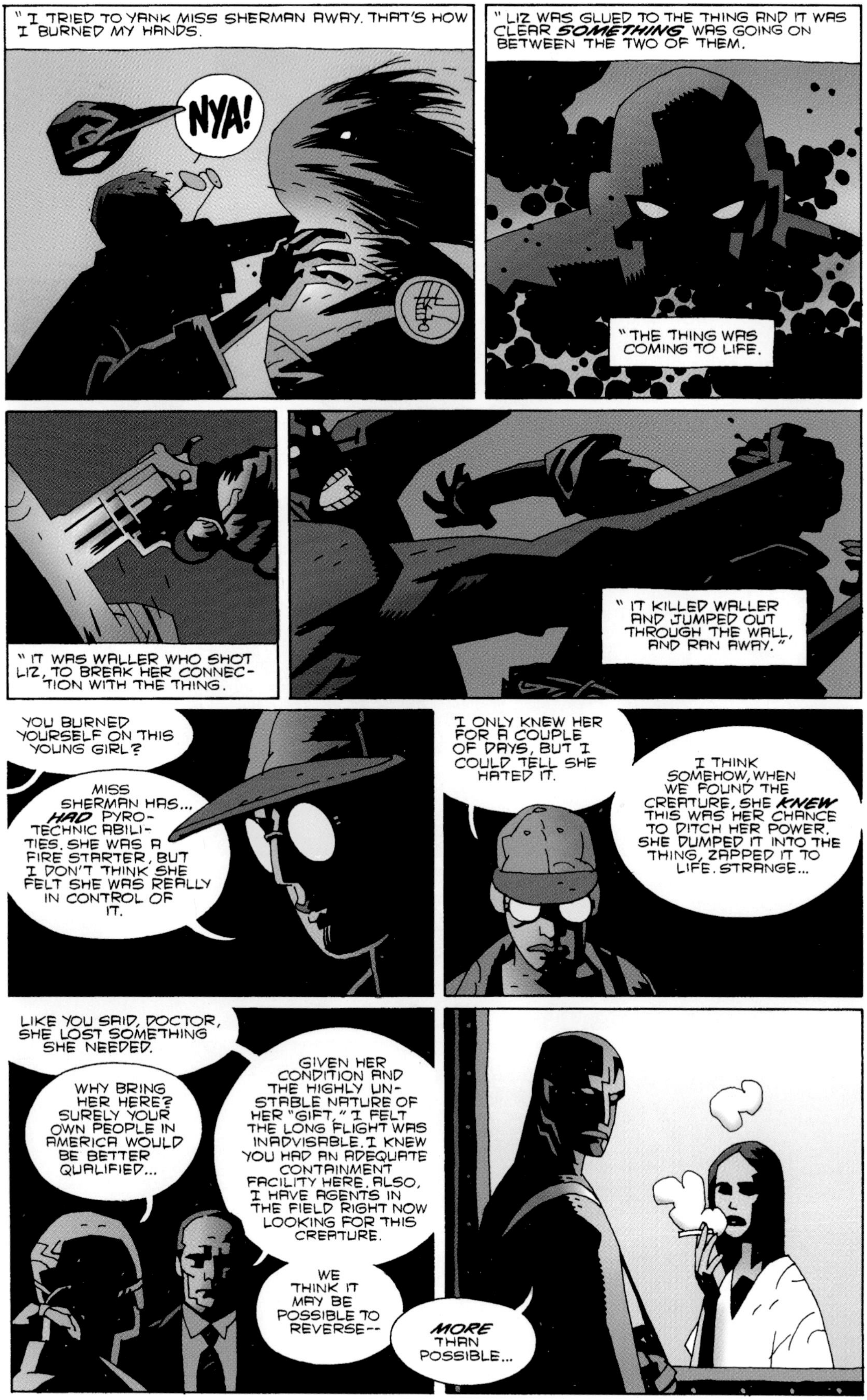

"I TRIED TO YANK MISS SHERMAN AWAY. THAT'S HOW I BURNED MY HANDS.
NYA!
"LIZ WAS GLUED TO THE THING AND IT WAS CLEAR SOMETHING WAS GOING ON BETWEEN THE TWO OF THEM.
"THE THING WAS COMING TO LIFE.
"IT WAS WALLER WHO SHOT LIZ, TO BREAK HER CONNECTION WITH THE THING.
"IT KILLED WALLER AND JUMPED OUT THROUGH THE WALL, AND RAN AWAY."
YOU BURNED YOURSELF ON THIS YOUNG GIRL?
MISS SHERMAN HAS... HAD PYROTECHNIC ABILITIES. SHE WAS A FIRE STARTER, BUT I DON'T THINK SHE FELT SHE WAS REALLY IN CONTROL OF IT.
I ONLY KNEW HER FOR A COUPLE OF DAYS, BUT I COULD TELL SHE HATED IT.
I THINK SOMEHOW, WHEN WE FOUND THE CREATURE, SHE KNEW THIS WAS HER CHANCE TO DITCH HER POWER. SHE DUMPED IT INTO THE THING, ZAPPED IT TO LIFE. STRANGE...
LIKE YOU SAID, DOCTOR, SHE LOST SOMETHING SHE NEEDED.
WHY BRING HER HERE? SURELY YOUR OWN PEOPLE IN AMERICA WOULD BE BETTER QUALIFIED...
GIVEN HER CONDITION AND THE HIGHLY UNSTABLE NATURE OF HER "GIFT," I FELT THE LONG FLIGHT WAS INADVISABLE. I KNEW YOU HAD AN ADEQUATE CONTAINMENT FACILITY HERE. ALSO, I HAVE AGENTS IN THE FIELD RIGHT NOW LOOKING FOR THIS CREATURE.
WE THINK IT MAY BE POSSIBLE TO REVERSE--
MORE THAN POSSIBLE...

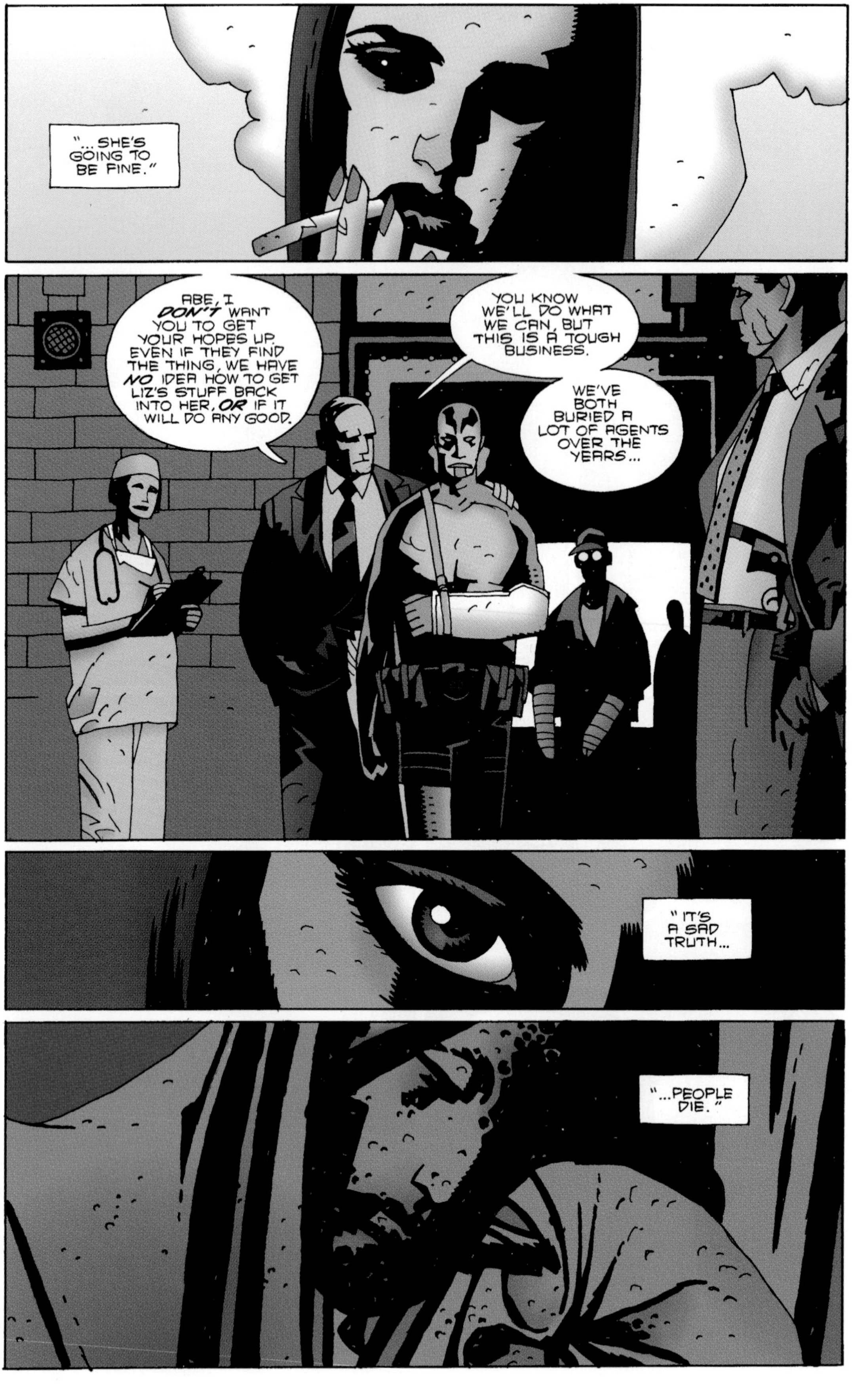
"... SHE'S GOING TO BE FINE."
ABE, I *DON'T* WANT YOU TO GET YOUR HOPES UP. EVEN IF THEY FIND THE THING, WE HAVE *NO* IDEA HOW TO GET LIZ'S STUFF BACK INTO HER, *OR* IF IT WILL DO ANY GOOD.
YOU KNOW WE'LL DO WHAT WE CAN, BUT THIS IS A TOUGH BUSINESS.
WE'VE BOTH BURIED A LOT OF AGENTS OVER THE YEARS...
" IT'S A SAD TRUTH...
"...PEOPLE DIE."

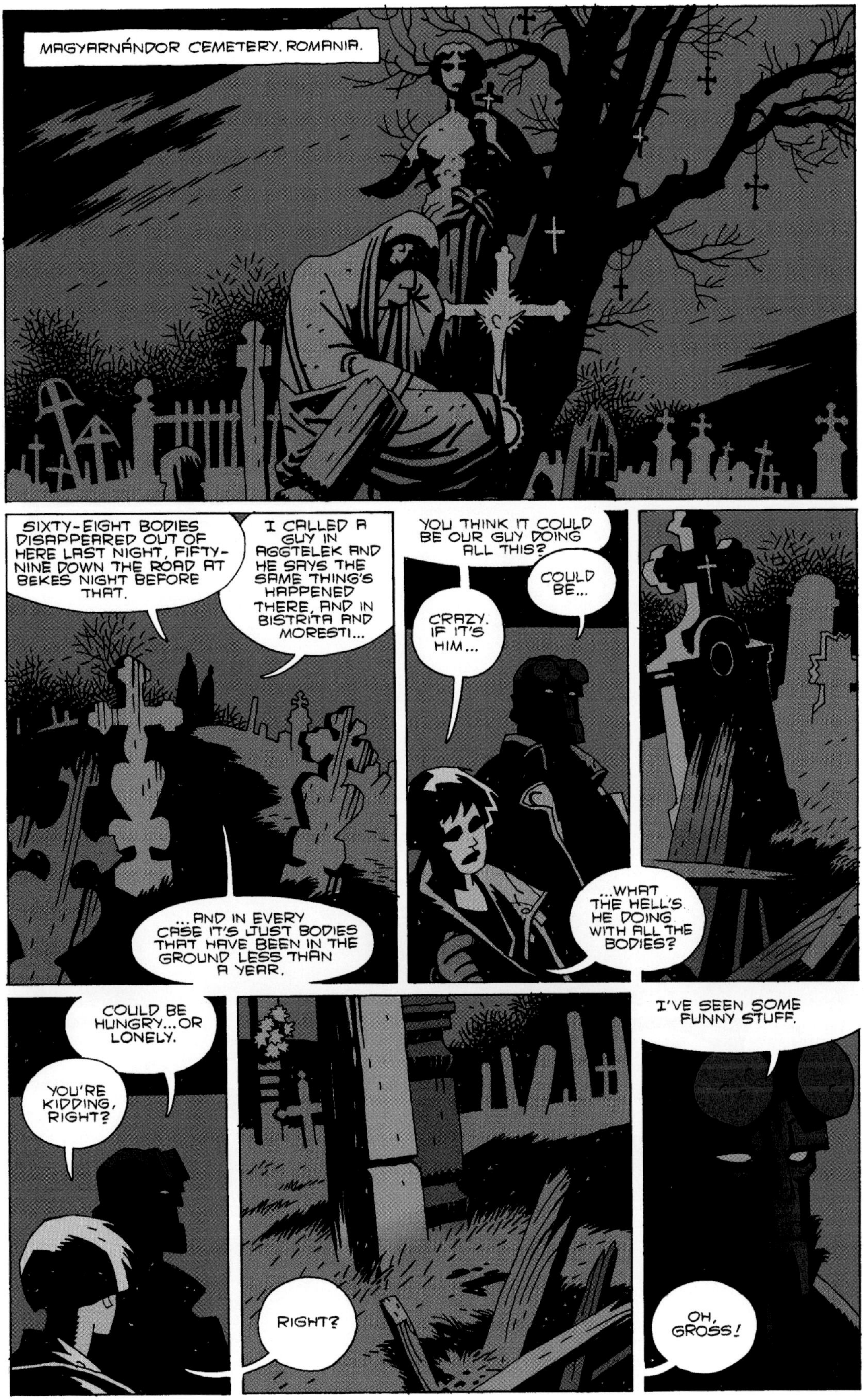
MAGYARNÁNDOR CEMETERY. ROMANIA.
SIXTY-EIGHT BODIES DISAPPEARED OUT OF HERE LAST NIGHT, FIFTY-NINE DOWN THE ROAD AT BEKES NIGHT BEFORE THAT.
I CALLED A GUY IN AGGTELEK AND HE SAYS THE SAME THING'S HAPPENED THERE, AND IN BISTRITA AND MORESTI...
...AND IN EVERY CASE IT'S JUST BODIES THAT HAVE BEEN IN THE GROUND LESS THAN A YEAR.
YOU THINK IT COULD BE OUR GUY DOING ALL THIS?
COULD BE...
CRAZY. IF IT'S HIM...
...WHAT THE HELL'S HE DOING WITH ALL THE BODIES?
COULD BE HUNGRY...OR LONELY.
YOU'RE KIDDING, RIGHT?
RIGHT?
I'VE SEEN SOME FUNNY STUFF.
OH, GROSS!

LOOK AT WHAT'S LEFT OF THESE COFFINS. SOMETHING DUG 'EM UP AND BROKE 'EM APART BY HAND. NO TOOLS...

AND NO WHEEL TRACKS ANYWHERE, SO HOW DID ALL THE BODIES GET CARTED OFF?

IF SOMETHING ATE THEM THERE'D BE *SOMETHING* LEFT OVER SOMEWHERE. LOCALS HAVE CHECKED THE WOODS--

SO MAYBE WE SHOULD BE LOOKING FOR ABANDONED BUILDINGS, CAVES--

HMM.

YOU THINKING ABOUT LIZ?

YEAH.

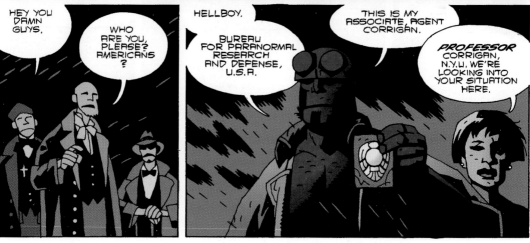

HEY YOU DAMN GUYS.

WHO ARE YOU, PLEASE? AMERICANS?

HELLBOY. BUREAU FOR PARANORMAL RESEARCH AND DEFENSE, U.S.A.

THIS IS MY ASSOCIATE, AGENT CORRIGAN.

PROFESSOR CORRIGAN, N.Y.U. WE'RE LOOKING INTO YOUR SITUATION HERE.

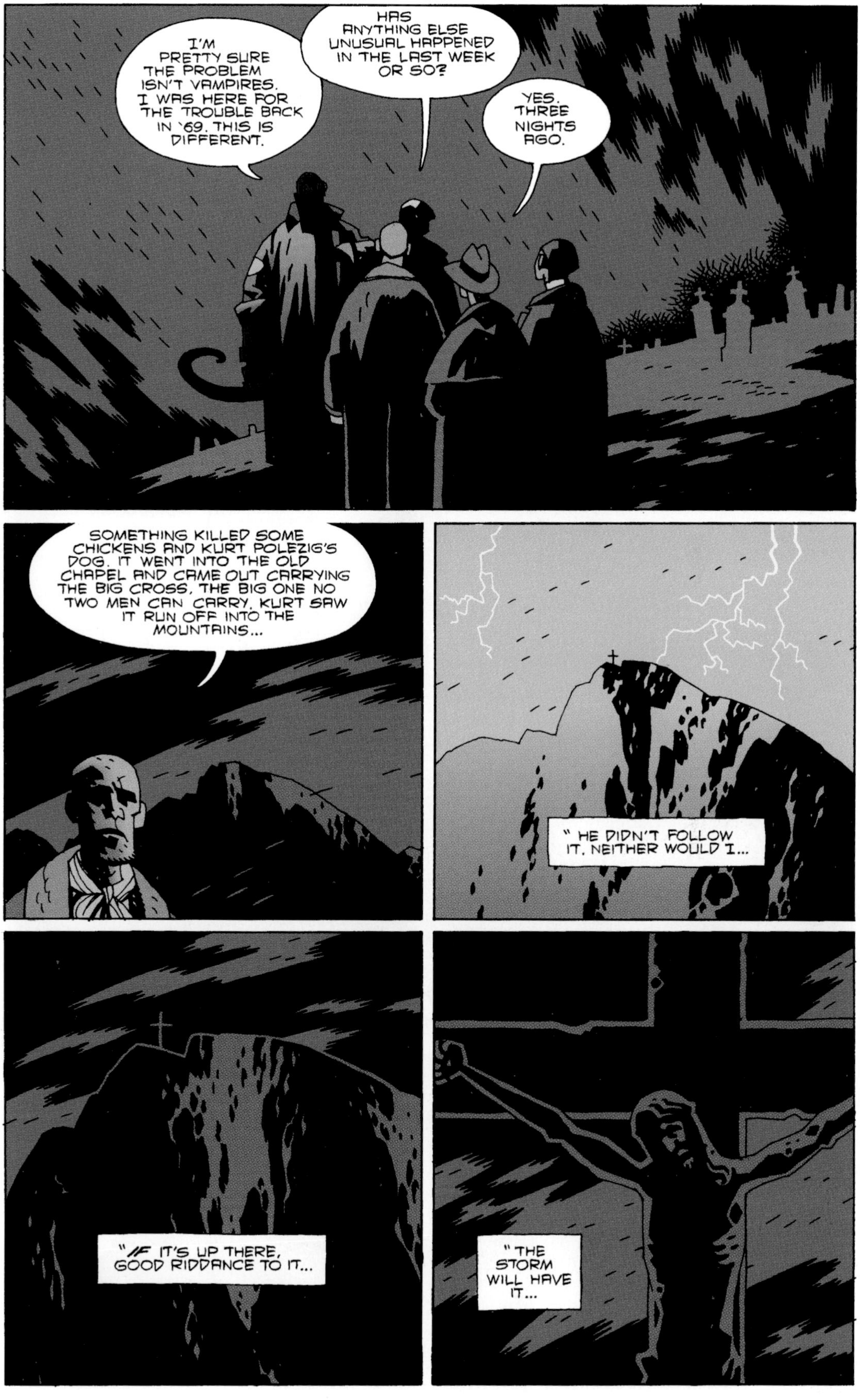
I'M PRETTY SURE THE PROBLEM ISN'T VAMPIRES. I WAS HERE FOR THE TROUBLE BACK IN '69. THIS IS DIFFERENT.
HAS ANYTHING ELSE UNUSUAL HAPPENED IN THE LAST WEEK OR SO?
YES. THREE NIGHTS AGO.
SOMETHING KILLED SOME CHICKENS AND KURT POLEZIG'S DOG. IT WENT INTO THE OLD CHAPEL AND CAME OUT CARRYING THE BIG CROSS, THE BIG ONE NO TWO MEN CAN CARRY. KURT SAW IT RUN OFF INTO THE MOUNTAINS...
"HE DIDN'T FOLLOW IT. NEITHER WOULD I...
"IF IT'S UP THERE, GOOD RIDDANCE TO IT...
"THE STORM WILL HAVE IT...

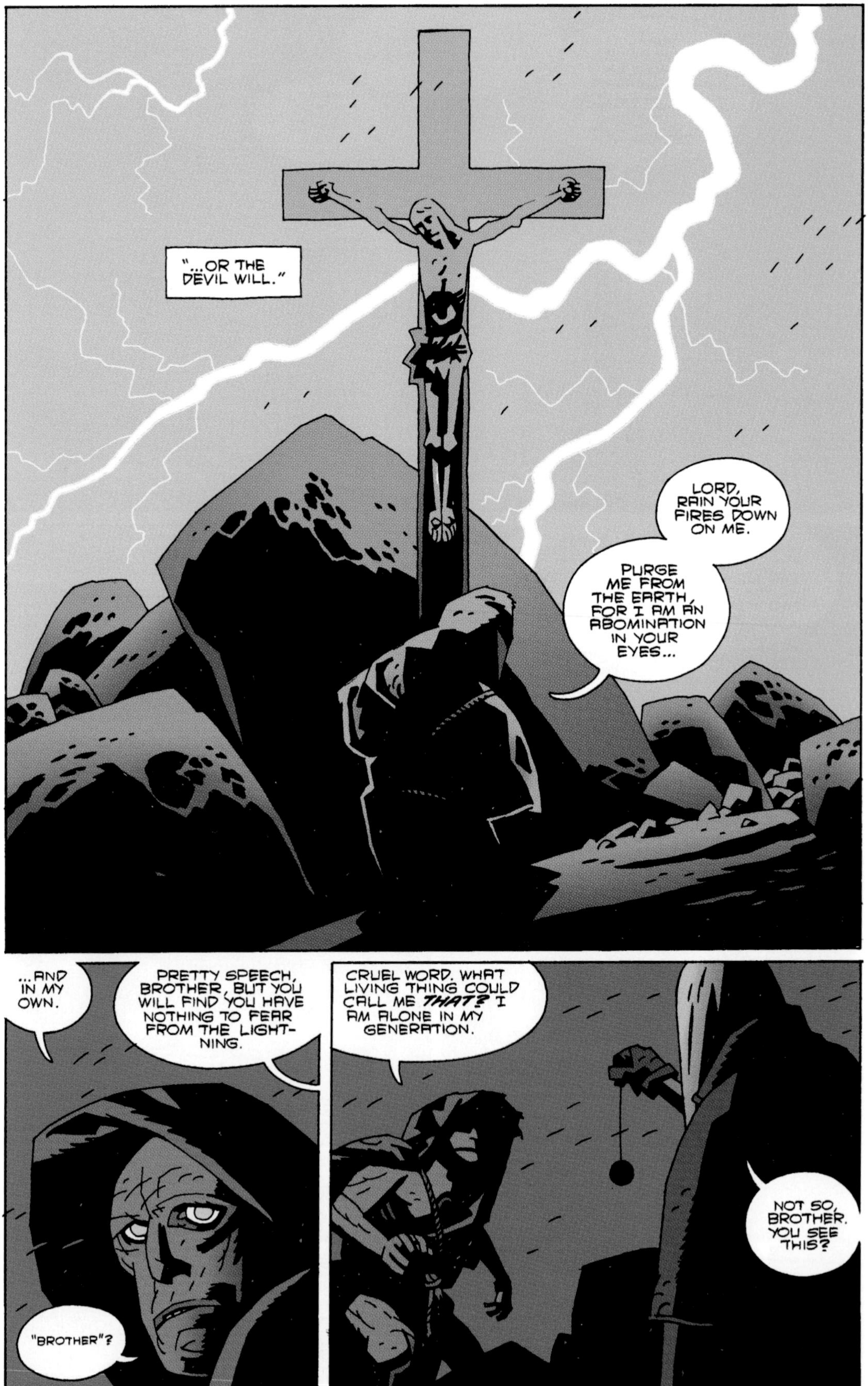
"...OR THE DEVIL WILL."
LORD, RAIN YOUR FIRES DOWN ON ME.
PURGE ME FROM THE EARTH, FOR I AM AN ABOMINATION IN YOUR EYES...
...AND IN MY OWN.
PRETTY SPEECH, BROTHER, BUT YOU WILL FIND YOU HAVE NOTHING TO FEAR FROM THE LIGHT-NING.
"BROTHER"?
CRUEL WORD. WHAT LIVING THING COULD CALL ME *THAT?* I AM ALONE IN MY GENERATION.
NOT SO, BROTHER. YOU SEE THIS?

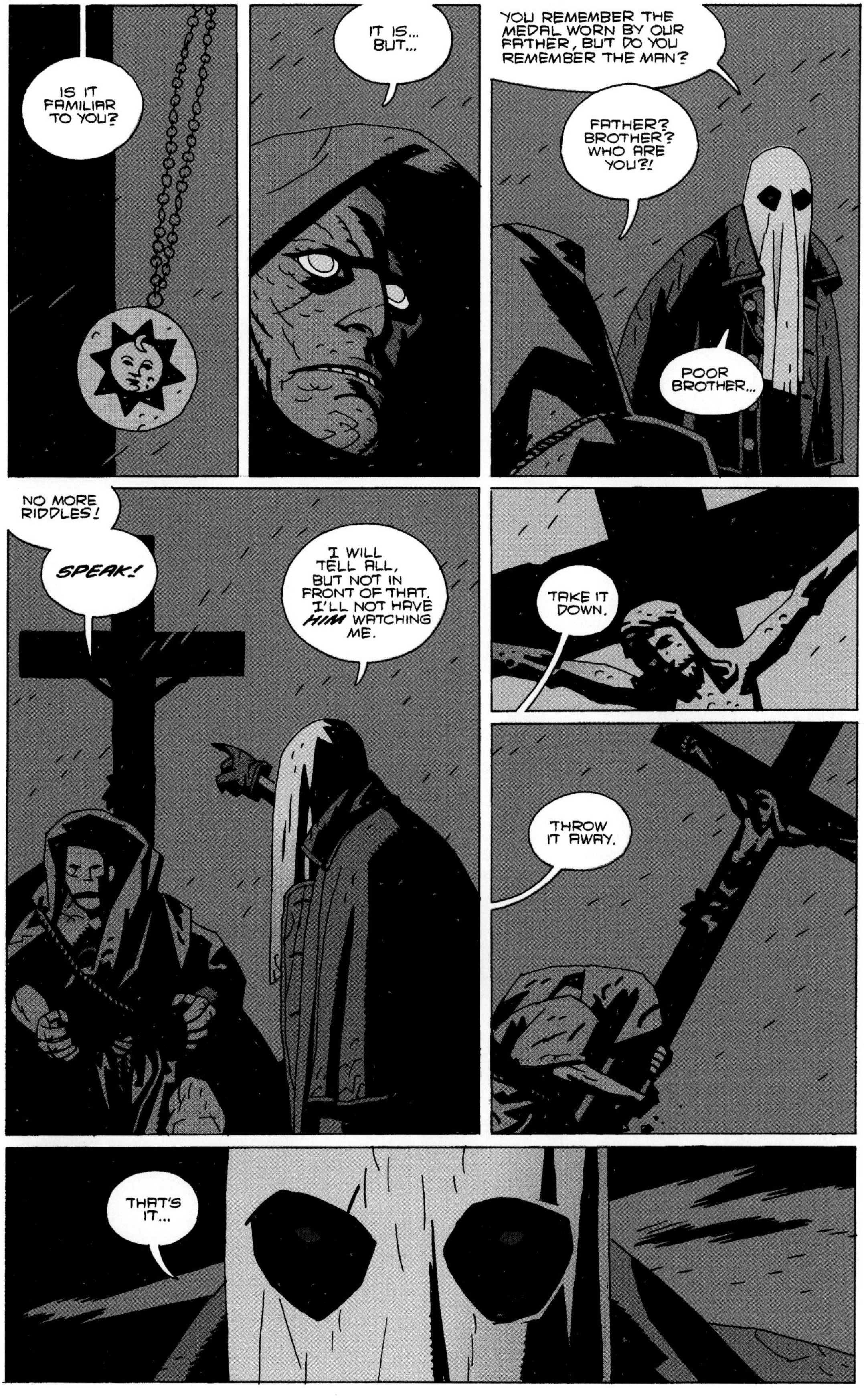
IS IT FAMILIAR TO YOU?
IT IS... BUT...
YOU REMEMBER THE MEDAL WORN BY OUR FATHER, BUT DO YOU REMEMBER THE MAN?
FATHER? BROTHER? WHO ARE YOU?!
POOR BROTHER...
NO MORE RIDDLES!
SPEAK!
I WILL TELL ALL, BUT NOT IN FRONT OF THAT. I'LL NOT HAVE HIM WATCHING ME.
TAKE IT DOWN.
THROW IT AWAY.
THAT'S IT...

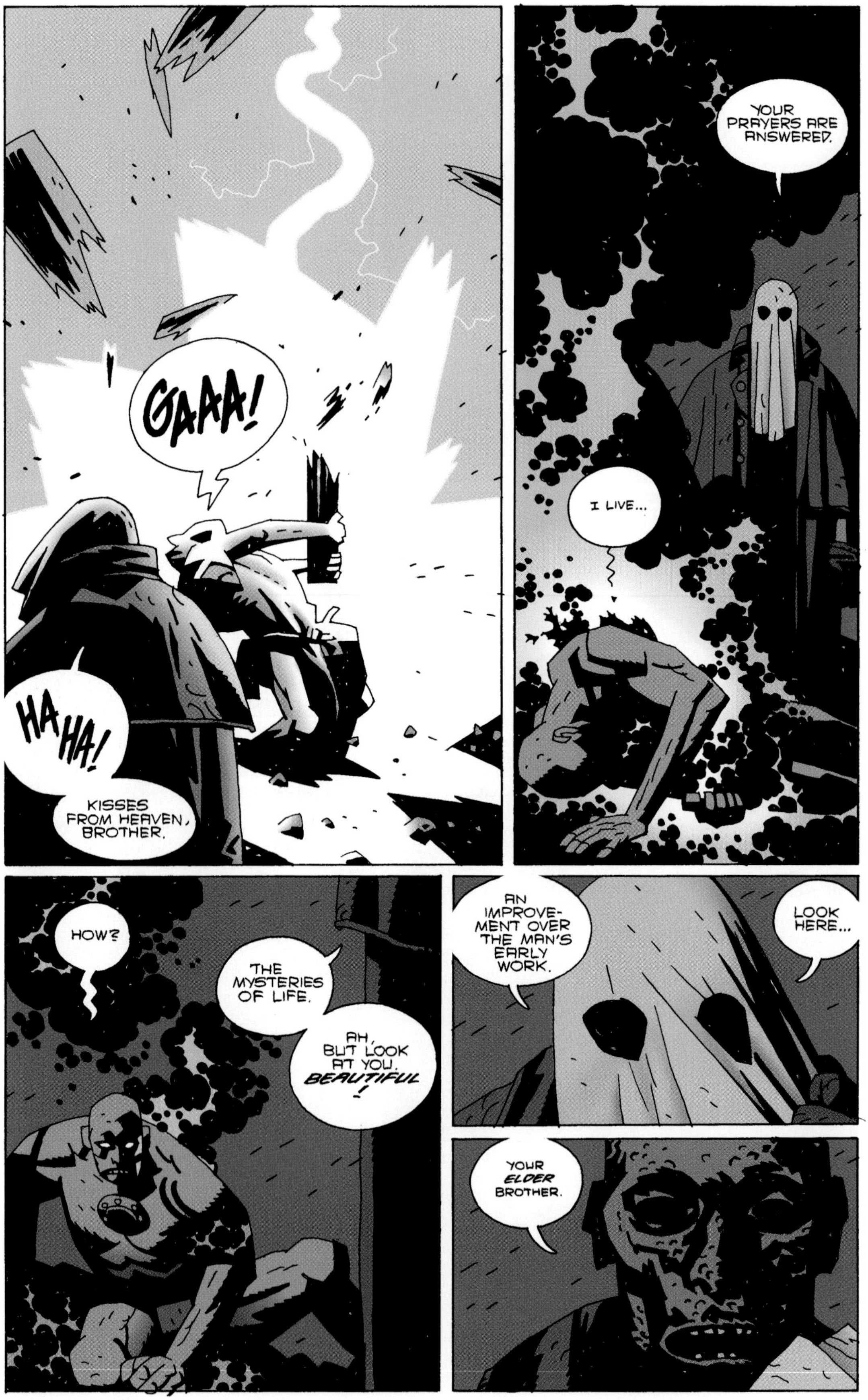
GAAA!
HA HA!
KISSES FROM HEAVEN, BROTHER.
YOUR PRAYERS ARE ANSWERED.
I LIVE...
HOW?
THE MYSTERIES OF LIFE.
AH, BUT LOOK AT YOU. *BEAUTIFUL*!
AN IMPROVEMENT OVER THE MAN'S EARLY WORK.
LOOK HERE...
YOUR *ELDER* BROTHER.

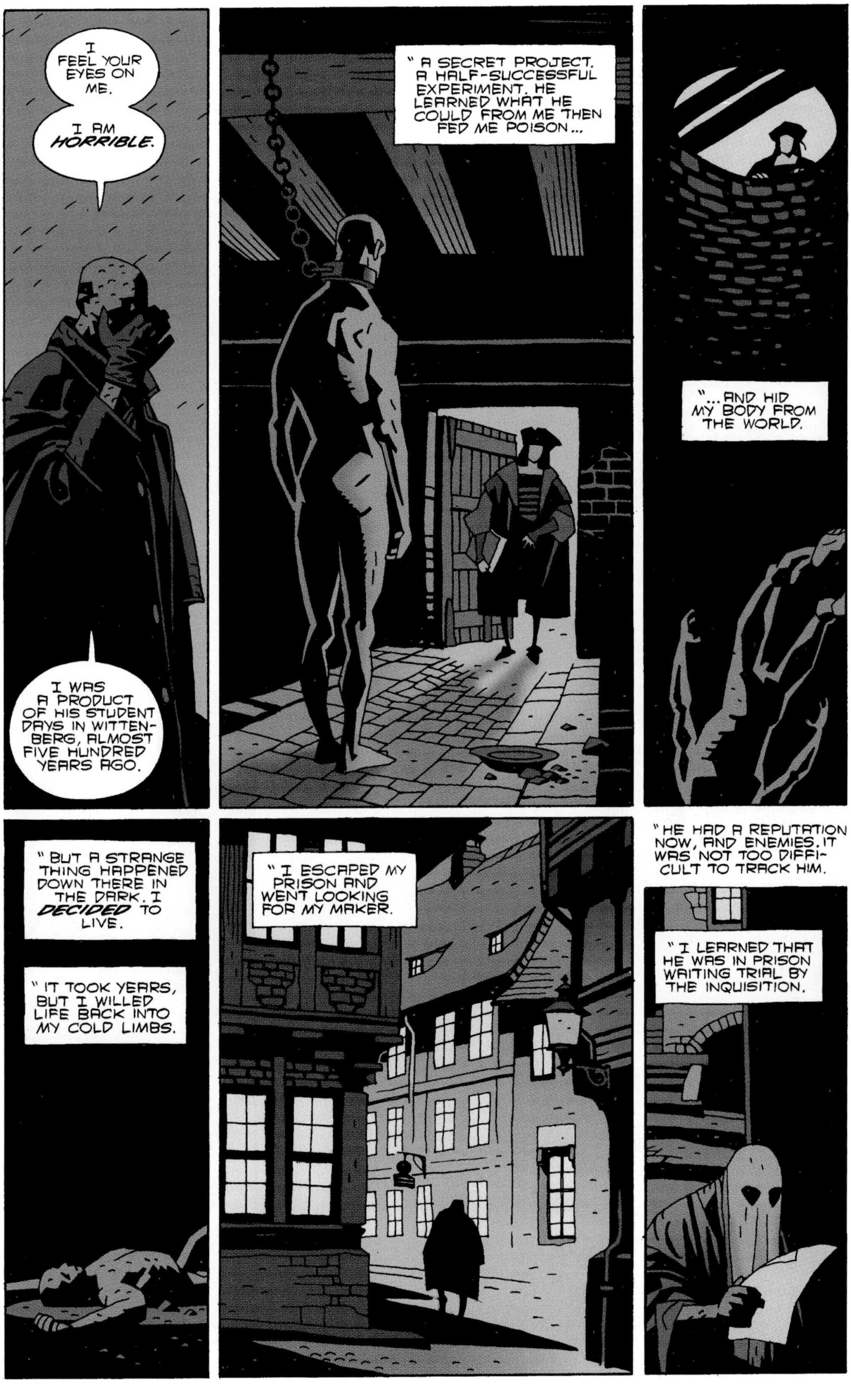
I FEEL YOUR EYES ON ME.
I AM *HORRIBLE*.
I WAS A PRODUCT OF HIS STUDENT DAYS IN WITTEN-BERG, ALMOST FIVE HUNDRED YEARS AGO.
"A SECRET PROJECT. A HALF-SUCCESSFUL EXPERIMENT. HE LEARNED WHAT HE COULD FROM ME THEN FED ME POISON...
"...AND HID MY BODY FROM THE WORLD.
"BUT A STRANGE THING HAPPENED DOWN THERE IN THE DARK. I *DECIDED* TO LIVE.
"IT TOOK YEARS, BUT I WILLED LIFE BACK INTO MY COLD LIMBS.
"I ESCAPED MY PRISON AND WENT LOOKING FOR MY MAKER.
"HE HAD A REPUTATION NOW, AND ENEMIES. IT WAS NOT TOO DIFFI-CULT TO TRACK HIM.
"I LEARNED THAT HE WAS IN PRISON WAITING TRIAL BY THE INQUISITION.

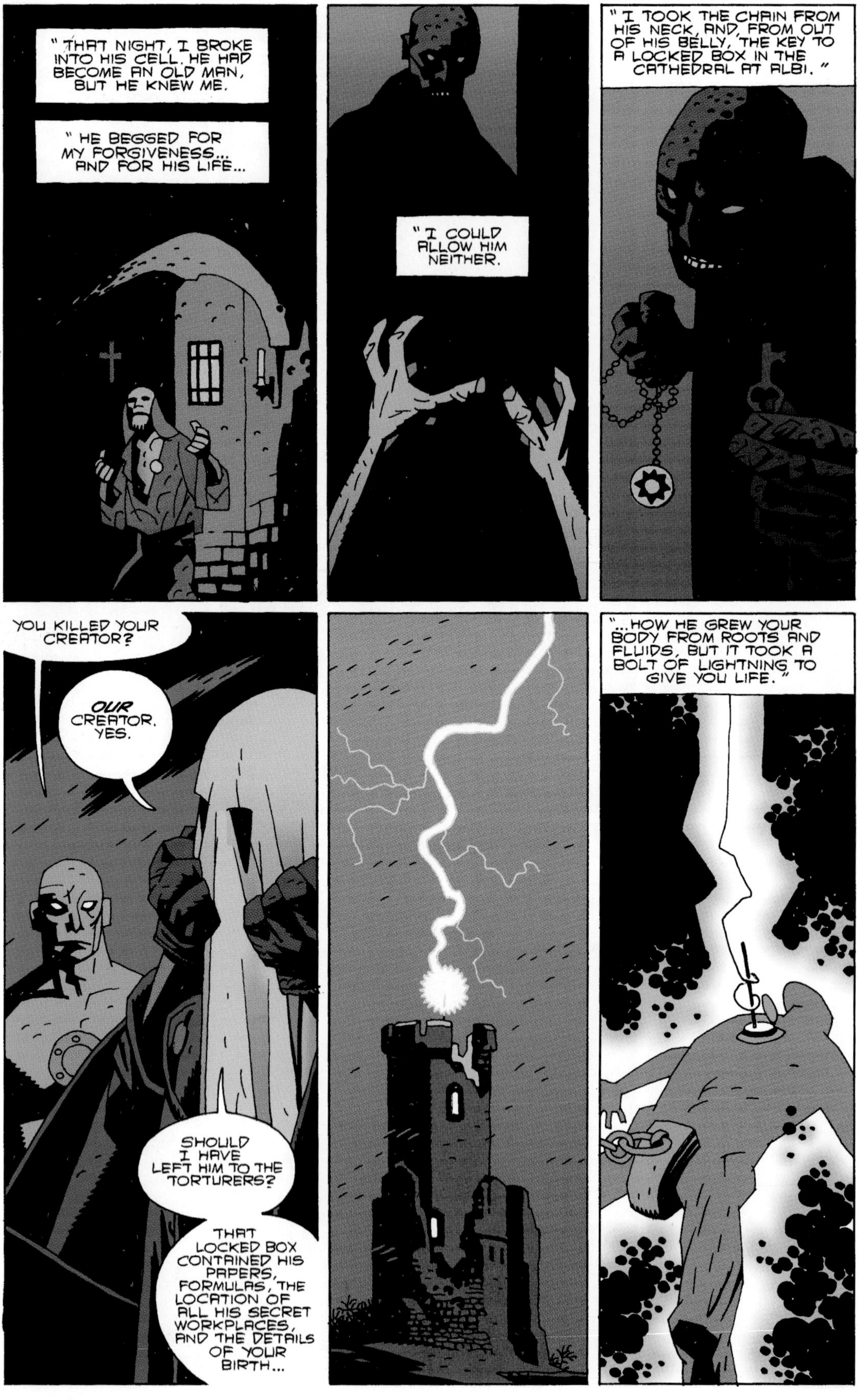
"THAT NIGHT, I BROKE INTO HIS CELL. HE HAD BECOME AN OLD MAN, BUT HE KNEW ME.
"HE BEGGED FOR MY FORGIVENESS... AND FOR HIS LIFE...
"I COULD ALLOW HIM NEITHER.
"I TOOK THE CHAIN FROM HIS NECK, AND, FROM OUT OF HIS BELLY, THE KEY TO A LOCKED BOX IN THE CATHEDRAL AT ALBI."
YOU KILLED YOUR CREATOR?
OUR CREATOR. YES.
SHOULD I HAVE LEFT HIM TO THE TORTURERS?
THAT LOCKED BOX CONTAINED HIS PAPERS, FORMULAS, THE LOCATION OF ALL HIS SECRET WORKPLACES, AND THE DETAILS OF YOUR BIRTH...
"...HOW HE GREW YOUR BODY FROM ROOTS AND FLUIDS, BUT IT TOOK A BOLT OF LIGHTNING TO GIVE YOU LIFE."

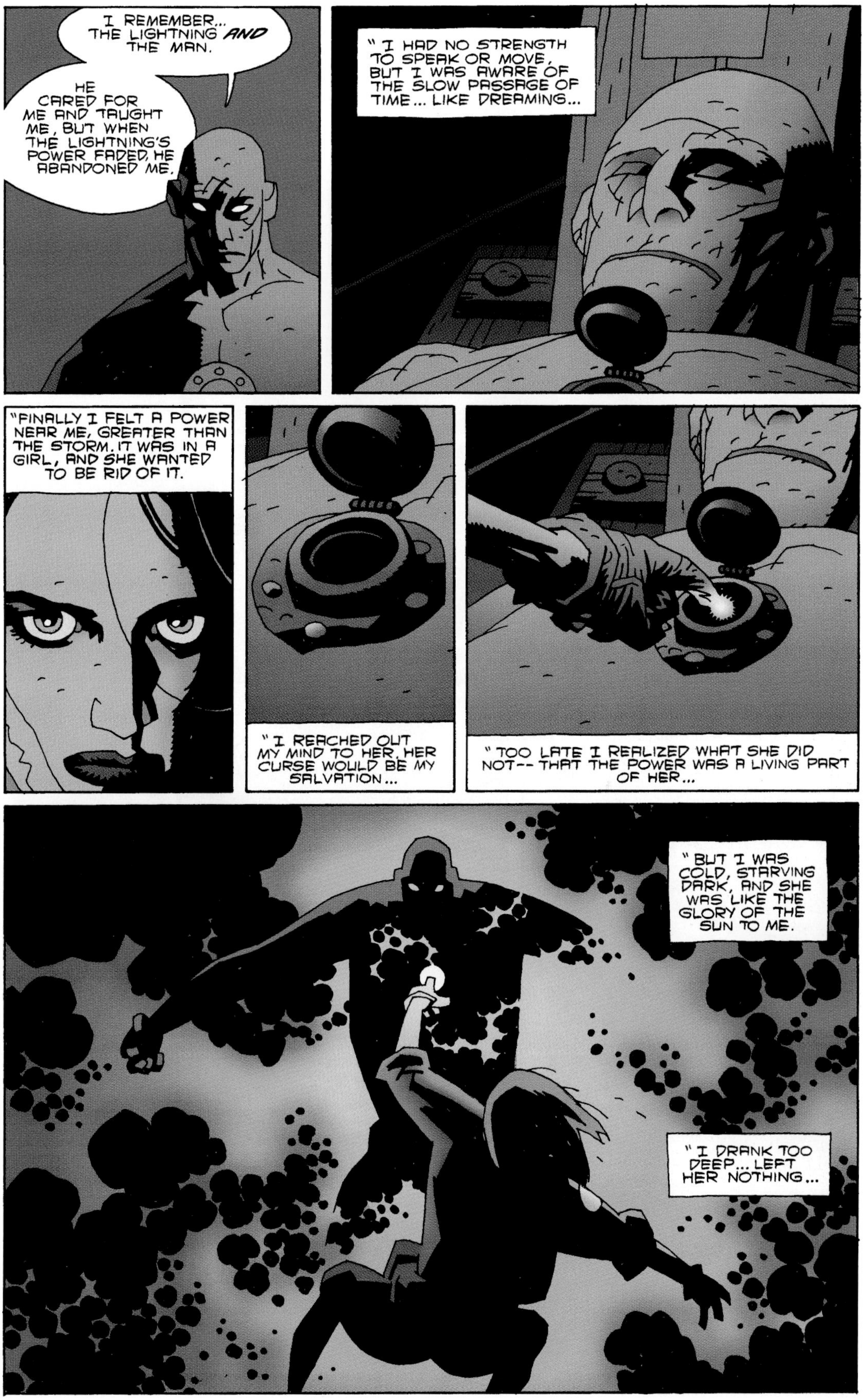
I REMEMBER... THE LIGHTNING AND THE MAN.
HE CARED FOR ME AND TAUGHT ME, BUT WHEN THE LIGHTNING'S POWER FADED, HE ABANDONED ME.
"I HAD NO STRENGTH TO SPEAK OR MOVE, BUT I WAS AWARE OF THE SLOW PASSAGE OF TIME... LIKE DREAMING...
"FINALLY I FELT A POWER NEAR ME, GREATER THAN THE STORM. IT WAS IN A GIRL, AND SHE WANTED TO BE RID OF IT.
"I REACHED OUT MY MIND TO HER. HER CURSE WOULD BE MY SALVATION...
"TOO LATE I REALIZED WHAT SHE DID NOT-- THAT THE POWER WAS A LIVING PART OF HER...
"BUT I WAS COLD, STARVING DARK, AND SHE WAS LIKE THE GLORY OF THE SUN TO ME.
"I DRANK TOO DEEP... LEFT HER NOTHING...

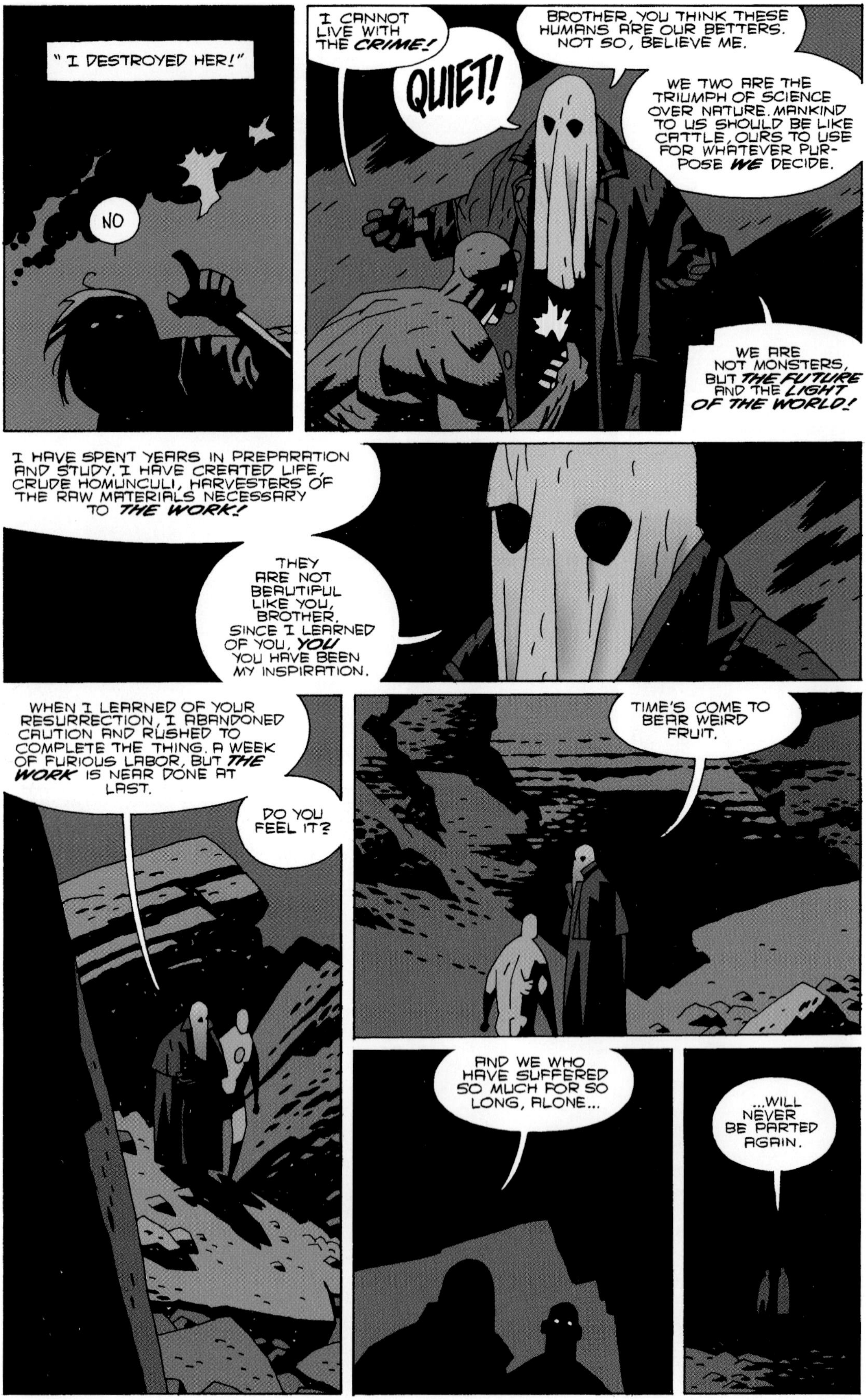
"I DESTROYED HER!"
NO
I CANNOT LIVE WITH THE *CRIME!*
QUIET!
BROTHER, YOU THINK THESE HUMANS ARE OUR BETTERS. NOT SO, BELIEVE ME.
WE TWO ARE THE TRIUMPH OF SCIENCE OVER NATURE. MANKIND TO US SHOULD BE LIKE CATTLE, OURS TO USE FOR WHATEVER PURPOSE *WE* DECIDE.
WE ARE NOT MONSTERS, BUT *THE FUTURE* AND THE *LIGHT OF THE WORLD!*
I HAVE SPENT YEARS IN PREPARATION AND STUDY. I HAVE CREATED LIFE, CRUDE HOMUNCULI, HARVESTERS OF THE RAW MATERIALS NECESSARY TO *THE WORK!*
THEY ARE NOT BEAUTIFUL LIKE YOU, BROTHER. SINCE I LEARNED OF YOU, *YOU* YOU HAVE BEEN MY INSPIRATION.
WHEN I LEARNED OF YOUR RESURRECTION, I ABANDONED CAUTION AND RUSHED TO COMPLETE THE THING. A WEEK OF FURIOUS LABOR, BUT *THE WORK* IS NEAR DONE AT LAST.
DO YOU FEEL IT?
TIME'S COME TO BEAR WEIRD FRUIT.
AND WE WHO HAVE SUFFERED SO MUCH FOR SO LONG, ALONE...
...WILL NEVER BE PARTED AGAIN.

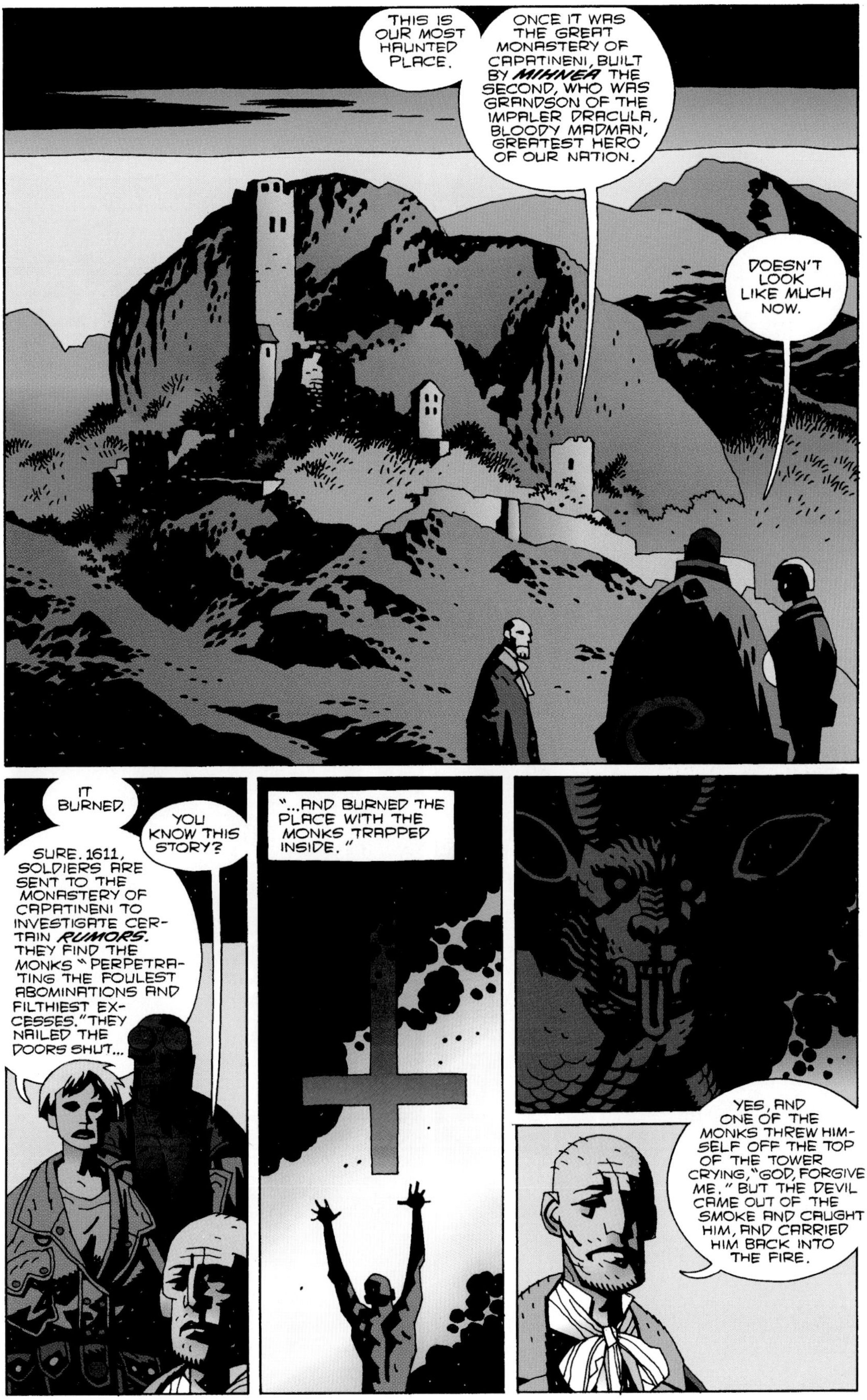
THIS IS OUR MOST HAUNTED PLACE.
ONCE IT WAS THE GREAT MONASTERY OF CAPATINENI, BUILT BY MIHNEA THE SECOND, WHO WAS GRANDSON OF THE IMPALER DRACULA, BLOODY MADMAN, GREATEST HERO OF OUR NATION.
DOESN'T LOOK LIKE MUCH NOW.
IT BURNED.
YOU KNOW THIS STORY?
SURE. 1611, SOLDIERS ARE SENT TO THE MONASTERY OF CAPATINENI TO INVESTIGATE CERTAIN RUMORS. THEY FIND THE MONKS "PERPETRATING THE FOULEST ABOMINATIONS AND FILTHIEST EXCESSES." THEY NAILED THE DOORS SHUT...
"...AND BURNED THE PLACE WITH THE MONKS TRAPPED INSIDE."
YES, AND ONE OF THE MONKS THREW HIMSELF OFF THE TOP OF THE TOWER CRYING, "GOD, FORGIVE ME." BUT THE DEVIL CAME OUT OF THE SMOKE AND CAUGHT HIM, AND CARRIED HIM BACK INTO THE FIRE.

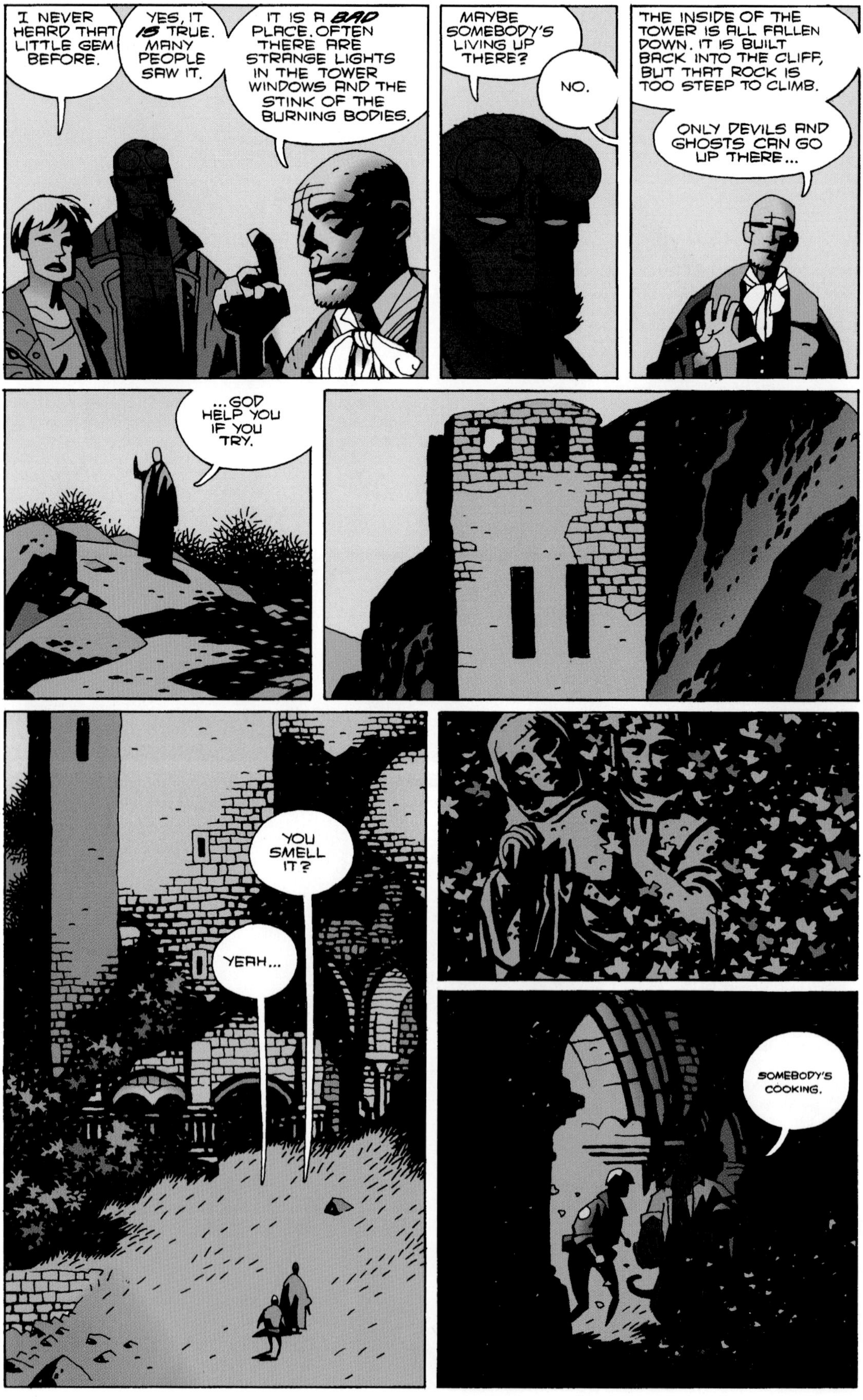
I NEVER HEARD THAT LITTLE GEM BEFORE.
YES, IT *IS* TRUE. MANY PEOPLE SAW IT.
IT IS A *BAD* PLACE. OFTEN THERE ARE STRANGE LIGHTS IN THE TOWER WINDOWS AND THE STINK OF THE BURNING BODIES.
MAYBE SOMEBODY'S LIVING UP THERE?
NO.
THE INSIDE OF THE TOWER IS ALL FALLEN DOWN. IT IS BUILT BACK INTO THE CLIFF, BUT THAT ROCK IS TOO STEEP TO CLIMB.
ONLY DEVILS AND GHOSTS CAN GO UP THERE...
...GOD HELP YOU IF YOU TRY.
YOU SMELL IT?
YEAH...
SOMEBODY'S COOKING.

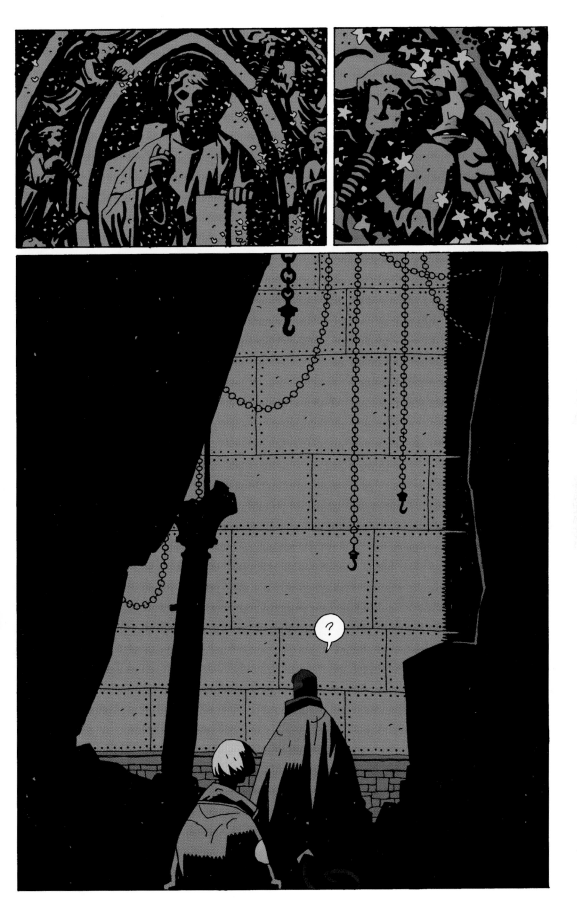

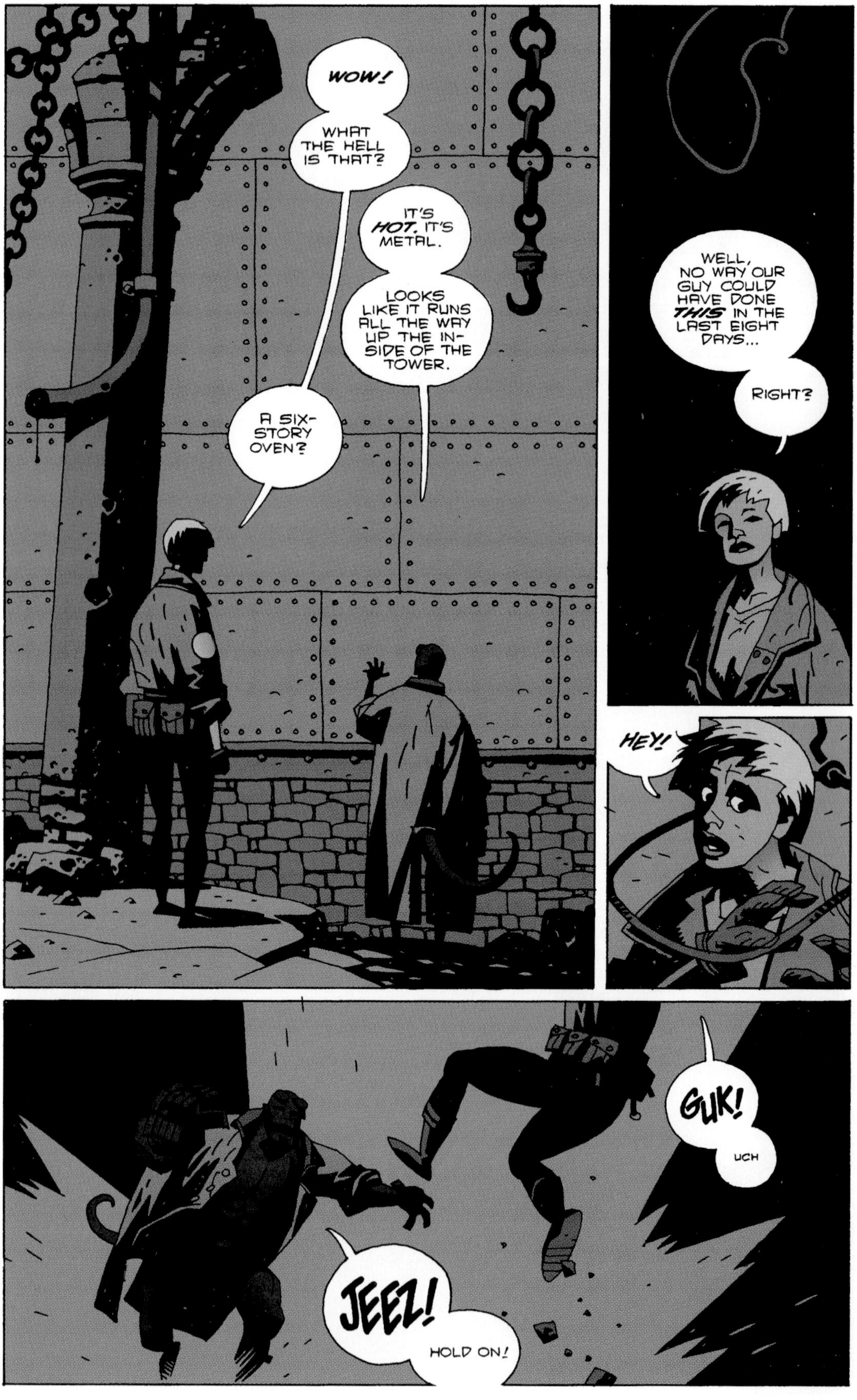
WOW!
WHAT THE HELL IS THAT?
IT'S HOT. IT'S METAL.
LOOKS LIKE IT RUNS ALL THE WAY UP THE INSIDE OF THE TOWER.
A SIX-STORY OVEN?
WELL, NO WAY OUR GUY COULD HAVE DONE THIS IN THE LAST EIGHT DAYS...
RIGHT?
HEY!
GUK!
UCH
JEEZ!
HOLD ON!

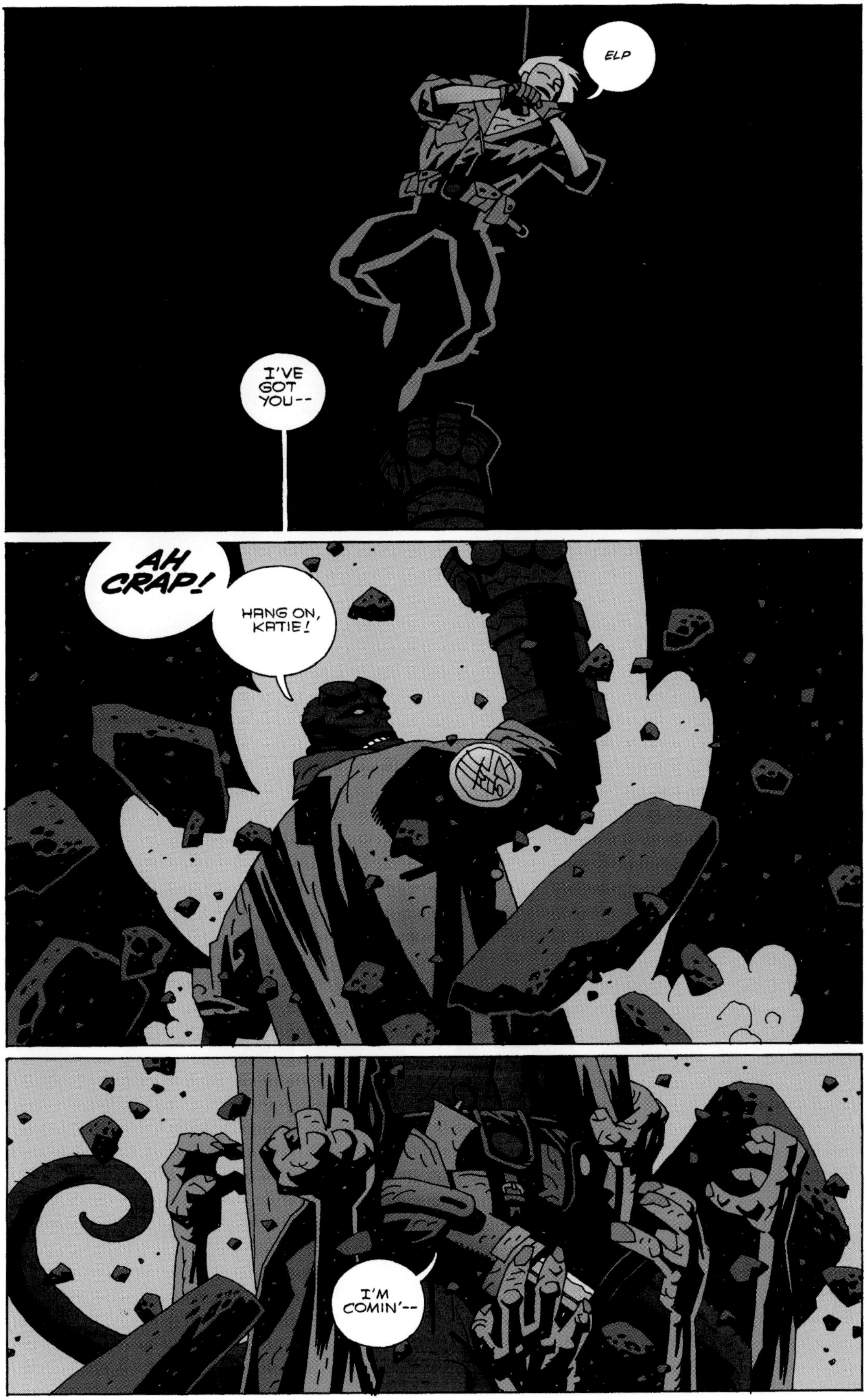
ELP
I'VE GOT YOU--
AH CRAP!
HANG ON, KATIE!
I'M COMIN'--

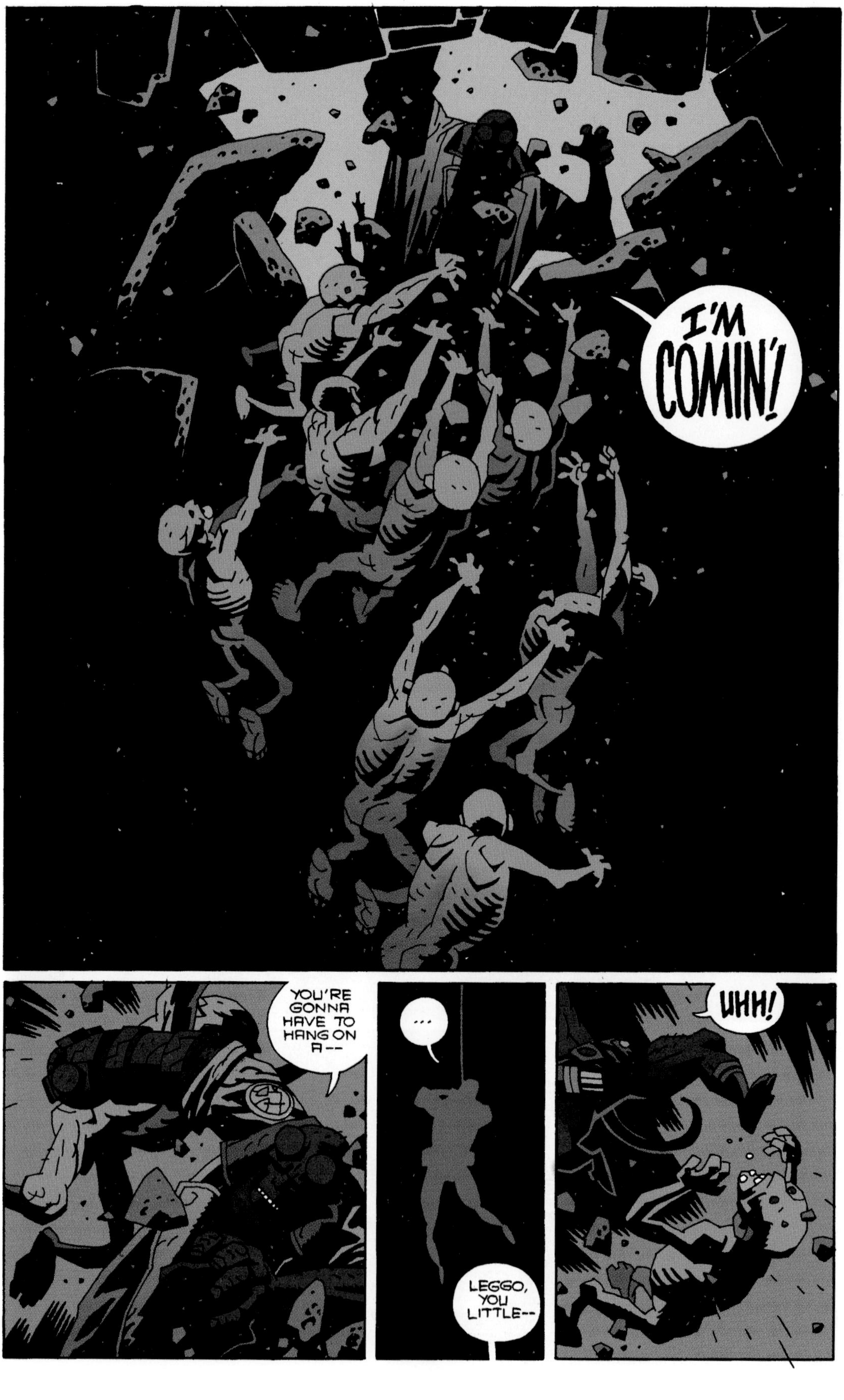
I'M COMIN'!
YOU'RE GONNA HAVE TO HANG ON A--
...
LEGGO, YOU LITTLE--
UHH!

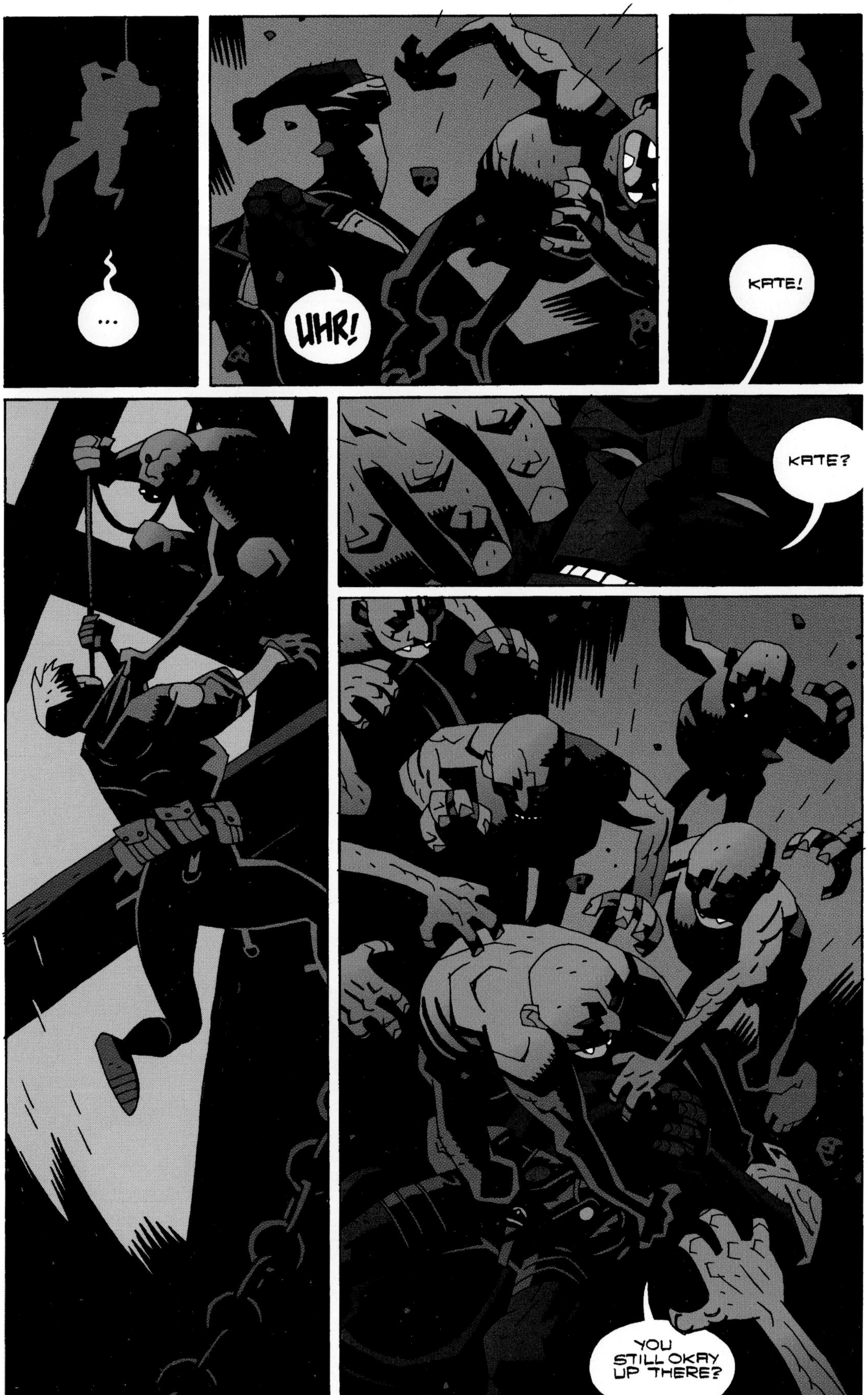
...
UHR!
KATE!
KATE?
YOU STILL OKAY UP THERE?

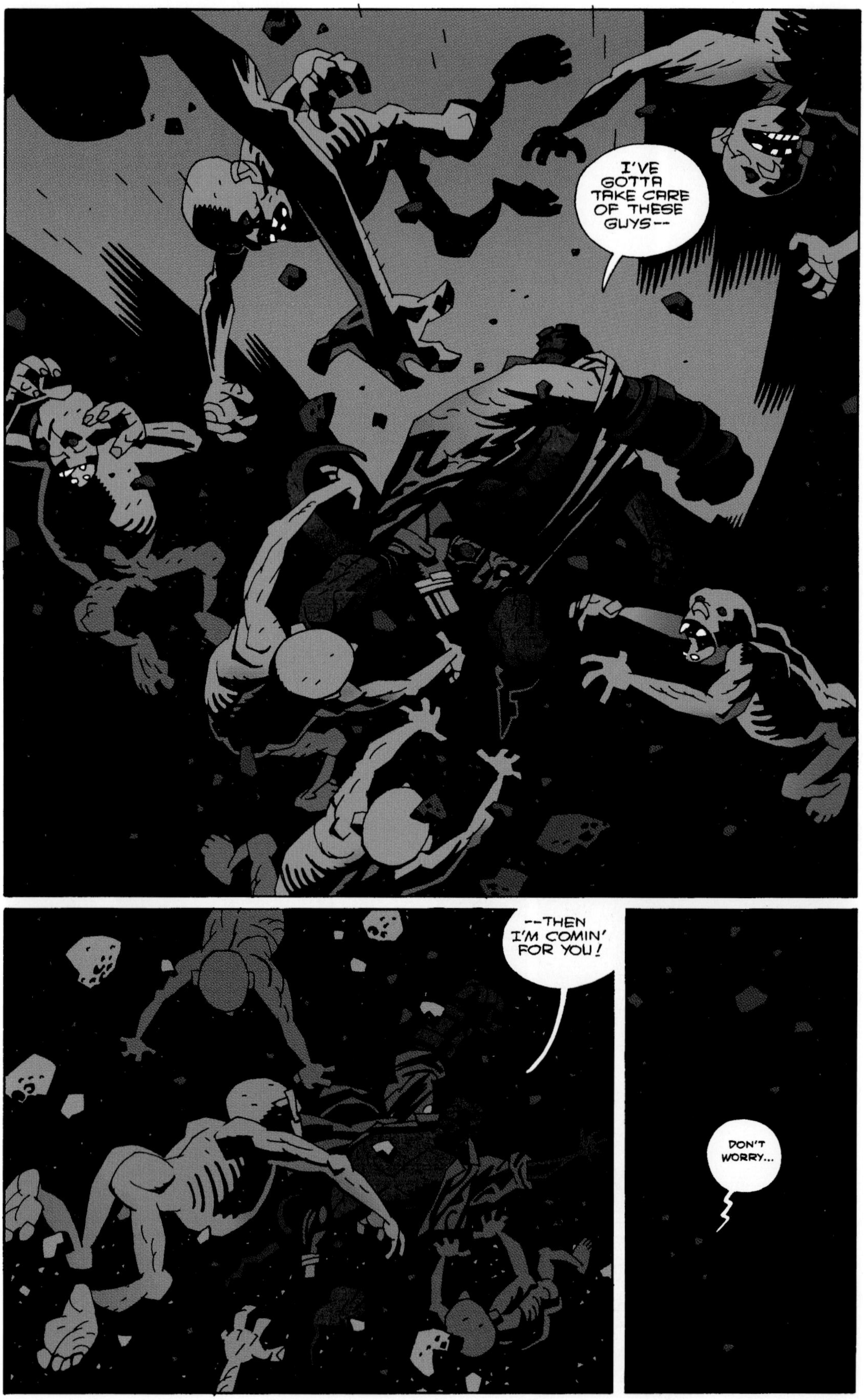
I'VE GOTTA TAKE CARE OF THESE GUYS--
--THEN I'M COMIN' FOR YOU!
DON'T WORRY...

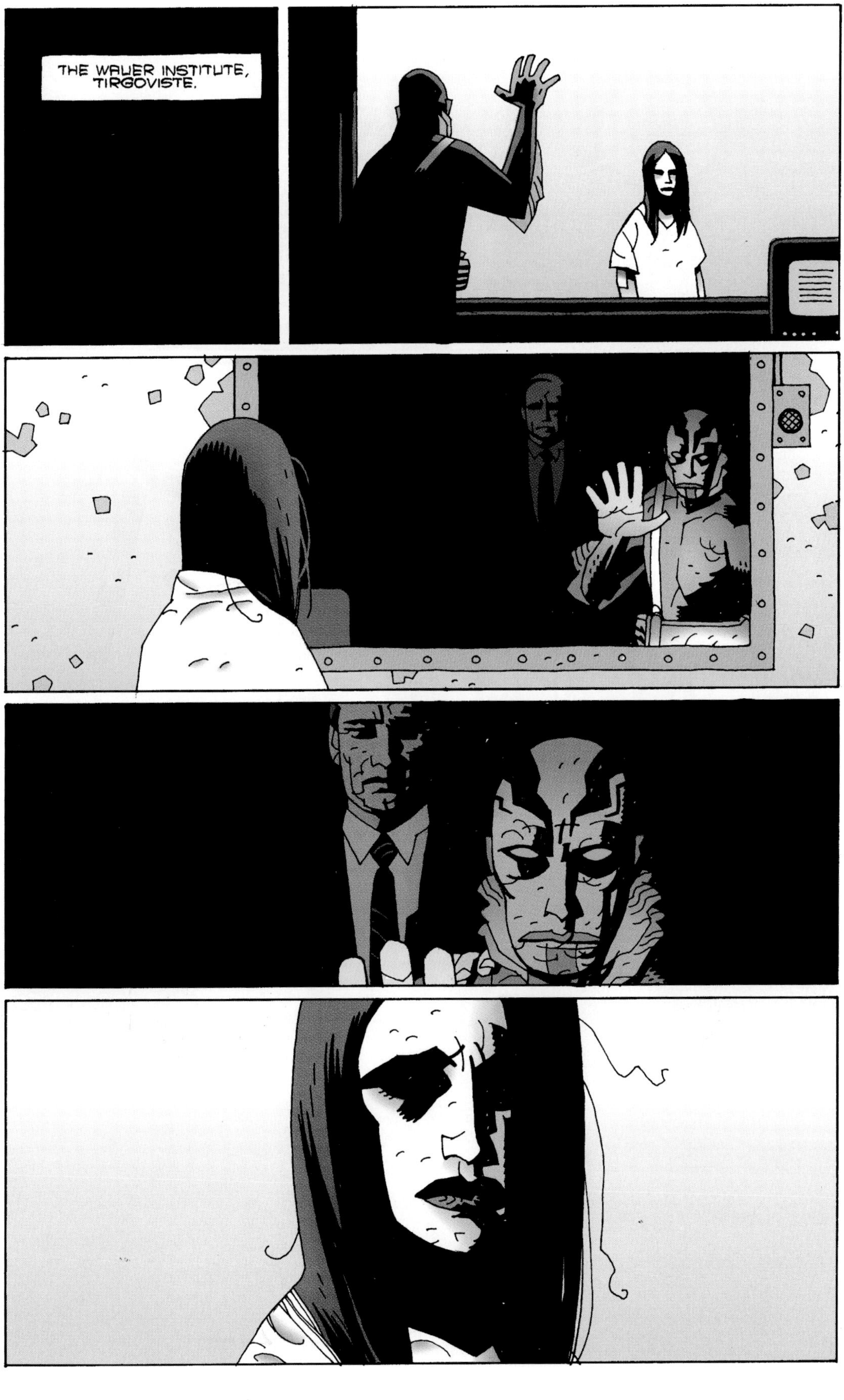
THE WALLER INSTITUTE, TIRGOVISTE.

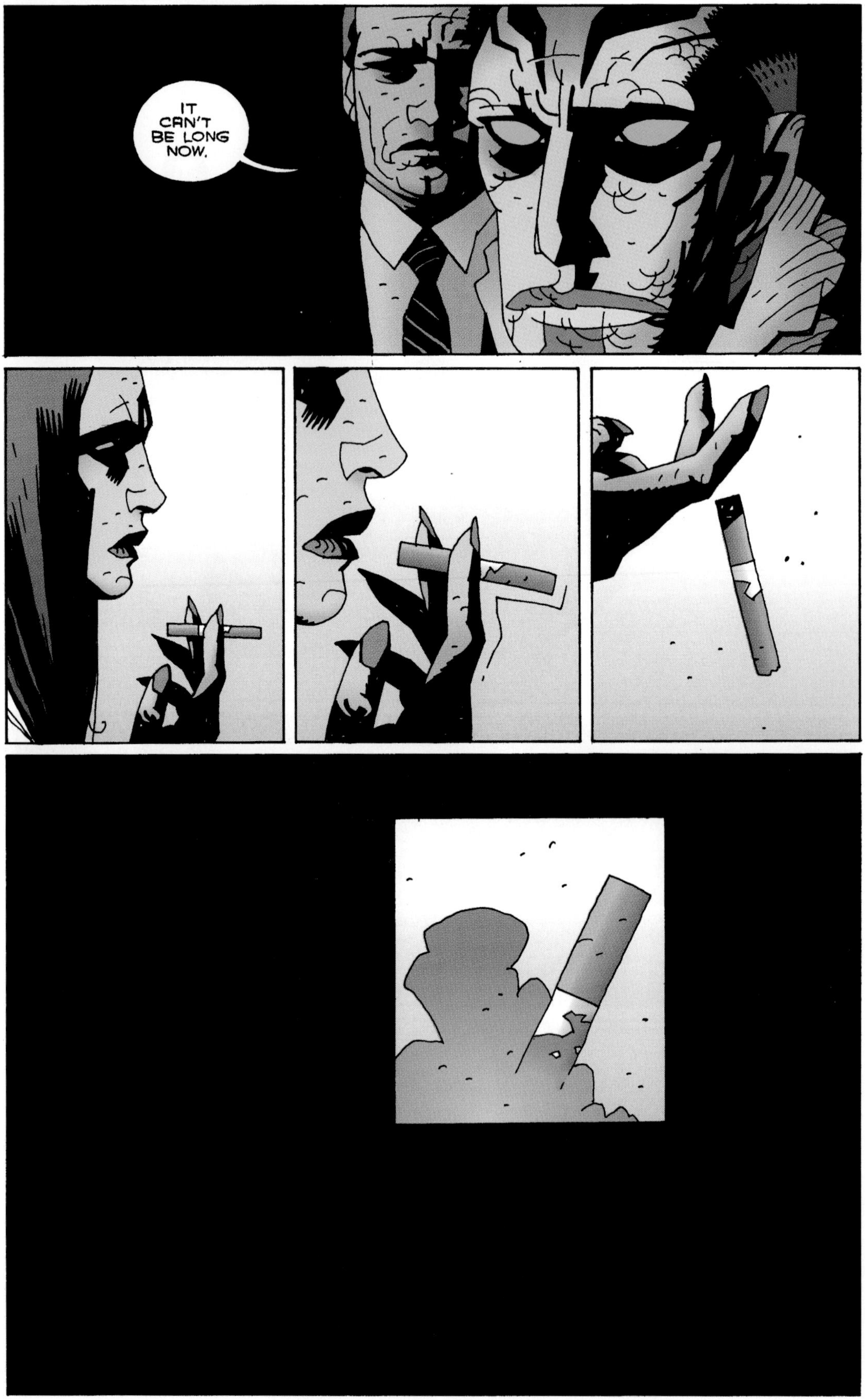
IT CAN'T BE LONG NOW.

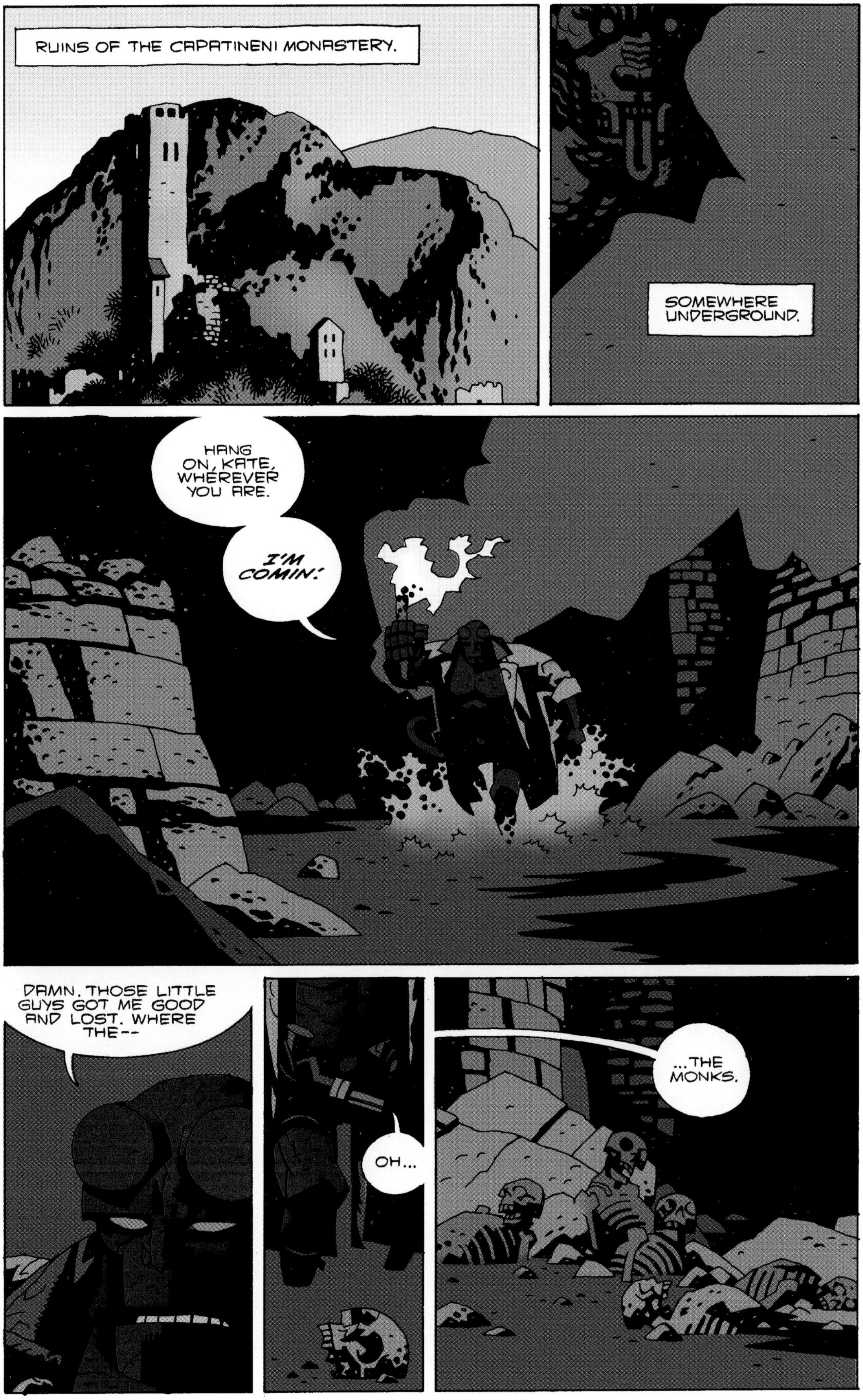
RUINS OF THE CAPATINENI MONASTERY.
SOMEWHERE UNDERGROUND.
HANG ON, KATE, WHEREVER YOU ARE.
I'M COMIN'!
DAMN. THOSE LITTLE GUYS GOT ME GOOD AND LOST. WHERE THE--
OH...
...THE MONKS.

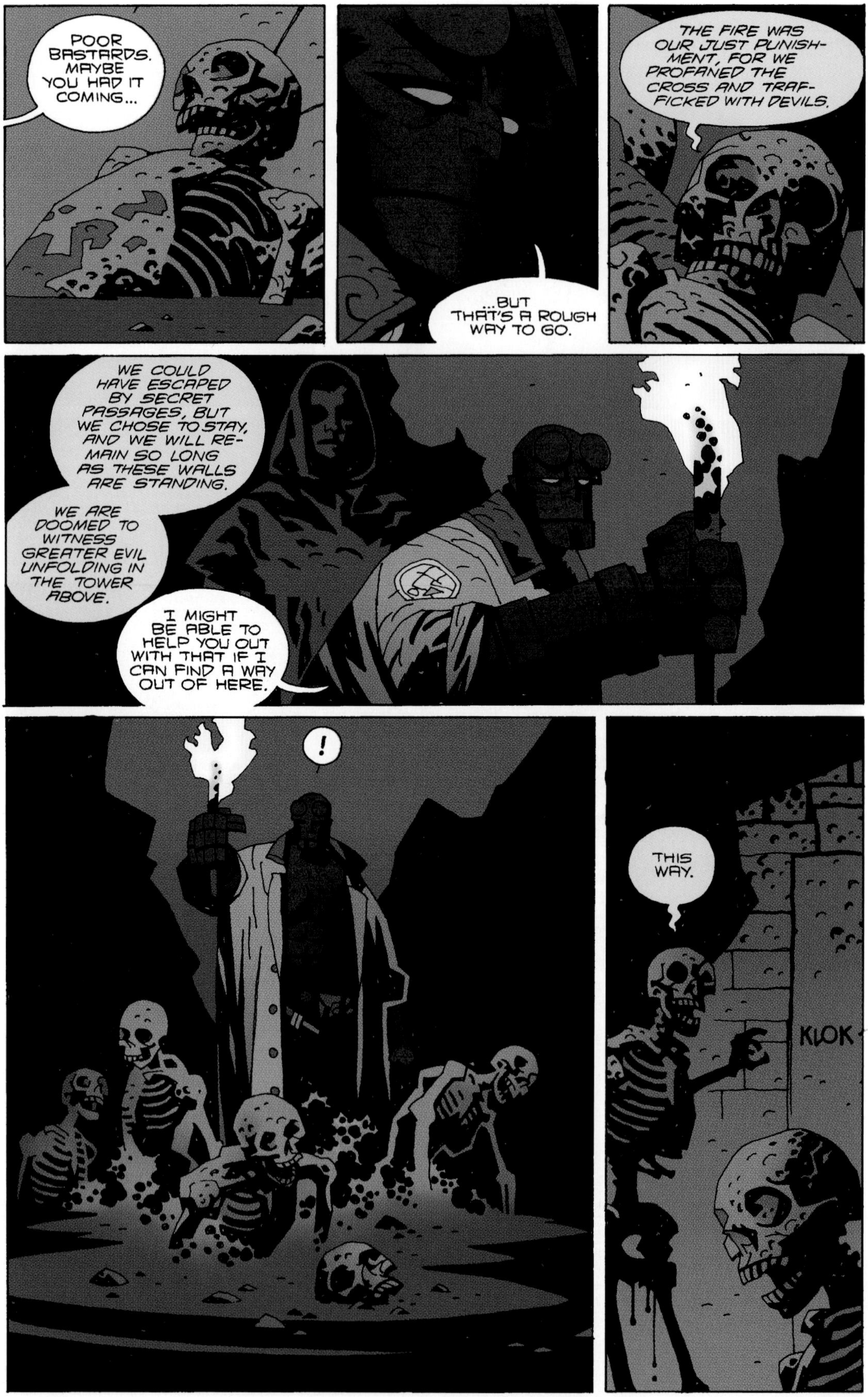
POOR BASTARDS. MAYBE YOU HAD IT COMING...
...BUT THAT'S A ROUGH WAY TO GO.
THE FIRE WAS OUR JUST PUNISHMENT, FOR WE PROFANED THE CROSS AND TRAFFICKED WITH DEVILS.
WE COULD HAVE ESCAPED BY SECRET PASSAGES, BUT WE CHOSE TO STAY, AND WE WILL REMAIN SO LONG AS THESE WALLS ARE STANDING.
WE ARE DOOMED TO WITNESS GREATER EVIL UNFOLDING IN THE TOWER ABOVE.
I MIGHT BE ABLE TO HELP YOU OUT WITH THAT IF I CAN FIND A WAY OUT OF HERE.
!
THIS WAY.
KLOK

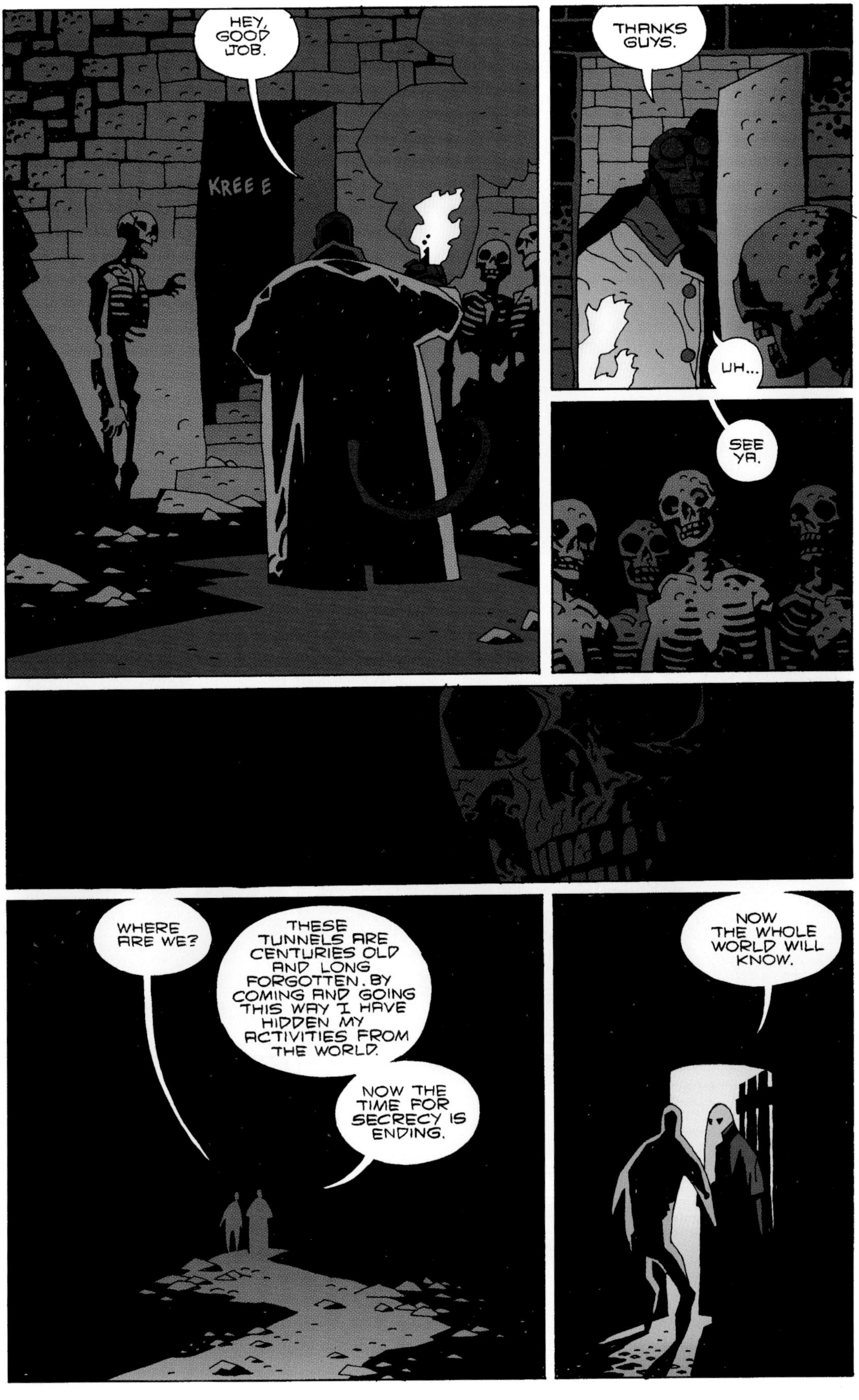
HEY, GOOD JOB.
KREE E
THANKS GUYS.
UH...
SEE YA.
WHERE ARE WE?
THESE TUNNELS ARE CENTURIES OLD AND LONG FORGOTTEN. BY COMING AND GOING THIS WAY I HAVE HIDDEN MY ACTIVITIES FROM THE WORLD.
NOW THE TIME FOR SECRECY IS ENDING.
NOW THE WHOLE WORLD WILL KNOW.

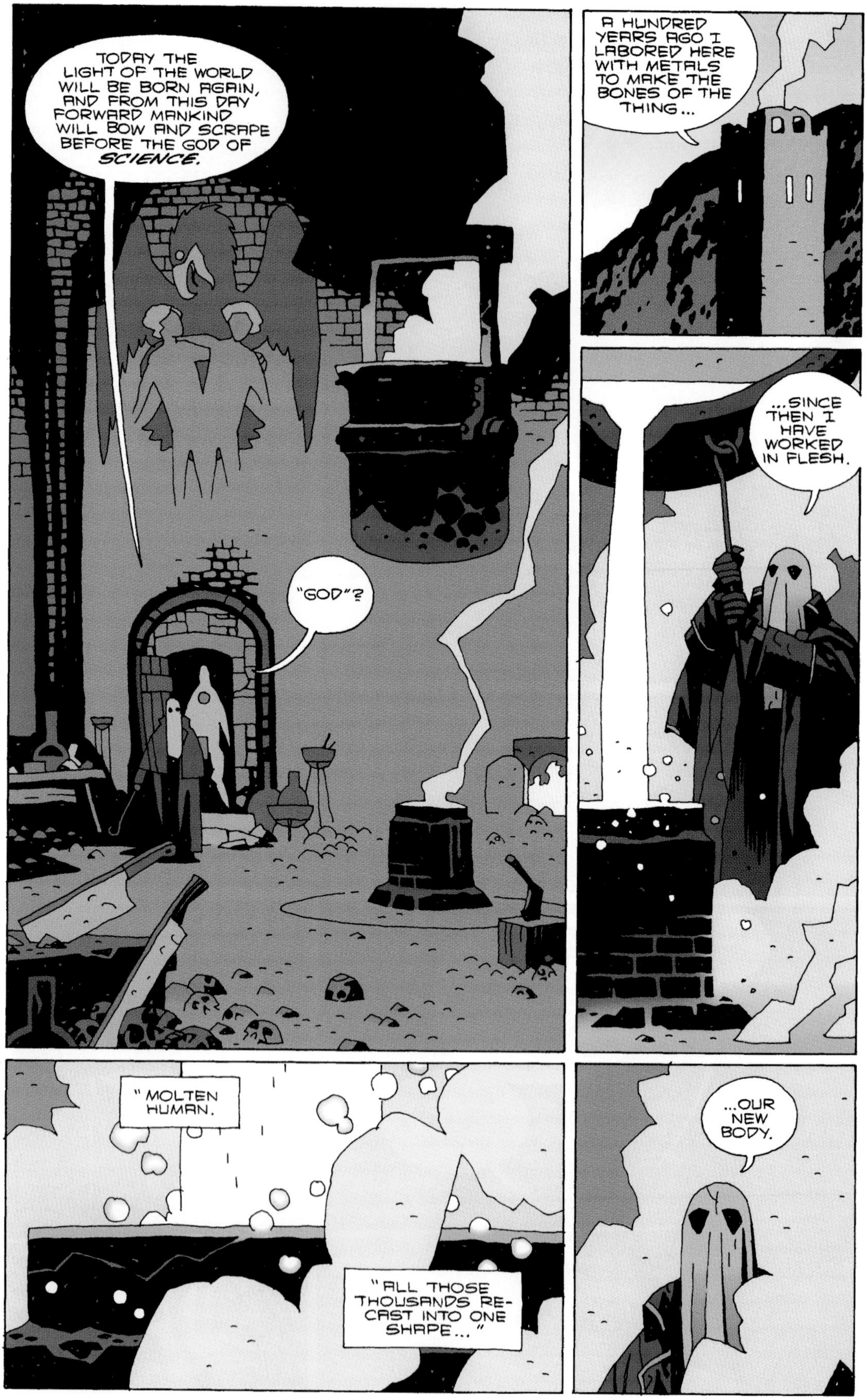
TODAY THE LIGHT OF THE WORLD WILL BE BORN AGAIN, AND FROM THIS DAY FORWARD MANKIND WILL BOW AND SCRAPE BEFORE THE GOD OF *SCIENCE.*
"GOD"?
A HUNDRED YEARS AGO I LABORED HERE WITH METALS TO MAKE THE BONES OF THE THING...
...SINCE THEN I HAVE WORKED IN FLESH.
"MOLTEN HUMAN.
"ALL THOSE THOUSANDS RE-CAST INTO ONE SHAPE..."
...OUR NEW BODY.

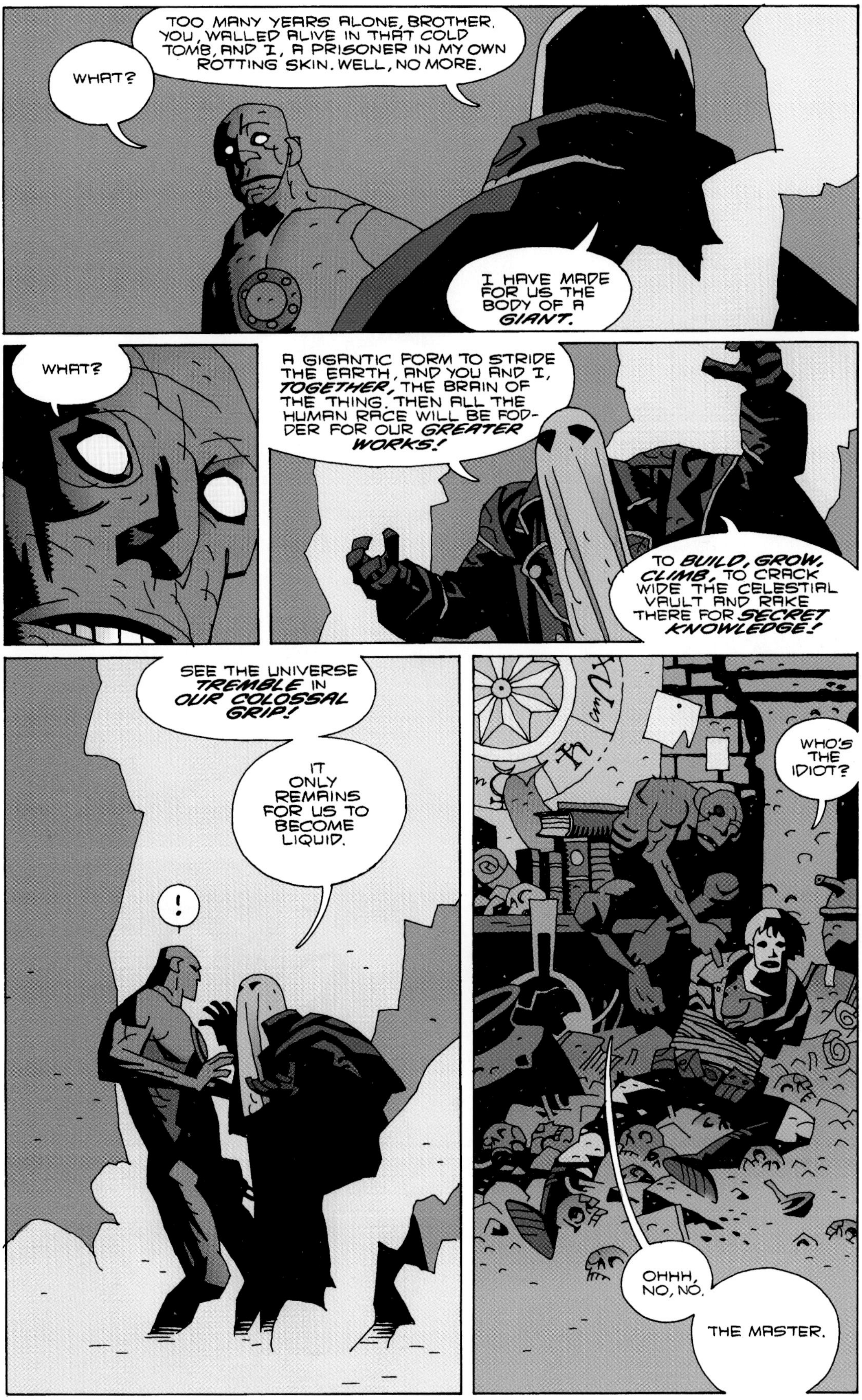
TOO MANY YEARS ALONE, BROTHER. YOU, WALLED ALIVE IN THAT COLD TOMB, AND I, A PRISONER IN MY OWN ROTTING SKIN. WELL, NO MORE.
WHAT?
I HAVE MADE FOR US THE BODY OF A GIANT.
WHAT?
A GIGANTIC FORM TO STRIDE THE EARTH, AND YOU AND I, TOGETHER, THE BRAIN OF THE THING. THEN ALL THE HUMAN RACE WILL BE FODDER FOR OUR GREATER WORKS!
TO BUILD, GROW, CLIMB, TO CRACK WIDE THE CELESTIAL VAULT AND RAKE THERE FOR SECRET KNOWLEDGE!
SEE THE UNIVERSE TREMBLE IN OUR COLOSSAL GRIP!
IT ONLY REMAINS FOR US TO BECOME LIQUID.
!
WHO'S THE IDIOT?
OHHH, NO, NO.
THE MASTER.

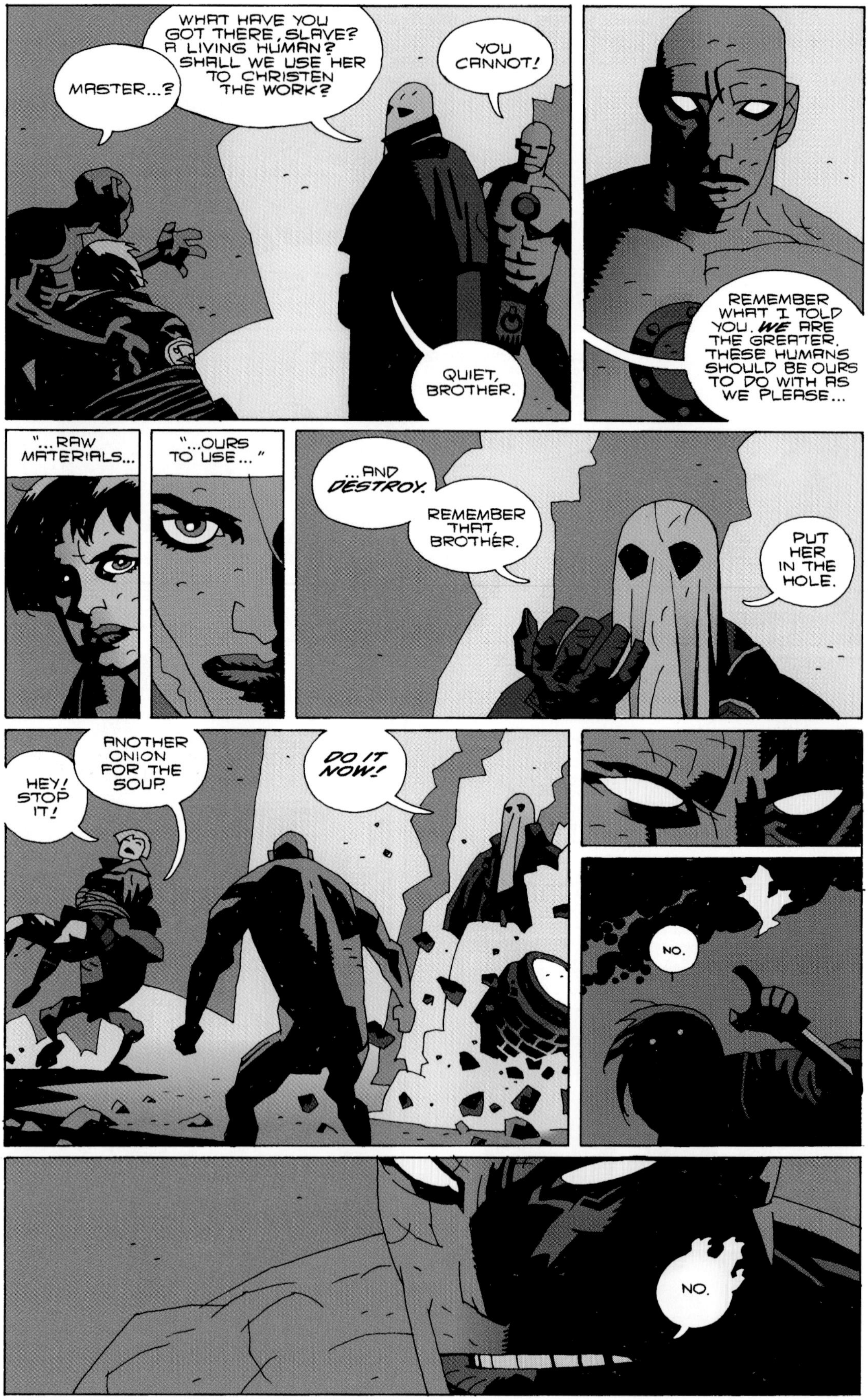
MASTER...?
WHAT HAVE YOU GOT THERE, SLAVE? A LIVING HUMAN? SHALL WE USE HER TO CHRISTEN THE WORK?
YOU CANNOT!
QUIET, BROTHER.
REMEMBER WHAT I TOLD YOU. WE ARE THE GREATER. THESE HUMANS SHOULD BE OURS TO DO WITH AS WE PLEASE...
"...RAW MATERIALS...
"...OURS TO USE..."
...AND DESTROY.
REMEMBER THAT, BROTHER.
PUT HER IN THE HOLE.
HEY! STOP IT!
ANOTHER ONION FOR THE SOUP.
DO IT NOW!
NO.
NO.

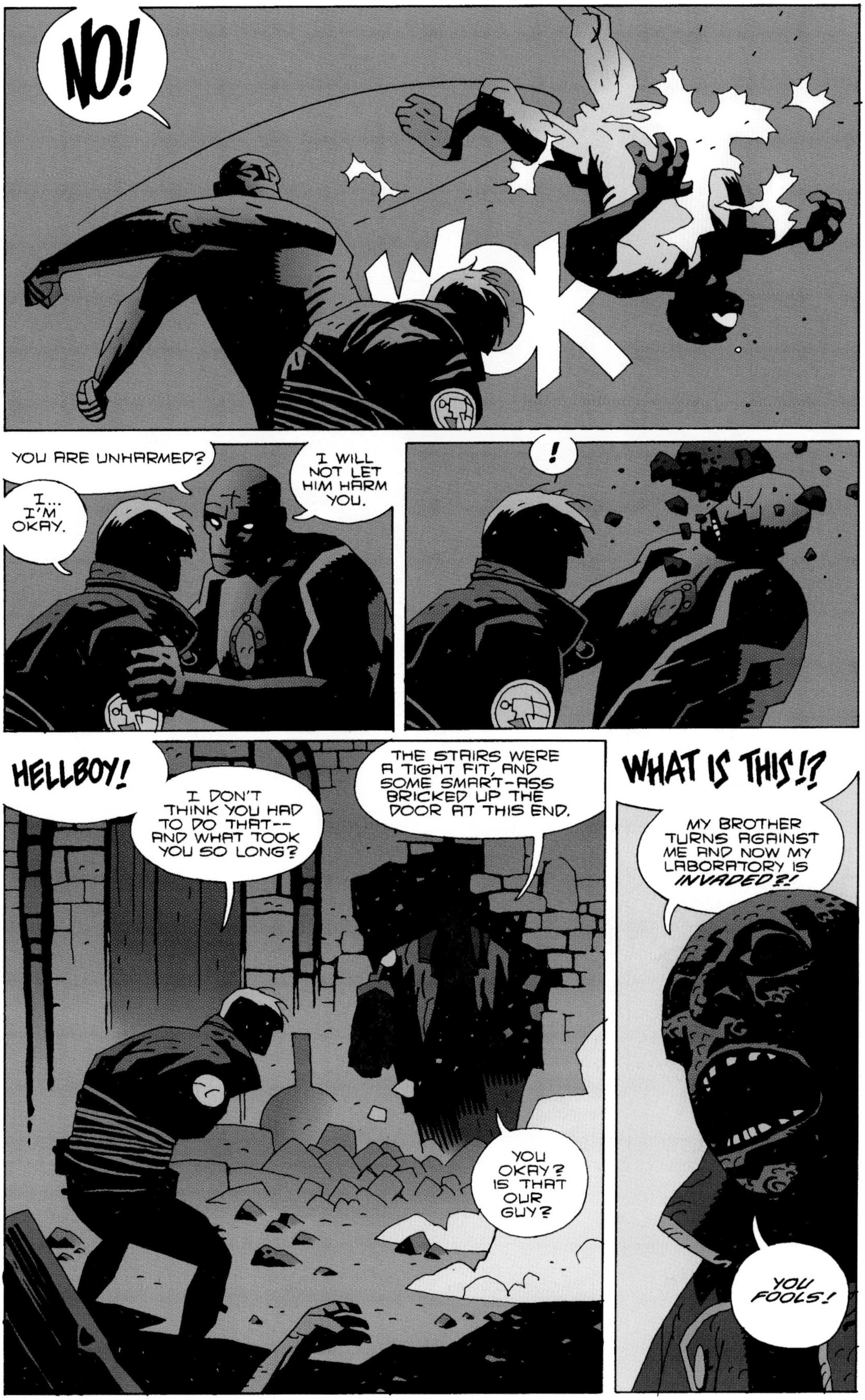

NO!
WOK
YOU ARE UNHARMED?
I... I'M OKAY.
I WILL NOT LET HIM HARM YOU.
!
HELLBOY!
I DON'T THINK YOU HAD TO DO THAT-- AND WHAT TOOK YOU SO LONG?
THE STAIRS WERE A TIGHT FIT, AND SOME SMART-ASS BRICKED UP THE DOOR AT THIS END.
YOU OKAY? IS THAT OUR GUY?
WHAT IS THIS!?
MY BROTHER TURNS AGAINST ME AND NOW MY LABORATORY IS INVADED?!
YOU FOOLS!

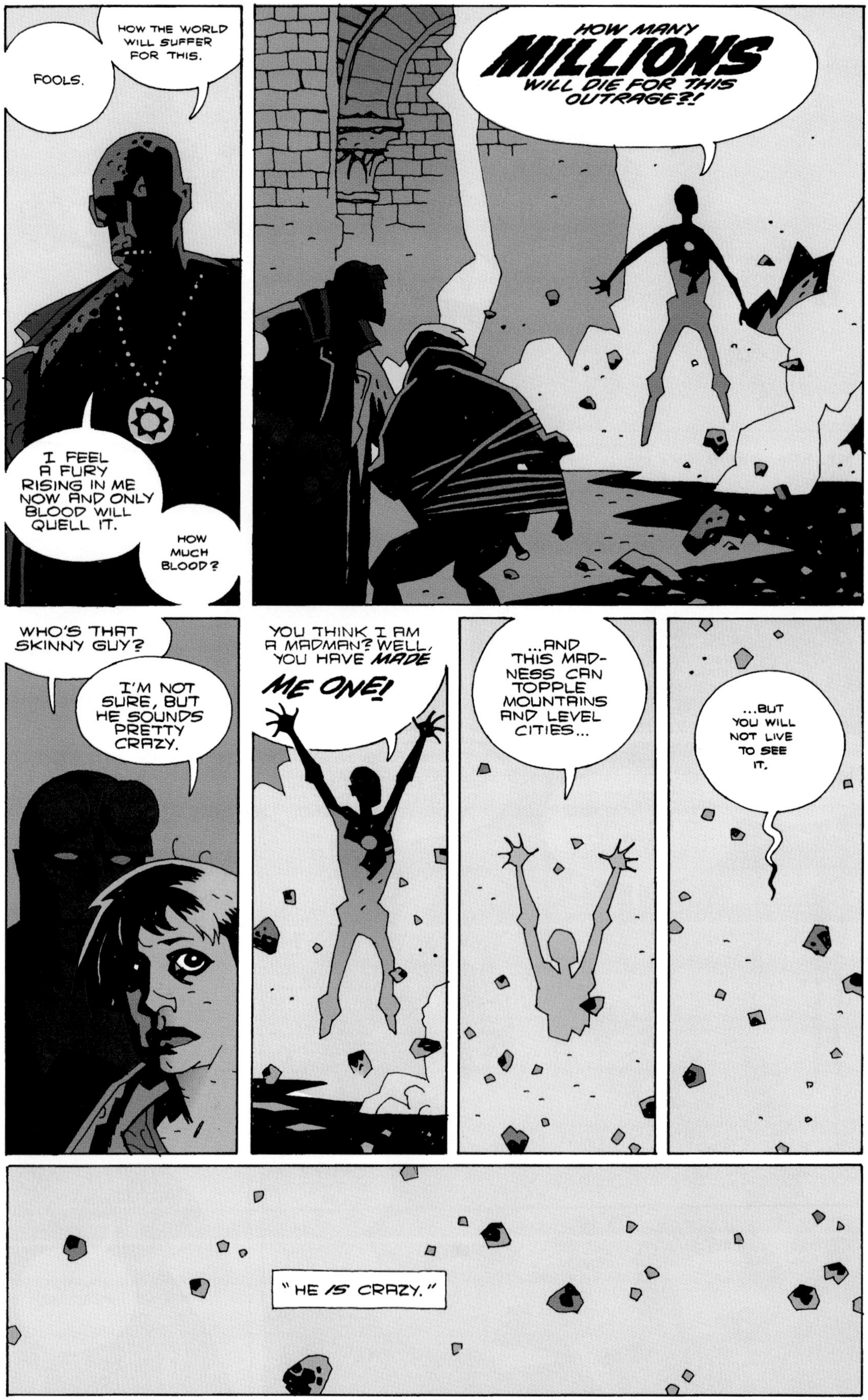
FOOLS.
HOW THE WORLD WILL SUFFER FOR THIS.
I FEEL A FURY RISING IN ME NOW AND ONLY BLOOD WILL QUELL IT.
HOW MUCH BLOOD?
HOW MANY MILLIONS WILL DIE FOR THIS OUTRAGE?!
WHO'S THAT SKINNY GUY?
I'M NOT SURE, BUT HE SOUNDS PRETTY CRAZY.
YOU THINK I AM A MADMAN? WELL, YOU HAVE MADE ME ONE!
...AND THIS MADNESS CAN TOPPLE MOUNTAINS AND LEVEL CITIES...
...BUT YOU WILL NOT LIVE TO SEE IT.
"HE IS CRAZY."

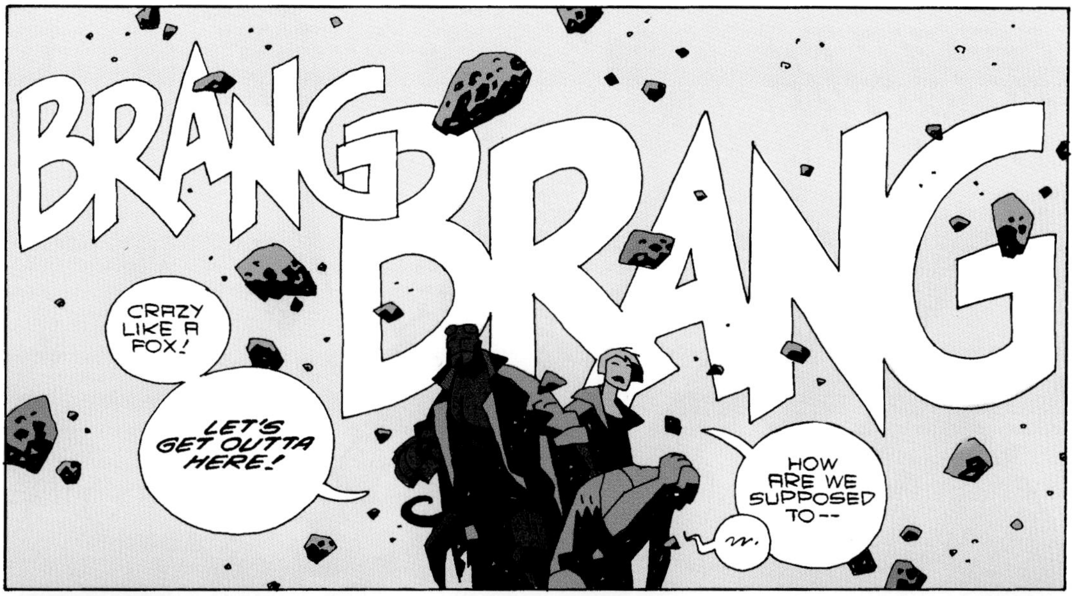
BRANG
BRANG
CRAZY LIKE A FOX!
LET'S GET OUTTA HERE!
HOW ARE WE SUPPOSED TO--

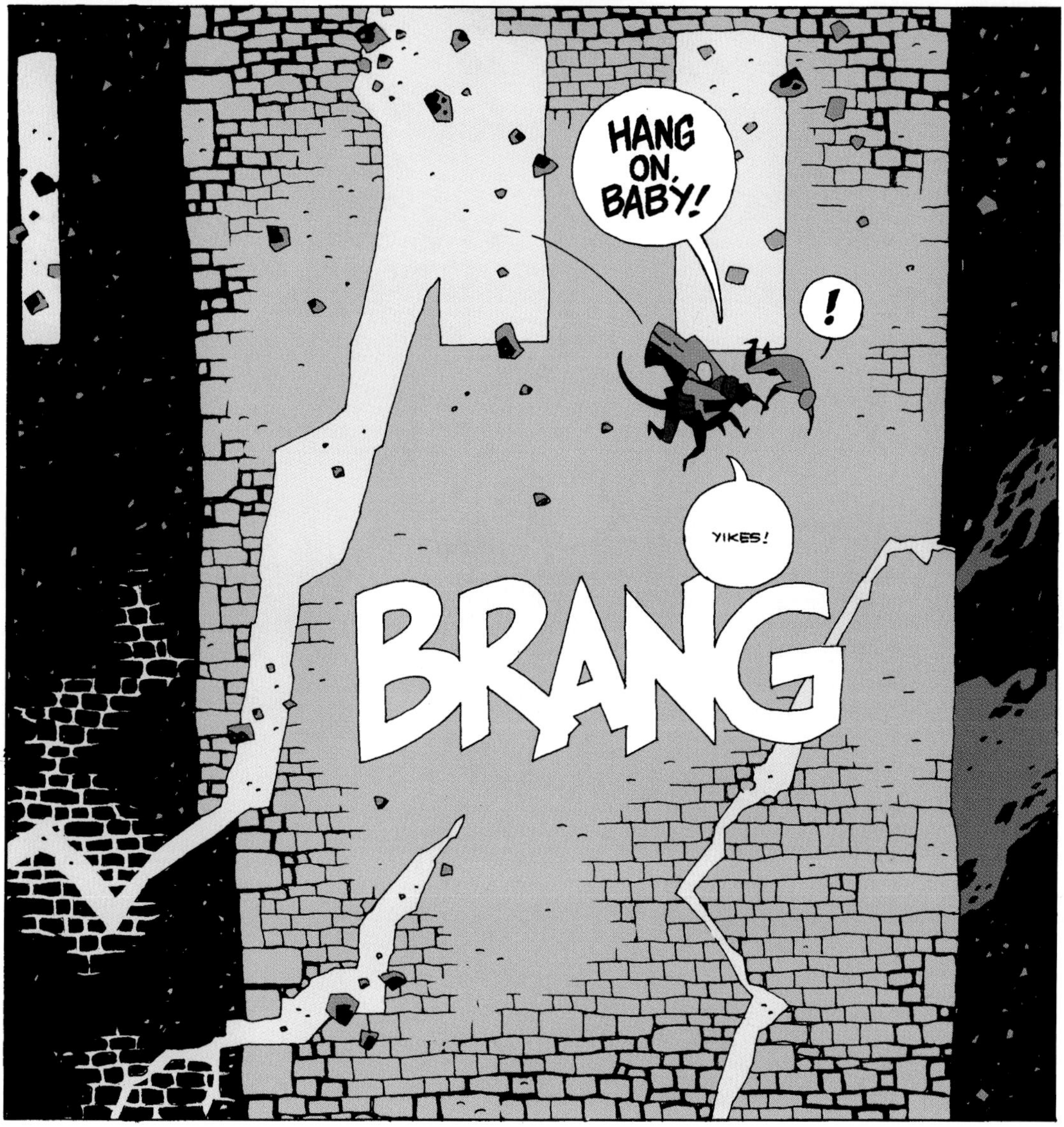
HANG ON, BABY!
!
YIKES!
BRANG

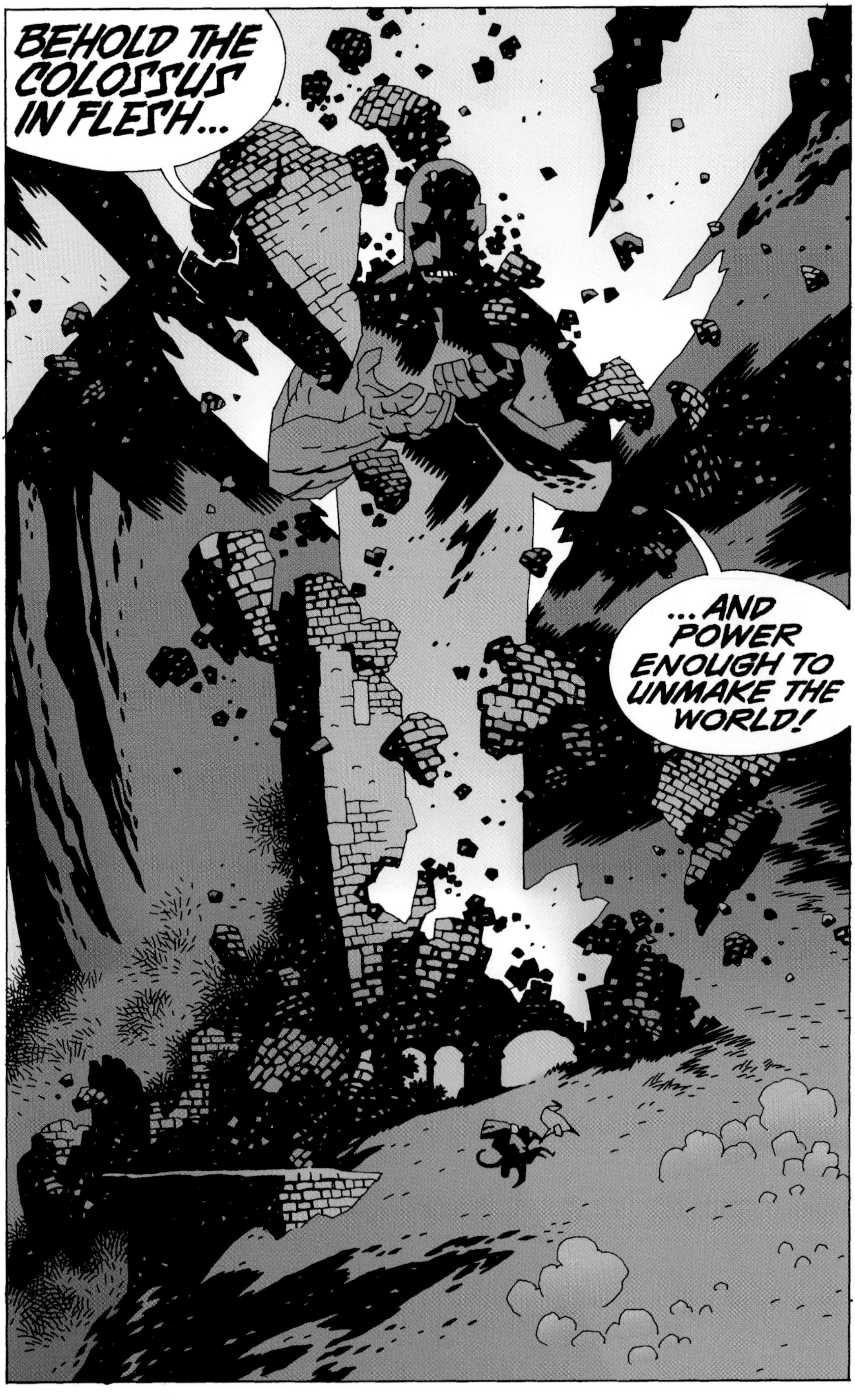
BEHOLD THE COLOSSUS IN FLESH...
...AND POWER ENOUGH TO UNMAKE THE WORLD!

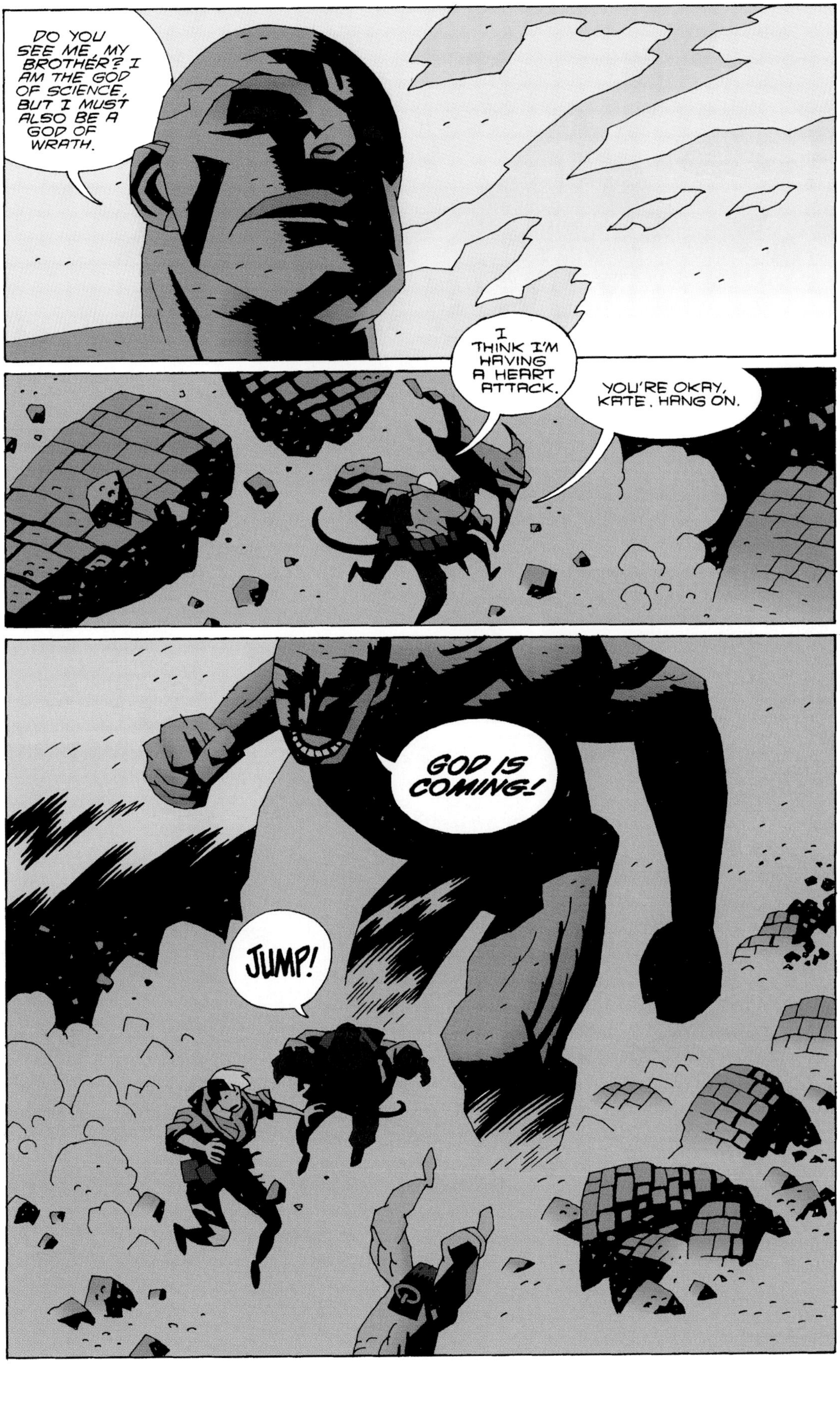
DO YOU SEE ME, MY BROTHER? I AM THE GOD OF SCIENCE, BUT I MUST ALSO BE A GOD OF WRATH.
I THINK I'M HAVING A HEART ATTACK.
YOU'RE OKAY, KATE. HANG ON.
GOD IS COMING!
JUMP!

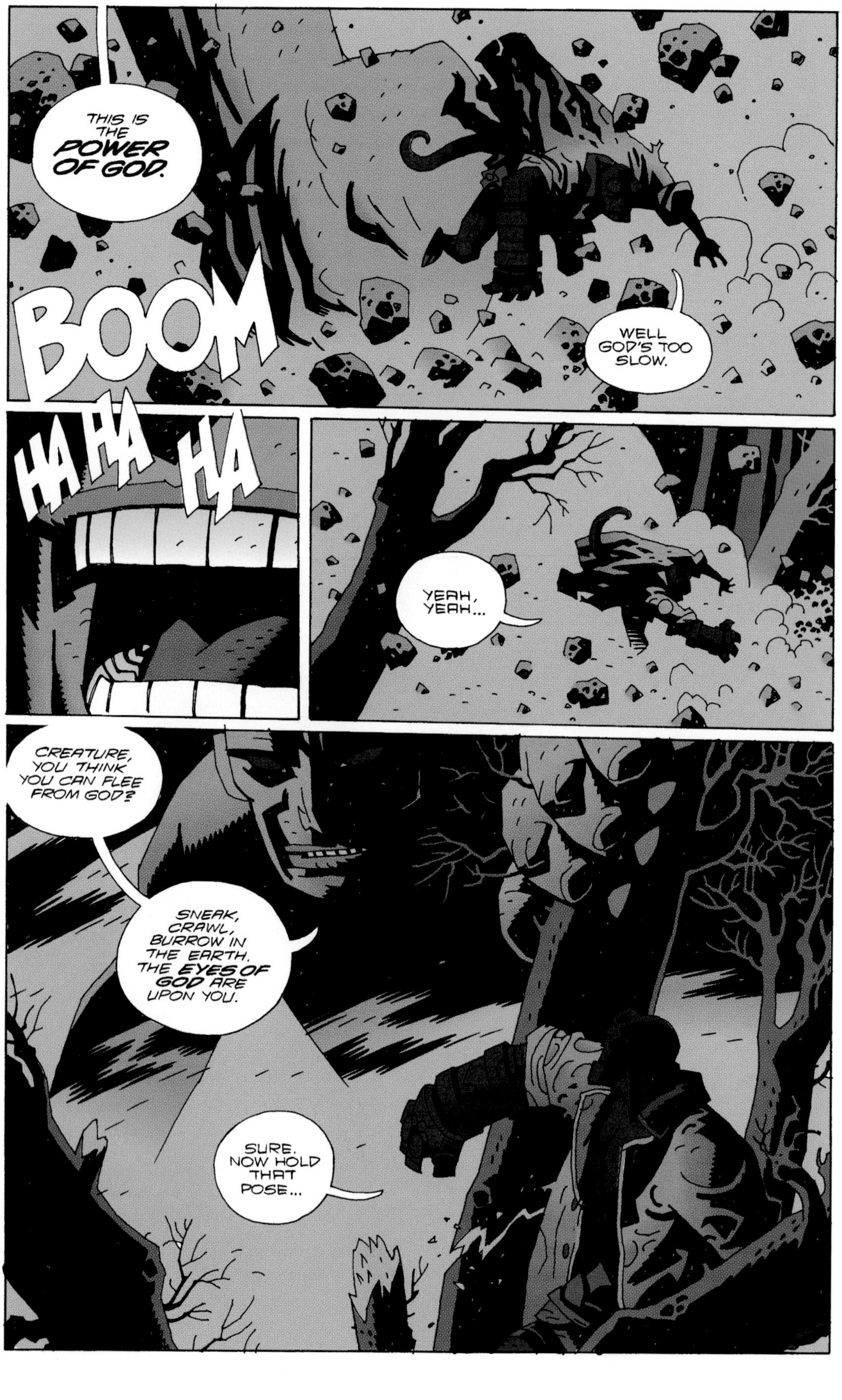
THIS IS THE POWER OF GOD.
BOOM
WELL GOD'S TOO SLOW.
HA HA HA
YEAH, YEAH...
CREATURE, YOU THINK YOU CAN FLEE FROM GOD?
SNEAK, CRAWL, BURROW IN THE EARTH. THE EYES OF GOD ARE UPON YOU.
SURE. NOW HOLD THAT POSE...

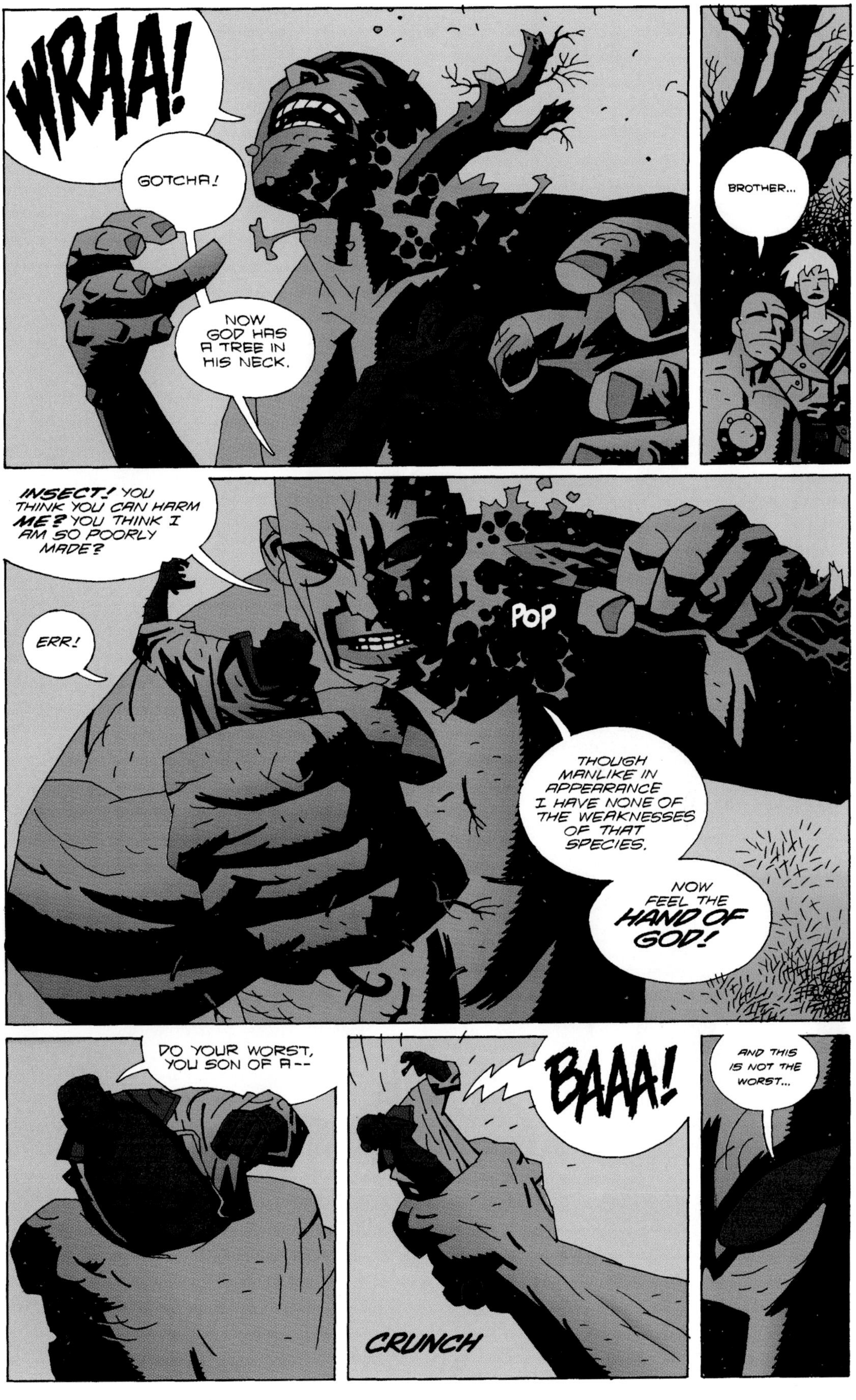
WRAA!
GOTCHA!
NOW GOD HAS A TREE IN HIS NECK.
BROTHER...
INSECT! YOU THINK YOU CAN HARM ME? YOU THINK I AM SO POORLY MADE?
ERR!
POP
THOUGH MANLIKE IN APPEARANCE I HAVE NONE OF THE WEAKNESSES OF THAT SPECIES.
NOW FEEL THE HAND OF GOD!
DO YOUR WORST, YOU SON OF A--
BAAA!
CRUNCH
AND THIS IS NOT THE WORST...

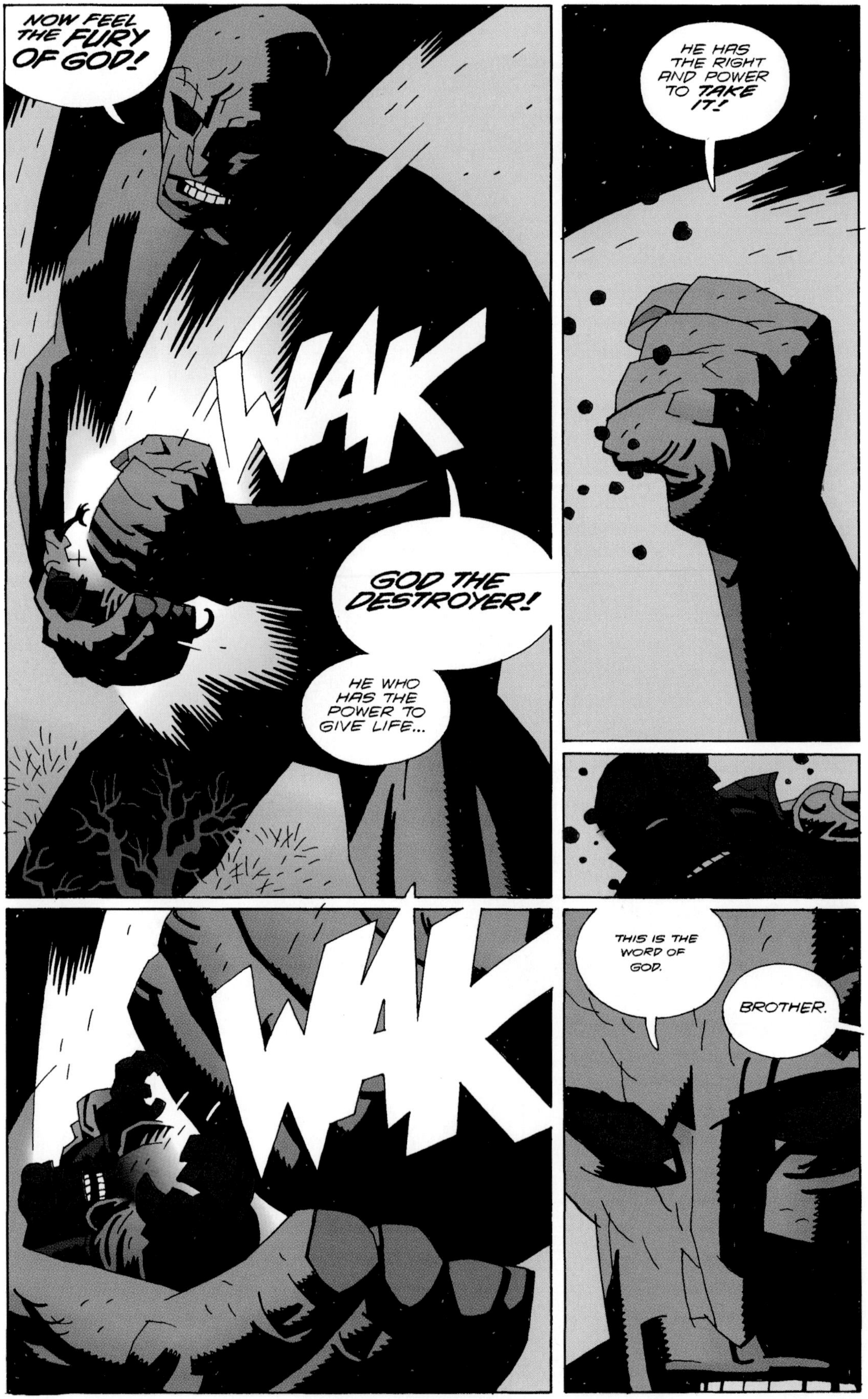
NOW FEEL THE FURY OF GOD!
WAK
GOD THE DESTROYER!
HE WHO HAS THE POWER TO GIVE LIFE...
HE HAS THE RIGHT AND POWER TO TAKE IT!
WAK
THIS IS THE WORD OF GOD.
BROTHER.

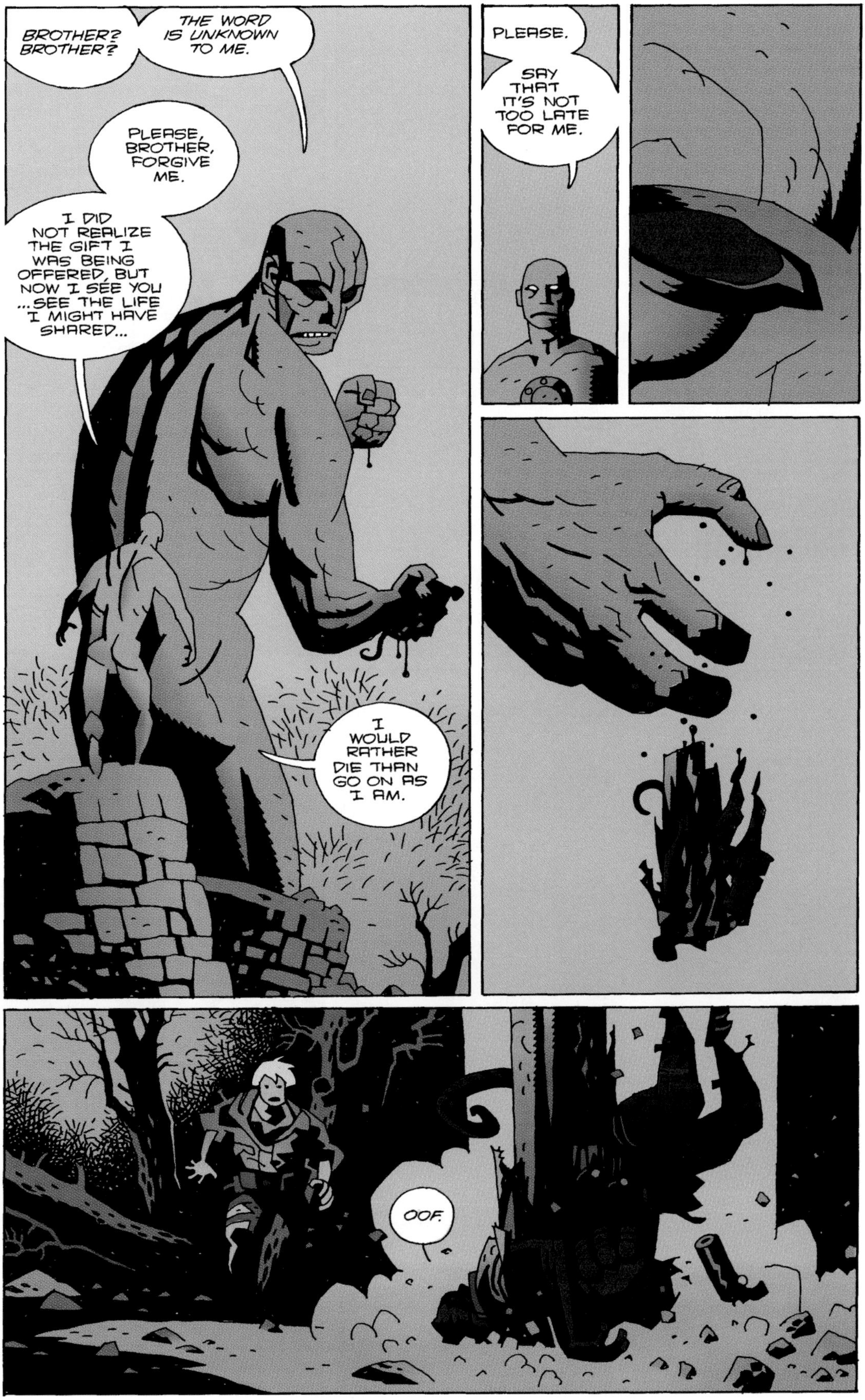
BROTHER? BROTHER?
THE WORD IS UNKNOWN TO ME.
PLEASE, BROTHER, FORGIVE ME.
I DID NOT REALIZE THE GIFT I WAS BEING OFFERED, BUT NOW I SEE YOU ...SEE THE LIFE I MIGHT HAVE SHARED...
I WOULD RATHER DIE THAN GO ON AS I AM.
PLEASE.
SAY THAT IT'S NOT TOO LATE FOR ME.
OOF.

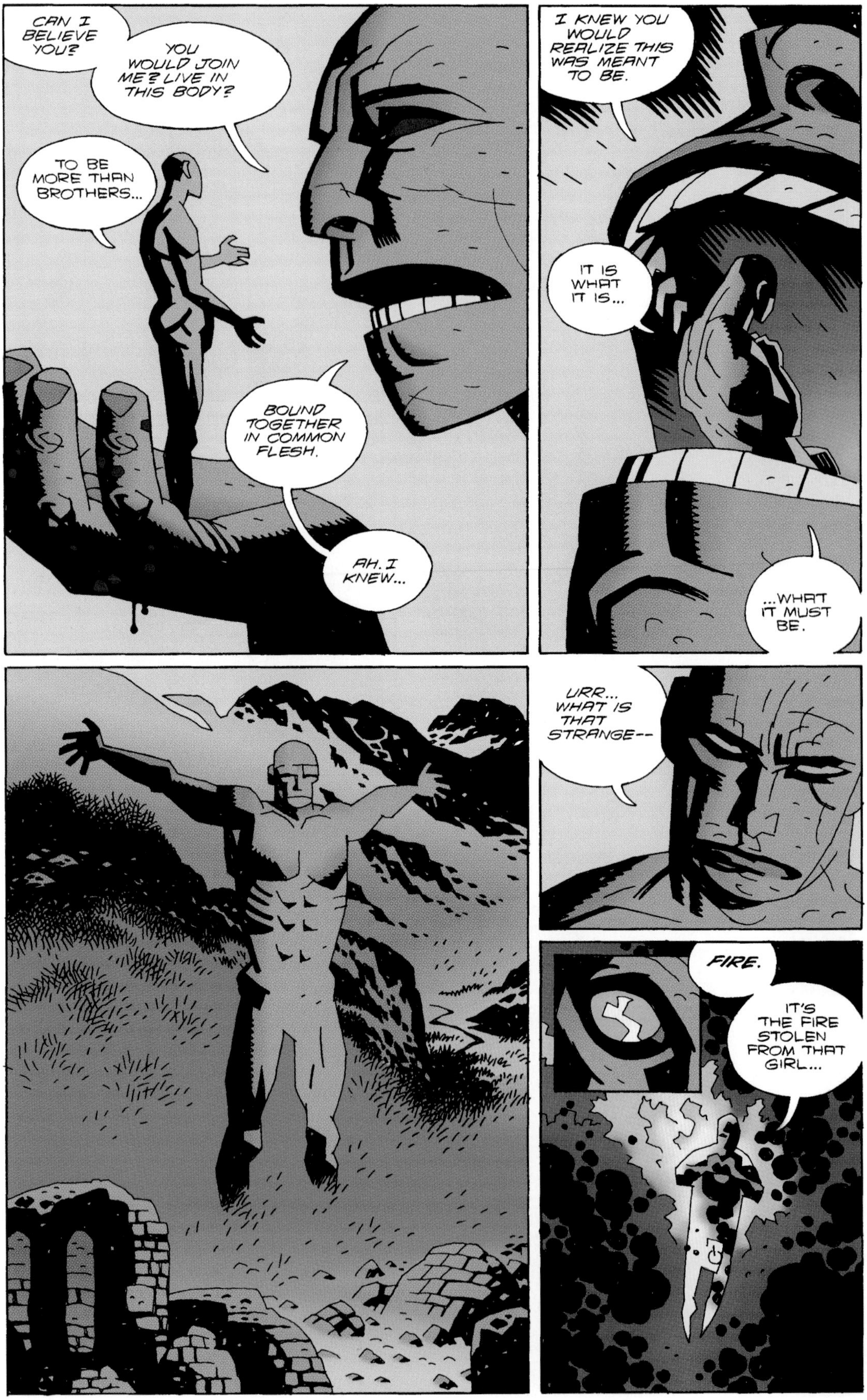
CAN I BELIEVE YOU?
YOU WOULD JOIN ME? LIVE IN THIS BODY?
TO BE MORE THAN BROTHERS...
BOUND TOGETHER IN COMMON FLESH.
AH. I KNEW...
I KNEW YOU WOULD REALIZE THIS WAS MEANT TO BE.
IT IS WHAT IT IS...
...WHAT IT MUST BE.
URR... WHAT IS THAT STRANGE--
FIRE.
IT'S THE FIRE STOLEN FROM THAT GIRL...

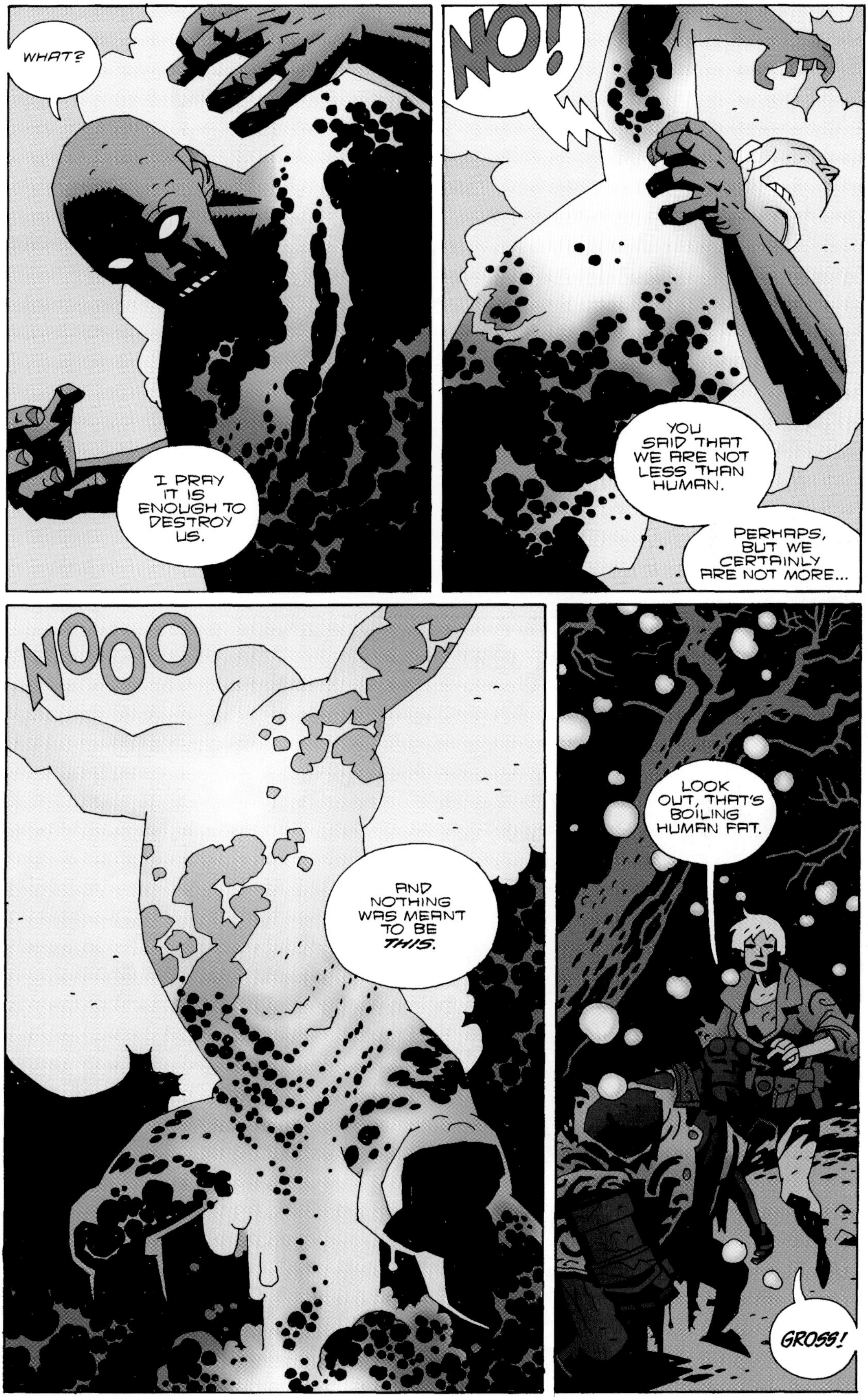
WHAT?
I PRAY IT IS ENOUGH TO DESTROY US.
NO!
YOU SAID THAT WE ARE NOT LESS THAN HUMAN.
PERHAPS, BUT WE CERTAINLY ARE NOT MORE...
NOOO
AND NOTHING WAS MEANT TO BE *THIS*.
LOOK OUT, THAT'S BOILING HUMAN FAT.
GROSS!

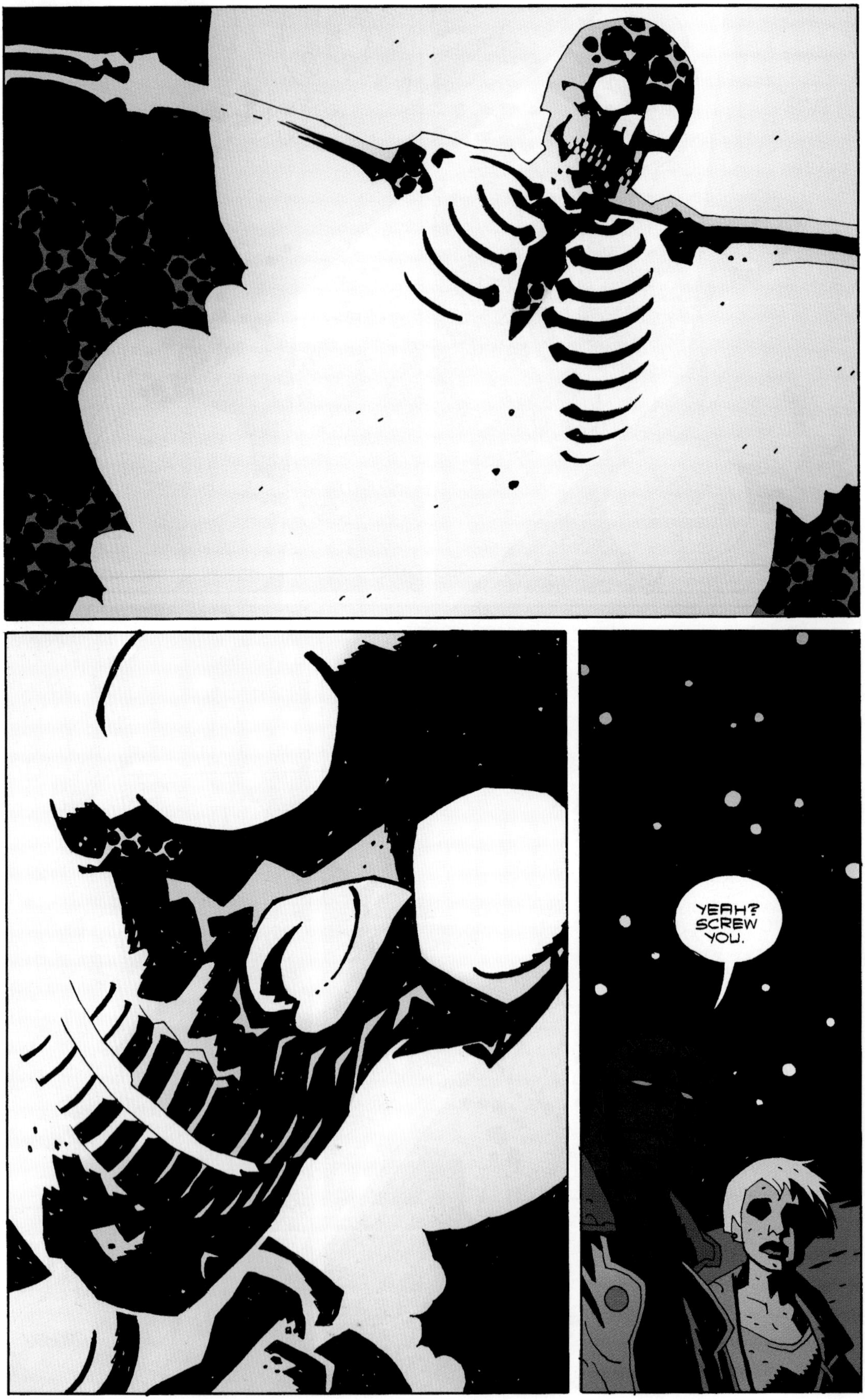
YEAH? SCREW YOU.

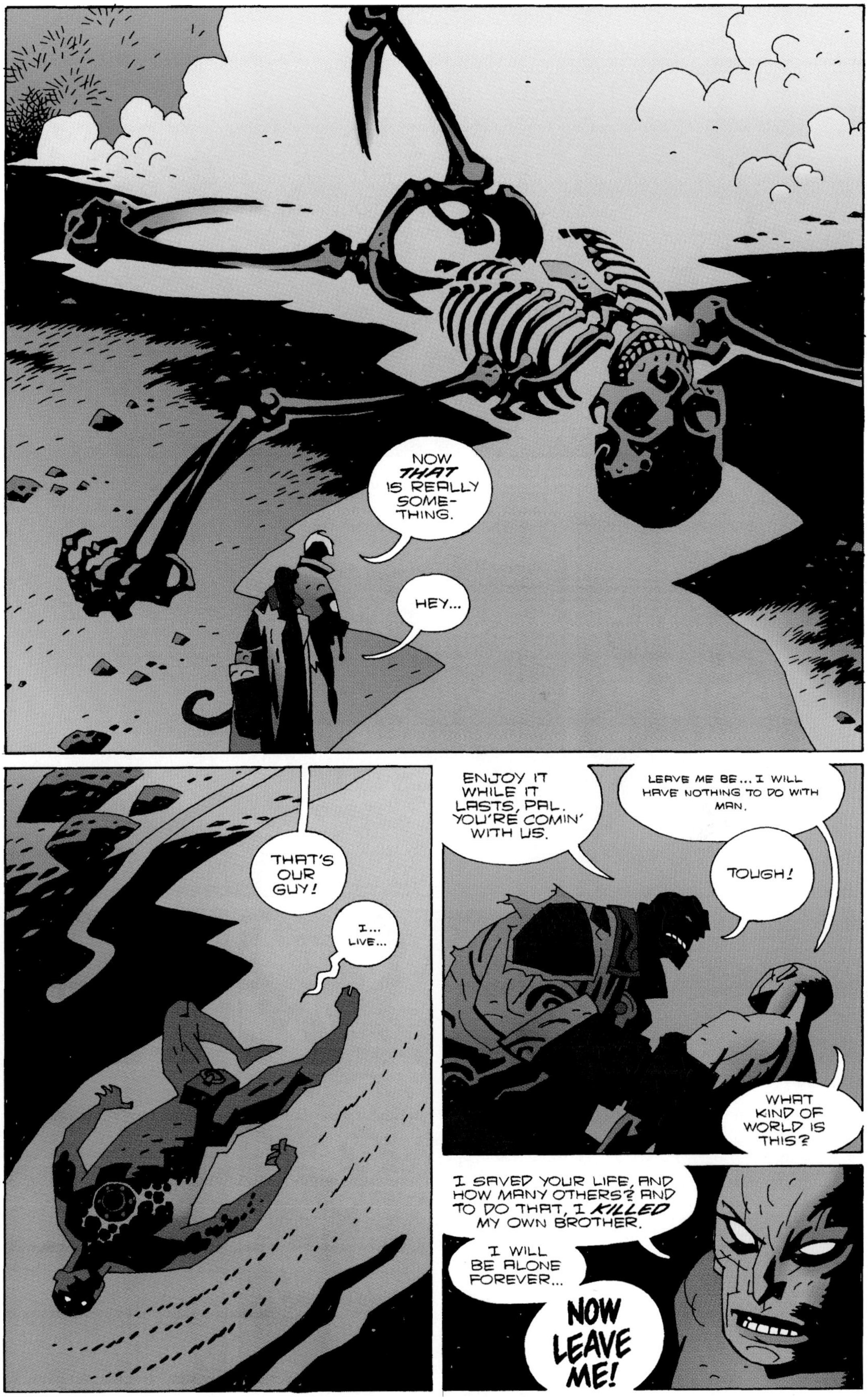
NOW *THAT* IS REALLY SOME-THING.
HEY...
THAT'S OUR GUY!
I... LIVE...
ENJOY IT WHILE IT LASTS, PAL. YOU'RE COMIN' WITH US.
LEAVE ME BE... I WILL HAVE NOTHING TO DO WITH MAN.
TOUGH!
WHAT KIND OF WORLD IS THIS?
I SAVED YOUR LIFE, AND HOW MANY OTHERS? AND TO DO THAT, I *KILLED* MY OWN BROTHER.
I WILL BE ALONE FOREVER...
NOW LEAVE ME!

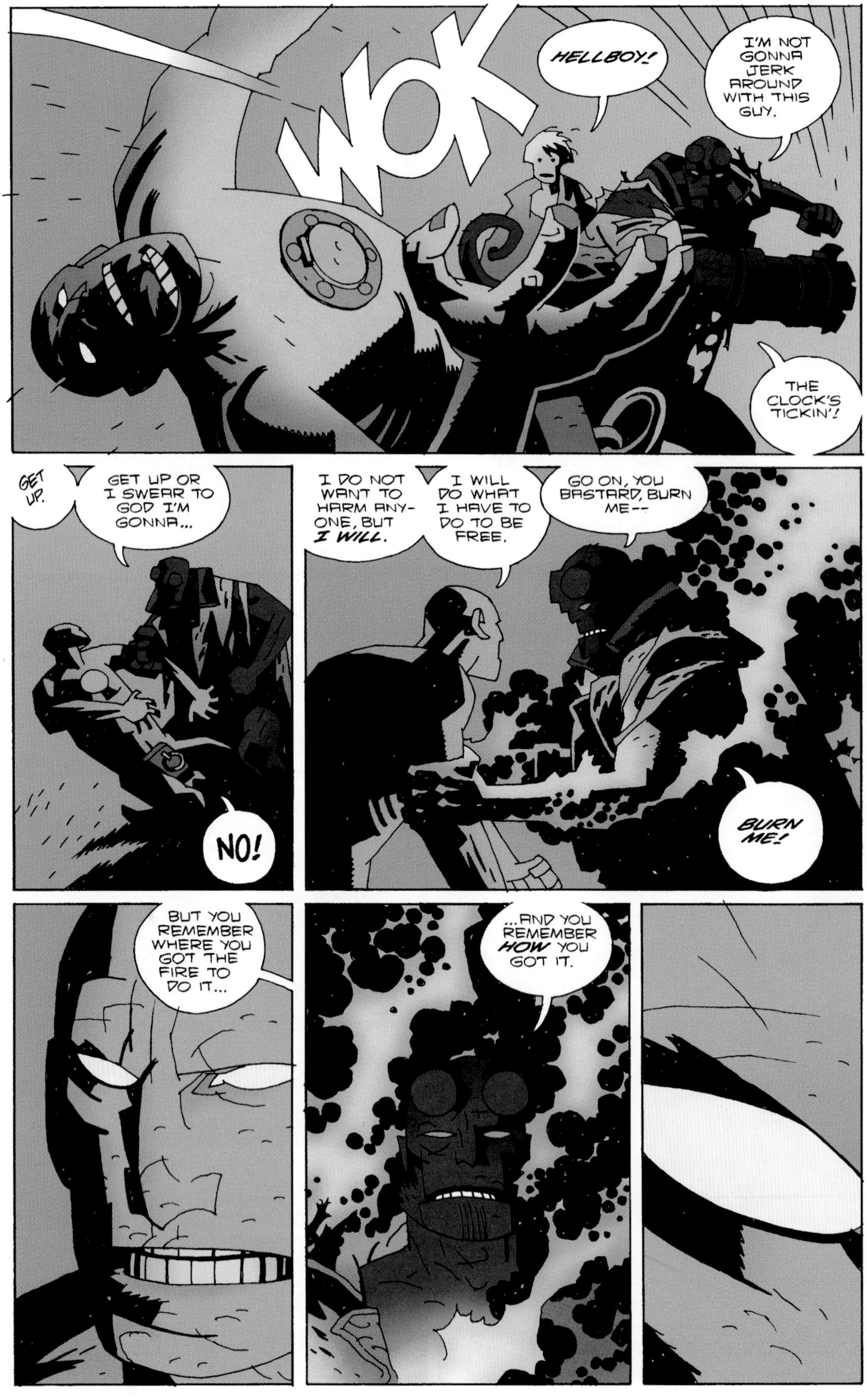

WOK
HELLBOY!
I'M NOT GONNA JERK AROUND WITH THIS GUY.
THE CLOCK'S TICKIN'!
GET UP.
GET UP OR I SWEAR TO GOD I'M GONNA...
NO!
I DO NOT WANT TO HARM ANY-ONE, BUT I WILL.
I WILL DO WHAT I HAVE TO DO TO BE FREE.
GO ON, YOU BASTARD, BURN ME--
BURN ME!
BUT YOU REMEMBER WHERE YOU GOT THE FIRE TO DO IT...
...AND YOU REMEMBER HOW YOU GOT IT.

THE WAUER
INSTITUTE,
TIRGOVISTE.

GANG
WAY!

COMIN'
THROUGH!

WHERE'S
LIZ?

HELLBOY...
SHE DIED A
COUPLE OF
MINUTES
AGO.

I'M
SORRY.

SORRY?

LISTEN,
NOBODY'S DEAD
AROUND HERE
UNTIL I SAY SO.
YOU HEAR ME?

NOBODY!

ABE?

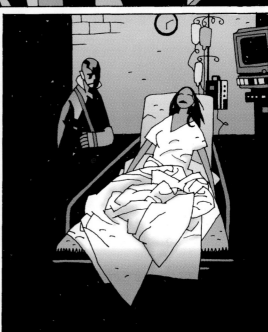

OKAY,
ROGER,
GIVE
HER THE
JUICE.

"ROGER"?

HELLBOY
NAMED
HIM IN THE
CAR.

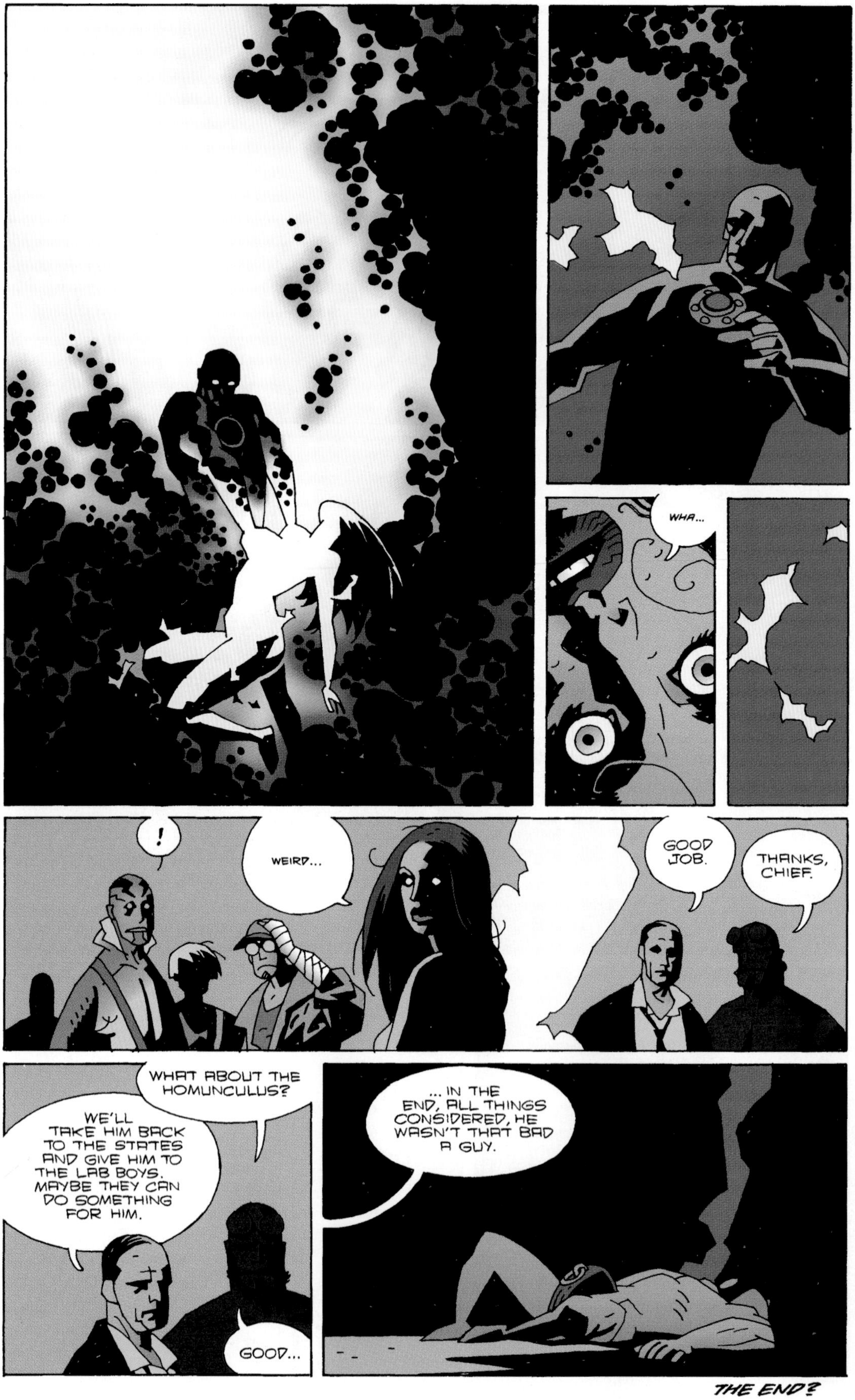
WHA...
!
WEIRD...
GOOD JOB.
THANKS, CHIEF.
WHAT ABOUT THE HOMUNCULUS?
WE'LL TAKE HIM BACK TO THE STATES AND GIVE HIM TO THE LAB BOYS. MAYBE THEY CAN DO SOMETHING FOR HIM.
GOOD...
... IN THE END, ALL THINGS CONSIDERED, HE WASN'T THAT BAD A GUY.

THE END?

HELLBOY™

GALLERY

featuring

KEVIN NOWLAN

MATT SMITH

DUNCAN FEGREDO

DAVE JOHNSON

THIERRY ROBIN

and

B.C. BOYER

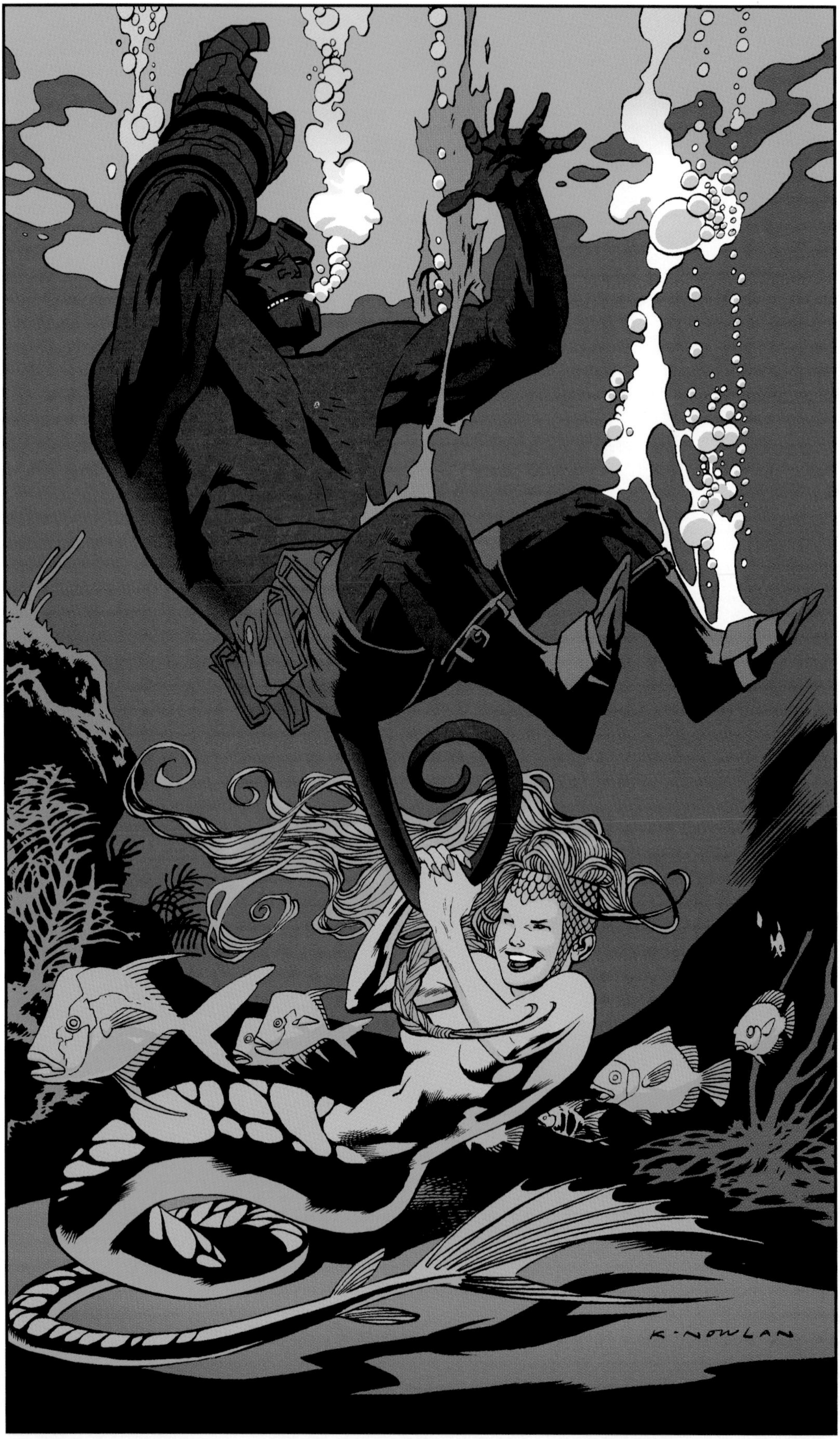
K·NOWLAN

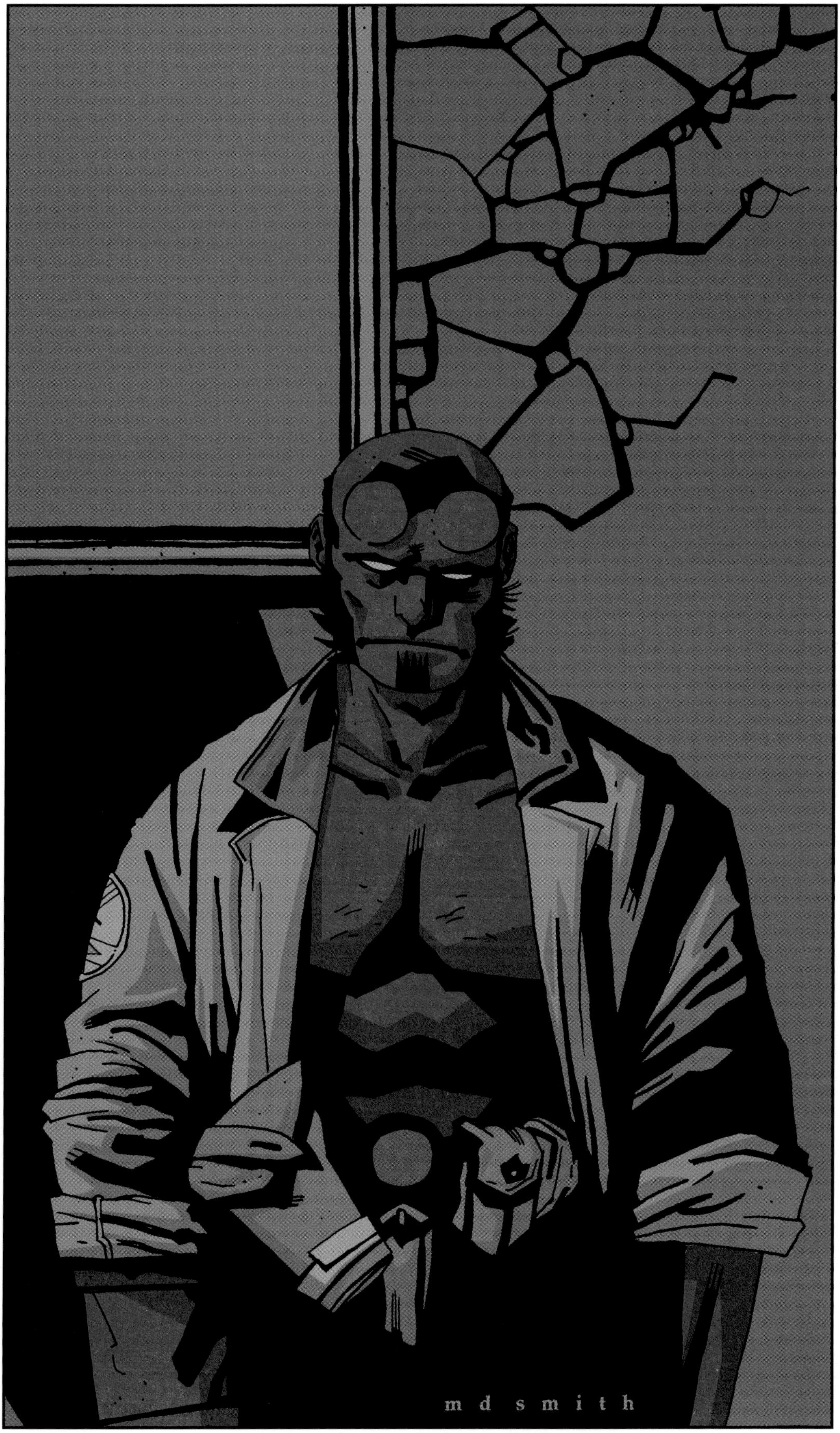
m d smith

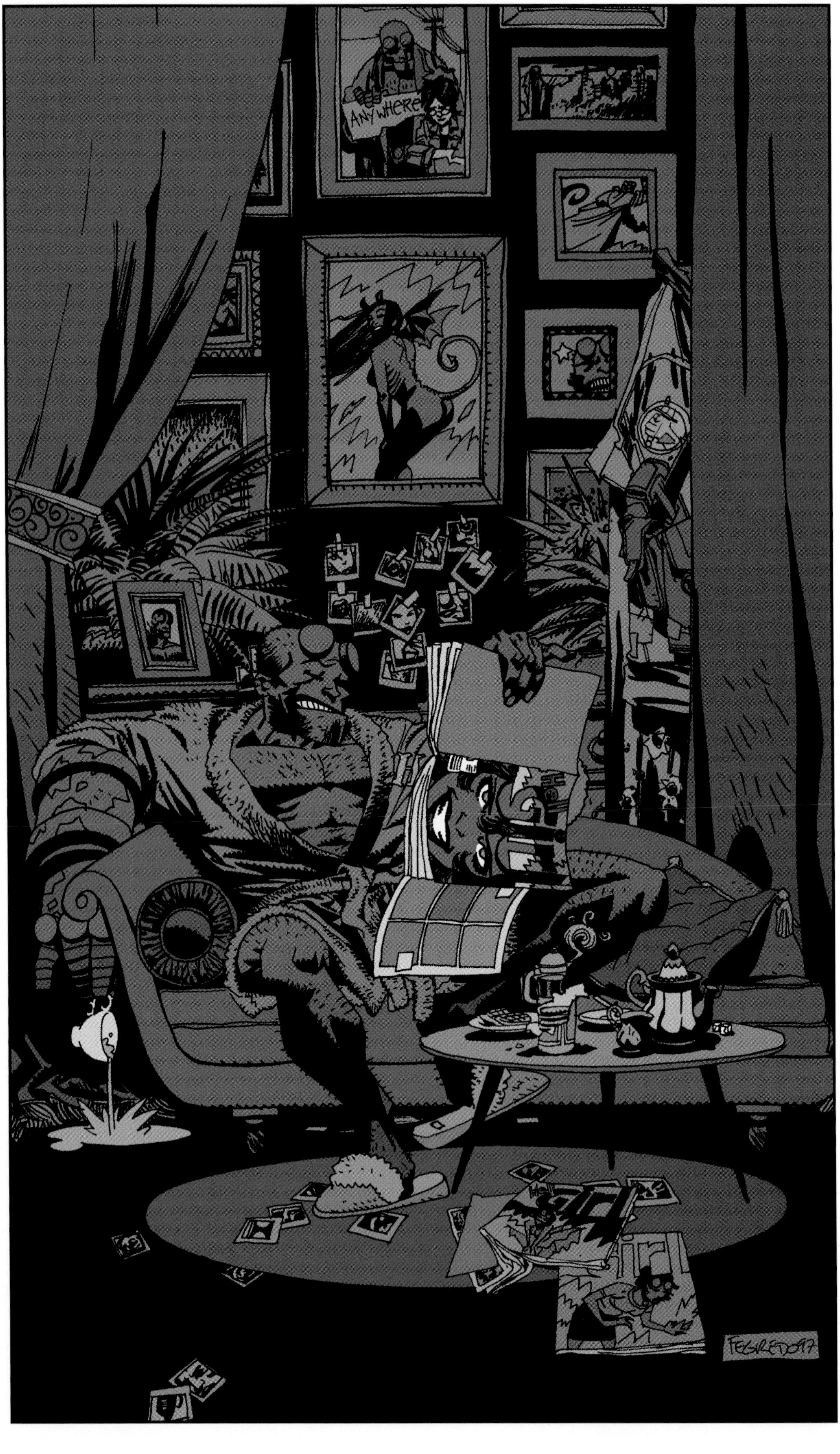
ANYWHERE
FEGREDO97

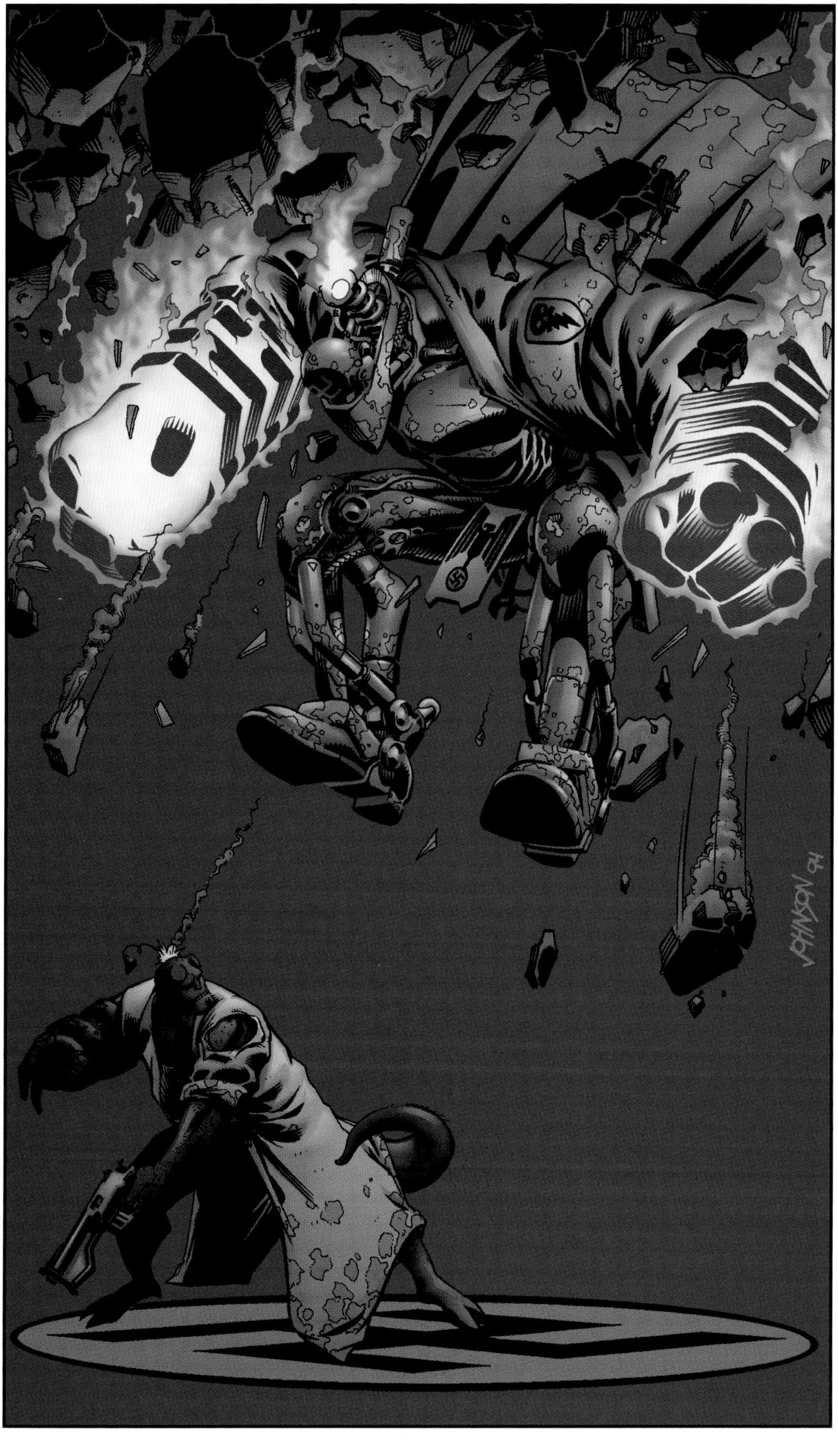
JOHNSON '94

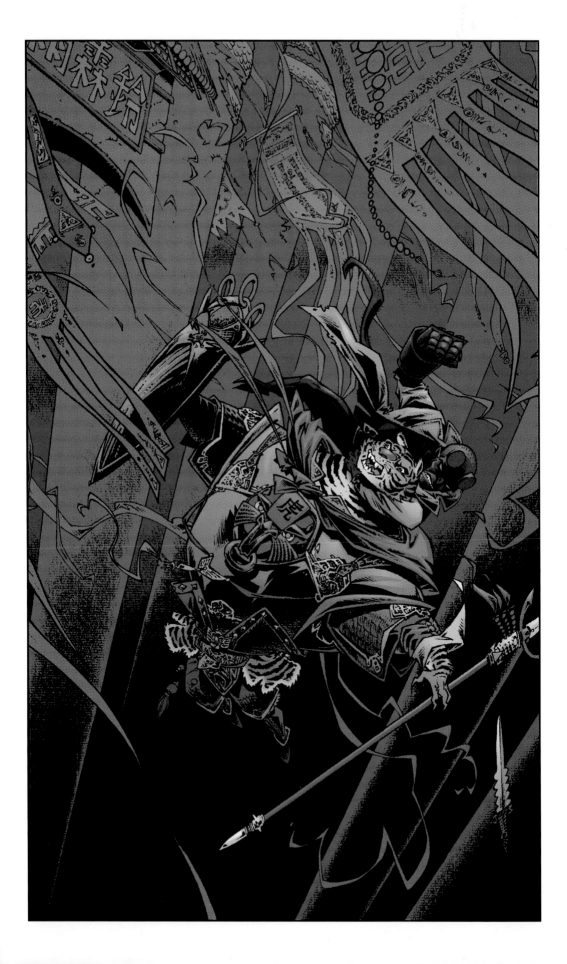

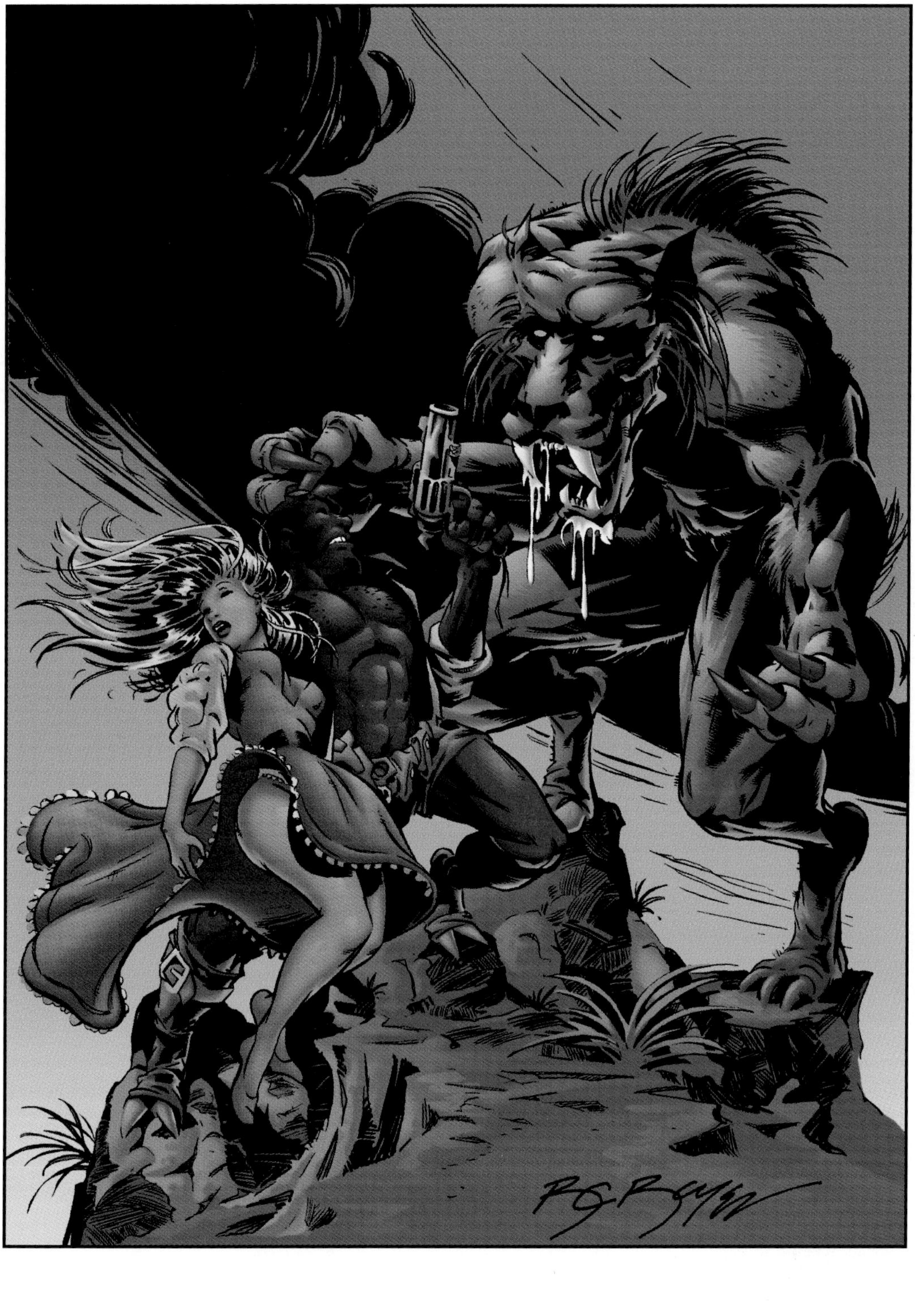

HELLBOY

by MIKE MIGNOLA

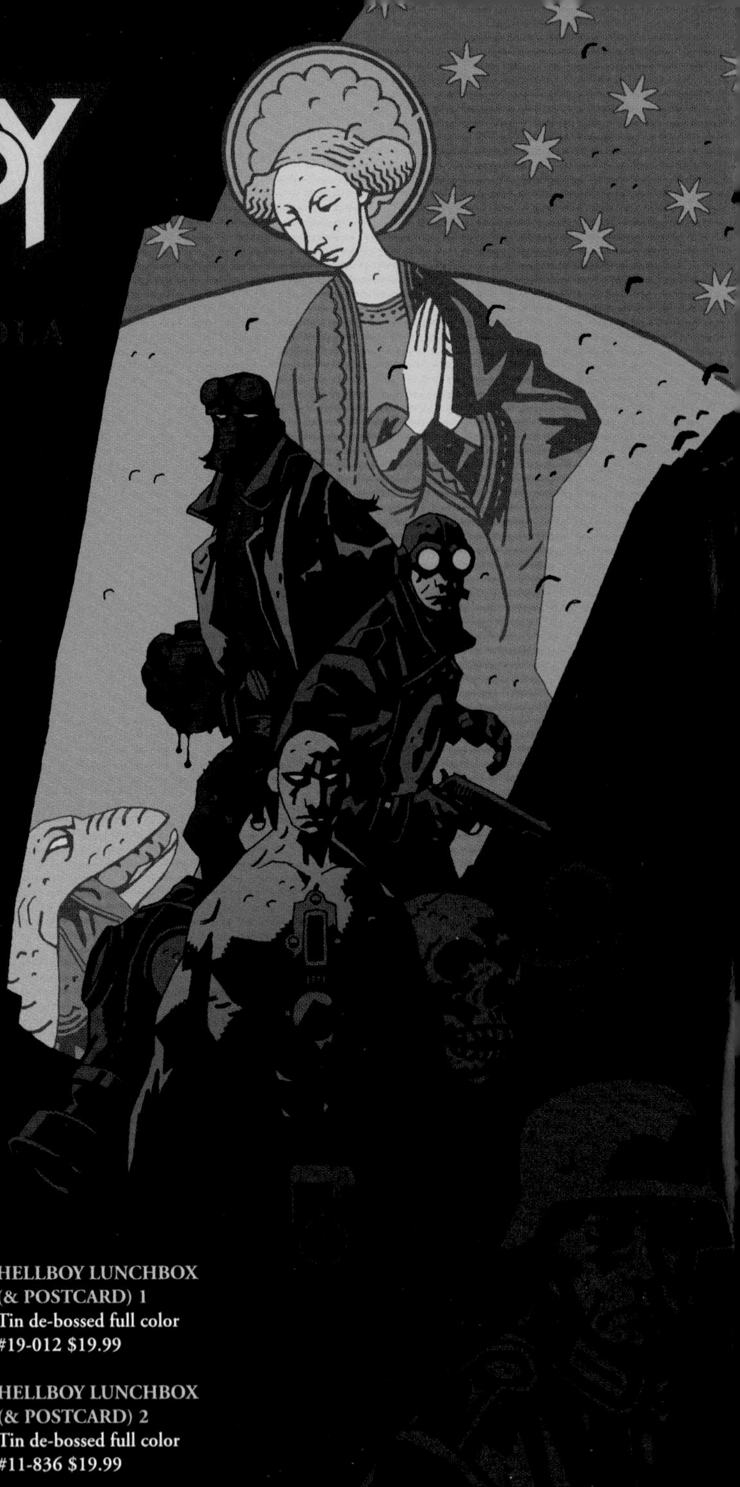

SEED OF DESTRUCTION
with John Byrne
ISBN: 1-59307-094-2 $17.95

WAKE THE DEVIL
ISBN: 1-59307-095-0 $17.95

THE CHAINED COFFIN
AND OTHERS
ISBN: 1-59307-091-8 $17.95

THE RIGHT HAND OF DOOM
ISBN: 1-59307-093-4 $17.95

CONQUEROR WORM
ISBN: 1-59307-092-6 $17.95

THE ART OF HELLBOY
ISBN: 1-59307-089-6 $29.95

HELLBOY WEIRD TALES
Volume 1
By John Cassaday, Jason Pearson,
Eric Powell, Alex Maleev,
Bob Fingerman and others
ISBN: 1-56971-622-6 $17.95

HELLBOY WEIRD TALES
Volume 2
By John Cassaday, JH Williams III,
P. Craig Russell, Jim Starlin,
Frank Cho, Evan Dorkin and others
ISBN: 1-56971-935-5 $17.95

B.P.R.D. HOLLOW EARTH
AND OTHERS
By Mike Mignola, Chris Golden,
Ryan Sook and others
ISBN: 1-56971-862-8 $17.95

B.P.R.D. THE SOUL OF VENICE
AND OTHERS
By Mike Oeming, Guy Davis,
Scott Kolins, Geoff Johns and others
ISBN: 1-59307-132-9 $17.95

ODD JOBS
Short stories by Mike Mignola,
Poppy Z. Brite, Chris Golden and others
Illustrations by Mike Mignola
ISBN: 1-56971-440-1 $14.95

HELLBOY BASEBALL CAP
#17-106 $14.95

HELLBOY LUNCHBOX
(& POSTCARD) 1
Tin de-bossed full color
#19-012 $19.99

HELLBOY LUNCHBOX
(& POSTCARD) 2
Tin de-bossed full color
#11-836 $19.99

HELLBOY PVC SET
#10-666 $39.99

HELLBOY JOURNAL
#12-309 $9.99

HELLBOY SWEATSHIRT
Red-and-Yellow Hellboy Logo
#12-411 $39.99

HELLBOY ZIPPO LIGHTER
#17-101 $29.95

HELLBOY BOOKS AND MERCHANDISE
CAN BE VIEWED AT www.darkhorse.com

To find a comics shop in your area, call 1-888-266-4226
For more information or to order direct:
•On the web: www.darkhorse.com
•E-mail: mailorder@darkhorse.com
•Phone: 1-800-862-0052 or (503) 652-9701
Mon.-Sat. 9 A.M. to 5 P.M. Pacific Time

DARK HORSE COMICS™ *drawing on your nightmares*